SCHOOL OF ORIENTAL AND AFRICAN STUDIES

University of London

THREE-DAY LOAN COLLECTION

This book is due for return not later than the last date stamped below.

INDIA
WAITS

INDIA WAITS

By Jan Myrdal

Photographs By
Gun Kessle

Translated By
Alan Bernstein

LAKE VIEW Press

Chicago

Lake View Press
p.o. box 578279
Chicago, IL 60657

The Swedish edition of this book was published
by P. A. Norstedt & Soners Forlag, Stockholm

Library of Congress Cataloging in Publication Data

Myrdal, Jan.
  India waits.

    Translation of: Indien vantar.
    Includes index.
    1. India. I. Title
DS407.M9313 1986   954   86-20069
ISBN 0-941702-06-5
ISBN 0-941702-07-3 (pbk.)

CONTENTS

Some Words as an Introduction

My publisher in the United States wants me to write some words of introduction in order to make *India Waits* easier to read for the North American public.

It is not a new book. The American edition is not the first English language edition. Readers in South and South-East Asia have been reading it in English for two years now. In English it has in India had two hard cover editions and is selling as a paper back. It is also being published in other Indian languages. But it has not—up to now—been available in the United States and Great Britain.

Why a new introduction? Are American readers so much more important?

First, I am inclined to refuse; this book already has a preface. That was written when the book was first published in India. It is still valid. Why should it not be? I have not basically changed. Neither has India. Ideas and books do not spoil and go bad like food left standing. There is really no logical reason to write a new introduction.

There were in the book a couple of questions that I wanted to clarify. For a new edition in Scandinavia I thus wrote two new chapters a year ago. They too are valid within the general framework of the book and I include them.

But to continue the discussion further than that I would have to write a new book. One day I will. (Granted that I still have a decade or so of work in front of me to dispose of; that the ongoing wars and the new wars in coming years do not make these journeys impossible; that I am not killed and that I am not struck by disease or accident.) *Urban India* is the title.

That is another book. The modern Indian state towards the end of this century. The high administration and the new technology. The new educated professionals; the technocrats. The industrial India. The working class, both the new technicians and the mass of laborers. The trade union struggles and the new trends. The huge cities. The pauperized peasant masses driven into the slums on the outskirts and then driven out by the municipal authorities. How the slum dwellers organize.

That book should discuss the further development of the state apparatus. The "encounters" in which urban civil rights activists and peasant militants are being eliminated—killed off—are the work of what can only be described as "death squads." How—and of what necessity—they and other such extra-legal state organs take form is worth a description. How the rising communalism, the plight of the minorities—the Muslims, for instance—is connected with the way in which the new computerized generation of bureaucrats are taking over the levers (terminals) of the modern state apparatus needs also to be discussed. That I will. But to write *Urban India* will take some years more. How many I don't know. But all these discussions presuppose this volume as it stands.

India waits could not have been written this year. Many of the people who helped me are in jail. Others are even dead. Many of the middle-class intellectuals who were then sympathetic to the peasant movement have since retreated into private life. Social contradictions are sharper. It would now not be possible to travel in the restricted areas as we did and I could not take part in public or semi-public discussions like I did. But at the same time the peasant struggles I describe have spread, become mass struggles and taken new forms.

On the other hand, to write about the new computerized state taking form in coming years without the background of the discussion in this book would not be meaningful. Here I discuss the tradition of the state and the role of history. It is also a personal record. Of course I am subjective. I have not stood aside looking at India. It is more than a generation ago I came to India and India then shaped me, made me see differently, made me take more definite stand on my own tradition also.

As it is I find this volume necessary. That is also why I am glad to hear from my Indian publisher that a new pocket edition is being printed there.

India is not only the third largest publishing market for books in English. It is also—as I have written—for an intellectual a country with an intellectual discussion as alive as that of Paris in the Eighteenth Century. This discussion, for the revolutionary intelligentsia in India now as for the Enlightenment in France then, is determined by the misery of the masses and the necessity for a great change. That is what then made and now makes the intellectual discussion vital. It matters what you as an intellectual say, and what you as a writer writes is of social importance.

But if I find the book necessary as it stands, why then write these words as an introduction for readers in North America, for them to read before the preface? Before the written book?

Well, I think it necessary to explain why a book in which I speak as an intellectual is published in one edition after another edition in India before being brought out in the metropolitan English speaking world.

At a time when the publishers, the movie makers and the critics in Great Britain—and from there to the United States—are finding it profitable to be nostalgic about the *Empire*, this book of course will seem odd to a public getting used to that nostalgia. I write on that Empire from another point of view—a more Indian point of view of the Empire, one might say, one that in reality is less odd than the nostalgia in the English media. Let me put it in another way:

Whatever the Czechs and the Poles and the Hungarians and all the other people living in what was once the Eastern parts of the German and Austrian Empires think about their present situation, and their present rulers, they would find a German and Austrian nostalgia for the Wilhelmine and the Austrian empires hard to accept. The nostalgia for Empire is as unusual in India as in Slovakia. And a Swedish film nostalgic about the dual kingdom of Sweden and Norway in the Nineteenth Century would find only a limited audience in Norway.

That might have to be said as an introduction.

Also: In this book I write rather little on Gandhi and non-violence and rather much on Bengali terrorism and the violent struggle against the British from 1857 onwards. Of course, I think that this stressing of the role of violence in recent Indian his tory is historically correct. I have also taken much of it from my first father-in-law, Kali Ghosh. But in Great Britain and in the United States it will seem strange. There the public is not only used to another picture of history; they even believe in it. In India this stress on violence and this homage to the Bengali terrorists and nationalists (for homage is what it amounts to when I write about Kali Ghosh and his experience) is not usual. But to an Indian audience I would not have to give this explanation. There people know that there is another history behind the official picture. The overwhelming majority have also in their poverty and in their oppression retained their capacity to doubt and mistrust. It is not in India—it is in Great Britain that it still is difficult to discuss historical personalities like Manabendra Nath Roy and Subash Chandra Bose.

There is still another reason:

I know that readers from America have asked why I hold peasant masses to be important in an age of computers. It seems peculiar. It also seems peculiar that I seem to think that the poverty ridden masses are less prejudiced than the young and educated executives of the West.

There is nothing peculiar about it. I too was once being brought up as an American, but at that time during the New Deal, as one in an anti-imperialist and popular tradition. That was the folk tradition and those the values that then were thought of as American. And as I read Mark Twain when I was young I later had no difficulty in understanding revolutions and popular struggles.

If I had been sure that the American readers had been brought up reading *A Connecticut Yankee in King Arthur's Court, King Leopold's Soliloquy* and other works in that American tradition, I would have had no need to write these introductory words.

But from what I read and from what I see these years, I find it necessary to write this.

Fagervik 1986
Jan Myrdal

Foreword

This book was to have been written during the Delhi winter of 1961-1962. But as the cold months passed to spring and then to hot weather while I wrote at my desk in Defence Colony, I felt the book slipping out of my hands.

Four years earlier, in January 1958, Gun Kessle and I had left Sweden to drive to India. I was to write. She was to take photographs. We were to do a book on India. We had arrived during the monsoon of 1958, and travelled up and down the sub-continent. With Delhi as our base, we visited Nepal, Burma, Sri Lanka, Pakistan and Afghanistan. We wrote on Burma, and re-reading those reports of twenty years ago, I still find them valid. We spent a long time in Afghanistan on our way to India, and we went back there from spring to late autumn 1959. The winter of 1959-1960 I spent in Delhi writing on Afghanistan. That book was later published in German and then all over Eastern Europe—until I wrote about Soviet Central Asia in 1965, and all my books disappeared from the shelves of book shops and libraries from Budapest to Vladivostok, and my very name was erased from all Soviet accounts of Swedish literature.

But the book on India that I had wanted to write ever since the War and that I had been preparing for all these years was too difficult to write. After four months of writing I was convinced that I knew nothing, understood nothing and could formulate nothing. When I received word that our visa applications for China had been approved and that Gun Kessle and I could go, I packed, sent my notes and books on India back to Sweden and left for China. A year later I had finished *Report from a Chinese Village*. I can almost say that this report on the life and revolutionary struggle of poor Chinese peasants in northern Shaanxi was the outcome of those years spent in India.

During the next two decades we went back to India several times. We travelled in the sub-continent in 1967, 1970, 1974 and 1975, and in December 1979, we returned once more.

This book is a travelogue of that journey in 1979 and 1980. To a great extent, it is a discussion about India and Indian social and historical reality. The book that I was not able to grasp twenty years ago could be written now. It had to be.

I have a personal involvement with India. I have spent important years of my life in India and I have Indian family relations. Kali Ghosh meant much to me, both intellectually and as a father-in-law through his marriage with Paula Wiking. But deeper than that personal involvement is the intellectual and political involvement.

For those of us in continental Europe who were young anti-fascists and anti-imperialists during the war against Hitler and fascism, India was a bewildering problem. Why?

After June 1941, not a word was to be heard from Moscow or from our communist parties about the Indian struggle for national independence. But German propaganda continued to hammer at us about Gandhi and Nehru. I still have several German documents and books on the Indian freedom movement directed at those of us who were anti-imperialist. I have read all this again while writing *India Waits*. I understand why it troubled me then. The arguments are good. But the conclusion—to support the Axis in its war effort—was wrong. We rejected the conclusion but were deeply troubled.

In England it was different. There socialists, communists, Indian patriots and democrats were debating, discussing, publishing. But on the continent—in pro-Axis, semi-neutral Sweden, or in Vichy-France or in the directly occupied countries, it was not that easy. Here the fascists were the ones who had the good arguments. I remember the way the young Nazi organizer at Bromma High School talked about the Bengal famine. I had no arguments to counter what he said.

China was another matter altogether. There the lines were clear-cut: Japanese invaders, and the communists around Mao in Yenan who were proving to be the true patriots.

Let me phrase the problem in another way so that a younger generation may understand. To struggle against fascism was necessary. Fascism was our most dangerous enemy. The enemy of not only the people of Europe but of the peoples of the World. But in this struggle we joined forces with democrats who were imperialists. We had to. Older comrades—

used to toeing the party line—told us not to think about it. The democrats we united with told us that in reality Gandhi was a fascist, that Nehru was prepared to be a Japanese collaborator, and that the British had to smash this fascist plot in India. And the fascists asked us to join their anti-imperialist struggle against Anglo-American imperialism.

The French writer and critic André Mathieu, who has a similar background, has told me of his utter confusion when as a member of the French resistance he was sent into battle for the first time . . . against Indian patriots recruited in the service of Hitler.

I never was able to resolve this contradiction during the War. I got around it by double-think. In later years I have understood that this conflict is typical.

Let me take another example: about one-seventh of the world's total population lives in India. Seeing India in this perspective makes her poor, an "under-developed" country, to use the expression that was common before the word "developing" came into use. But count out those outside commodity production, those below the poverty line, those who are, economically speaking, non-existent, and India becomes a well-to-do and truly developing state somewhere between Spain and France on the international scale.

But can one count out the overwhelming majority? That depends of course on who this "one" is. Everything that is real is reasonable, said Hegel. Thus everything that is reasonable will become real, as the Marxists put it. But if it is reasonable for the rulers to count out the overwhelming majority as non-existent, what would the corresponding reality be?

Every time I have come to India I have seen prosperity increase for the top slice. The suburbs become nicer. The air-conditioned trains better. The standard of living higher. While the (economically speaking non-existent) masses sink deeper into poverty.

I used to say that this is not the result of capitalist development. Rather, I said, it is pre-capitalist, feudal impoverishment. The Indian bourgeoisie had not become independent. It continued as an appendage of feudalism.

India became politically independent in 1947. The colonialists did not put up an armed struggle to retain their domination. Colonialism was no longer profitable. Already in 1934, the Indian textile industry produced seventy-five per cent of all industrial textiles. Seventy-five per cent of all the steel used in India was produced locally. The Second World War gave Indian trade and industry what passed for an explosive economic expansion. But if India had gained political independence, the structure was still semi-colonial.

Nehru inherited the state that the British had taken over from the

Mughals. The British who ran the machinery were partly displaced by their Indian pupils, partly crowded out by Americans who in turn were later crowded out by Russians, while all along Indian capital collaborated and kept to its subordinate position.

The cities swell and decay as development goes nowhere and the oppressed become ever more numerous and poor. But, what if the Indian ruling class is now crowding out the foreigners and becoming independent? What if semi-feudalism is taking a leap? What if it will make a new order real?

I am asking myself this because from India I went, as I did twenty years ago, to China and to the poor and economically backward countryside where the 800,000,000 peasants—the old-hundred-names—are now being left behind, outside the new type of economic development in the post-Mao era. Or rather where fifteen per cent of peasants producing commodities are being included in the new society and the eighty-five per cent pushed out among other leftovers in the hinterland.

I do not pity either the Chinese or the Indian people. The masses are not pitiful. Whatever happens, I remain convinced that in the long run it is the people who constitute the driving force of history.

It is true that the masses in India are poor. It is true that there are flies crawling over what has been eyes of the blind boy begging in Calcutta. But that is not the truth about the Indian people. The Indian people are a rich and strong people. The fact that they are often portrayed as apathetic, and pitiable and poor—rich only in soul—says more about the class stand of the portrayer than of the reality of those portrayed. As the March Hare would say, they think what they write.

The truly stimulating intellectual discussions today are not to be found in Stockholm or Berlin—or for that matter in Paris, London, New York, Moscow or Tokyo—but in cities like Bombay, Calcutta, Delhi, Hyderabad or Madras. And the future of India will be decided in the vast Indian countryside, in those half million dungheaps called villages—as Gandhi put it—by those masses who are economically non-existent and often portrayed as apathetic and caste ridden.

But if the truly stimulating intellectual discussions are to be found in India, there is also a dangerous ambiguousness in this intellectual tradition. The difference between West and East is not that the West has a tradition of reason while the East has one of spiritualism opening towards mysticism. The Indian tradition is intellectual. There are of course mystics in India, but the intellectual attitude is one of unflinching belief in reason. The emancipation of the mind and the spirit of contradiction which characterize Indian intellectual circles also lead to a willingness to go to the furthest extremes.

This intellectual tradition is a caste tradition of the intellectuals in Indian society. And here it becomes ambiguous. M. N. Roy writes about the free, Dionysian individual. Kali Ghosh explains it himself to a certain degree. There is in the Brahmanical heritage a dangerous tradition of Nietzschean reason "beyond good and evil." Or as Johann Jakob Meyer described Kautilya's *Arthasastra* in 1926, when he wrote that it was "uncivic, non-civic and supra-civic, like the Brahman himself...."

If it is necessary to point out that the intellectual tradition of India is that of reason, it is also necessary to add that the Indian village was never static and unchanging. On this point Marx was wrong. His articles on India in 1858 for the New York Daily Tribune were brilliant journalism. They were not revelations. Marx would have been horrified if he had been told that a century after his death his words were to be treated as revealed Truth. Indian society has a history and that history is known.

(He who doubts what Marx wrote and checks his statements follows Marx; he who trusts Marx and believes his words breaks with Marx!)

This time Gun Kessle and I made a journey from Delhi to Bihar, and then through Calcutta, over Orissa to Andhra Pradesh, and southward and up through Karnataka to Bombay. Earlier we had visited almost all of India.

On this occasion we also visited the disturbed areas in Andhra Pradesh. But as this could not be done openly, and as we were under police surveillance, we left Andhra Pradesh and then went back on the quiet from Bombay.

For our convenience the Royal Swedish Embassy in Delhi had, in December 1979, given an account of our itinerary to the Indian Foreign Ministry. The Embassy staff were not aware that we planned to interrupt our journey in Bombay and go back to Andhra Pradesh and to the disturbed areas and the armed squads in the forest, instead of proceeding to Gujarat. They are not responsible.

The friends with whom we travelled in Andhra Pradesh during our first visit did not know that we would return. They did not learn of our second visit until we were back in Sweden.

We have lived long enough in India to have different contacts at different levels. The fact that I refrain from making known exactly who these contacts are is just as natural as my not publishing the names and addresses of the "safe houses" that we used. The precaution is as necessary in Indira's India as it was in the France of Louis Bonaparte. India is not a fascist dictatorship. Neither was Bonapartiste France. But it is a country in which the people and the political workers live under close surveillance.

Hence, after having gone from temple to temple in Karnataka, we returned unseen (I believe) from Bombay to Andhra Pradesh. Old friends aided us. Then for fourteen days we travelled in the disturbed areas. We stayed in villages and small towns and in the camps of the armed squads.

There are different opinions in India, there are different political groups. Gun Kessle and I do not take sides in these discussions. That is not for us. We are foreigners and have no right to say which of our friends is correct. That will be decided by the Indian people. But we do take sides when it concerns the Indian people. They are not only hospitable and friendly; however oppressed and poor—downtrodden, beaten up, violated, exploited, pushed into ignorance and casteism, swindled and despised—they are strong and wise. They are the future of India as they have been the driving force in its past. It might be noted that if the police had caught us in the villages or forests of the disturbed areas nothing much would have happened to us. A beating maybe. But our hosts would have had a difficult time.

The villagers with whom we stayed and who gave us food, the political workers, the people who helped us, were typically Indian. Openhanded and proud. Thinking about them and about all our friends with whom we have been travelling and talking all these years, I am convinced that however many turns and twists there are along the road, the future reality of India will finally be decided by what the oppressed masses of India see as reason and not by what the ruling class sees as reason!

It is here in the third world poverty of the thousands upon thousands of villages in India that the future is being born. Without the city—as it has been written—the true wrath tramples the grapes. Here a wine is being trodden in this century that shall deluge the world.

To begin this personal description of a journey in India in the eighties, I go back to my diary twenty years ago.

Jan Myrdal

INDIA
WAITS

Work Diary, Winter, 1961-1962

Defence Colony 129-A, New Delhi

November 6, 1961

The Foreigners' Registration Bureau wondered how I support myself. I wonder, myself, at times.

"You have been tourists in India for a long time now."

November 8, 1961

Peter Schmid's book *Indien mit und ohne wunder (India With and Without Wonder)* arrived from Sandberg's bookstore in Stockholm by airmail book-post. The Customs had not opened the package, which is lucky because they would have confiscated it. It is banned. That is why I ordered it.

Schmid is Swiss, but the book is published in West Germany. It is still quoted at regular intervals in Parliament. There was a diplomatic incident when West Germany's ambassador, Dr. Wilhelm Melchers, praised it. Mitra says that Melchers was, at one time, a Nazi party member. He has it from the East Germans.

The book is very, very German. I understand why it was banned. Its humor belongs to a late round at a gathering of former SS-men. Two particularly shocking passages led to the ban:

> *page 7—On the subject of Indian traffic:* I am speaking from experience: what I bagged during a month's journey through India was two dogs, a kid goat, a rooster and a cyclist.
> *page 126—A German Supervisor at the steelworks in Rourkela about the Indian workers:*
> Instead of building blast-furnaces, we should build gas chambers for four hundred million Indians.

Apropos German humor—the only thing specifically German about this kind of humor is that it seems to be easier to find a publisher for it in Germany. In Africa and Asia, it is considered to be generally European and American. It can be heard at any foreign party.

I'm no liberal! The Indians are right. That sort of book should be banned!

November 14, 1961

Luc wants us to attend the official opening of the industrial trade fair. He designed two of the pavilions and has invitation cards. Dr. Radhakrishnan will make the inaugural speech. Gun does not want to go. She has heard him before, she says.

I was at the Embassy to pick up the affidavit for Foreigners' Registration, certifying that we will not become public charges of India.

November 15, 1961

In the newspapers, I read that the Vice President said what we had expected him to say:

Vice President Emphasizes Spiritual Values

Dr. Radhakrishnan quoted the Upanishads and stressed that the amassing of wealth must not be the goal of labor. He has recently visited Holland, Germany and Hungary, and the leaders of these countries had confessed to him *with uncommon unanimity* that their people were better off than ever but were not at all happy. *This proves that man needs more than just material well-being.*

At Foreigners' Registration, they study meticulously Ambassador Böök's affidavit stating that no cost related to our stay in India *will touch any Indian governmental authority, national or private institution or other Indian party.* So we are once again armed with proper resident permits. Pavel was right when he used to say in Moscow:

"Human beings are made up of three parts: body, soul and passport. You can get rid of your soul, and your body can be in really bad shape, but just try to get along with a bad passport!"

November 20, 1961

In the evening at Mitra's house. Among those present, a member of Parliament from the CPI [Communist Party of India]. He speaks enthusiastically about the "peaceful road."

"Nowadays, all roads lead to socialism. In ten years, India will be the first socialist country with a genuine people's car!"

He has something to do with the Panda Committee and says that in a few short years the public sector can begin production of the Indian people's car.

"It won't cost more than 6500 rupees, everything included."

When he drops his notes, he calls to the servant to pick them up. Mitra smiles slightly. On the way home Gun says: "They sure don't make communists the way they used to."

December 6, 1961

It is not until late in the morning that the mist over Delhi begins to lift. Standing on the verandah, I feel in the air a harsh taste of winter. The morning papers write of war. Southbound train traffic in the direction of Bombay has been interrupted. Troops are being transported to the border of Goa. Yesterday, Nehru spoke in the Lok Sabha: "War with China cannot be ruled out," he said.

One of the women who carries bricks to the construction site on the other side of the street has put down her child on a pile of gravel. It is as thin as a beanpole. It lies completely still. At first, I think it is already dead. Then I see that it is still alive. It lies there naked, shivering slightly. It can only be a couple of months old. The child is a girl. She will be dead by Christmas.

Suddenly rage is upon me. It is like a hammer blow to the larynx, and my mouth grows dry. The brick-carrier is a serf. She has been brought here from her village in Rajasthan by a contractor. Delhi's new suburbs are mortared with the blood of children.

When I first came to India in 1958, all the problems I perceived seemed clear to me. I knew the essential features of the subcontinent's history. Indeed, I even had a Bengali father-in-law, Kali Ghosh. Because of him, I was deported from Great Britain as an undesirable alien in 1950. But even if I knew quite a bit about the art, culture and politics of India in 1955, I had never experienced seriously the rage. The rage which has shaken me these years in India. This remarkable, helpless rage which nauseates me, rings in my ears and shakes my body, as I sit here at my typewriter and see the child lying there, dying in the gravel.

December 8, 1961

This morning the demolition squad tore down the dairy in the coolie colony by the railroad. It was a pucca house. Brick walls and a sheet-metal roof. The owner had fastened an Indian flag onto a pole and raised it above his house. The flag drooped over the roof. Four coolies labored with picks to break the walls down. Two policemen supervised the work. The women from the colony had gathered in a group. They looked on in total silence. The man sat on his *charpoy* smoking. The number of on-lookers kept growing.

"Why doesn't he do something?" Gun asked. "Why doesn't he defend himself?"

There now remains nothing of the house but an unsorted pile of bricks. The police have confiscated the flag and taken it away.

In the evening, I see that the man has raised a *shamiana*, a colorful tent used on festive occasions. It looks odd. It is as if he were going to celebrate a wedding.

December 9, 1961

Early this morning, they had begun to rebuild the dairy. All the neighbors of the colony lend a hand. They gather up the bricks. Tomorrow the house will stand there as usual.

Kiran comes calling. She says, "The man bribes the police to have his dairy there. Then the police tell him that they must tear it down anyway. They have received their orders and it cannot be put off any longer. Then they tear it down. He must scrape together new protection money and pay them again. Then he can rebuild his dairy. After four months, the whole process starts again. The police tear down the house once more. If they didn't pull it down from time to time, he would start feeling safe and stop paying them off. Then, how would they survive?"

"Well, what does he say when the politicians tell him that India is in danger?" I ask. She does not answer, but begins to talk about the Chinese threat.

December 10, 1961

A young peasant agitator, arrested by the police during a demonstration in Kerala, has died. The demonstrations are getting bigger. People do not believe in these sudden heartfailures.

December 11, 1961

Down on Lodi Road, a sweeper stands with the corpse of a child in his arms. The corpse is wrapped in red silk paper. It looks like a large Christmas package. The sweeper holds it in his arms and weeps. The burial cortege consists of two more men. Naturally, they too, are sweepers. Barefooted, with ragged clothes. Behind them are the hovels of the sweeper-colony.

The man carrying the corpse of the child crosses the street. The little cortege walks towards the illegal crematory of the sweeper-colony, beyond Link Road. The newspapers have written that this place is a nuisance to the house owners in the neighborhood (people who need the sweepers to scrub their floors and clean their toilets).

In the evening Åse says: "Death does not cause Indians pain as it does us." She makes me sick.

What is the use of going on about a thousand people having frozen to death, five thousand children dying or another eight thousand people succumbing to cholera?

"Indians don't feel the pain of death the way we do. They are fatalists. They are different."

The experts rake in their tax-free five thousand every month and pursue their relentless struggle for the right to duty-free whisky, and the right to fly the pennant on the car so that the President's bodyguard will present arms when they drive through Rashtrapati Bhavan. No one cares about a poor devil of a lowly sweeper, crying in Lodi Road with his dead child wrapped in red silk paper.

December 12, 1961

The India known to Europeans is inhabited by the following groups: 40 percent poor lowly lepers, 40 percent energetically happy community developers, and the rest, porters, "boys" and touristguides.

December 16, 1961

Singh from Punjab National Bank got in touch with me yesterday at Luc's. He began by talking about his cars. Then he wondered if I would not like to draw up a new design for Wearwell's bicycles. It seems they are too heavy and unwieldy. Their center of gravity is too high and, what is more, their gears do not function properly. They would pay me well.

"But I know nothing about bicycles."

"The bicycles should also be equipped with foot-brakes."

"I used to cycle a lot, but I really know nothing about bicycles."

"Indians will use bicycles for the next two or three hundred years. The market is enormous. They won't be able to afford anything other than bicycles. And, besides, traffic problems would be unmanageable if all of them had cars."

Luc laughed and said: "If you don't watch out, you'll end up dressed in *khadi* with a Congress cap on your head, talking about spiritualism and a socialist pattern of society, and rich as a king. You'll be as happy as a rat in the cheese."

He went on. "I have been working here for two years. Designing houses, factories and town plans. The last four months, I have associated only with industrialists. They grow increasingly wealthy. That is the only development I can see. Fatter rats, and more of them, in the big cheese. The situation is reminiscent of pre-revolutionary Russia. And we're heading for the same end."

December 17, 1961

It is still dark outside when the alarm goes off. The room is cold. I switch on the electric heater. When I go out onto the verandah, I see that it is raining. The sky is slowly turning grey with dawn and the wind is cutting. In the faint morning light of winter, wet yellow leaves fall heavily on the stone pavement. I sit at my typewriter and look out. Three scrawny, stray cows shiver under the peepul tree. The sweeper-girl goes by. Her rain-soaked sari flaps heavily around her legs. Two coolies run by with large scarves wrapped about their heads. The landlord comes out onto the stairway. He has his army coat over his shoulders. He looks out into the rain and then goes back inside. The smell of *chapaties* floats in the air.

I have a hard time working. I blame it on the electricity being shut off. The room is dark and the grey light from the window is cold and faint. I can hardly see the keys of my typewriter. Suddenly the light comes on. The heater begins to radiate heat. Then the light goes out again. It is raining all the while. Water seeps in under the verandah door. I roll up the green rug and push it up against the door.

The electrical mains are over-taxed. And, of course, we in the less posh areas are the first to be shut off. The cows are gone. Out in the sweepers' colony, they are trying to light their *chulas*. Acrid, white smoke in the morning rain.

I think about my discussions with Kali in the summer of 1950. At that time, we were living in Kaffatorp, in the south of Sweden. We talked about India. I was leaving in the fall, though later it turned out that I was unable to get together the money for that trip. We ate fermented Baltic herring which reminded him of Bengal. We walked in the beech wood and talked only of India.

He had worked underground in Bengal in the late 1920s. He refused to say whether it was in Jugantar or Anushilan, but he had been a Bengali nationalist, a terrorist. He had written in the *Swahinata* of that time and had been jailed in the great police sweep following the attack on the Chittagong Arsenal in 1930. In time, he was deported from India to England and had not been home in twenty years. He discussed terrorism with me. He had abandoned it. For many years now he was a Marxist. But he held that one had to see terrorism in its historical context. And he was not in total agreement with the official communist line on terrorism. Why, he had been a terrorist himself. It was the terrorists who had given back to the Indian people their self-confidence. It was important for people to see their masters run like scared rats.

We sat on the banks of the Immel, the peace of summer around us. He spoke of the splits and divisions and of the horrible reciprocal slaughter between Hindus and Muslims. He believed that these divisions would be surmounted.

Last year we met in Delhi. We drank tea together. He was dressed in a dark suit and was very British. I did not ask him what his politics were but he writes for *Blitz*. He is coming again to the West, I hear.

From the outside, it was always easy to understand and talk about India. Take 1956 as a case in point. That whole summer in Geneva, we used India as an example. The Italians, particularly, found this example extremely useful. Nehru and the Congress Party had declared socialism to be India's future. We took them at their word. We used them to make our case. There was not just one road; life offered alternatives. Several different roads led towards the future. Out of Nehru's words we fashioned a theory.

Now I understand what Nehru meant. He used words to decorate. Like the rose in his buttonhole. Like his smile.

It has stopped raining. The Rajasthani women are carrying bricks to the construction site. One of them used to carry a child with her to work. Now it is dead.

December 18, 1961

Last night, Indian troops marched into Goa. Finally! The troop movements were already completed several days ago. Everyone was just waiting. Twice, the marching orders were rescinded. I had almost begun to believe that "the voice of reason" would succeed in stopping the liberation of Goa. But the pressure on Nehru from the African countries and the Indian people became just too strong. Listen to the radio. The declaration by Menon. But why these unnecessary excuses? At present, it appears that the pressure is easing off.

In a conflict between India and Portugal, or between India and Great Britain, I would support India, of course. Even the existing India.

The India of the rulers, the existing India, is totally different from the India of the ruled. The India of the rulers is full of slogans, luxury, affluence and phrases about India's love of peace and its unique brand of socialism. The India of the ruled is destitution, privation, starvation and death.

Today, however, I feel joy because the India of the rulers has sent its troops into Goa. Colonialism is dying. Things have gone more rapidly than I thought possible in the 1950s.

December 21, 1961

Yesterday evening, the moon was enclosed in a lunar halo. The moon was full. Cirrus clouds formed a strange pattern. They seemed to emerge from the southwestern horizon in long layers across the sky. Today the clouds are heavy and it is very cold. The newspapers report that "Operation Goa" is terminated.

I was with Luc and Michelle last night. We talked about South Indian temple sculpture. (Art as an escape. I did not agree.) Then about the racist ideas of the Swedish agricultural expert's wife.

Michelle was of the opinion that the ideology of race which is characteristic of her entire social class is not just an attitude or even an ideology, but is a neurosis. The fact that it is a collective neurosis and that the neurotics lack any awareness of the disorder does not make them any less dangerous.

"Didn't you notice how she reacted?" says Michelle. "When she began talking about the Indian character and personality, her breathing grew heavier. Her gaze began to wander. Her face reddened. Her words were marked by a strong emotional tenor. The more rationally you spoke of the number of sweat glands and lack of correlation between skin color and behavior, the more she was forced to make rationalizations. Obscure emotions were at work. Looking at her, I got the feeling that she was really talking in order to drown out fantasies of rape. That's what makes her so dangerous."

I agree only up to a point. Certainly racism can appear in that sort of individual expression. It is also possible, I believe, to show a relation between the racial attitudes of the agricultural expert's wife and her repressed, shame-shrouded, erotic fantasies. But what is decisive is that racism is a necessary and functional ideology, serving to preserve the position of the rulers. The empires of past and present-day neo-colonialism must create their racist ideologies in one form or another. And because it is irrational, this racism is also related to illogical, vague and barely conscious feelings of anxiety.

Michelle thinks that they should be helped by letting them speak out. I am in total disagreement. One cannot help anti-Semites by letting them speak about their anti-Semitism; one cannot cure racists by letting them spread their racism. (We have seen the experiment performed. In Germany, the anti-Semites were allowed to "speak out.")

Michelle's liberalism is dangerous. I am of the opinion that the fomenting of racial hatred should be outlawed. Outlaw the symptom and fight the theories with arguments. This FAO official who accepts being married to such a wife should be threatened with immediate dismissal. That would silence her. That would not cure her, but it would stop the spread of the disease.

The very process of decolonization can result in a growing racism in our countries.

December 27, 1961

I met Al Parsian Turkes from the Turkish embassy. This is an intelligent fascist.

"We have lodged a protest against India's invasion of Goa. We are a member-nation of NATO and we have the deepest misgivings about the use of force."

He laughed and continued: "But when we captured Smyrna, it was a lot bloodier than when Nehru took Goa. Although, at that time, we were not members of NATO, of course."

December 28, 1961

Visited Babu in the afternoon. A member of Parliament from the Congress Party was there to solicit a contribution to his campaign fund. The candidate for Parliament was *harijan*, an untouchable, from a rural electoral district in Punjab. He was a back-bencher. He spoke not more than once a year in Parliament. He was poor. So poor, in fact, that this morning, when five important visitors from his home district suddenly dropped by, he had to send his servant out to borrow money with which to buy sugar and milk. He had taken the five visitors over to Babu's, so that Babu would offer them something to eat. He asked Babu not to reveal how poor he was. He had big problems.

"I get five thousand rupees from the party to cover election expenses. But our Chief Minister, Kairon, has demanded that each candidate give him five thousand rupees in exchange for his support. So it evens out. Besides, each collector must raise a hundred thousand rupees for the party in his own district. Kairon has demanded it. It is illegal. But who's going to say anything? You know how Kairon is. He will always be re-elected, but the person who protests will lose his livelihood. It has happened many times.

"My campaign costs will be thirty thousand rupees. It is not much, but mine is a poor man's district of untouchables. You know what it costs to be elected! I have to spend five thousand rupees on liquor and women. I can't get by with less. And even so, they'll have to settle for the cheapest girls. Women just get more and more expensive. I have to rent a jeep for six weeks, and jeeps are expensive at election time. I have already hired two agents. They cost me one hundred rupees per month apiece. I'll have to hire more. Publicity and such things also cost money. Then I have to give bribes, too. The money which is left over I'll use to buy votes with. You know a *sarpanch* here has to spend ten thousand rupees to be elected. He has his expenses and has to get back what he has spent. That is understandable. But that causes the price of votes to go up. The opposition parties try to outbid us. We'll pay such and such a price for a block of votes, they say. Then I have to calm the village leaders and tell them that Congress pays better. But I'm the one who has to pay. It won't be easy."

When he had left I asked Babu, "How much does he earn as a Member of Parliament?"

"Four hundred and fifty rupees a month, plus twenty-one rupees a day in allowance for expenses. But only for those days he is here in Delhi."

"In other words, seven hundred rupees a month!"

"Hardly! It's unusual that anyone is present everyday. He must also see to his electoral district."

"But he has to have thirty thousand!"

"That's the minimum."

"So how can he be an honest politician and Member of Parliament?"

"There is no such thing!"

"But Nehru. . . ."

"He wears a rose in his buttonhole, and at a word from him, we were once ready to face death. But times have changed. Have you met an honest official? He would have to be extremely rich and have numerous poor peasants sweating for him, if he is to pursue a bureaucratic hobby as uncommon as incorruptibility. Everyone is corrupt. Don't you understand what he said? If you defy Kairon, you lose your livelihood. I have personally heard Kairon say to a police inspector, 'Arrest that man and put him away or you'll be out on the street without a job the next time you see me.' That's the way it is."

Later that afternoon, Gun and I stand on the kitchen verandah and look at the construction site across the road. The old brick-carriers walk with heavy loads on their heads. Their breasts flap to and fro. These old women are younger than we are. They are serfs and are worn out. Their children play among the brick piles. A five-year old places a brick on the head of a three-year old. They pretend that they are working. It's icy cold. The old women carry their loads in a long line under our verandah.

"How wonderful for them that they live in the world's largest 'democracy,' " says Gun. "The contractor might give them a few paisa to celebrate with when he has sold their votes."

December 29, 1961

Sun. No longer so cold. Last night only four people froze to death. They are trying to round up the homeless. Patrols pick them up from their sleeping places on the streets. Yesterday, the Rotary Club held a fundraising lunch for the poor. At the same time, the destruction brigade pulled down six houses.

Nehru held a press conference yesterday. He was asked how he judged reaction to the invasion of Goa: "Nothing in the past fifteen years has so delighted every sector of India's people; every party, every class, every group (although I can't speak for every individual) has been delighted by this event. . . . In Goa, these events have been greeted with joy by the entire population. Not just by Hindus, but even by the Catholics and other Christians."

He looks old. He searches for words when he answers. His smile now appears a little out of place. It flashes charmingly, but fades quickly.

New Year's Eve, 1961

Sun. The cold spell is over. So far, seven hundred and twenty-eight people and thirteen thousand farm animals have frozen death in U.P. and Bihar. During the operations in Goa, Diu and Daman, seventeen Portuguese and twenty-two Indians died. One Portuguese is reported missing.

Gun wants me to write to the publishing company and propose that I translate Moti Chandra's *Technique of Mughal Painting*.

January 10, 1962

Yesterday evening, an ox-cart tipped over on Link Road, across from the cremation site. The cart was broken and the load of cauliflower spilt over the road. Traffic piled up and drivers honked irritably. A man wrapped in a grey blanket stood next to the pile of cauliflower.

He did not reach the market. He will be forced to sell the load at a reduced price. The cart must be repaired.

Late at night I saw him again. He was still standing next to his ruined cart and spilt load of cauliflower. I could see his thin legs beneath the grey blanket. He waits.

January 15, 1962

Mitra returns from a visit to Calcutta.

"In Bengal, they only asked me what I thought of Albania." He has also met Surendra, who was so intensely revolutionary when we lived and worked together in Budapest and Bucharest in 1953.

"He has joined his uncle's firm and become a manager. He hardly said hello."

March 23, 1962

I shall be leaving India in a few days. Travelling on. I pack manuscripts and notes.

The New Raj

We are back in India once more. A generation has passed. It is December 1979 and only yesterday we arrived at Palam airport. We drove through the outskirts of Delhi and I had trouble getting my bearings. All the landmarks have been submerged in buildings. The great burial grounds have become new residential districts. Prosperity now reigns in this barren and rather ugly area west of the Jamuna river. It is the prosperity of the tax collectors, for here lies the capital of vast India.

Here there have been many capitals. In the past every new conqueror from the northwest had to pass the North Indian plain between the Jamuna and the great Indian desert. Delhi had to be captured to ensure domination over Hindustan. Here the rulers erected their camps of stone and masonry and here they raised their mausolea. From here they taxed the villages of their empire.

On the eastern side of New Delhi, in Sundar Nagar market, we buy Indian sweets and look at the brassware in the stalls. Before driving on we look in at Mohenjodaro. It is still *the* curio shop and antique market for the embassies and foreign experts. The prices have skyrocketed and the selection is limited.

"Everything has been bought up."

The brass figurines, twenty years earlier still considered scrap to be melted down, have now become antiques, gone up in price, and vanished from India into the international market.

It is said that somewhere in this vicinity lay the first Delhi, a chief's village on the burn-beaten land. In the *Mahabharata*, Yudhisthir and his four brothers burnt the woods and founded the city of Indraprastha, according to traditional dating, some three or four thousand years ago. It was at the time of the tribal feuds which have provided the subject matter for an epic as voluminous as sixteen *Iliads*. Historians say these feuds probably occurred somewhat later, around two thousand eight hundred years ago. At that point, eight hundred years had passed since the fall of Mohenjodaro and Harappa. The great cities on the Indus and all their trading stations in the direction of what is today India had long been abandoned and forgotten when that first Delhi was founded. Almost two thousand years were to pass before the city became important. There were other cities of importance: rich trade centers along the coasts and in the agricultural hinterland. Delhi was out of the way. Its era of greatness began with the emergence of a strong centralized government and the growing poverty of empire.

In 1011 A.D., at the time of Mahmud of Ghazni's tenth plundering expedition into Hindustan, the Raja of Delhi attempted to unite the country's many rulers for their self-defence: "For if this raging torrent is not stopped, all of Hindustan will soon go under and every state, big or small, will be destroyed."

But they were unable to unite and Mahmud of Ghazni carried out six or more expeditions into Hindustan. It was the strong feudal state which destroyed the high-living small princes. But the plundering was of such proportions that it transformed the society. The new, strong feudal state was an army of plunder on the march, and where it passed it also destroyed the independence of the towns, the autonomy of the villages and the guilds of the craftsmen.

Following the death of Mahmud of Ghazni, a new, fortified Delhi was built as a barrier against invaders from the northwest. It was a Hindu garrison town. It was also a springboard for the attempt at unifying Hindu North India by armed force. However, in 1193 when Ghorian armies had crushed all resistance, and the Hindu princes had been killed, or had fled or capitulated to the Muslim conquerors, General Qutb-ud-din Aibak, Muhammed of Ghor's slave, installed himself as Viceroy in Delhi. He was still a slave in 1206 when his master was murdered and he had himself proclaimed Sultan.

This signified not just a change of religion or dynasty: the Sultanate of Delhi was a new, effective regime. Instead of the small Hindu principalities bickering among themselves, in place of an economy where royal festivals and temple construction siphoned off resources from the army, came a tightly centralized, militaristic world power with economic and cultural ties with Western and Central Asia.

Six cities were built here after the demise of Hindu rule, one more magnificent and mighty than the other. Enormous irrigation works were constructed. Commerce and handicrafts thrived. The sultans had thousands of weavers and masons to work for them. Tax revenues poured in from all over the realm.

On occasion, this tax-based empire was shaken by an invasion and new rulers replaced the old. Between the ruler's retinue, seeking to become hereditary nobility, and the powerful central bureaucracy, tensions became explosive. At times the court was moved from Delhi. Occasionally, the city was sacked. In 1327, the ruler had the inhabitants rounded up and expelled. They were ordered to travel one thousand kilometers towards the south to Daulatabad where they were to build a new capital city. But a few years later, Delhi was more magnificent than ever. The city was necessary to the empire.

In 1398 Delhi was captured by Tamerlane's troops. The city was sacked and put to the torch, and its population massacred. When the troops departed, the city lay blackened, abandoned, empty and without a ruler. But it was rebuilt as always. The entire plain between the Jamuna and the desert was once city land. The monuments survived even when the surrounding cities were burnt down or pillaged.

Nadir Shah captured the city in 1739 and plundered and massacred so thoroughly that his name became a term of abuse. But the city recovered. In September 1857, during the Indian war of independence, the British captured the city using exceptional brutality and banished its inhabitants. The British officers and soldiers looted the riches of the deserted city. Displaying true mercenary shrewdness, they permitted the inhabitants to return individually the following year, on the condition that they paid the British a fee of 25 percent of the value of their real estate if they were Muslims and 10 percent of their real estate if they were Hindus. All their other property had already been carried off by British gentlemen and soldiery.

But from this, too, Delhi recovered. In 1911 the British moved the capital back to Delhi from Calcutta and began the construction of their imperial Delhi, intended to house the military officers and tax-collectors who would rule their India.

Today the tenth Delhi sprawls, a formless agglomeration of houses across the plain of ruins. The air is heavy with pollution. The lines of cars swell out in the direction of the winding roads of the expanding suburbs. A stench rises from the sewers. Delhi has not become a real industrial or commercial center. But the city has grown at a tremendous pace, since it is from here that one seventh of humanity is taxed and ruled. This is the hub of the new empire, capital of independent India. Here flock those trafficking in power, influence and government contracts.

Villas in the manner of post-war Italian architecture and bungalows in the gas-station style of California push out over the burying grounds to the south. On the remnants of a thousand years of warlords, emperors, government officials and saints, the suburbs of the new middle class throw up before them a brownish scum of slum dwellings.

When we lived in Defence Colony it lay on the outskirts of the city. Today Defence Colony is situated towards the center and beyond it sprawl huge new residential districts. New homes for a new class. Draftboard designs from the architectural academies of the whole world materialize here as shoddy buildings of stone-scrap brick walls and huge, humming air-conditioning units in place of insulation. Never has imperial Delhi been as populous as it is today. About six million people have congregated here. And this, the latest and greatest Delhi, has engulfed all its predecessors. Here accumulates the wealth leeched by politics from India's poverty. India is now independent.

At the turn of the century Delhi was but a provincial market and railroad center. It fit easily within the confines of the Mughal Shahjahanabad, up in the northwest corner of this landscape of ruins. The British garrisons were located north of the city. It was a North Indian cantonment with an illustrious past. The great monuments could be used as background for spectacles such as that when Queen Victoria was proclaimed *Kaiser-i-Hind*, on January 1, 1877; or when the Indian princes arrived mounted on elephants at the durbar on New Year's Day, 1903, held so that Lord Curzon could proclaim with great pomp the inebriate Edward VII emperor. The pageants were expensive but false, just as the empire itself was embroidery. But the monuments were the real thing.

In 1911, when the British decided to move the seat of government of their Indian empire from Calcutta to Delhi, the city had a little more than two hundred thousand inhabitants.

As for the reasons behind this move, the contemporary European press such as *Hvar 8 Dag* of January 21 reported:

> If the innermost feelings of an ancient civilized nation are offended, practical reforms will do little good. Now, however, the critical act of redress seems to have come. The moving of the Indian seat of government to the ancient Indian imperial city, sacred Delhi, must be considered a magnanimous act of wise and liberal statesmanship. It would seem that King George, by means of the proclamation at the durbar in Delhi, has at one stroke put right all that which for so many years has caused the people's dissatisfaction and taken a firm hold on its most profound sentiments. Certainly, no concrete reform act, however extensive, could have aroused such general and intense satisfaction throughout the country and so effectively strengthened British rule. In the eyes of the native population this

will now appear as a direct continuation of the country's ancient traditions of government and will be invested in a religious and historic sanctity which it could never achieve in the more European than Indian, commercial and industrial city, Calcutta.

It is possible that those who were responsible for this move believed in these mystical explanations. In point of fact, the British were fleeing from an increasingly politically active Bengal. But in the official communication of August 25, 1911, from the Indian government to their superiors in Britain, the simple and obvious reasons for the move were enveloped in fanciful speculation that "Delhi is a name to work miracles." The Muslims would be incredibly happy if Delhi recaptured "its proud place as the center of the empire." As for the Hindus, Delhi is the ancient Indraprastha and is near the great battlefield of the *Mahabharata* and "therefore intimitally associated with sacred legend in the minds of the Hindus."

The Bengali terrorists, however, warned the British in their *Swadhin Bharat (Free India)* leaflet, and the inveterate imperialist Lord Curzon derided this over-hasty, panic stricken, secret decision to "exile India's government to Delhi's crumbling graves."

Even for those who believed in omens, the move was inauspicious. On December 7, 1911, George V was to make his solemn entry into Delhi. From the station he was to proceed to the Red Fort. There he was to receive the ruling Indian princes. But the large reception pavilion had burnt down the week before. He was to make his entry into Delhi from the Red Fort and then proceed to the "ridge," held by the British in the summer of 1857 and from where they captured the city in the autumn. From there he was to go to the large group of tents put up behind it. But no elephants could be procured, so he had to ride a horse. And the people brought there to cheer him did not notice when he passed. The monument to Edward VII was unfinished and could not be properly inaugurated. George V had to settle for placing a commemorative plaque between the scaffolding.

At the great coronation durbar held on December 12, the king-emperor proclaimed that the seat of government would be moved from Calcutta to Delhi, and a few hours later the P&O Line's proud ocean liner "Delhi" ran aground in the fog off Tangiers. On board were the King's elder sister, her husband, the Duke of Fife, and his daughters, the princesses Maud and Alexandra.

On December 15, the King-Emperor and Queen-Empress ceremoniously laid a cornerstone each for the new capital. Unfortunately, they placed the cornerstones in the tent town, an area which turned into marsh during the monsoon season. The stones later had to be carted clear across the city, to be placed on more solid ground up on Raisina Mound.

The following year Lord Hardinge, the Viceroy, was to move formally to Delhi. When he left Government House in Calcutta, a bolt of lightning struck the flagpole and the flag was torn to shreds. When he arrived at the railroad station in Delhi, fifty elephants were waiting and Lord Hardinge took his place in the silver-ornamented royal *howdah*, the elephant saddle. Above the Viceroy, the state parasol, the symbol of authority, was held. He sat as if on a throne in the boat-like *howdah*. Bobbing along on the elephant's back, he noticed that the imperial crown in front, which rested on a cushion above the great Star of India, had worked itself loose. It wobbled back and forth to the elephant's gait.

When the procession passed through Chandni Chowk, the Bengali revolutionaries were already in position. On the roof of the Punjab National Bank, Rash Behari Bose waited with a bomb assembled by Manindra Naik of Chandernagore. At 11:45, the Viceroy reached the spot and Rash Behari Bose threw the bomb. The servant carrying the state symbol was killed instantly. The state parasol broke over the Viceroy, whose eardrums were shattered. He was wounded and lost consciousness due to loss of blood. Rash Behari Bose escaped and the whole magnificent pageant was transformed into an occasion of mourning.

The omens could not have been clearer. No wonder the statue of George V, which stood in the imperial city he had proclaimed, was to be taken down and put away before he had been dead twenty-five years.

However, the seat of government was not moved for the sake of symbolism. There were weighty motives which had to do with domestic politics. The British had deliberately played Hindus and Muslims off against each other. At a time when the greatness of the empire was beyond question, its spokesmen could express themselves as Lord Elphinstone had towards the end of his life. *"Divide et impera* was the motto of the old Roman empire and it should also be our own." Fifty years later, when Bengal was to be partitioned into a Muslim and a Hindu state so that they could make things difficult for each other, Lord Curzon warned of discussing these matters publicly: "What I can safely say within the walls of this council chamber is not necessarily appropriate to be shouted from the rooftops."

However, within a few years, the attempt at using and encouraging these contradictions would result in such a profound political crisis that the British were forced to partially rescind the decision on Bengal's partition, and, what is more, to move the seat of government from restive Calcutta to tranquil Delhi. In Delhi, where the new age was only represented by a railroad station and a few steam-mills, no bourgeoisie, no proletariat and no unruly, agitating intellectuals were to be found.

Feudal tranquillity and poverty reigned about Delhi's sepulchral monuments. In Bengal during the partition, between 1905 and 1911, the Muslims had their own Muslim East Bengal. Now it was thought that the Muslims should be compensated for their loss of a separate state, by placing the seat of government in the classical capital of Muslim India.

In Russia and in Europe, there was speculation about Britain's foreign policy motives for the move. It was thought that Italy's war against Turkey and Anglo-Russian rivalry for control over the disintegrating Ottoman empire might make it necessary for the British to move their capital nearer the Middle East.

That theory was hardly correct. Nine months of the year, the British government of India was located in Simla, in the mountains north of Delhi, in close proximity to Afghanistan, Russian Turkestan and the Middle East. It was only during the winter that the government was in Calcutta.

Actually, Delhi was a larger Simla with better means of communication. The higher British officials were able to bear living in Delhi seven months of the year. India had been ruled by the British as a bureaucratic autocracy. The situation was that described by Harold Cox in *The Graphic* of January 13, 1912:

> The Europeans dwelling in Calcutta maintain that it is only when the Indian government is in Calcutta that it is at all subject to influence by an independent public opinion. Up in Simla the high officials live in a rarefied bureaucratic atmosphere, considering themselves to be demigods whose every word is law. After nine months of this self-glorification they return to Calcutta where they encounter an educated and successful European population which does not worship them, which does not even know who they are.

By moving from Calcutta the bureaucrats fled from Bengal's radical mass agitation and, at the same time, liberated themselves from the "educated Europeans who did not treat them as divine images but as normal human beings."

Instead, the bureaucracy could take the princes and Legislative Council with it. The reforms of 1909 had given the Legislative Council twenty-seven elected members. This was not a majority (the Council had a membership of sixty) but it was a broad enough minority to be expected to use its right to move and discuss general questions in a manner more advantageous for the bureaucracy than would European public opinion in Calcutta. The latter was certainly both educated and well to do, but it exercised its duty of criticism in a spontaneous and peevish manner in private clubs and at official banquets. Besides, as the bureaucracy pointed out, they were only a special-interest group. The elected members of the Legislative Council, on the other hand, came from all over India. They were nominated by provincial councils and bodies such as chambers of commerce and associations of landowners. They, together with the princes, represented that public the bureaucracy needed in order to allow for a meaningful decision-making process. The move to Delhi signified a self-realization of the bureaucracy. It was the apotheosis of the state in a new imperial city of red sandstone. British India's administrative structure was here to shape the plan of the city.

And the city turned out accordingly. New Delhi is a systematic city. It is a city of boulevards laid out in a hexagonal pattern. Human beings do not think in hexagons. They think rectangularly, in a grid or in blocks as in the moves of the knight across a chess board. As a result, it is impossible to find one's way in New Delhi. But the city was laid out so as to make it easily defensible. It was adjoined to Old Delhi, but connected by only three streets. These could be quickly sealed off and held by a couple of platoons. The whole city could be held in check by a handful of well-disciplined troops, who armed with machine guns at the hexagons, could keep the boulevards clear of mobs. The mopping-up operations could then be carried out area by area.

Along the boulevards lie the civil service departments and official residencies. Strictly following the list concerning order of precedence, residencies were built in the greenery for the high officials, princes and representatives. The higher one's rank, the closer to the center of town and the bigger the bungalow. In the back of the bungalows lay the alleyways inhabited by the servants. In its backyards, high society cultivated slums.

But this, British imperialism's last and most accomplished urban development in colonial India, began to crumble at the first rain. New Delhi's exemplary bungalows were shoddy from the very beginning. Their foundations were bad. The walls cracked. The roofs began to leak after the first monsoons and the servants had to be sent up to try to tramp them water-tight. The sewage system was underdimensioned, fat rats ran right across the reception halls of the residencies, and after the monsoons the septic tanks overflowed and it stank in the princely apartments. The impressive colonnades proved to be false fronts. The plaster cracked, peeled off and was covered with grey patches of mould. Large English-style fireplaces of marble and brick sat in state in the salons. But when it turned cold and the servants lit the fire, the whole thing burnt up because it was all built of marbleized wood. The bureaucratic structure which materialized in this new capital was already rotten.

In the very center of this city, the Viceroy's palace was to sit enthroned on Raisina Mound. A magnificent vista would be created where the immense parade route formed a main artery in the direction of a palace intended to surpass Versailles and Schönbrunn. Lutyens designed it and the construction went on for decades. It was Mughal-ornamented classicism for 1,000,000 pounds. This sum was so enormous that a half a century earlier, a similar amount had purchased from the British all of Kashmir for the cavalryman Gulab Singh, thus making him a Maharaja and founder of a dynasty.

However, long before the palace was completed, the bureaucracy had government offices, the administrative buildings designed for them by Herbert Baker. These enormous edifices were placed in front of the palace. The bureaucracy also decided that the slope up to the palace should be steep. And now, as we move up the parade route and follow the main artery of the vista, the palace sinks before us and the government offices rise toweringly above us until only the crest of the palace can be spied between the two massive, red buildings where governmental power makes its will known in official papers, notes and memoranda.

As an afterthought, a bit to the side and outside the great vista, beyond the northern office building and below the Sun temple and Anglican cathedral, sits the parliament. It was not planned from the beginning. One could say that it hangs like a large carbuncle from the walls of power which rise above the main artery in the picture's center. Such is this ninth Delhi, built by the British for themselves and abandoned sixteen years after its formal inauguration in 1931.

However, the ninth Delhi, which the British left behind, still had a population of only half a million people. Administration, retinue, officialdom and democratic apparatus was not more numerous than that. It is today that Delhi grows and expands. And this Delhi of the new middle class is a city marked by a curious fear. It was not like this twenty years ago. People say that the streets have grown dangerous.

"It's not like it used to be."

"Be careful! You could be murdered."

"Now they even rob foreigners."

At Palam airport, the police record the passengers' names and destinations and the registration numbers of the taxis.

"It's a safety precaution."

"Why?"

"So that nothing will happen en route."

It is said that in the new residential districts gangs of city dacoits run amuck. They arrive in stolen cars. They loot. They empty entire houses in broad daylight. They assault women and pull the jewelry off them. The victims have to be grateful that they are still alive.

"They grabbed a little boy because he had a gold ring on his finger. When they couldn't remove it, they cut off his entire hand and drove away with it so that they could get at the ring later."

"Where did that happen?"

In Defence Colony, a few days ago. Up on B-block. The boy got gangrene in the stump and they had to amputate the whole arm. He may not live."

Evening has come and the streets are filled with cyclists. They are the petty clerks, on their way home to the suburbs of the poor. Everything is as it used to be and, yet, the mood is another. A new raj rules Delhi now.

The Rise of the Lumpen-Bourgeoisie

Jama Masjid in Old Delhi used to stand in a swamp of slums. This magnificent mosque, built for the Mughal Emperor Shah Jahan between 1644 and 1658, was surrounded by filth and squalor. It was to these overcrowded bazaars that we used to go to buy mutton. But also to find spare parts for the car or to go into the Hindu junk-merchants' shops to see if there were any interesting brass figurines among the scrap to be melted down.

It was the Partition which created this genuine slum. When the British finally left India because the empire was no longer profitable, their method of "divide and rule" had been practiced to the extent that their departure resulted in a bloodbath, in which poor Muslims and poor Hindus killed one another and great torrents of refugees poured out over the subcontinent.

"Hindus," says Akbar Adil of Karachi, a decade after Partition: "Don't tell me about Hindus! They got hold of my aunt and hacked her to pieces. Before burying her we had to put the corpse together again from sixteen pieces. And still there were parts missing."

While several hundred thousand Hindus and Sikhs fled in the direction of Delhi, Muslims were being hunted down on the streets of the city. In the beginning of September 1947, when the Indian government had Gurkha troops evacuate Muslims from Delhi and send them west to Pakistan, the Indian officials supervising the operation reported that the corpses of men, women and children lay in the by-lanes. Many of the

Muslims who chose to remain in Delhi sought refuge in the shadow of the great mosque. The slum was a haven of refuge.

The British had divided in order to rule. Methodically and on a large scale, they had systematically fomented schism in 1905 when they partitioned Bengal and in 1909 when they introduced electoral registers separated according to religion. Thus the British quickly succeeded in bringing about established political structures divided along religious lines. This policy led eventually to the bloodbath which took place in 1947 and 1948.

It is hard to say how many people lost their lives. Perhaps it was no more than a half a million. Perhaps it was three times that number: 500,000 Muslims, 500,000 Hindus and 500,000 Sikhs. In any case, the killing was well-organized. Sikh patrols, jathas, cleaned out village after village in Punjab. Not even infants or old people survived in the villages. On September 22, 1947, these jathas stopped a train filled with refugees from Delhi. It was just outside Amritsar. For three hours the refugees were cut down by swords, stabbed with spears and shot down with firearms, while the Indian guards looked on with interest. Two days later, thousands of Muslims stopped a refugee train carrying Hindus to the east. It was forty kilometers west of Lahore. Some 340 Hindus were killed, 250 wounded. But the Pakistani patrol defended the refugees. Seventy-eight of the attackers were killed and after forty minutes the train was able to continue towards Delhi. However, on January 12, 1948, when a train with 2,400 Hindus and Sikhs from Bannu, up in the north-west frontier area, was to travel to India, 1,650 of the refugees were killed and most of the survivors were wounded. There were a great many such incidents. The British left in the middle of an orgy of blood which effectively prevented social change. People killed each other for the glory of God, and 14,000,000 people took to the roads, soon to be followed by another 3,000,000. That is why Jama Masjid in Delhi stood mired in the slums and why Old Delhi resembled a rat's nest. Six hundred thousand people were crowded into a city built for 60,000.

Old Delhi was, in fact, the Mughal Shahjahanabad. The Emperor had the Red Fort built for himself. It is a massive imperial residence, in red sandstone, with an interior like melted Persian dreams in marble. In 1648, he took possession of his Red Fort. He then ordered a city to be built for the population. For the ninth time, the building of Delhi began once more. The first town wall was built in only four months in 1650. It was of clay and could not withstand the monsoon rains despite its having cost the Emperor 150,000 rupees. So the Emperor ordered a new town wall to be built of stone and mortar. It took seven years to build and when it was completed in 1658 it had cost 400,000 rupees. The wall was 4 ells wide and 9 ells high, its circumference was 6,664 ells and it was defended from 27 bastions. The city had fourteen gates and all fourteen were of equal height and grandeur. Each gate had a name. There was the Kashmir gate, the Kabul gate, the Ajmer gate, the Turkman gate and many more.

For his own use and for that of the inhabitants of the city, Shah Jahan ordered the construction of a mosque as magnificent as Emperor Akbar's in Fatehpur Sikri. It was built of red sandstone, white marble and black slate. 5,000 masons, stonecutters and laborers worked here everyday for six years until the mosque was finished. The work cost the Emperor 1,000,000 rupees then.

It was a monumental edifice for the city of which it was said:

> Kase rā zindgāni shād bāshad
> Ki dar Shae-e-Jehan ābād bāshad

The man who has the good fortune to live in the city of Shahja-hanabad lives a happy life.

However, the French doctor and philosopher, François Bernier, did not share that opinion. In the middle of the monsoon heat, on July 1, 1663, he was in Shahjahanabad, and wrote of the city to the philosopher, Francois de la Mothe le Vayer in Paris:

> Of what I have written you can ascertain if the individual who would live a good life should leave Paris to come to Delhi. To be sure, the mighty lords have everything they desire, but that is because of their numerous servants, their long whips and the fact that they possess a large amount of money. That is why I once noted that in Delhi there is no in between: either one is a mighty lord or else one lives a life of misery.

Delhi was a city of rulers.

About the mosque, Bernier writes in the same letter:

> It is not displeasing to the eye. Everything is well thought-out and carefully executed, with properly well-balanced proportions. I am convinced that were a church to be built in Paris with the design of this temple, it would be admired. If for nothing else, then for its unusual architecture and singular appearance.

In 1857, when the British quashed the great uprising, they also debated whether the great mosque should be blown up. The Muslims were the cause of so much trouble. William Howard Russel, correspondent in India for *The Times*, wrote on June 8, 1857:

> If we could eradicate the traditions and destroy the temples of
> Mahomed by one vigorous effort, it would indeed be well for the
> Christian faith and for the British rule. But such an effort cannot be
> made by man; and any attempt to effect the object will only add to
> the difficulties which always lie thick enough in the way of our faith
> and in the progress of our government.

Moreover, he was glad that the mosque had not been blown up because
he had an appreciation of architecture, and the mosque was

> one of the grandest temples ever raised by man. There is a chaste rich-
> ness, an elegance of proportion, and a grandeur of design in all its
> parts which are in painful contrast to the *mesquin* and paltry architec-
> ture of our Christian churches.

But so that the Muslims would not get any ideas, the British billeted their
troops in the mosque and ate pork at its *mihrab*. It was five years before
Muslims were once again allowed into their great sanctuary.

Fleeing Muslims flocked to this mosque in the bloody year 1947 form-
ing a slum around the monument. But all of Delhi changed religious profile that year, and its Muslim population dropped from 45 percent to 10
percent. This slum, too, became a dwelling place even for Hindus and
Sikhs. Around the mosque lay the junk shops. Old Delhi had become
one giant slum. Half of the population did not have drainage in their
homes. It stank. The tourists held their handkerchiefs to their noses
when they came to look at the monument. It was bad publicity for India.

Prime Minister Nehru paid many visits to the slum districts. He was
photographed wandering through the squalor. The people gathered
around him and he said:

> For the last few years I have been deeply interested in the slums of
> Delhi. Every time I have visited them, I return with a certain feeling
> of numbness and an urgent desire to have something done to re-
> move these slums. Action is initiated, but progress is slow because
> of innumerable difficulties.

Yet today, the slums around Jama Masjid are gone. The tourists can photograph the monument from a distance and still enjoy the view.

A grass-covered park lies where until recently refugees cluttered the
view. Delhi, too, has been beautified. What Jawaharlal Nehru was unable
to achieve in twenty years due to innumerable difficulties, was done in a

few months by his grandson, Sanjay Gandhi, under Indira Gandhi's state of emergency from 1975 to 1977.

Statistics speak for themselves. During the thirty months preceding the state of emergency declared on June 25, 1975, the authorities in Delhi pulled down 1,800 buildings. During twenty-one months of the Emergency from June 25, 1975, to March 23, 1977, the authorities in Delhi pulled down 150,105. The average number razed increased from two houses a day to two hundred and forty a day. The number of inhabitants per building in Delhi's slum districts varies somewhat, but on the average it is 4.8. During the years just prior to the Emergency Powers Act, the demolition brigades had forced nine or ten people to move everyday. This increased to an average of more than 1,150 people who were forced to move each day.

The people whose departure had beautified the city were working people. The fact is that other families—those without income—just disappeared. 30 percent of the slum inhabitants were gainfully employed. Of these, 13 percent were unskilled laborers, 18 percent small merchants and peddlers, 38 percent skilled laborers and artisans, 11 percent clerks, and servants of various kinds accounted for 9 percent, transport workers 8 percent and other categories 3 percent. The average income of the slum's inhabitants was, however, lower than that of the general population, and the percentage of illiterates was larger than for Delhi's population as a whole. The reason they lived in the slums was partly that housing costs were low and partly that the slum housing was near the places where they work.

The difficulties in clearing these slum-districts that Jawaharlal Nehru referred to were, in his own words:

> the lack of accommodation....We have to provide housing for them before we can ask them to vacate...to take them far away means to uproot them from their work. Also, whatever new accommodation might be provided is likely to have a higher rent, even though it might be subsidized.

In theory, people could not be forced to move from the slums unless the authorities could, at the same time, provide them with somewhere else to live. The project for clearing Delhi's slums also had to first be approved by the Prime Minister. Of course, what really happened was not quite so pretty. But, on the average, not more than a few families a day were cast out of their homes.

Legally, the demolitions had to be announced in advance. Regulations prescribed by law had to be followed concerning expropriation procedure. Ratified plans could only be altered in a stipulated manner. The courts could intervene. That was the way it was in theory. Reality was something else. Indira Gandhi's Emergency Powers Act swept all these formalities out by the door. The destruction of buildings in Delhi became a mass phenomenon without anyone being able to show later how, and by whom, the decisions had formally been made.

At the beginning of the Emergency, Kotha Raghuramiah was the minister in charge of building. Afterwards, he continued to be an influential member of the government during the entire period of the Emergency. He was a witness before the inquiry commission held after the Emergency and claimed that he had not made any of the decisions concerning the demolition of buildings in Delhi. He also claimed that he had been unaware of the extent of the destruction. In fact, the decisions had been made entirely outside normal channels. The orders had come from the household of the prime minister.

It was Sanjay Gandhi who directed the operations against the slums. At that time he held no position of authority. However, being his mother's son and his mother being Prime Minister, Sanjay became a powerful young man. He took an interest in birth control and urban renewal among other things. He tried to create for himself a name as a politician among the youth. Government officials and politicians called on him and he issued orders. To the authorities in Lucknow (with a copy to the head of government in Uttar Pradesh) went a telex-message expressing his wish that "the clearing of the city of stray cattle, illegal buildings and beggars should be completed within six months, so that the city during the cold period, which is the tourist season, will give a cleaner impression." He wanted action along the same lines in Varanasi. As for Delhi, Sanjay had taken over the municipal government. He lived in the home of his mother and the high government officials had to go there to get their orders. Sanjay decided to beautify Delhi.

Slum clearance was also politically opportune. In these slum districts Indira Gandhi and her Congress did not have many friends. Here lived a whole nest of opposition elements. The opposition was often religion-based. The Jan Sangh and RSS were strong in the slum. But to make sure that the slum clearance should not seem a program to benefit the Muslims, the demolition brigades also struck in Muslim districts. The area around Jama Masjid was cleared and made attractive for tourists. Besides, Sanjay had no intention of allowing the creation of "a second Pakistan" there.

The demolition proceeded quickly. Block after block was cordoned off by the police and the houses were torn down before the inhabitants had a chance to protest. Those who by chance managed to lodge a protest in time were threatened with prison. MISA was in effect. And MISA, the law on internal security, granted the authorities the right to jail people.

Delhi's middle class was subject to great inconvenience during the slum clearance. They thought it outrageous that their servants, washerwomen and night watchmen were deported from the city in this fashion. Letters of complaint reached Prime Minister Indira Gandhi from various well-known personages, letters describing the suffering of the people. She responded by either warning or dismissing from office those who complained. Those who went to her home to make a personal appeal had to meet Sanjay who briskly asked them, for their own good, not to stand in the way of progress. Sanjay Gandhi personally inspected the operation around Jama Masjid. Wrapped in his shawl, he gazed out over the area.

"Standing there, he tried to give his lips the haughty curl of his grandfather," said Saxena, British-educated, with a keen legal mind. "He was like a Roman imperator displaying his profile. He acted like a little boot, on his way to becoming a Caligula. Why, his grandfather was India's Augustus and his mother was the country's ruler."

We sat in Saxena's study in December 1979. It was a cold, raw winter's evening, but inside, the electric heater glowed in what passed for a fireplace. On the stone floor lay a Kashmiri rug and the walls were covered with bookshelves. High up against the ceiling were bound annual volumes of *Modern Review*. Then, black volumes of juridical literature, followed by paperback government publications. The titles were written in ink on their covers. The lower shelves were filled with bundles of documents. A picture of Nehru in a silver frame still stood on his desk. The window held a large air-conditioning unit, now in total silence. We sat in deep, comfortable club-style armchairs at a table with a glass top. We drank whisky. Imported whisky. Old Smuggler.

"I am as good a patriot as the next chap," said Saxena, "but one has to draw the line somewhere. I draw it at Black Knight."

The bearer came in carrying a bowl of warm cashews. The bearer had aged. He was a Christian and wore a turban and white cotton gloves. But he was not barefoot. He had on white, rubber-soled tennis shoes.

In the past, Saxena usually spoke of Nehru with an admiration bordering on adulation. He had first met him just before the war broke out.

"Gandhi was the nation's father. For him we probably would have been willing to walk around in homespun if it would have helped. But Nehru was different. I had just returned to India then. You know, whatever I had thought about Congress and its policies, I must admit that it had been correct to take responsibility for the establishing of provincial governments. Indians had proved themselves capable of governing, and Congress had instituted basic reforms for law and order in the positive sense. Why, it was these Congress administrations which gave us freedom of speech and freedom of the press. Whatever I might have said as a student about Gandhi, I had to admit that I had been mistaken. Then I met Nehru. When he walked into the room, I thought to myself that I had never before seen such a beautiful human being. He resembled a young Krishna. I was immediately affected, like a girl who is dumbstruck with love. Since then I have been his supporter. If he had not existed, I would have supported Subhash Chandra Bose. But Nehru showed how we could fight the British, and even go to prison for what we had to do in 1942, without helping either Hitler or Hirohito. Gandhi acted according to his instinct and that often led him right, even if he acted in a manner none of the rest of us understood. But if it were he, and not Nehru, who had determined Congress policies in 1942 and thereafter, then Japanese military police would now be patrolling these streets. Nehru was the only person strong enough and smart enough to be able to stand up to Gandhi and get away with it."

Now, twenty years later, Nehru still sat in his silver frame on the desk, but Saxena scarcely mentioned him. Instead he talked about what he called "the new dynasty." Elections would be held, but Saxena did not consider the chances good for stopping the growth of the dynasty: "Indira is not gifted. But she is shrewd and doesn't forget things easily. She has the name and unlimited economic resources. Heaven knows where she gets the money. As you know, there are many foreign interests in India. And what of her opponents? Political curs wrangling over the offal! The Dynasty takes over. Motilal begat Jawaharlal and Jawaharlal begat Indira and Indira begat Sanjay and India got the ruler it deserved.

"Just look at what happened around Turkman Gate! For forty years they had been wondering how to beautify the area. Plan after plan was produced. The slum grew. But finally they slowly started to clear the slum and move the inhabitants from the area. That was in February 1974. Then the Emergency went into effect and Turkman Gate came to Sanjay's attention. In mid-April the police cordoned off the neighborhood. The sterilization buses were brought in. Panic spread. The houses were demolished by bulldozers and people were rounded up and driven out of town to the other side of the Jamuna. Sanjay Gandhi directed the operation from his mother's residence.

"On April 19, the people started to protest. The rampage of the demolition brigades and the sterilization platoons filled them with fear. It was the women and children who began to throw stones first. They were the target of tear gas, and the police received orders to attack them with lathis. When the men tried to defend their women, children and homes, the police were ordered to shoot with live ammunition. It is hard to say how many were shot down. Various figures have been reported. The police placed the fatalities at six, but it is more probable that at least fifty slum-dwellers were killed and about one hundred wounded before their resistance was broken and the authorities could get them together and then get them out. That evening when the curfew had gone into effect, the authorities put up a floodlight and called in six more bulldozers. This went on for a week. Sanjay went there to inspect the operations on the evening of 20th April.

"Sanjay Gandhi is behaving like a Mughal prince. In 1658 when Shah Jahan was deposed by his son Aurangzeb, the inhabitants of Delhi were insolent towards the new ruler. When Aurangzeb put his elder brother Dara on public display in Delhi before having him beheaded, riots broke out. But Aurangzeb had the troublemakers put to death and Delhi was silent once more. Sanjay believes he is the man to beautify the city like Shah Jahan and to put down the mob like Aurangzeb. At times I think he will succeed. He is uneducated, ill-mannered and like his mother does not forgive easily. He is also totally heartless. He will help her to get re-elected, and then we have but to wait for the new constitution: India will be ruled by Indira Gandhi until her demise or dethronement, when Sanjay Gandhi will take the helm of state for the rest of his days.

"But he is no Mughal prince. Or to be more precise, he is not like any of the great Mughal princes. He lacks both their genius and their erudition. He is no Babur, Akbar, Jahangir, Shah Jahan or Aurangzeb. If he resembles any of them, it is one of the late princes: a Jahandar Shah. His reign marks the beginning of the fall of India.

"We are in the process of relapsing into a new Mughal rule. What did the British leave behind? A free press, modern education, an effective and relatively honest administration. Say what you will, this was the European heritage we adopted. If you read only the writers of the Bengal Renaissance and look only at appearances, you might think that this heritage has become a permanent part of us. But it hasn't. The Emergency illustrated what was "normal" for India. The widespread sycophancy is also typical. All of official India began to flatter Sanjay during those years. No order was needed. He was treated as the successor. Radio and television were filled with reports about the young leader's appearances and about the hundreds of thousands who cheered him. Neither law nor ordinance applied. Here we have the typically Indian. It's the Mughal within us."

The bearer came in with a tray full of plates. On the plates were small, warm snacks. Some very spicy, some mild. Saxena poured out more Old Smuggler and went on: "Elphinstone wrote someplace that Shah Jahan's reign had been the best during the Mughal epoch and that the times under that ruler had been good, tranquil and secure. He thought that many of his readers might have difficulty believing this, considering India's poverty. But that was the fact. According to Elphinstone, it was a mistake to compare Mughal India under the rule of Shah Jahan with modern Europe. What Elphinstone meant by "modern Europe" was his Europe, eighteenth and early nineteenth century Europe. Shah Jahan's reign, in his opinion, had been good for the people in the way times had been prosperous for the Roman people during the rule of the better soldier-emperors. It is in this light that Sanjay should be seen. The prosperous times we can look back on will be the good years under a Severus. Sanjay's reign will be the time of twilight and disintegration. Even the ritual of a free press and honest administration will barely remain.

"What will I do? I'll survive. I'll serve the dynasty. If Sanjay comes to power, I'll speak of our young and brilliant leader. Believe me, it's safest. Any talk about civil courage belongs to another time. Today is not like the thirties when we had the masses with us in our demands for freedom of the press, freedom of speech, rule of law and representative government. Now the British are gone and our independence was won long ago. Our new rulers are now doing away with all the gains we won in our struggle against the British, all we achieved by taking over the western tradition, learning from the nineteenth century radical renaissance in Bengal, and the secular and rationalistic Nehru. The people are either too uninterested, too ignorant or too oppressed to do anything and we must look out for ourselves."

We take a taxi to the hotel. We drive through Old Delhi, Shahjahanabad. The emperor's Red Fort rests in the night and the silhouette of the Jama Masjid he barely saw completed before he was deposed can be seen behind the new park. But in the morning when we return to Jama Masjid we see that the area is beginning to fill up with peddlers. The slum is creeping back from the outlying suburbs.

That day, we eat lunch with Narayan, a Bombay journalist, at the Volga in Connaught Place. "All that talk is not worth paying attention to," he says. "Those are the words of a brown sahib. Roman emperors, Mughals, the Bible and the march of History, just to prove that there is nothing to be done. There's nothing remotely remarkable about Sanjay. He is an uneducated, spoiled, ignorant son of a prime minister, who wants to get rich quickly and who has discovered that he can turn his mother's power to profit. One needs neither Roman emperors nor Mughal princes to explain it. I've met the same sort of person in Europe, but that hardly had me talking about Charlemagne."

Sanjay Gandhi (no relation, by the way, of Gandhi, the nation's Father) was born in 1946. The marriage of Indira and Feroze Gandhi was a failure. In 1949, Indira moved back home to her father, the Prime Minister, and dedicated herself to caring for him and her own career. If young Sanjay was mentioned at all towards the end of the fifties, it was to comment on what an unbearably ill-bred and spoiled child he was. If anyone had told me then that in a few years he would be a powerful man who would cause the highest functionaries to tremble, I would have dismissed it as typical anti-Nehru, anti-Indian, cocktail party chatter. "Nehru is no Mughal potentate."

Sanjay was enrolled in exclusive private schools. But he was dull and unimaginative. At most, he seemed interested in cars. Finally, he was sent to Rolls Royce in England. They were doing a great deal of business with India. He was to go through their four-year apprenticeship programme. Once a week, he would attend the local technical high school. Things seemed to go well enough the first year. Then he moved out of the student dormitory and rented a house in Crewe with two boys of his own age. He was eighteen at the time. From then on things went downhill. A representative of Rolls Royce was eventually forced to request a meeting with India's High Commissioner in London to ask that India call Sanjay home, for his own sake and the company's. He was not yet twenty-one and had not completed his apprenticeship. This was in September 1967.

In India the protracted discussions about the production of an inexpensive Indian car were still in progress. It was expected that the new middle class would need hundreds of thousands of new cars. The contest was between an Indian Renault, an Indian Mazda and an Indian Fiat. The problem was that this project could not entail the importing of capital goods, parts or raw materials.

Sanjay, being idle, began to build his own car in a backyard shed. He worked in the garages in North Delhi. Soon minutes began to circulate between the ministries about Sanjay's mini-car. It was to be a two-door compact with a two-cylinder, air-cooled engine. The sales price was to be 6,000 rupees and Sanjay figured on an annual production of 50,000 cars. Enthusiastic reports began to appear in the newspapers. Sanjay was compared to the youthful Ford or Edison.

Thus was born the Maruti. And while various functionaries with growing concern sent minutes back and forth seeking permission for Sanjay's car company, Indira Gandhi spoke of her son, presenting him as an example for the youth of India. The Hindustan Times reported on September 24, 1968, her speech of the day before in Ahmedabad. She praised her son's enterprising spirit, and the report went on:

> She had urged all young men to show initiative even before her son began to construct a car. Her son was a sensitive young man, but he had used his money and energy to build a car. It was not a luxury car but it was quite comfortable and suited to Indian conditions. It would be appropriate for the middle class, she added.

Step by step, young Sanjay's car project was steered through the vast labyrinths of the Indian bureaucracy. Maruti was to be a large Indian car company. Unfortunately there remained a problem; to wit, no such car existed yet.

After playing for time, Sanjay, with the help of summoned technical assistance, was able to produce a prototype that could be sent to undergo inspection. But the prototype did not correspond to the technical description. The car had an imported engine. The whole thing was to a large extent assembled from imported parts. During the test runs new problems arose. They were repaired and forgotten. On June 24, 1974, the steering column broke and the car landed in a ditch. Eventually, the inspection was suspended before the tests were completed. On July 25, 1974, Sanjay Gandhi was granted his licence.

So far, the story seems quite innocuous. A spoiled, confused young man, assembling car parts and dreaming of becoming a Ford, has the misfortune of having as his mother the country's powerful Prime Minister, so the daydreams turn into a bureaucratic circus and a real honest-to-goodness factory. But, in fact, the story is neither harmless nor simple.

Sanjay became very rich off Maruti. His relatives and close associates also got rich. His interest in cars waned when he acquired a company with which to speculate. He had the simplest of methods for garnering capital. The coal-merchant Narh Gotewala, for example, was summoned to Sanjay Gandhi in December 1975. Sanjay informed him that he had a choice of either investing 100,000 rupees in Maruti Ltd. or of being arrested under MISA, the law for internal security. The coal-merchant was short of ready cash. He asked for understanding from the authorities when it came to his business dealings so that he could obtain the money. Sanjay agreed to this. The coal-merchant bought shares in Sanjay's Maruti Ltd. for 50,000 rupees. Thereafter, he received an allocation of 20,000 tons of coal and Sanjay insisted that he buy more shares.

In Delhi the authorities had granted refugees permission to establish shops along Janpath, the great main thoroughfare. These shops prospered. Suddenly the businessmen were told that the buildings were to be pulled down. But if they bought shares in Maruti Ltd. their shops would be spared. They subscribed and escaped ruin.

Some businessmen subscribed for very large sums in exchange for not being arrested or in order to get out of prison. What is still more interesting is that several people on the rolls as shareholders knew nothing of their possession of these shares. Many names were fictitious, listed as living in non-existent houses or on non-existent streets. Where the capital originated is unknown.

Sanjay Gandhi designated retailers for this car which did not exist. These individuals paid great sums of money as security. Rattan Lal in Chandigarh paid 250,000 rupees as security. But no cars were delivered.

Still, he did not dare demand his money back. He knew that retailers who had demanded their money back had landed in jail.

S.C. Aggarwal paid 600,000 rupees for distribution rights in Hissar and Gauhati. When he wanted to give notice of termination of the contract, Sanjay Gandhi threatened him with imprisonment and S.C. Aggarwal had to get down on the floor, grasp Sanjay Gandhi's feet and beg for forgiveness. Approximately 100,000 of S.C. Aggarwal's 600,000 rupees were later converted into shares and the rest was never repaid.

Prakash Gupta who also requested the return of his money was imprisoned under MISA. There are many such examples. Sanjay Gandhi was no innocent car-enthusiast who happened to bite off more than he could chew. The entire Maruti Ltd. affair was a base swindle in which political power was used to make a fortune.

"Sanjay Gandhi is not stupid," says Narayan. "The other political families are just as corrupt. But his methods are cruder. Neither is Sanjay encumbered by political, religious or social convictions. Politics don't interest him except in the sense that he likes to deal in power and make that power profitable.

"Possibly, one might say that he thinks the poor too numerous and troublesome. He would like to have a society where the poor are as inconspicuous as they are in Europe. That's why he wants to remove them from the cities and do away with them through birth control. The poor cause trouble and consume resources. Read Marx! Similar societies produce similar social phenomena. In this expanding Delhi, where all of India's dealers and racketeers congregate, Sanjay Gandhi grows increasingly powerful. In his support he organizes his loyal Youth Congress, his December 10 League. The feebleness of the Indian bourgeoisie gives its lumpen elements their chance. They are as loyal to him as these elements can be to anyone, for he is their salvation. What they have in common is that they, like Sanjay, feel an irresistible urge to practise charity on themselves at the expense of the nation's working people. So forget Rome and the Mughals! Consider Louis Bonaparte! Sanjay is a type. Replaceable by his brother. Or by someone else filling his function."

Gathering in the Chill of Christmas Day

Christmas Day 1979 is cold and windy in northern India. The sun shines feebly, radiating little heat. The election campaign is in its last laps. A meeting is to be held in the open space outside of Vithalbhai Patel House in New Delhi. The lawn has been covered with tarpaulin. A thousand people or more can be seated there. Behind this area and towards the sides, chairs have been arranged in double rows. Up front, by the podium, colorful canvas has been stretched out. Seats of honor are placed in a long row, with bright canvas strung up behind and overhead. This could be the scene of a grand wedding. The biting wind snaps at the canvas and sets the banners to flapping:

NATIONAL FRONT AGAINST AUTHORITARIANISM
FIRST NATIONAL CONVENTION

Indira Gandhi was toppled from power in the spring of 1977. This astounded her. After having introduced the state of emergency and crushed all open opposition, she had heard nothing but servile homage. In the end, she had begun to believe her own propaganda. Why, she was India's Indira! She was descended from Jawaharlal who was descended from Motilal. She believed the elections would ratify and legitimize her power. And then the poor stood up and voted her out of office.

On that occasion, before she would accept her election defeat to be a fact, it seems she made inquiries to see if the army would help her re-establish and maintain the orderly conditions of the Emergency—a time when the trains were on time and no strikes were allowed, and the papers printed only sympathetic news. But the army refused. They, too, opposed her and could not be trusted if she attempted a coup with their assistance.

She was deserted by all. When she fell, there was no hand willing to help her. She had provoked a storm of protest. Even her own henchmen would have nothing to do with her. In the end, only Sanjay and his goonda friends remained. She had been defeated and Sanjay had been proven right. He had advised her to declare an Emergency and to rule in defiance of the courts and the opposition. He had warned her about the politicians. Elections were a dangerous gamble, he had said, and now when they stood alone following their election defeat, he advised her to make the most of the situation. She should rid herself of all those who had wavered, who had doubted, who had tried to acquire insurance outside the family. The party machinery should be made up only of those whose entire political—and often even civil—livelihood was dependent on Indira and Sanjay. Only lackeys were to be relied on. This was the only way the momentarily unified opposition could be split and the family regain power. Later, Sanjay would say that only those who had been jailed and who had suffered for the movement and the family could count on receiving political positions of trust. In spring 1977, when people believed that Indira and Sanjay Gandhi would be tried and convicted for crimes against the state and the civil penal code, opposition to them was a massive popular storm.

Not since 1947 when the British left had the Indian political opposition been so unified. The year 1977 was the second liberation. All the sundry forces had been able to unite. And this unity had been forged in Indira's prisons. There the men of the Gandhi movement had shared cells with liberal bosses, and Hindu fanatics from the RSS had been locked up with Charu Mazumdar's tortured peasant-revolutionary Naxalites.

Even CPI, the wholly Moscow-dominated communist party, had turned against Indira in the end. The Russians had been worried by Sanjay's antipathy towards communists and his contempt for Russians.

A new era, an era of democracy, was expected to begin in the spring of 1977. Editorial writers around India, Europe and North America wrote of the Triumph of Democracy and the Victory of the Will of the People. And so it was, if by that one meant that the people did not want to be sterilized against their will and that they did not want to be assaulted, jailed and tortured when they protested against poverty and miserable conditions. But now the new era was already two and a half years old and the gilt was wearing off. This was no new era. It was just the same, old, normal, wretched Indian political era of oppression, corruption, falsehood and fraud. Now as in the past, politicians lined their pockets at the expense of the poor. They were embroiled in intrigue, and Sanjay played them off one against the other. There was a succession of financial scandals. The police raped, tortured and murdered in the same old way. One might even say that the landowners took the opportunity to kill and burn even more people than they had in previous years. True, most of the political prisoners had been released during the joyous days of liberation in spring 1977. But not all of them. Censorship had also been abolished and the newspapers could print pretty much what they pleased.

"India's corrupt politicians are like Paris' prostitutes," said Gun. "For a time they ply their regulated trade according to the rules, watched over by the authorities. Then comes a great moral reform, and they sell themselves under every streetlamp."

The loudspeakers are being tested. They crackle and shout. The volunteers who carry chairs and set up tables covered with pamphlets and flyers, are young They are excited and full of expectation. They are students. We have spoken about democracy. They say that it is necessary to defend democracy and the fundamental democratic rights. All positive forces must be united, no matter what, in the defence of democracy.

"It's not true that Indian democracy is just a humbug. Nor is it something just given to us by the British. The fact is that it was the people who fought for freedom. The peasant movement played the decisive role in the struggle for our freedom. Law, political rights and due process are not unimportant for the people. Just to the poor person if he can be arrested by Sanjay's goondas and have his spermatic ducts severed no matter how much he protests, or if normal civil legal conditions prevail. This was also why the poor made use of their right to vote and swept Indira and Sanjay from power. It is not a matter of indifference whether India is a bourgeois democracy or not. Better a democracy tainted with corruption, privation, electoral rigging and occasional violent electioneering, than no democracy at all. Better an imperfect bourgeois democracy than an effective fascism. Don't you agree?"

Yes, I agree. But there are still very few people at the meeting. In half an hour the writers, lawyers, journalists, teachers and trade union workers' first convention against authoritarianism will begin. It is the last phase of the campaign. Those who have been able to unite here are the remnants of what was once a massive popular protest movement. The politicians brought to power by this popular movement proved to be petty, incompetent and corrupt. They accused each other of opportunism, crime, stupidity and treachery to their country. In *Surya India*, the journal run by Sanjay Gandhi's wife, Maneka Gandhi, one scandal after another was exposed since June 1977. True, this is the lowest form of gutter-journalism, but smart and well-informed. Maneka Gandhi combined total ruthlessness with the most accurate of sources. The unified opposition to Indira Gandhi has been demolished by the use of the weapon of scandal or the threat of scandal. As Prime Minister, Indira Gandhi built powerful and effective police organizations. They are of use to her even now at the time of defeat; they are her tools.

"Maneka gets her information from her contacts in RAW. That's how she can destroy her opponents."

RAW, the Research and Analysis Wing, with a large annual budget and powers above and beyond the law, is the most mysterious and clandestine of the various parallel police organizations set up by Indira Gandhi. The tradition and experts were already there. The British Criminal Intelligence Departments in the provinces of what was then British India and their Intelligence Bureau were well organized. The reports they compiled on nationalism, communism and terrorism are still the best source of material for the student of the history of the workers' and nationalist movements in India. The reports are well-written besides, in a style of steady objectivity. The British political police was not loud and clumsy like the Gestapo. It was effective. And it was this effective apparatus that Jawaharlal inherited in 1947 and that his daughter, Indira, expanded and improved during the years before 1977. Her opponents could not hope for any indulgent silences about their most innocent embezzlement, bribery or erotic escapades. After June 1977 she allowed Sanjay Gandhi to split, crush, scare or buy over her opponents by any means possible. Those who had hoped for a new era in the spring of 1977 saw instead how the country continued to stagnate and how the leaders surrendered themselves to venality, debauchery, intrigue and incompetence. India's new leaders after Indira Gandhi's fall proved to be, if not fascists, at least takers of bribes and small-minded reactionaries. After a while, people were ready to believe every accusation. There was no charge against the country's politicians that was considered too far-fetched to be believed.

Those who are beginning to assemble here this cold Christmas morning are the intellectuals who led the opposition to Indira Gandhi's Emergency. Many of them spent time in prison while she was in power. I recognize several of them as they arrive one by one. Some of them were already active in the thirties. Intellectuals with a sense of civil courage. Old men wrapped in woollen shawls. Women with gray-streaked hair. No great crowds rush to attend this meeting. The noise of the campaign thunders and rolls across the whole country, but here the mood is spiritless. Indira Gandhi has once again promised to fight for the poor. Her propaganda is populistic like that of Louis Bonaparte or Benito Mussolini. But the people are morosely suspicious.

"Politicians!"

The word is used as a term of abuse. In private, people talk about those who have sold themselves to the Russians or the Americans.

"Jagjivan Ram is a CIA agent!"

"H. N. Bahuguna is working for the KGB!"

Bahuguna led the exodus away from Indira Gandhi in 1977 as leader of the Congress for Democracy. He was placed in charge of the oil, chemical and fertilizer industries in Morarji Desai's government. Charan Singh, who was minister of the interior, informed Morarji Desai that Bahuguna was a KGB agent. But later, when Charan Singh, with the assistance of the Russians and Indira Gandhi, toppled the government and made himself Prime Minister, thereby bringing on the new elections in the summer of 1979, he appointed Bahuguna his minister of finance. Then, in October 1979, Bahuguna went over to Indira Gandhi and became her party's general secretary during the election campaign. (Later he defected again.)

"Now who can trust politicians like that? Who can even keep track of their shifting alliances and various manoeuvres? Just intrigue and corruption. Politics is business."

The crowd is still thin. The chairs are mostly empty. Liberals, senior officials with their honor still intact, lawyers, writers, professors. The cold wind blows across the thinly-scattered audience. There are also empty chairs up on the speakers' platform. The volunteers remove them. They try to create a feeling of unity by rearranging the platform. The election campaign is in its very final stage and it is only now that it has been possible to achieve any kind of unity. The press conference was held the day before Christmas Eve. They had come together to "resist Indira's and Sanjay's fascistic boss-rule." Campaign workers had been sent out to various electoral districts such as Rae Bareli, Medak and Amethi, to oppose the campaign apparatus built up by Sanjay. Any candidate would do, just as long as Indira was prevented from returning to power! That is the sum of what they have agreed on. It is not much of a platform and hardly inspiring.

There are many who have refused to go along. Can one cooperate with those suspected of sympathizing with Hindu extremism? Can one work with people who have shown sympathy for Naxalites? Can one support corrupt politicians? Up on the podium sits Satyanarain Singh, former general secretary of the Marxist-Leninist party. He has lost that position because he believed that one had to unite with as many as possible in order to oppose Indira Gandhi and the Russians. Some refuse to attend this meeting because he is going to speak. Others are not there because, out of principle, they cannot unite with X or Y. V. M. Tarkunde is going to speak. He is one of India's most prominent liberal lawyers. Because he is speaking, India's second most famous liberal lawyer will not attend. That is the way it is. Even though both would say the same thing. Still, My Grace and Your Highness cannot find happiness under the same shamiana, even if they hear fascism howling outside the door.

V. M. Tarkunde opens the meeting. He commands a great deal of legal and moral authority. He has been a judge. He is a lawyer at the Supreme Court, and his civil courage is such that it was he who led the commission of inquiry into the police murders of youth accused of being Naxalites.

"It is imperative that we take up the struggle in defence of fundamental values. It is impossible to preserve democratic rights and freedom in an undemocratic society.

"The declaration of the Emergency was made possible when all the political parties betrayed their responsibility. Politicians switched opinion, party and political conviction for reasons of pure self-interest. What faith can one have in those who constantly betray our confidence?

"Blind Faith is dangerous. Without an informed citizenry democracy cannot survive. Blind faith is accorded every leader who can create an aura of mystery about his or her person. The individual holding blind faith wishes to be delivered from his freedom; it makes one want to follow the leader.

"Every dictator speaks of a strong society. Every dictator promises a strong government and stability. Every slavish soul, and those lacking self-confidence, are taken in by their propaganda.

"Hero-worship is dangerous. Personalities, and not issues, take center stage. Reason is drowned. Fascism is the result."

The sun gives no warmth. As I write in my notebook, my fingers grow stiff with cold. What Tarkunde is saying is valid, liberal and humanistic, and I agree with him. India's rulers cannot be accused of lacking force. The authorities kick, beat and torture with incredible force. Tarkunde is right. It is the lack of democracy, representative government, law and the equality of the poor citizen, that oppresses the people of India. I try to count those attending this first national manifestation. Maybe two hundred. Tarkunde is one of India's foremost lawyers. Among the two hundred spectators there are many of India's most prominent people. But the public is missing. The one that was to pack the open area. Tarkunde makes sense. But he is not inspirational or charismatic.

He speaks of the Emergency between 1975 and 1977. Indira Gandhi demolished the free press and introduced censorship. She proved that she respected neither the laws nor the promises and ideals she had used to win votes. The prisons were filled with political prisoners. They ranged from party leaders and Members of Parliament to humble peasants and workers. The party leaders did, however, get better cells. At a time when Gandhi's diplomats were speaking of Indian democracy and Mrs. Gandhi's fight for human rights, she held more than 150,000 political prisoners in her over-crowded jails, maintaining strict censorship so that nothing leaked out.

V. V. John, a Christian and an educator, comes from Kerala. He complains: "Even this meeting is held under a flag of convenience. Just what is anti-authoritarianism? Are we opposed to authority in general? It is cowardice not to openly and clearly state that it is tyranny and despotism that we oppose. If we do not even dare call despotism by its right name, will we be able to resist that despotism? Terms such as 'anti-authoritarianism' are only signs of compliancy and cowardice.

"We gained our political independence thirty-two years ago, but our intellectual elite has still to understand the relationship between democracy and freedom. This elite played a miserable role when Indira Gandhi introduced the Emergency. It is not shouldering its responsibility!

"Do you know what happened at the University? All those who struggled against the authorities and who courageously defended their right to refuse to take part in examinations and who claimed that we professors oppressed them by requiring them to study and show proof of knowledge, and who shouted that this was class struggle and revolution, all of them became terrified rats when the Emergency came into effect. They shouted about revolution as long as it was permitted. When things got serious, they shut up. Now that the Emergency is behind us, they are shouting once more. That sort of behavior is anarchy, not democracy. The fact is, they cannot distinguish between authority and despotism. So they serve despotism by opposing reasonable authority!

"It is high time intellectuals wake up to their responsibility. But our intellectuals don't talk politics. Instead, they busy themselves with some sort of political star-gazing. They are astrologists! Who is going to win? Who is going to lose? Who will receive these many votes? Who will receive that many votes? Who will make a deal about what with whom? Who will arrange this or that? It is useless! The intellectuals in our country must realize that it is not some sort of lottery, or of finding the winning combination, or of intrigues, but of right or wrong. It is a question of truth, scruples and responsibility."

All two hundred of us applaud, standing there on behalf of Greater Delhi's ten million, and India's seven hundred million people. Attorney-General Soli Sorabjee mounts the rostrum:

"We have taken things so much for granted that we do not appreciate our civil liberties until we lose them.

"What is important when we judge the merits of a politician? What are the decisive questions? The important thing, I believe, is how they view the freedom of the press and the independence of the judicial

branch. The existence of a free press and an independent judiciary guar-
antees even the poor citizen a chance to assert his claim.

"Indira Gandhi holds the freedom of the press and the independence
of the judiciary in contempt. She is despotic. She introduced censorship
in 1975. The freedom of the press has been threatened in the past, but
she did what was not done even when our country was at war: she subjected the press to pre-publication censorship and had even the most innocent news items policed.

"And what of Indira Gandhi's performance with regard to the independence of the judiciary branch? Sixteen High Court judges were transferred against their will. They were sent to places where they did not
speak the language or know the customs. She ignored some orders of
promotion and promoted those judges who did her bidding. And what
mistake had those forced to move made? They had ruled independently
of the will of the government. Not a word of this was printed in the
newspapers. Nor was it mentioned on the radio or television, where one
could only hear reports about our beloved young leader, Sanjay Gandhi.
And if it was mentioned in Parliament, we would have known nothing,
because it was forbidden to report anything from there not in the interest
of, or flattering to, the Prime Minister. We could only hear the news on
the BBC or Voice of America. The judges were refused passports for journeys abroad. They were kept under surveillance. Indira Gandhi punished them because they had done their duty, obeying the law and not
just her Ladyship's wishes.

"Now in 1979, she is trying to make a comeback. She openly attacks
the independence of the judiciary. She considers it to be a reactionary
concept. Her supporters say that a free press and the rule of law are ob-
stacles, to be done away with.

"We have opposed, and must continue to oppose social untouchability. But we would do well to introduce a political untouchability for those
politicians who have demonstrated a lack of respect for the community
founded on the rule of law, and who have shown themselves capable of
brutally transgressing against all the most fundamental values, if given
the opportunity and if it is in their self-interest."

The list of speakers is long. Well-known and prominent personages
speak in English and Hindi. The audience listens, shivering in the winter
chill, and applauds. This is liberal India. Senior officials who do not accept bribes. Lawyers who assert the principles of a society governed by
law. Newspapermen who believe in the freedom of the press. Writers,
union officials and people from the schools and universities. But the
chairs are few and the wind is cold. Out on the streets, vans mounted
with loudspeakers drive by. From time to time, the words of the speaker
are drowned out by the thundering slogans from Sanjay Gandhi's

loudspeaker-squads. A number of those present were jailed for their opinions during Indira Gandhi's Emergency; some of them had already spent time in prison under British rule. They were the group which provided inspiration for the massive popular movement against the despotism of Indira Gandhi which toppled her in 1977. Now they sit, a small group of intellectuals, on a lawn in New Delhi, and listen to each other say the right words.

Indira Gandhi feels contempt. She despises those gathered here because they are few in number and weak. But her contempt runs deeper than that. Indira is supercilious. She has always been so. She is no brilliant thinker. She is intellectually slow. But she does feel scorn and has reason for that scorn. She has inherited from her father the governing establishment left behind by the British. Its functionaries obey. They must obey. They are not citizens, they are subjects. And paragraph nine in the Central Civil Services Conduct Rules reads:

> No government servant shall in any radio broadcast or in any document published in his name or anonymously or pseudonymously or in the name of any other person or in any communication to the press or in any public utterance make any statement of fact or opinion which has the effect of an adverse criticism of any current or recent policy or action of central or state government.

According to paragraph 311, second passage, section C, the right of a government official to appeal his dismissal and to defend himself against the accusations upon which his dismissal is based is suspended, "provided the president, or provincial governor finds that it is not in the interest of the state to allow such an appeal." No wonder that there is so little civil courage to be found among Indian functionaries. Even senior, internationally known Indian officials such as B. K. Nehru, High Commissioner in London, or T. N. Kaul, Ambassador in Washington, went far beyond what could be demanded of a diplomat during the period of the Emergency. They grovelled before Indira Gandhi. They sold and dishonored themselves, openly and consciously lying. As I sit here in the cold, looking at this crowd-few and shivering—I feel both Indira Gandhi's scorn for her functionaries and a deep respect for this handful of people who maintained their integrity.

Writers, journalists and actors were not very different. Indira had hardly even to pay them. They turned coward. No wonder Indira Gandhi said to Oriana Fallaci: "What do you want me to do? I am surrounded by a bunch of idiots. And as for democracy. . . ."

I understand her contempt. With whip in hand, one need only let the lash snap in the air to make a T. N. Kaul shrink, smile and obediently say what he did in Washington on October 31, 1975. There he declared that only "fifteen leaders and approximately one thousand others have been arrested." He informed his American listeners that three of the fifteen leaders and three hundred of the thousand had already been released. And all the while he knew that this was not only a lie, but that among the arrested and tortured were to be found those he had once associated with and had called friends. He had heard the whiplash crack and was a man lacking in civil courage.

On the other hand, here sat those who would have a hard time getting ahead. An unexpected number of them are lawyers. It was they, in fact, who had shown admirable civil courage between 1975 and 1977. Not all of them, perhaps, certainly a far cry from the majority, but enough so that among left-wing revolutionaries one might hear words such as Kumar's, spoken during a pause in the meeting:

"Our opinion of judges and lawyers was incorrect. Our analysis was superficial. We took into account only the fact that jurisprudence was part of the superstructure. We didn't consider the fact that the conservative judge who followed the law under those circumstances was, in fact, siding with the people against the authorities. But now we have learnt this."

B. G. Verghese expressed the same thought in another way, when he spoke of authoritarianism from a traditional Gandhian position:

"Which members of society need the fundamental political rights? Indira Gandhi says that these rights are an obstacle to the country's progress. She says that the rule of law curbs development. But who needs political rights and who needs the rule of law?

"It is the poor. It is the 'harijans,' the untouchables, who need them. Thus we witnessed how the poor used democracy to topple Indira Gandhi in 1977."

The last to speak was Satyanarain Singh. He spoke of the poor peasants' and farm laborers' struggle for their legal rights. The landowners had turned the laws regulating the maximum size of landholdings into a farce:

"They sign over the property to aunts and cousins. They sign it over to the oxen. Why, even the landowners' dog is the legal owner of a piece of land. This is not the distribution of land, it is a fraud. The poor struggle for their legal rights against the landowners. It is the poor who represent law and order! It is Sanjay's goonda-politicians and the feudal barons who are upholding lawlessness and disorder! We have common interests when it comes to the defence of democracy. We must all unite against the fascism which threatens us."

He speaks first in Hindi and then in English. An experienced orator, dressed in a heavy winter overcoat. The intellectuals listen to him. He makes coarse and pointed jokes in Hindi, but speaks with effort and in abstract terms in English. It is already late in the afternoon. The audience begins to thin out.

"What did the state of emergency mean? The workers lost their right to strike. The poor suffered forced sterilization. The intellectuals were the victims of censorship. Russian influence grew. The peasants were prevented from demanding their legal rights. Women were demeaned. Fascism represents a threat to us all."

The loudspeakers crackle and the words echo across the now almost deserted open area.

"The defence of democracy and the upholding of democratic rights must also mean opposition to feudalism in the countryside and support for the poor peasants in their demand for land and personal freedom."

Crinkled flyers now blow about in the wind between the rows of increasingly empty chairs.

"Indira Gandhi's cynical collaboration with the Russians is a threat to our national independence. Therefore: Up with democracy and democratic rights! Down with feudalism, goonda-tyranny and national humiliation!"

Everything said here today was excellent. I agree with most of it. It is what I have heard from good and sensible people as long as I can remember, and it is what I have read of what good and sensible people have said in the past when faced with great crises. Now I sit here at this meeting which is no mass meeting and hardly even a gathering, and the cold wind blows down my spine. I am chilled to the very marrow. When I look around I feel the cold within me.

The resolution adopted was correct and wise. It pointed out the growing wretchedness, and the increasingly open and cynical corruption of the Indian politicians. It mentioned the betrayed hopes and the dangerous political indifference it had caused. It showed how this very situation was making it possible for Indira Gandhi, using a combination of brutality, physical violence and phrasemongering social demagogy, to seize power. It was fascism which was taking shape in her policies, thus making her much more dangerous than the others who were only corrupt, cynical and incompetent in the usual way. She was the greater danger.

The now chilled, old and middle-aged liberals and the expectant young students adopted the resolution unanimously, while Sanjay Gandhi's loudspeaker-vans dominated the streets and his people organized street meetings. People gathered around the loudspeakers and the slogans were drummed out. But the faces of the onlookers were reserved and unsmiling. The shouts and cheers came only out of the loudspeakers.

"They were right, of course, about what they said today," remarked Gun. "But they don't stand a chance. It's already too late. And this time she won't need any Emergency. She has already crushed all her opposition. The bourgeois liberals have shown themselves to be divided and isolated. And the revolutionaries are disunited and weak."

The Indian Dichotomy

"I'm no Hegelian," said Suraj. "There are no abstract forces determining history."

We had spent five hours at his house, a small group, drinking coffee and discussing Indian developments. That is, the others discussed and I took notes and asked a question now and then. Suraj is from Andhra Pradesh, a diminutive, dark wiry man with sparkling eyes and a quick intelligence. A university professor, he had been jailed several times since 1970, for being a Naxalite and having participated in the peasant movement in Srikakulam.

"It is the people who shape history through their struggle. The people are the driving force in history and it is right to rebel. That's why I believe it is nonsense and a dangerous misreading of Marx to write as some academic Marxists have, on the subject of capitalism's destruction of the Indian village: 'Social progress is achieved, as history shows, through the amoral action of historical forces.' The fact that Marx could write something to this effect, living as he did in the England of the 1850s, can be explained. He did not have enough facts on India and so could believe the myth of the unchanging village and the passive masses. Part of the explanation might be found in the official Hegelianism of a Europe under the Counter-Revolution. However, the majority of Indian intellectuals as quick as, say A. R. Desai, let the struggling people disappear behind the abstract forces of history. There is more to this than just their having read Marx. I mean, they have not taken up wine-drinking, even though

Engels wrote about wine. They choose selectively and that choice is socially determined even for Marxists. They are victims of the Indian dichotomy.

"It can be outlined in this way," he said. "Note that when I use the term culture, I don't mean art but the entire cultural superstructure with all its customs and laws. In other words, I use the term in the same sense as Mao did when he spoke of cultural revolution."

The Dichotomy

Period	Socio-cultural role	Political role
Nineteenth Century Renaissance movement	progressive	pro-British
War of Independence 1857	none	anti-British
Gandhi's Nationalist movement	reactionary	anti-British
Ambedkar and the struggle of the untouchables	progressive	pro-British
The Communist movement 1920-1941	none	anti-British; for the working class
The Communist movement 1942-1948	progressive	pro-British; for the working class
The Dravidian movement	progressive	pro-British;
Telengana Rebellion	none	against the Nizam; for the peasants.

"Then fill the actual struggle at the grassroots under each entry! (How the Marxist-Leninist and Naxalite struggle of 1967-1979 should be classified can be debated.)

"If you are seeking an explanation for the repeated defeats suffered by the people, I believe you can begin to find it here! The two movements do not join!"

The discussion had started as a general conversation on the present situation. But as it went on it became more structured and more concerned with the roots of the present. I then started taking notes in earnest, asking my friends to talk in turn. The conversation had become a seminar, as it so often does among Indian intellectuals.

Kumar had the flowing beard of a peasant—or a revolutionary—from the Punjab. He too is a professor, though not in India. He is an economist. He comes from one of the former princely states of Rajasthan where his father had a high hereditary post in the service of the court. Kumar was educated in England. He is heavily built and looks as if he has toiled on the land all his life.

"Democracy" he said, "democracy was not the gift of the British. To believe that is to make a mistake. A mistake that the British administration was always anxious to see us make. It leads us to sectarianism and failure.

"The official writing of history becomes peopled by heroes and villains. The words the British educators made us talk and think. What is a villain? A villain, a serf! In official history the masses comprise only a passive or backward element. The active ones are treated as villains. And it may seem that some shining heroes fought for our independence and that the British administration gave us Democracy and Law and Order.

"On closer examination we find that the real active force, the real heroes, are the masses, the villains as the British would say, the peasants. They rise up. They struggle. They revolt. Each British reform becomes a crying necessity after a rebellion or the threat of rebellion. In the nineteenth century, too, it was the masses who acted. The British waded in blood to hold them down and they had to pass one reform after another in order to remain in power.

"As for Gandhi, of course he was important, but only as long as the masses supported him. He was able to compromise, slow down and check developments for a time, but in the end the masses surged right on by him. When the Indian Navy mutinied in February 1946, the British realized that they had to leave India and hand over the government to the Congress and the Muslim League as quickly as possible, if the masses were to be prevented from liberating the country themselves and driving both the government and the urban-dwelling rulers out of India. When it comes right down to it, both independence and political democracy are the fruit of the struggle of the Indian peasant masses. This must be accepted if one is to do meaningful political work."

"It isn't so much a question of accepting it, as of being able to see it in the first place," said Santosh. He is from Bengal, a thin chain-smoking journalist. He had been out in the forest with the early Naxalites for some years and then spent some years in jail.

"Those of us who grew up in educated families and who come from intellectual backgrounds admired the men of the Bengali Renaissance and their tradition. Why, it was Ram Mohan Roy and those who followed, up to and including Rabindranath Tagore, who in a hundred years of intellectual endeavor created a new Bengal and dealt a heavy blow to evil tradition and harmful customs.

"Today, as in the past, it is important for us to bear in mind that it was our own intellectuals like Ram Mohan Roy who led the struggle against degrading feudal customs such as *sati*, infanticide, polygamy and child marriage. It was also they who supported educational reform and the right of girls to schooling. However, the Bengal Renaissance was not just a reform movement pushed by the new Bengali middle class in the 1820s and after: it was a true renaissance.

"Foreign influence played an emancipating role—comparable to Arabian influence during an earlier epoch in Europe. Students at the Anglo-Hindu school directed by Ram Mohan Roy studied Euclid and Voltaire, astronomy and mechanics. When, from 1815 to 1817, he translated the sacred Vedantic writings, from Sanskrit to the popularly-spoken Bengali, and then followed up the reform work with a merciless polemic against orthodoxy, he played the part of a liberator. He was aware of this. He considered it his duty, as he said, to save people from imposition and servitude and promote their comfort and happiness. When Tarkunde and the other liberals at the meeting the other day spoke of the danger of blind faith, they were echoing Ram Mohan Roy and the Bengal Renaissance of a hundred years ago. As he said, 'Irrationalism and blind faith destroy the texture of society.' We are still building on the foundation of that cultural revolution."

"There is more to India than just Bengal," said Suraj, "even if it often seems that Bengal is India when the conversation turns to lyrical poetry, philosophy and revolution. The Renaissance movement was a country-wide phenomenon. Abroad, you are too quick to equate the debate in Calcutta with the Indian debate. But Bengal is only one part of India and the Bengali debate is only one of a number. You should also bear this in mind when discussing today's revolutionary movements! As for the Renaissance, it was a necessary intellectual liberation struggle, conforming to the laws of societal development. Telugu, my native tongue, is a rich language with a great tradition. For us, it was Veerasalingam Panthulu who became the renaissance personality, the preeminent figure, the liberator. In pure, straightforward prose, he wrote for us our language. He rejected totally the cumbersome, erudite Sanskritized language which hindered and shackled the new concepts. He served the people. He was our Lu Hsun. He translated Shakespeare and Kalidasa, he wrote our first novel and first modern play, and founded periodicals. He became our first journalist and essayist, wrote his autobiography and was a polemist. His writing was to the point, and people understood what he wrote. The earlier antiquated language crumbled around him. And he was a committed intellectual. He opposed child marriage and argued for the right of widows to remarry. He took up the dowry problem and prostitution. He exposed the corruption of the officials and their oppression of the people. At the same time, it was he who wrote about our great, classical Telugu poets, introducing them to the people. If you could only read Telugu, you would understand. Yet this writer of world stature is confined to a language spoken by sixty million, a language less known outside India than either Finnish or Norwegian, even though our writers are at least as good!

"And although he died in 1919 at the age of sixty-seven, the reactionaries still abuse him, maintaining his writing was just out-and-out communism."

"It's true that India is many things," said Kumar, "and, certainly, the Renaissance was a countrywide phenomenon. The new Indian middle class produced pioneering intellectuals all over the country during the nineteenth century. Some are truly Renaissance figures, while others remain well-intentioned bourgeois reformists. We could talk about Mahadev Govind Ranade of Bombay towards the end of the last century, about both his greatness and his limitations. All the same, the fact is that it was in Bengal, in seething Calcutta, that this Indian renaissance began soon after the Napoleonic Wars. Ram Mohan Roy initiated the Bengal Renaissance, and he can still be considered the model of the liberal, progressive Indian bourgeoisie."

"By saying that," said Santosh, "you are saying that Ram Mohan Roy played two completely different roles. Consider his relationship with the Muslims. We are all Bengalis. The same people; the same language; the same traditions. Religious conversions were taking place all around him, and he was able to note that the branch of the family which converted to Islam developed into freer and physically stronger human beings than those who remained faithful to Hinduism, repressed by all its rules and strictures. He struggled to loosen its fetters. He also spoke both Arabic and Persian, and was familiar with Islam.

"Observe that his first religious-philosophical work, written in 1804, featured a preface in Arabic, while the main text was in Persian. It might have been written by a Muslim who had evolved into a rationalistic deist," said Kumar.

"He also respected the Muslims," said Santosh. "He maintained that the Muslim jurists at the courts were more honest than, and superior to, their Hindu counterparts. Yet he praised the British for breaking the Muslim domination of the Hindus, and for putting an end to nine hundred years of Muslim affronts to Hinduism. And it is right here—at the very beginning of the Indian renaissance which is to develop into a reform movement and bourgeois nationalism—that we also have the beginning of communalism, the contradictions between communities which the British were to turn into such a horrendous tragedy for Bengal and for all of us."

"You know why Ram Mohan Roy suffered this duality," said Kumar. "It's hardly a matter of religion or philosophy. It goes much deeper. Who was he? In spite of everything, he was a high-caste aristocrat and land-owner. Who became Muslims? The untouchables, the lower castes, the poor. They converted to Islam, for the same reasons that Dr. Ambedkar urged his untouchable brothers to become Buddhists. It was a way out of the worst feudal degradation. However liberated Ram Mohan Roy wanted to be, he wasn't able to take the leap out of his class. Thus his po-litical voice spoke for the responsible elements: the large zamindars, the landowners, the highly respected merchants, the muftis and the head native officers, the new Indian middle class striving for greater power for themselves, the power that was guaranteed by British rule. He should both be admired and critically appraised in the light of history. If we don't do this, we shall never solve the problems of Indian democracy."

"I think," said Santosh, "that most liberal, humanistic intellectuals in India today recognize this duality Tarkunde sees it. However, even today the Bengal Renaissance is a liberation for Indian middle class intellectu-als. Consider a young student growing up, out in some mofussil-hole, trusting the elders and heeding the teachers, and suddenly he runs into Ram Mohan Roy! He is liberated!

"What is it that we are constantly being told? Spiritualism is India's greatness, our teachers told us. We have shaped the concepts *moksha*, *karma*, *yoga* and, of course, *ahimsa*. *Moksha*—spiritual liberation through the practice of self-denial; *avidya*—the blindness to ultimate truth out of which the material world arises and which is abolished in the soul's total consciousness; *karma*—the law which holds that each being reaps the fruits of its actions in previous existences good or bad, so that the poor person is suffering his punishment, while the rich person is enjoying his goodness; *yoga*—the system of breathing exercises and bodily training which bestows more than natural gifts and insight on the practitioner; and *ahimsa*—refraining from the taking of life, which can be translated into vegetarianism or Gandhian politics. These are ideas and concepts which keep people fettered. Who can revolt against *karma*? If reality is only ignorance and delusion, why struggle? This is feudal ideology. But it is enough to read Ram Mohan Roy to dispel the trammels of this crip-pling web. And when, as a young student, one first encounters Derozio and the Young Bengal of 1830, the sense of freedom and exhilaration makes one want to shout."

"Aren't you being just a bit too rationalistic now?" asked Suraj. "While it is true that people have believed in *karma* and *moksha*, and still do, that doesn't stop them from taking part in the struggle. I've just come back from Warangal where the peasants are struggling in spite of *karma* and police troops. On my way here I read Emile Zola's *Lourdes*, which I bought at the train station in an English paperback edition published in Bombay. I don't see much difference between Lourdes and Vemulawada, where they also deal in miracles and pilgrimages. One must not allow oneself to be taken in by the ideologies. What's important is to see what is actually taking place: the growing agrarian revolution!"

"Don't underestimate the power of liberating criticism," said Kumar.

"I don't," said Suraj, "but one should place a couple of big question marks alongside this European rationalism. Not because it's rational, but because it's European. Let's return to our young student out in the West Bengali countryside, the one Santosh was talking about. First, he gets hold of Ram Mohan Roy, then discovers Young Bengal and the great critical liberation of a hundred and fifty years ago, and then he gets to Marx's *Manifesto*. If he is the normal Bengali intellectual, he has by this time, put a very great distance between himself and the Bengali masses. Why, they can't even read the *Manifesto*. The first legally published Indian edition which appeared in 1944 was forced to include the complete—and otherwise excellent—annotations of Rjazanov. In other words, first a 16 page introduction, then the *Manifesto* itself covering 32 pages, followed by 160 pages of explanatory notes and an appendix of 86 pages. All this was necessary for the Bengali intellectual, raised in India a hundred years after the text was written, to understand what it's about. On top of all that, one has to be educated at a mission school to understand all the Biblical references made by Marx and Engels. And Aron, who teaches German, maintains that one can't really read the *Manifesto* correctly if one doesn't understand the allusions made to Goethe, Heine and the classical German writers! Yet what Marx wrote was a straightforward and terribly forceful text—in Europe—in 1848. What Mao did in China, we must do here. He 'Sinosized' Marxism, rendering it comprehensible and effective in China and turning it into the tool of the Chinese masses. We must 'Indianize' (I don't want to say 'Hinduize,' as it sounds communalist) Marxism so that it can become the tool of the Indian masses. This has nothing to do with some kind of local Andhra-chauvinism or India-fixation. It's a question of the people's needs. Translation is not sufficient. One must serve the people. Rationalism and Europeanization leads away from the people.

"Let's take an example in the opposite sense. Here in India, we speak of *ahimsa* and different kinds of non-violence. All over the world people write about Gandhi's philosophy. Then people wonder how the very leaders who have spoken so much about non-violence could be so quick to resort to violence against our neighboring countries. But the problem is not quite so difficult for the individual raised in the Hindu tradition. It is in the *Bhagavad Gita* that we encounter *ahimsa*. Just what is this text? It is the lofty dialogue which opens the great and bloody battle in the *Mahabharata*. Krishna has to convince Arjuna, the hero of the Pandavas, to go to war. *Ahimsa*, the noble principle of nonviolence, is then an argument for violence and killing. Why shouldn't Arjuna participate in the great slaughter? Bodies are just the clothing of the souls which are taken off and exchanged for new. Those who are killed are already doomed to die, their death being but the carrying out of the inevitable. For us, this is not even worth pondering over. It's not half as weird as the trinity of the Christians. But it is a problem for those who have not grown up steeped in the myths and who regard *ahimsa* as a theory. Thus, things go badly for all these foolish Europeans and Americans who wander around India, begging, using drugs and pretending to be Hindus."

"But the object is to free ourselves of all that," said Kumar.

"One can only be free by liberating oneself in one's own culture," said Suraj. "It's a simple matter for me to free myself from the Finn's *Kalevala* by reading a footnote on it. It's so easy, because I know so little about it. On the other hand, it would take a protracted and purposeful struggle to free myself from the ideological hold that a hundred feudal generations exert on me by means of my own culture's traditions, customs and beliefs. Derozio and Young Bengal can't do this for me."

"I don't agree," said Santosh. "Neither India nor Andhra is that unique. Calcutta is an international crossroads. It was already so in 1830. To a large degree, it was due to Derozio and his followers that Calcutta in 1830 was not just any intellectual center, but an intellectual hotbed where the young Bengalis found themselves occupying some of the most advanced intellectual and political positions.

"On December 10, 1830, two hundred liberals and young intellectuals met in Calcutta. They gathered to honor the July Revolution in Paris. They rallied around the tricolor. It was Derozio who inspired them. He was eighteen when he began teaching at Hindu College in 1826. A brilliant and magnetic personality, he was an Eurasian and an Indian patriot. He had been brought up in Calcutta by an exiled Scot, a free-thinker and republican. He encouraged his students to question everything. They debated free will and determinism, the existence of God, the right of women to education, religion as a ruse of the clergy, the French Revolution, the Greek struggle for independence and the duty to seek truth and obey one's conscience.

"He taught, he wrote, he debated. He was an early Indian intellectual, one of a new kind, and the older, orthodox Bengali fathers were appalled at the decadence he spread. Nothing other than the truth was sacred for Derozio's disciples. They read Voltaire, Bacon, Locke, Hume, Bentham and Thomas Paine. But the authorities were horrified over the rumor that the young people violated all the sacred commands by drinking wine and eating beefsteak. One story went that a father had taken his son to the temple of the goddess Kali. But the son had not fallen on his knees and prayed to the goddess. Instead, he had just said, 'Good morn-

ing, madam.' It was said that Derozio's students had become atheistic
scoundrels. Well, the debate clubs were shut down, the publications
banned. Derozio was fired and died of cholera soon after, at the age of
23. But the Young Bengal he created, lived on. One might say that the
spirit of Derozio is still alive in Calcutta. It was in Calcutta, and in
Bengali, that Thomas Paine, damned and hated in England, America
and the whole 'respectable' world, was published. In 1832, *The Age of
Reason* was published in Calcutta.

"Thirty-three years were to pass before the first Swedish edition could
appear," I remarked.

"Yes," said Santosh, "even if the Reaction was harsh and seemed at
times to get the upper hand, intellectual Calcutta has since the 1830s
been marked by the presence of this rebellious, rationalistic intellectual
tradition of truth-seeking. And, if you will forgive me, it is rather typical
that Thomas Paine appeared in Swedish thirty-three years after being
published in Bengal. The situation is not very different today. With all
due deference to Helsinki, Stockholm, Oslo and Copenhagen—all pleasant cities—they are not as intellectually alive as Calcutta."

"It's true that Derozio was a great person," said Suraj, "and we have
every reason to bear the deepest respect for the Derozians. They had
great integrity and they persevered for many years in an arduous struggle against the Reaction. But I must point out that, on the whole, what
happened to them was what happened to their contemporaries, the
Saint-Simonists of France. They drifted from revolt into senior government positions. Careers were made possible in India by the Charter Act
of 1833, and many Derozians became liberal, Europeanized, incorrupt-
ible functionaries in the service of the colonial power, just as many Saint-
Simonists became the men of Louis Phillipe and Napoleon Ill. There is
the gist of the problem.

"As for criticizing the students who came to be known as Young
Bengal, I, for my part, would stress something else. Around 1830, these
students were attacked partly for mimicking *firangis*, but also for convert-
ing to a heterodox, non-Vedic system of thought, which on top of everything, was not the partially accepted Buddhist or Jain philosophies, but
the totally damned, materialist school: Charvaka. This represents something very important for the future of India, because with all due respect
for Thomas Paine whom I hold in esteem, the fact that Indian materialism reemerges in the 1830s, is proof that our renaissance really was a rebirth. If the people are to triumph in India, we must also take up the
struggle within our own philosophic tradition. Basing ourselves on popular Indian materialism, we shall defeat both *moksha* and *karma*!

"However, what is really decisive here—and I'm taking for granted
that you agree—is that this entire renaissance, whether in its moderate

manifestation like Ram Mohan Roy's disciples or radical like Derozio's Young Bengal, sided with the British against the masses when it really counted.... Their own class interests guided them, just as Ram Mohan Roy's class interests moved him towards what was to become communalism."

"Yes," said Santosh, "that is the main thing. And this is the point I've been wanting to make. Our Bengal Renaissance took a stand against the peasants. But to comprehend just how tragic this was, one must remember the greatness of this renaissance. When the British crushed the Sepoy Rising of 1857, they had the backing of the entire Indian elite. One can read in books that there were exceptions. Some claim that Harish Chunder Mukherjea was one such exception. In *Hindoo Patriot,* he was supposed to have shown sympathy for the rebels. But now that Benoy Ghose has reprinted these articles written in 1857, we can be sure that Mukherjea was in total agreement with the British. Quite natural, when one considers that he had advanced in their service from being a clerk earning 25 rupees a month to Assistant Military Auditor paid 400 rupees. The only difference between him and the British bloodhounds was that he did not describe all natives, both Hindu and Muslim, as born criminals and inferiors."

"He did demand severe punishment for the rebels, however, and called for more European soldiers and officers to keep the Sepoys under control," said Kumar.

"One mustn't be an idealist," said Suraj, "because then one judges too harshly. How could Mukherjea in Calcutta, working for the British and writing in a journal meant for the English-speaking, Westernized and educated class economically dependent on the British, support this rebellion which threatened the very foundations of British rule? We should instead consider his position during the Indigo Rebellion. To supply the British textile industry, indigo was cultivated by British planters in Bihar and Bengal. Their methods were not unlike those later developed on the cotton plantations in the southern states of America after slavery. The *ryots,* or peasants, were forced to grow indigo, which was then purchased at the lowest possible price. It was blatant exploitation and undisguised oppression. For half a century, the exploited poor peasants fought against this system. And it was over this question that the Bengal Renaissance was to split. The moderate elements, such as Ram Mohan Roy and Dwarkanath Tagore, defended the plantation owners; they personally profited from that system—as Dwarkanath Tagore innocently pointed out. That part of the renaissance was directly dependent on brutal exploitation, and wanted the forces of the British government to protect their interests. However, when the exploited peasants rebelled in 1860-1861, they were supported by those like Harish Chunder Mukherjea,

and by a large section of the new Indian middle class. It lay in their class
interest to do away with the plantation system and to develop agriculture. Harish Chunder Mukherjea made a great contribution here. Call it
humanitarian, if you like. This was within his power. And he should be
given credit for it. But we shouldn't be idealists and believe that he could
(or that his modern counterparts can) act against his own immediate
class interests."

"That's where we don't agree," said Kumar. "I wouldn't work on the
assumption that a broad unity is impossible to fashion. And I don't believe that the revolution of 1857 was doomed to defeat. The reason that
we now have to carefully discuss both the Renaissance and 1857 is that
we have yet to solve the problems we faced a hundred and fifty years
ago."

"The masses are the driving force," said Santosh. "I agree with that.
Here in India, it is the tribals, the untouchables, the lower castes, the
landless and the poor peasants who make up the masses, and it is they
who today and in the future are the motive force of history. We know
how the urban middle class feels about that. Why, we can read what they
have to say about Pol Pot! They are afraid of the hatred of the masses.
When the peasants rise, the same thing happens today as it did during
the Santhal Rebellion in 1855-1856. I have seen that with my own eyes.
The British officers who led the punitive expedition recounted that when
the money lender was captured by the peasants, they first cut off his feet
and shouted that that was four annas of the rupee. Then they took off his
legs and considered eight annas to have been repaid. Then they cut the
torso in half and said it was twelve annas and finally they chopped the
head and shouted that now all sixteen annas of the rupee had been repaid. And it is said that in 1855 when the wealthiest money lender in the
district, Deendayal Roy, could not escape in time because of his obesity,
his servant Jagannath Sirdar stepped up with an axe in hand and
chopped him into pieces, saying: 'These fingers you used to count interest with! This hand you used to take food from the poor!' I have seen the
same things happening in the present agrarian struggle. It is easy to talk
about unity and to say that the middle class should join forces with the
masses, and that its blows should be directed at the main enemy. But the
fact is that a large portion of the Indian urban middle class is as terrified
at the thought of the masses revolting as Mukherjea was of the Sepoys in
1857. That's why their uprising remained leaderless. They almost succeeded in toppling British rule without leaders."

"It is not easy to say where the classes stood in 1857," said Kumar.
"On the whole, one can say that the revolt was supported by the peasants, and small and middle-sized feudal landowners. Their interests
were threatened, and they revolted. It was not just a military uprising, it

was supported by the masses and spread nationwide. But the new middle class, those with a European education, turned against the uprising."

"Note that, on the whole, the large feudals refused to participate in the rebellion and supported the British," said Santosh. "Although 1857 is described in some books as the princes' struggle to maintain the Hindu right of adoption and hence the princely houses' right of inheritance, the princes generally supported the British and were later rewarded for that support. That's why we got to keep the princes until independence. Because they had helped the British oppress the people, the British gave their descendants the chance to oppress the people in their own turn. Lakshmi Bai, Rani of Jhansi, was forced to participate in the war. She became a heroine, in spite of herself. But there's no denying that she was brave...."

"She was a woman of historical stature," said Kumar. "There were also other members of the feudal class, such as Nana Saheb, who became leaders. Still, it can be said that with the death of Tippu Sultan during the assault on Seringapatnam, on April 28, 1799, the last feudal leader of historical calibre passed away. 1857 was a national uprising, a national war of liberation, but the old ruling class was no longer able to lead the struggle, and the men of the new Indian renaissance took the side of the British against the peasants and Sepoys."

"Events in the south were typical," said Santosh. "There the feudal barons rebelled but were soon bought off by the British. The leadership of the national uprising fell into the hands of representatives of a dying class who betrayed the Sepoys. And this explains the whole course of the war between 1857 and 1859. The Sepoys were good soldiers who knew their tactics, but they did not have leaders with a strategic comprehensive view. So they passed over to defensive warfare after capturing Delhi, instead of spreading the war to all parts of the country with Delhi as a base and the Mughal emperor as a legitimate symbol."

"There are," said Suraj, "two other aspects which are characteristic and which should be remembered. One is the tremendous courage shown by the Sepoys. They were like the Santhal rebels about whom the British said, 'They know all weapons, except one: the white flag.' Even when the Sepoys were captured and executed in the most brutal fashion, they did not lose their dignity. This bearing and bravery which tended to continue the struggle long after all hope was lost has been handed down from generation to generation in the Indian peasant uprisings. Even today it inspires the youth, the Naxalites, who are captured, tortured and taken out into the forest to be shot. In colonial literature, Indians are portrayed as simpering, begging, intriguing and the like, but in fact, generation after generation of Indian rebels, peasant leaders and revolutionaries, have known how to die with dignity. This is a great inspiration for our people, while it is a source of hatred for the rulers.

"The second point is that the reprisals by the rulers have always been the bloodiest possible. That is how it was in Santhal and in 1857, and how it has continued to be. The 1921 Mopla uprising in Malabar was scarcely noticed outside India. Naturally, Gandhi disassociated himself from it. Those involved were poor Muslims who had already rebelled thirty-five times against the British. But in 1921 they rose up because they believed in Gandhi's words about *swaraj*. Naturally, some tried to impose a communal character on the uprising. But after nine months of struggle, the British troops succeeded in resuming power and crushing the rebellion. Their losses totalled forty-three dead, a hundred and twenty-six wounded. Do you know how many poor peasants died? The British admitted to three thousand, but in truth, the number was greater than ten thousand. On November 19, 1921, seventy captured poor peasants were shut into an air-tight railroad car. The doors were not opened until all of them had suffocated. Those were the proportions always.

"When one speaks of the cruelty of the rebels and of what they do to moneylenders, one should not forget the real brutality, that shown by the British, and later by the Congress, to their victims. To this day, the official version of history describes the Moplas as outlaw tribes.

"If in 1857 those who represented the new ideas and the necessary transformation of the entire superstructure were with the British in Calcutta, and the great uprising lacked both leaders and progressive sociocultural aims, then the situation was even worse for the poor peasants of Malabar in 1921. Gandhi and his movement opposed the British, but they repudiated both the justified struggle of the poor peasants, as well as all progressive socio-cultural reforms. The Western-educated, so-called progressives vacillated between support for Gandhi and some third alternative. But they didn't unite with the poor peasants either."

"Gandhi, however, did appeal to the peasants' emotions," said Kumar. "When it came to cultural and social questions, he was an ultra-reactionary, and he attempted to win over the peasant masses with his reactionary stands. But the educated and the intellectuals, who considered themselves progressive, were not even able to talk to peasants."

"Because of this," said Santosh, "the Indian Communist Party remained divorced from the masses. The only one among their leaders during the interwar period who even seemed to consider a role for the peasant masses was M. N. Roy. He, at least, was aware of their existence."

"Yes," said Suraj, "what was it that was typical of these Communist leaders? All of them were from the comprador class, who had grown up in the cities and been educated in London!"

"How did they see 1857?" asked Kumar. "During the entire period when the principal task was immediate national independence from the British, Communist leaders were not able to accept 1857 as a national uprising. Palme Dutt and M. N. Roy shared the view of repudiating the uprising, implanted by the intellectuals of Calcutta. They considered it reactionary. In this they were, incidentally, in complete agreement with Jawaharlal Nehru. It was only after the Navy Mutiny in 1946, independence in 1947 and the Telengana struggle in 1946-1951, that they began to be able to see the conflict of 1857-1859 as the Indian war of independence. Those who were able to perceive this were the likes of V. D. Savarkar, who evolved into ultra-reactionaries and pro-fascists. There is the problem. A communist party which can see neither the masses as they are, nor the nation, and which can't even take up the struggle for bourgeois democratic demands, is bound to be left trailing behind the mass movement time and again, and to find itself in no position to play a significant role."

"We face the same problem today," said Suraj. "We have movements which are socially progressive but politically reactionary. And then we have the political left which cannot formulate the real problems, still less the necessary solutions. The Naxalites, too, have confined themselves to negating the past."

"It was not until now, after 1974, 1975 and the serious defeats that we have begun these discussions. For the first time, we have begun to seriously discuss questions concerning the last century's cultural renaissance and national liberation war. In several social arenas, such as the struggle against the giving of dowries, for women's right to education and widows' right to remarry, the truth is that the communist movements of this century have been less advanced than the nineteenth century reformists. Veerasalingam Panthulu was labelled a communist by reactionary and feudal elements, but the communists did not realize that this was a challenge to them. It is with the coming of the revolutionary cultural movement that we are beginning to bring together our various tasks."

"Just look at what's happening," said Kumar. "The Marwaris supported what was called the enlightenment. But the Marwaris are not just people from Marwar in general, they are real *baniyas*, merchants, moneylenders and shopkeepers. They are a caste of merchants, and one can find moneylending Marwaris not just all over India, but all over East Africa and Southeast Asia. The Marwaris are like Europe's Jews, their caste function is that of the usurer and merchant, even if individuals among them have taken up other occupations. Well, they generally supported enlightenment and western education. Those like the Birla family which control a large portion of the Indian economy have shown a great interest in this education. But just what is their cultural ideology? On August 15,

1947, when India got its independence, all the Birla employees received a special 'tie allowance' so that they could dress properly—like Europeans—for the ceremony. It was not a matter of culture in general, but of comprador culture!"

"We had no Mao in the twenties and thirties," said Suraj. "There was no communist or peasant leader capable of making an analysis the way Mao did of the Hunan peasant movement, where he united the cultural demands with the social, and identified the forces which could liberate China. Nor has anyone been able to produce a similar summary of that which is historically predetermined and inevitable in India. We have been content to spread Mao's thought and Mao's analysis of Hunan, which does serve some purpose, since similarities do exist between China and India. But the differences are so great that one cannot use Mao's description of Hunan as a guide to Andhra Pradesh or Bihar.

"Mao was able to speak of both the oppression of women and politics. But a person like Dange could never do that. He can speak of working class trade union questions but not about their social and cultural problems. It was not just that these leaders could not speak about important issues, they could not even see them. When the struggle was at its bittermost in Telengana and the peasants had established a broad unity against feudalism and taken up armed struggle, the party's General Secretary B. T. Ranadive made a ruthless public attack on them. He refused to accept the unity and struggle against feudalism. He called the struggling communists in Andhra reformists and class collaborators. And he openly attacked Mao Zedong. He criticized Mao for the very analyses which were just then proving themselves correct in practice. While the Indian communist leader B. T. Ranadive was denouncing Mao Zedong's policy of 'new democracy' as un-Marxist, the Chinese People's Liberation Army was marching to victory, guided by that very theory."

"Hold on a minute," said Kumar. "We must not forget that China's communists rid themselves of direct Soviet control in 1935, and could thus become a significant political force in their own country. We cannot blame the defeat of the Indian Communist Party on a foreign country, but neither should we neglect to take foreign influence into account in our analysis. The Indian Communist Party was held so tightly in check that it didn't have the chance to formulate its own analysis. Perhaps M. N. Roy could have done it. Some of his writings in the late twenties led to his being criticized at the Comintern's Fourth World Congress, and the result was that he was driven out of the Communist world movement. But these writings contained a lot of truth. In any case, they were more correct than what Kuusinen said against him.

"Indian revolutionaries were held in a kind of colonial dependence by Great Britain's Communist Party. India suffered because this hindered independent development. China adapted Marxism to its own conditions and had its own revolution, but we remained mired in a colonialized Marxism and had no chance to go our own way.

"As for B. T. Ranadive, it is probable that he had Soviet advisers. At that time, word within the party was that Tito and Gomulka had just been declared enemies, and that some big blowup was about to take place in China. Apparently, B. T. Ranadive had been told something to this effect and had taken the opportunity to launch the opening attack on Mao. But Mao's strength had caused the Soviet leaders to back down. It was intrigue like this that impeded the progress of the popular democratic movement in India. And when these foreign advisers and directors had brought the party to the point of schism, and many communists began to take the road of Naxalbari and the peasant revolution, it took place with the slogans: China's road is our road! China's Chairman is our Chairman! Finally, Chou En-lai was forced to step in and criticize this."

"They were wrong in every situation," said Suraj. "At the outbreak of World War II, they were so slavish in following the slogans about 'struggle against the imperialist war' that they made contact with the German and Italian espionage organizations in Kabul and placed the party in their service. It was not until 1942 that they were able to make a break, while some were never able to sever connections. But when all of India rose up against the British in 1942, the party had already made a complete about-face. Instead of giving this struggle a correct, popular and democratic orientation, they supported the British.

"What the party did succeed in achieving during the years of the war was to establish an influential cultural movement. They were able to carry forward the work of the nineteenth century renaissance, while pursuing such a reactionary pro-British political line that it entailed active opposition even to the economic strikes of the working class.

"And if there is reason to criticize the Telengana struggle, it is not because a broad, anti-feudal united front was created, but because the demand, 'land to the tiller!' was not combined with progressive, anti-feudal, socio-cultural demands. There you have the difference between Telengana 1946 and Hunan 1927!"

"Don't forget that caste and class generally coincide," said Kumar. "90% of the national leadership of the still-united communist party was made up of *brahmans*. Today, the situation is the same for both CPI and CPI (M). This relationship between caste and class has been decisive. It is easy for *brahmans*, who have turned atheist to be of the opinion that the struggle of the untouchables to worship at the temples is reactionary. When they speak of India, they mean high caste India. They know nothing else. So how can they even raise the correct demands in this socio-cultural struggle?"

"I experienced that myself," said Santosh, "when I joined the peasant movement and revolution following Naxalbari. I had thought that the land question was foremost on the minds of the poor peasants and the landless. Ultimately, it is. But what was the immediate cause of their struggle? Their *izzat*. Their honor. Their personal dignity. The right to stand upright before the landowner and look him straight in the eye. The right to walk in front of his house. The right to refuse to bend down and pick up the cigarette butt he has cast aside. Revolution is the struggle for human dignity!

"The issues must merge at the grassroots. Political, cultural, economic. What was never achieved by the leaders, has always proved to be a necessity for the local cadres even if they were not able to formulate this need theoretically. But then, it's at the grassroots that policy becomes clear. Take the dowry question, for example. We opposed the giving of dowries. It is a burden on the people. In the areas where we annihilated or chased away the landowners and the police, and where we had begun to establish people's power, no dowries were given. After the government went in with a large police force, we were defeated and forced to pull out. Our political errors, we can discuss another time. Right now, I just want to tell you a story.

"Soon after the landowners had been returned to power and the police had taken control of the area, I was given the assignment of returning illegally to a village. I was to get in touch with the comrade in charge. He was a poor peasant. A good, politically conscious young comrade. He had just got married. He had received a dowry. I asked him how he could accept it, since it was against our policy. He replied that both he and his sisters were to be married. At first he had refused a dowry. Then his mother had spoken to him, saying that if he did not accept the dowry, the family would have to give up its last piece of land for the girls, and their lives would be ruined. And the mother had said that the giving of dowries was indeed a heavy burden on the families, but that he had to realize that by himself he could do nothing. If he acted on his own he would succeed only in ruining the lives of his loved ones without having achieved anything. Since then, I have often thought about this incident because what that woman understood, what the people know, is often beyond the comprehension of the intellectuals in positions of responsibility. What is decisive is not individual heroism, a few brave acts by individuals, but the collective struggle of the masses. And it is not just for immediate economic gains that the masses struggle. They are struggling for their human dignity."

"As for Naxalbari," said Kumar, "it meant, objectively speaking, that some ten thousand young people from high caste, upper class and intellectual homes, broke with all traditional caste standards and class rules by joining the revolution. In their words, it was a matter of 'integrating without being leaders'! In this, we learnt a lot from the Chinese political campaigns. We ate together, worked together, talked and fought together. You could say that by breaking all caste rules in this way and by beginning a new life, these young people also became Indians instead of *brahmans, kshatriyas* and such. Those who participated in the revolution were transformed."

"Well, let's not exaggerate," said Santosh. "There are many who spent time in the forests and fought during those years in the late sixties and early seventies, and who returned without having been arrested or jailed. I met one of them this morning. He's a car salesman. He owns a house and leads a normal upper middle class existence. I asked him how that had come about. He said that he had only to return home, open the door to his room, put on his clothes and step back into his family relationships. One thing led to another. Alone, one cannot break with one's past."

"There's a lot in what you say," said Suraj. "Not all revolts are the same. I've been out in the forests and in jail, and I smoke like a chimney. And even though my father knows all this, I could never light a cigarette in his presence. I wouldn't want to show disrespect. I don't think it's wrong. I respect him. But he's orthodox."

"That kind of respect isn't wrong," said Kumar. "But if we aren't able to combine the political and economic struggles with the struggle for human dignity, India's people are doomed to defeat again and again."

"And remember," said Suraj, "that it isn't some abstract force which is decisive. I am no Hegelian. There are no abstract forces that determine the course of history. History is shaped by the struggle of the common people."

Then he outlined his dichotomy, the one that had to be overcome, the one that had to be seen first in order to be surmounted.

It had grown late. Santosh and Kumar left to catch their bus. Suraj poured out another cup of black, South Indian coffee and said, "We were speaking of *ahimsa*. It's interesting. In *The Origin of the Family, Private Property and the State* by Engels, I was reading about Scandinavian mythology. He quotes from your *Völuspa*, 'brothers will wage war against one another and become each other's slayers, and sisters' children will break bonds of kinship.' As you can imagine, that is very interesting to us, because the entire *Mahabharata* is about how the clans were destroyed and replaced by the new power. And the *Gita* is, in fact, a slippery and ugly piece of casuistry. Arjuna is to be convinced that it is proper and morally correct to violate the most sacred commands, that is to 'break the bonds of kinship.' Whereas, until then, the taking of the life of a family member had been unthinkable, *ahimsa*, non-violence, is now trans-

formed into a principle, which interpreted casuistically, justifies the killing of family members in the service of higher interests. In India, we've
discussed this question at some length. Dange wrote a totally absurd
book in which he made up a piece of Indian prehistory. But D. D. Kosambi and Debiprasad Chattopadhyaya have written much of great interest and ingenuity on this subject. It is necessary for us to reach an
understanding of the ideologies of our own culture. Scandinavia is still a
bit peculiar compared to the rest of Europe. You have kinships and a
number of pre-feudal and tribe-influenced traditions, it seems. And I
have done a little reading on the subject. For example, the fact that the
crime of trespass does not exist today because of the old tribal right of access means that you have the legal right to enter private land and such.
What about your discussions in leftist circles? Is there a lot of debate
about *Völuspa?*"

Train to Patna

We push our way through the crowd towards the platform. The evening air is chilly. People lie huddled up against each other. The porters shout. It is noisy. The smell of oil, coal and people is in the air. It is like being at the Gare de l'Est in Paris in 1946. We are about to take the night train from New Delhi to Patna: the 156 Tinsukia Mail. Leaving New Delhi at 10:15 p.m., it goes through Aligarh, Kanpur, Allahabad, and past Benares at Mughulseraj, arriving the following day in Patna at 12:50 p.m. From there it goes on to Calcutta.

We hoist up our luggage. Gun crawls into a corner near the window. The window pane is broken. Somewhere a stone was thrown at the train. The windows in the corridor are also shattered.

"Where are the bedrolls?" asks Gun. Then I remember that I have forgotten to make reservations. It is already 10:03 p.m. and too late to find bedding at the station.

"It's going to be a cold night," Gun says. "But, no worse than flying, I guess."

The compartment door is pulled open and a man of about sixty steps in. He is thin-haired and wears gold-rimmed glasses. He looks around. "The upper bunk is mine," he says. He unpacks a blanket from his suitcase. It's green with blue stripes. He takes out an inflatable rubber cushion. He blows it up and makes up his bed. Then he looks at me.

"I believe I saw you at the meeting," he says. "If I recall correctly, your wife was taking pictures. You are Myrdal, aren't you? My name is

Chowdhury. I believe we've met before." He hands me his visiting card. He lives in Poona. I cannot recall having seen him before. No matter how hard I try, I cannot seem to place him.

"As you see, I am no longer working for the government. I have a consultant firm. That's why I'm travelling to Patna."

He carefully closes the compartment door and locks it. He fastens the safety latch.

"One can't be too careful," he says. "One never knows what might happen. Especially around Patna. Four train robberies just yesterday. Did you hear about it? At Jhajha, all the passengers in a second-class car on the 39 Up Howrah Delhi Janata Express were held up. The dacoits were armed with revolvers. But they didn't shoot, only stabbed a passenger who tried to resist. And at Manpur, the 7 Up Toofan Express was robbed; at Neora, they stopped the 142 Down Bhojpur Shuttle and took absolutely everything from the passengers, while at Fatwah they emptied the baggage car on the 67 Up Howrah Bombay Janata Express. They don't usually hold up first-class coaches or foreigners, but one can't be too careful. Especially now during the election campaign. The number of train robberies always goes up before elections. Train robberies mean bad publicity for the sitting provincial government, and Indira wants to win in Bihar.

"I am not one to speak too badly of her, but she does play rough. I was working in the ministry for a time during the Emergency. Mostly with questions concerning oil. I think one could say that she really wanted to do her best for the country, but she had bad advisers. She was not kept informed of what was happening. If she had been, she would never have called for elections in 1977. Why, she actually thought she would win. She had bad advisers and inaccurate information."

The compartment is cold. We put on sweaters and wrap ourselves in our raincoats.

"You can't be relied on," says Gun. "You said you'd reserve tickets and bedding and now you've forgotten the bedding. Just don't complain about the cold!"

"It's nice to have travelling companions who do not smoke," says Dr. Chowdhury.

"There's a lot of talk these days about off-shore oil outside of Bombay," he says. "We read in the papers about the energy crisis, environmental protection and how we should use our resources. But the whole thing is just a battle between Russian and American interests. Will it be the Russians or the Americans who will control our oil and gas? The Russians' technology is not as good, but they have more political clout. The Americans have the more advanced technology, but their standing in the corridors of power is not as high as that of the Russians right now. But these things are not talked about. Instead we are served up a discussion about environmental protection and national independence. It's said that Indira Gandhi favors the Russians. I don't know. I think she favors Indira. But then, she does have bad advisers.

"Of course we oppose authoritarianism. Who wants to be bossed around? But just how much do you think the people care about what is said at those meetings? Why, they don't even attend them. Do you think the man on the street cares about lofty principles and human rights, or about what happens to this or that magistrate? Do you? I know what the man on the street wants. He wants order and stability. He wants security for himself and his property. He doesn't want to be robbed when he is obliged to take the train. It is law and order he is after.

"Last autumn, I had to go to Ranchi. I was planning to take the bus. But then I heard about what had happened to one of my friends. A gang of youths stopped the bus. They stood in the roadway so that the bus was forced to stop. They refused to pay their fares. They just laughed when asked to pay. One of them pulled out a knife and put it to my friend's throat. No one dared to do anything. They took his wallet. No one even dared to sneeze. Then, laughing, they ordered the driver to stop, jumped off and disappeared. The police? The police did nothing. There's nothing we can do, they said.

"All the politicians talk about law and order. But what do they do when they travel by train? They lock themselves in their first-class compartments and don't open up no matter what. They pretend that nothing is happening. No one does anything.

"Last week, I travelled from Bombay. The train was late. Do you know why it was late? Someone had pulled the emergency brake just before the train pulled into the station. We came to a halt. When I looked out, I saw a whole carload of ticketless passengers get out of the train and walk in the direction of the slums. That's where they live. It was closer for them to get off right there in the middle of the tracks. And besides, they could then avoid a clash at the ticket gate. Two railroad policemen stood on the embankment. They carried rifles. But do you think they shot at the ticketless passengers? Do you think they did anything? Do you think they said anything? No, they didn't. I spoke to the conductor and asked him why the train employees didn't do anything. "What would you have us do," he replied. "Who gets into trouble if there's a fight, gunfire and someone gets shot? We do. It's always us. You yell at us because the train is late and the newspapers criticize us if we do anything. And we can be killed if we interfere." That's how it is.

"The man on the street wants law and order. He wants the trains to run on time. Do you think he cares about all those fine words about the freedom of the press and the irremovability of judges and lofty principles? I don't. Indira Gandhi is now promising law and order, and we'll see what happens."

The train pushed on through the night. It clattered at the rail joints and the bunk heaved and squeaked. I looked at Dr. Chowdhury. His gold-rimmed glasses shone. He had removed his tie and shoes, and made himself comfortable. Perhaps I had really met him before.

"You were here during the fifties, weren't you? The fifties and early sixties? Since then you haven't lived here, just visited. Isn't that so? Well, then you haven't seen what has taken place. You were here during the good years. Things have gone poorly for India since Nehru died. Yes, perhaps they had already begun to turn sour before his death. Jawaharlal Nehru did not give us a strong government, but while he was in power our industrial growth rate was 9.5 percent. Then we got a strong government. The annual growth rate dropped to 4.9 percent and annual price increases rose from 4.2 percent to 7.5 percent. This is very important. It's this that brought down Indira Gandhi.

"If the Janata had been able to pursue a different economic policy, the people might have put up with the confusion and insecurity. But prices kept rising and the black market grew. What do people start thinking about at times like these? It's then that they call for law and order. We were talking about train robberies. We aren't the ones robbed. We can lock ourselves in. The newspapers report that when the Patna-Samastipur Express was robbed on Tuesday at Bachhawara, the dacoits got away with a lakh of rupees. A lakh is 100,000. The daily wages of 3,000 farm laborers. In this case, it wasn't farm workers, but junior clerks, workers, peasants and their families who were robbed. How do you think they will vote? The following day, the passengers on the Mithila Express were "relieved" of 1.5 lakhs. There are many people who expect prices to keep rising no matter what. In their view they would rather have a harsh government which will jail the black marketeers, shoot the troublemakers on the spot, enforce law and order, and make things run on time, than a lax regime which allows things to drift and can't even maintain order in the streets.

"No matter what government we get, we've got rough years ahead. We had a somewhat healthy balance of payments the last few years. Mainly because so many people have gone abroad to work in the Arab countries and sent home some of their earnings. That source is now drying up. Meanwhile, the price of oil continues to climb. And inflation is no laughing matter. You were here in 1960. That is a statistical base year. If the price index is set at 100 in 1960, by now it has reached 390. It won't be easy to maintain stability in this country in the future.

"India is a parliamentary democracy and that's a good thing. Pakistan and other military-ruled countries are not exactly inspiring examples to emulate. But all the politicians are trying to remain on good terms with the military. The number of banners, ceremonies and parades is constantly increasing. Did you know that we now have five hundred generals in India? Recently, seven hundred majors were promoted to lieutenant-colonel, receiving an extra star and a monthly raise from 2,000 to 2,500 rupees. The same thing happened in the other military services. 1,200 majors or their equals were promoted at one stroke. And still, the junior officers are not satisfied. It's going too slow for them. It takes six years to become a captain and can take up to thirteen to become a major. But since the number of senior officers has grown so large that we don't know what to do with them, and lieutenant colonels have been assigned to clip military train-tickets out in the sticks, civilians have shot by them in the order of precedence. Not even a brigadier general is looked up to any longer. A young district collector on his first assignment in a little district of no more than a lakh of people or so has a higher standing than a brigadier general old enough to be his father, grown grey on active duty during the course of four wars. That is not right!"

The train comes to a halt. We are in Aligarh. It is midnight and the train is on time. Dr. Chowdhury unfastens the locks and safety catch and pulls open the door. He speaks to some railroad employees on the platform. They stand facing each other and Dr. Chowdhury speaks in a loud voice. Then he turns and gets back into the train. When he comes into the compartment he says, "I tried to arrange for some bedding. But they said it should have been reserved beforehand. Besides, the stop is only for five minutes. That's how things are! If they were worth their salt they would certainly have come up with some bedding. But that's how it is nowadays. No one wants to accept responsibility and put things right."

The train shakes and jerks as it slowly pulls out of Aligarh.

"Never mind," I say. "We have enough clothes on. My wife is already asleep."

"Well, good night then," he says. "I'll turn out the light, if you don't mind."

The dust annoys me. I can't sleep. It itches. It clogs all the pores. I have difficulty breathing. In spite of the cold, I go to the shower room to wash off. The entire first-class coach is asleep. All the doors are carefully locked. I shower. The Indian wide-tracked railroads allow for comfortable coaches. This first-class coach was built in 1977. But almost all of the windows have been broken and badly repaired. The train looks as if it has done service in a war. But, in fact, it has only been on the Delhi-Calcutta line for three years.

I put on another sweater and wrap myself in my raincoat. I have made a pillow of a pile of clothes. Dr. Chowdhury is sleeping soundly. I hear short, authoritative snores.

I can't sleep. I think about the meeting of the other day and of the discussion with Kumar, Santosh and Suraj. A broad unity must be forged and the dichotomy bridged. But isn't it easier said than done? Isn't this one of the impossibilities of Indian politics? In August 1942, when all of India rose up against the British—more extensively and more violently than Gandhi, Nehru and the Congress could imagine—the peasants liberated large tracts of land where the train now rolls. In what is now Uttar Pradesh, Bihar, West Bengal, Maharashtra, and down towards what is now Tamil Nadu, the British authorities were chased away and the peasants established their own power. In some districts, they held power for several years before the British were able to reestablish their authority and rule. The masses were totally united. But the Communist Party of the time, a party claiming to want revolution, had no time for the peasants, and considered the peasant revolution wrong and theoretically muddled. Instead, it buried itself in what was otherwise excellent, anti-fascistic cultural work. And as for the Congress, they wished to see the last of the British, but hardly wanted to do away with the landowners, since the landowners were their fathers, brothers and cousins—in other words, the financial mainstay of their political activities. That is if they were not landowners themselves.

The situation was similar in the 1830s. Widespread, heroic peasant uprisings took place outside Calcutta. The peasants fought valiantly and the British authorities were obliged to bring large forces into action before they were able to quell the uprising and jail, torture, hang and shoot the surviving rebels. But in the city of Calcutta, the intellectuals assembled to celebrate freedom: the freedom guaranteed by England in the Reform Bill of 1832.

The morning dawns, overcast and cool. The train moves across the vast, flat countryside. There is severe drought. The ground which should be covered with verdure is burnt instead.

"It's going to be another difficult year," says Dr. Chowdhury. "Hunger, too, plays a part. One should not always interpret incidents as a political settling of accounts or caste conflicts. It may also be the work of dacoits. I recently read some reports on a few such incidents while in Delhi. In Dahanabiha, not far from Patna, there were between twenty and twenty-five people armed with homemade bombs, rifles and knives, who robbed a Babu and made off with about 5,000 rupees in valuables. Last Tuesday, a battle took place not far away in the village of Braunti. A band of forty-five people attacked the house of a certain Parmeshwar Singh. They made off with 15,000 rupees, killing one of Parmeshwar Singh's household and injuring two others. This may, of course, have been a political, caste or Naxalite action, but from my quick look at the report, it appeared to have been perpetrated by more traditional dacoits.

When times are bad, that sort of thing becomes more common."

The train is late when it pulls into Danapur at around 1:00 p.m. We end up sitting there for more than an hour. The cause is an unannounced strike by the railroad workers. A worker at the locomotive sheds has died. All traffic on the Eastern Railway has been stopped. There is some violence, a fight, some injuries, and many are hurt. It was said that the railroad workers were acting strange. Irrational.

The strike was not all that strange. The strikers wanted the family of the deceased to receive benefits from the railroad company. They maintained that it was the company's responsibility because the man had died while on duty. The superintendent of the Danapur section had rejected their demands, saying that compensation might be considered by the railroad authorities according to the rules and regulations, but only after a doctor's report had proven that such consideration would be in accordance with established rules. The railroad workers in Danapur heard this response and walked out in a lightning strike that shut down all traffic.

"There you see for yourself," said Dr. Chowdhury. "They are undisciplined. No wonder the man on the street is demanding law and order."

The Land of the
Ancient State

We have rented a car in Patna, the capital of Bihar, and intend to drive towards Rajgir at dawn. But the rains have come in the night. We do not set off before seven in the morning. Still, the city is half asleep and silent behind drawn shutters, the streets empty. The asphalt glistens.

The winter rain falls on the plain. Heavy grey curtains of moisture move across the land. The palms look cold in the morning chill. From time to time, the Ganga can be seen towards the north. This rain is eagerly awaited. But it has been a long time coming. The fields are scorched by drought and are yet to be turned green by the rain.

As the main road turns south at Bakhtiarpur for Rajgir the villages begin to show signs of life. People stand wrapped in blankets, waiting. An old man crosses the road. A girl stands shivering in a doorway. She stares after us. The air is damp. In the cold, the morning rites take a long time. But Indian cities and villages are late risers, and the day's work does not usually begin before late into the morning.

We are driving through an old India. It might be called the earliest real India. The great cities of the Indus civilization are, in fact, pre-Indian. Mohenjodaro and Harappa were declining far from here about three thousand five hundred years ago. They gave rise to no immediate successors; although the tradition survived, development was interrupted. Vedic India up in the northwest, the Aryan chariots, herds of cattle and singing priests, never reached here during Vedic times; they only reached about as far as where Delhi stands today. Now, as we drive from

Patna to Rajgir, we are travelling in the oldest India of unbroken tradition. Here, between the sixth and third centuries B.C., the Indian state, which is still a model for India today, began to take form. We drive through the Indian heartland—the land of Buddha, Chandragupta and Asoka.

This, India proper, is not the India of the Bible or Classical Antiquity, as mentioned in the Book of Esther:

> Now it came to pass in the days of Ahasuerus (this is Ahasuerus who reigned, from India even unto Ethiopia, over an hundred and seven and twenty provinces)...

The Book of Esther was written when the history of the Persian Empire and Alexander's military expeditions was already the subject matter of legends. Ahasuerus is Xerxes, and Biblical India was confined to the twentieth satrapy of the Achaemenidian empire, that is the Indus valley and the area west of the Indus, what is today western Pakistan.

This region remained under the rule of that empire for a period of two hundred years. From this India an efficient administration collected for the Persian state treasury an annual tribute of three hundred and sixty talents (from *talentum*, weight) of gold dust. From here were also recruited the Indian archers who won glory for themselves at the victory of Thermopylae, 480 B.C., and who heroically defended Plataea the following year against more advanced Greek forces, only to be crushed by the irresistible frontal attacks of the heavy Greek phalanxes. In 480 B.C. for the first time Indian colonial forces fought on European soil in support of the dominant empire.

This Achaemenidian experience came to signify a great deal for India's future development. But the ancient India we now cross this rain-grey, winter's morning is the India neither the Persian emperors nor Alexander reached. Alexander appeared on this horizon not as a world conqueror but as a bandit-chief raiding outlying districts of the empire. He is not mentioned in contemporary Indian writing. It is not until the whole story of Alexander reaches India in the form of legend and popular tale that he begins to show up in Indian material.

At the end of July 326 B.C., when Alexander passed what is now Amritsar, reached the Beas and stood before this India, his troops mutinied, refusing to follow him further.

Plutarch gives their reasons:

> The battle with Porus depressed the spirits of the Macedonians, and made them very unwilling to advance further into India...(and) they now most resolutely opposed Alexander when he

insisted that they should cross the Ganges...For the kings of the
Gandaritai and the Praisiai were reported to be waiting for him
with an army of 80,000 horses, 200,000 foot (soldiers), 8,000 war-
chariots and 6,000 elephants.

This mutiny probably saved Alexander from defeat and allowed him
three more years of life, to end with malaria in Babylonia, sick with drink
and fast becoming a god-king. For the situation was as described by Plutarch; a comparison of the opposing forces was not in his favor.

Nor was this any exaggeration, for not long afterwards Sandrocot-
tus, who had by that time mounted the throne, presented Seleucus
with 500 elephants and overran and subdued the whole of India
with 600,000 men.

I will get back to Sandrocottus-Chandragupta later. Alexander's expeditions were not lacking in importance for India. But this road we are
taking towards Rajgir is the ancient trade route of merchants and the
campaign track of generals. This region witnessed the triumph of progress and the viable despotic-state a century before Alexander and Chandragupta, and began to develop the strong, bureaucratic society which
became the Indian ideal.

Large parts of the vast Gangetic plain were then still primeval forests.
Here and there were glades of pasture and habitation. The trade route to
the northwest passed through inaccessible and dangerous regions, but
by then the first markets, where iron from the east was reloaded on its
way west, had already taken the leap from village to commercial town,
while silver coins maintained a standard weight and fineness. From their
primeval forests, roving hunters still threatened the rural districts, roads
and commercial centers of the settlers, but the settlements expanded,
commerce increased and the plains grew renowned for their wealth.

A thousand years had passed since the Aryan tribes had broken in
over the Indus valley and the Land of the Five Rivers. They had "freed
the rivers" from the demonic barriers which had stopped the waters.
They had flooded the countryside. The developed irrigated agriculture of
the Indus valley was destroyed when the Aryan warriors, in the name of
Indra, razed the dams so "the stones rolled away like wagon wheels"
and the water flowed freely off the vast, fertile pasture-lands of the
Aryan herds. Barbarism had triumphed over civilization.

When the invading tribes, with their horse-drawn chariots, trains of
ox-carts, singing shamans and thundering male gods, occupied their
new land, a line was drawn between free man and slave, between Aryan
and *sudra*. The free men fought, sang, sacrificed and deliberated, the

subjugated labored. For a long time, society remained so primitive that the *sudras* could not even be called slaves.

As the Aryan tribes pushed further east, their living conditions changed. Not much remained of the blood ties. The Aryan warriors had never allowed *sudras* to mix with Aryan women; they, however, had children with those women available. New groups grew up within the tribes, and the four *varnas* of the caste system took shape: *kshatriya*, the rulers, warriors; *brahman*, the shamans, the priests; *vaisya*, the shepherds, the farmers; and then the caste below the castes, *sudra*, not part of the tribe like the other three, but only belonging to it the way the livestock did. Out of tribal society crystallized social classes, and the further east the new society spread, the sharper grew the class divisions. The reason for this phenomenon was that the agricultural method of burn-beating no longer sufficed. In the new areas, the land was fertile, but heavy and in need of iron to make ploughshares. Iron could only be obtained from the east, in trade for other goods. And at that crossroads Vedic civilization developed, with all its philosophers, poets, great thoughts and incipient grim exploitation. Towards the ninth century B.C. not much of the original barbarism was left.

There further to the east, by the Ganga, where Vedic India had never reached, a rapid Aryanization took place. Religion, language and caste structure was adopted, transformed and developed to meet local needs. And it was here that Hindu India began to emerge. Krishna—the black one—who in the *Rigveda* was still a demon, Indra's enemy and the symbol for the Aryan's adversaries, became the principal deity, replacing Indra. After a thousand years, those who worked the land, the *sudras*, with their Krishna and their irrigation works, had triumphed over the Aryans. This they had achieved, however, by making themselves *brahmans* and Aryans. They had swallowed up and assimilated their conquerors. They had systematized the caste system, the rituals and rules, and in the process had transformed admonitions into prohibitions, changing both form and content. If the pugnacious, hard-drinking, bloodthirsty shamans who wandered down towards India had seen what was called Aryan down by the Ganges one thousand years after their passing, they would not have recognized very much. And the *brahmans* and *kshatriyas*, who set off for the northwest to meet sages and acquire the proper Sanskrit accent and vocabulary, were shocked and appalled by what still remained of barbarism and—to them—filthy customs among those primitive pastoral tribes. Not only did the *brahmans* go to the fields and plough, even the barber could turn up the next day in the guise of a *brahman*.

Here in the growing affluence by the Ganga, classes crystallized. For the ruling class and its castes, work became both harmful and immoral.

Labor became low and vile. Labor became dishonorable, something for slaves, members of lower castes and servants. Physical labor was so disdained that in the stories even the slave felt ashamed about the meanness of his labor, while the high-caste philosopher—living off the labor of others—agonized over life's wretchedness, which demanded of him the physically strenuous inhalation and exhalation of breath for survival. This contempt for work, the contempt for labor which slave society and the caste system created in their own interest and which later helped to maintain feudalism remains a heavy burden today. And not just in India!

The rain has turned into a stubborn, silent drizzle as we walk through the large excavations at what was once Nalanda. On the steps of the main temple, school classes from Patna jostle with Nepalese pilgrim groups and Japanese tourists. For eight hundred years the monastery at Nalanda was the great Buddhist university where students from all over the known world congregated. On his travels to the west, the Chinese monk Hsüan Tsang spent a total of two years here, during several visits between 637 and 642 A.D. At that time, ten thousand monks studied here. More than a thousand of them had a good grasp of twenty holy texts with annotations, more than five hundred had a good grasp of thirty books, and ten monks, among them Hsüan Tsang himself, had a profound knowledge of fifty books. The day did not have enough hours; they were spent in discussion and conversation. The younger and older monks helped one another and, according to Hsüan Tsang, all India looked upon these monks as models worthy of emulation.

Students came from all over the world, seeking to be enrolled in the university. They wished to "put an end to their doubts and then become celebrated." For, as Hsüan Tsang pointed out, he who was known as a monk from Nalanda was honored everywhere he went.

Most of the foreign students who came to the seminaries had to return home, since the subjects which were discussed there were often too difficult. Only those with a profound knowledge of ancient and modern teaching were admitted. Hsüan Tsang noted that only two or three out of ten were admitted.

More than one hundred classes were taught each day and not a moment was wasted. The mood of the monastery was naturally grave and dignified.

Both the major vehicle—*mahayana*—and the minor vehicle—*hinayana*—with its eighteen schools, as well as the profane classics, such as the Veda scriptures, were studied. The commentator reports that logic, grammar, medicine and mathematics were also part of the curriculum.

The rains have picked up once more and we have sought shelter in a little shrine with a large Buddha image, beside the ruins of a temple. People hurry by under umbrellas. Many of them are wrapped in plastic coverings. They have come from all over India and from the Buddhist countries of Asia. Since being dug out during the interwar period, Nalanda has again begun to be a place of pilgrimage.

As long as Buddhism seemed uncontroversial, there was no university here. Although Fa Hsien, who came here at the beginning of the fifth century, mentions the place, Na-lo, and notes that Buddha's disciple, Sariputta, was born there, it was to the monasteries at Patna that the scholars then went. In 427 when the Emperor Kumara Gupta established the monastery at Nalanda, India was at the beginning of its transition into feudalism, and the new, reformed Hinduism began to displace Buddhism. The university at Nalanda soon became world famous—renowned throughout the then known and civilized world—and developed into a leading Buddhist centre, while Buddhism continued to lose ground in a society which was being transformed beyond the monastery walls. Nalanda survived even when in 1197 triumphant Hinduism itself was defeated by the Muslim conquerors. Following the Muslim conquest of Bihar, but before they had time to establish the authority of the Sultanate of Delhi over the entire area, the Tibetan monk Dharmasvamin (Chag lo-Tsa-ba Chos-rje-dpal) travelled through northern India. He studied a year at Nalanda and then, in April 1234, left for home in Tibet. Nalanda had already been burnt and sacked by then, but because it was built of brick, it was still inhabitable, and seventy monks studied there under the guidance of the ninety-year-old Mahapandita Rahulasribhadra. But as Dharmasvamin sadly notes: "In general, one can say that in India the non-Buddhists were numerous, the Sravakas (the Jain laity) were fewer, and the followers of the Mahayana even fewer."

With those words, Nalanda disappears from history, and for Hindus the ruins become the remnants of the city of Kundalipura where the father of Krishna's wife Rukmini ruled. When that indefatigable traveller Dr. Francis Buchanan visited Nalanda around 1810, he found a temple dedicated to the goddess Kapatesvari. A statue of "a fat male" was worshipped there. Today, even that temple is gone, and all that remains of its tradition is the name of the village Kapatya. However, thanks to the excavation, Buddhist Nalanda has once again become a place of pilgrimage and tourism.

Out of the rain, we sit and watch the tourists hurry by, and the dignified pilgrims wandering devoutly in the ancient temple.

Gun says, "Each age searches out its history from the past."

"Yet, there is always an objective base for even the loftiest learning and deepest piety," I say.

"Somebody had to toil and sweat if ten thousand learned monks were to spend all their time discussing spiritual matters," says Gun.

And she is right. The past really happened. It cannot be changed no matter what historical tradition the age emphasizes. The commentator, the monk Hui-li, who wrote Hsüan Tsang's biography, says when discussing the monks at Nalanda:

> The king gave the revenue of more than one hundred villages to support them, and each of the villages had two hundred families who daily offered several hundred *tan* of rice, butter and milk. Thus the students could have the four requisites (clothing, food, bedding and medicine) sufficient for their needs without going to beg for them. It was because of this support that they achieved so much in their learning.

The world famous learning of the monks, their renowned seminaries and dignified gravity reposed on the daily backbreaking toil of twenty thousand families.

In Rajgir, we visit the town wall and caves and follow in Buddha's footsteps. The city was already old when it became one of Buddha's favorite places and when Mahavira, the Jains' last Thirtamkara, spent fourteen rainy seasons here. Nalanda was a suburb, but Rajgir was the capital of the kingdom of Magadha. King Bimbisara, the first to have a standing army of his own, expanded his realm and lent his support to both Jainism and Buddhism. Here was the center of the new power and new ideas. Here was shaped the bureaucracy, and even ideology, of the realm. Bimbisara was of humble birth. He was of tribal origin and only out of courtesy could he be considered a *kshatriya*. The new state was founded here a thousand years before Nalanda became the center for the highest learning of the time. That state needed iron for its foundation; iron made the state a necessity.

It was this iron-state of the sixth century B.C. that frightened Alexander's Macedonian army and which, even today, serves as a model for India's rulers. That state made possible tremendous economic advances; it gave scope to new, revolutionary ideas and, with a grim despotism, destroyed the past. To the south lie today's large Indian iron ore deposits. We drive through the spurs of the mountains towards the southwest.

The ferric oxide forms a crust on the rocks. The northernmost of these deposits are to be found here, near Rajgir. They are easily exploited.

Since the ninth century B.C. the tribes around the Ganga had been going through a process of change. Agriculture generated more wealth than in the past. This was due to the fact that the blacksmiths, using a type of bellows first used in Egypt seven hundred years earlier, worked the iron ore from Rajgir and the mountainous tracts to the southwest. With the new tools which were produced, the jungles could be cleared. Production rose: rice, cotton, sesame, wheat, millet beans, lentils, indigo and gourds were grown. Axe, hoe and ploughshare forced back the jungle. Harvest followed harvest. The states around the Ganga were now already more prosperous than the older, Aryan areas to the northwest. But when the agriculture around the Ganga and towards the Deccan to the south began to employ irrigation techniques, it leapt past even the irrigated agriculture of the Indus valley once destroyed by the Aryans.

It was here that the third irrigation technique was developed—the one suited to a monsoon climate.

The first irrigation technique diverted or dammed river water, or drew off the water. The second technique began with wells and developed into the *qanat* or *karez*, the huge underground water system.

The third irrigation technique was tank-building. Reservoirs were excavated. The monsoon rains were stored and during the dry season the water was let out to irrigate the fields. This technique was now developed here, and together with the first irrigation technique it spurred further agricultural production. The importance of animal husbandry declined.

Shipping grew on the Ganga. Two-wheeled ox-carts rolled along the roads, caravans of donkeys loaded with merchandise began to be seen, and this became the economic center of the subcontinent. Handicrafts developed in the cities. There was a rapid rise in both luxury artisanship, destined for trade with distant lands and for the very rich, and in the production of everyday commodities. Goldsmiths, jewellers and pearl-embroiderers, but also carpenters, cartwrights, blacksmiths, coppersmiths, bronze-founders, basket weavers, tanners, rope-makers, arch-makers, potters, weavers and dyers populated entire city neighborhoods, had their own lanes and began to organize themselves into guilds.

The new agriculture destroyed the pastoral collectives of the clans. Newly cleared land became private property. Big landowners followed in the wake of the ploughshares, and these new landowners lived in constant fear of their slaves, day-laborers and the poor. They were forced to set up private armed forces to keep the rabble under control. This growing prosperity created wealthy classes from among the old clans, and tribal society became entrenched in an ever more rigid hierarchic order. The old rulers—the free born and prominent—organized against this new wealth. Social standing, rights and duties were determined at birth. The common people, the slaves and rabble had no right other than to work and obey orders, even if there were occasional rare cases of a few becoming rich through frugality, sweat and cunning.

According to tradition, there were sixteen *janapads* or provinces—from Gandhara up in the northwest towards the Hindu Kush, to Anga near Bhagalpur in what is today Bihar. These *janapads* were not states, but tribal territories. They were quite heterogeneous. Some remained in the time of the pastoral peoples and warrior tribes. One might consider them genuinely Aryan. Even then, they were considered impure by the learned, sacrificial priests of the Gangetic valley. He who travelled to the northwest was obliged to undergo expensive purification ceremonies before he could return to his own clan. Economic development was so disparate between the *janapads* that what was genuinely authentic and traditional was even then considered unorthodox. These areas had now also been conquered by the Persian empire, and it was their tribal warriors who fought and died in the European wars of the Persian king.

Under the influence of great wars and internal conflicts, the new economy remade the governmental structure. Of the sixteen *janapads*, there remained only four at the time of Siddhartha. Two had already evolved into monarchies; these controlled the Ganga and the rich agricultural areas. Kosala, to the west, was the oldest and mightiest kingdom; it had just fought and destroyed Kasi and taken Benares. Kosala controlled both the trade route south, towards the Deccan, as well as the route towards the northwest. The second realm was Magadha to the east, the capital of which was the impregnable Rajgir. The other two *janapads* Malla and Vrijji were situated to the north and northeast of the Ganga. Arrian describes them in his history of Alexander's military expeditions:

> ...they conducted their own political affairs in a regular and constitutional manner. For the multitude was ruled by the aristocracy, who governed in no respect contrary to the rules of moderation.

Malla and Vrijji were oligarchical, tribal federations. A small number of oligarchs ruled over an agrarian population. There was equality among the oligarchs and decisions were made at meetings. All the oligarchs were equal and neither wealth, courage nor learning placed one above the other. In general, the non-free agricultural laborers were not members of the tribe; they remained outside, and below, clan society. While their struggle with the free men grew increasingly bitter, the struggle within the oligarchy itself also grew more relentless. The newly affluent fought for their privileges, and the ambitious young men quit the equality of the tribe to seek success, honor and power at the royal courts. Still, Malla and Vrijji were mighty: they had their warriors and controlled the northern trade route from the Ganga.

Besides these *janapads*, organized as states, there still existed independent tribes which refused to yield and which retreated ever further into the wilderness. Within the new, more strictly organized kingdoms were also to be found virtually independent tribes which only recognized the suzerainty of the king. One of these was the small, republican Sakya tribe, which still did not admit caste divisions, but only differentiated between free and non-free. It was into this tribe that Siddhartha—called Gautama because his was the ox totem—was born, in or around the year 560 B.C. He would later be known as Buddha, the enlightened. In modern encyclopedias, he is called a prince. And it is true that his father and relatives, like other free men, could serve as headmen-rajas. But Siddhartha was a free-born aristocrat, not a prince of a royal house. The authors of the encyclopedias are shackled by their own inability to think as anything other than subjects. At this point in time, when the triumphant state swept all before it, and his own tribe was destroyed, when values changed radically and many people were cast out into darkness and misery, while others swung up on the wheel of fortune to prosperity and honor, the fact that Siddhartha was born a free man held importance for the future. After this age of destruction and freedom when it was a joy to be alive, thought became shackled, and remains so to this very day.

Although the new tools and new techniques first made forced labor profitable and, through a general enslavement, created an enormous surplus for the free-born, this surplus in turn, destroyed the life of the old society. In the past, Indra had ripped up the cities of the Indus valley the way one tears old cloth. Then Indra himself had been shoved aside by the demons he believed he had defeated, while the new cities destroyed the remnants of the society once established by the Aryans.

Where the tribal collectivity once worked the land—Siddhartha's father also tilled the soil—the forests were now cleared by slaves and day laborers. New classes came into being: landowning small peasants, slave-owning middle peasants and large land barons, masters of large tracts of land and served by slaves. The slaves no longer belonged only to those born to that station; they might also be debtor-slaves.

This was the golden age of commerce. Caravans wandered northwest carrying crude iron, rice and sugarcane molasses from further down along the Ganga. The handicrafts of the cities flourished. The merchants lent money against mortgaged property and demanded interest, compound interest. And all the ancient, sacred customs and traditions were eroded by usury.

These new power-holders, who now make their appearance, demanded law and order—their brand of law and order. They were not of high birth, but of common origin. They did not hold the free-born in especially high esteem. They made their loans and demanded their rights in the face of all the ancient customs. They needed the state to protect their interests against the clans. The standing army crushed the tribal militias. A standing army needs pay. Money is what motivates and guides that army. So taxes had to be collected. But since the tax-collectors had to be supervised, a bureaucracy was necessary. The bureaucracy too had to be watched over and spying made part of the system. This new monarchy lacked the religious content held in the past by the holy kings. The new kings themselves were of lowly birth. They made their own way, directing the openly despotic, bloody governments which severed all ancient social ties and opened up prosperity's floodgates.

For a time, it seemed that Kosala would attain the dominant position in the Gangetic region. It was that power which finally destroyed Siddhartha's whole tribe. Predominance instead passed on to Magadha. The other three *janapads* were crushed, for Magadha controlled both the richest iron ore deposits and trade routes. With the destruction of its rivals, this new power swelled in all directions. The jungles were cleared. The forest tribes were driven further. The whole world was to be under its rule. At the time of Xerxes' victory at Thermopylae, Magadha had become the dominant power in the Gangetic region. When Alexander stood at the Beas in July 326 B.C., Magadha had emerged as an empire with its new capital, Pataliputra, well on its way to becoming a world metropolis.

Bimbisara was the first in the line of kings who led this advance towards world domination. It is believed that he came to power in 546 B.C. His parentage is disputed. He was succeeded—and, perhaps, murdered—by his son Ajatasatru. During the reigns of Bimbisara and Ajatasatru both Buddhism and Jainism emerged in Magadha. Both Buddha and Mahavira were active here. During Ajatasatru's reign, the first Buddhist council was also held. He died in 416 B.C. and was eventually succeeded by five kings, each of whom is thought to have murdered his father. Another three kings, of the same or a closely related dynasty, ruled until 362 B.C. Then Mahapadma Nanda, believed to be the son of a *sudra* mother, or perhaps of a barber and a prostitute, but in any case known to be of the lowliest of births, ascended the throne. He is known as the ruler who finally crushed the free-born and who was later recognized as a *kshatriya*.

Thus, during a span of a dozen reigns, a new society was created. It was radically different from the one it replaced. Although cruel and despotic, it offered scope to talent. While the slaves were worked beyond endurance, the landowner could expect no mercy if he speculated with borrowed money and gambled wrong. When the debt fell due, he might have to pay with his own freedom and become a slave. Production increased, and although the poor starved, they were still better off than the tribes which had been driven further into the inaccessible forests where the new agriculture had not yet found it profitable to penetrate.

This was indeed a great transformation. All vows were broken. All the gods fell and Ajita Kesakambali answered King Ajatasatru:

There is no such thing, O king, as alms or sacrifice or offering. There is neither fruit nor result of good or evil deeds. There is no such thing as this world or the next. There is neither father nor mother, nor beings springing into life without them. There are in the world no recluses or *Brahmanas* who have reached the highest point, who walk perfectly, and who having understood and realized by themselves alone, both this world and the next, make their wisdom known to others.

A human being is built up of the four elements. When he dies the earthly in him returns and relapses to the earth, the fluid to the water, the heat to the fire, the wind to the air, and his faculties pass into space. The four bearers, he on the bier as a fifth, take his dead body away; till they reach the burning-ground men utter forth eulogies, but there his bones are bleached, and his offerings end in ashes. It is a doctrine of fools, this talk of gifts. It is an empty lie, mere idle talk, when men say there is profit therein. Fools and wise alike, on the dissolution of the body, are cut off, annihilated, and after death they are not.

This is a time of great intellectual effervescence. Everything is debated. Everything is questioned. Spirits are free and Sanjaya Belatthiputta answers.

If you ask me whether there is another world—well if I thought there were, I would say so. But I don't say so. And I don't think it is thus or thus. And I don't think it is otherwise. And I don't deny it. And I don't say there neither is, nor is not, another world. And if you ask me about the beings produced by chance; or whether there is any fruit, any result, of good or bad actions, or whether a man who has won the truth continues, or not, after death—to each or any of these questions do I give the same reply.

It was at this time and in this intellectual environment that Siddhartha Gautama became the Buddha. More important than all his teaching was the organization he created. And it was here that his being free-born played a vital role.

Everything had fallen apart. There was no escape for the people. It was at this point that Siddhartha Gautama established his *sangha*. From the Sanskrit *samhan:* to join together. We see these associations today in the militant peasant movement. The revolutionaries build their *ryotu-coolie sangham,* and it is the same association as Siddhartha's, drawing on the same popular, tribal solidarity. For forty-five years Siddhartha led his church. It was created as a retreat from the world's wretchedness, into a secure illusion. The destroyed clan-community re-emerged as a religious communion. The freedom of the monks was that of the free-born in clan-society. Democracy characterized relations within ascending Buddhism; the congregation discussed and made decisions as the clan had once done. The adherents were propertyless as the clan members had been earlier. They were provided for and spent their time in exalted service. Although one was not born into this congregation as into the clan, one was admitted as a clan member might be admitted into the inner circle of men.

Siddhartha laid down the ritual himself. The sangha as a whole performed the ordination, after the candidate had been presented and the congregation asked three times if anyone objected. When the sangha assembled and proposals were put forward, they were accepted if no one protested. If anyone were against the proposal, the majority ruled. The sangha itself appointed vote-counters. Here then we have the re-emergence of the democracy of the clans.

Although this organization was a refuge in a chaotic world where the new reality destroyed all conventions and where people's fear and suffering was as intense as the tempestuous joy and new inebriating sense of freedom, still Siddhartha's association was not revolutionary. It was not a threat to the new rulers. On the contrary, the kings protected and aided Siddhartha's sangha. It was a source of pleasure to them.

It could never move from illusion into real life, by becoming a democratic association of the truly tormented and suffering. The fact of the matter was that the great truth that existence meant suffering did not include everyone.

Siddhartha expressly prohibited the ordination of slaves. And in this new society where even the free-born could become slaves if they were unable to pay their debts, Siddhartha also prohibited the ordination of debtors. The existence of the new society could only be guaranteed by means of a standing army, unburdened by the old traditional morality. Since many of the soldiers abhorred the deeds they had been compelled to perform in the name of the king and authorities, it was not unusual that such enlisted men sought to join Siddhartha's sangha. But Siddhartha was dependent on the favor of the king, and his sangha, too, was protected by the army of the new power. So Siddhartha declared that soldiers could not be admitted. They could not desert the army to seek shelter in his democratic serenity and other-worldliness. And King Bimbisara was grateful and showed his gratitude.

At the time Alexander was advancing toward the Indus, Buddha's organized church had grown strong along the Ganga. It had already experienced its first schisms and held its first decisive councils. The kingdom in which the church was located was mighty. It stretched from what is now Orissa in the east, to Punjab in the west, and from Nepal in the north to Andhra Pradesh in the south. Both the church and the standing army had grown; 20,000 horsemen, 200,000 foot soldiers, 2,000 chariots and 3,000 elephants stood guard over this new state of bailiffs and tax-collectors. Its ruler was the low-born Mahapadma Nanda's descendant, Dhanananda.

When Alexander reached Taxila in the spring of 326 B.C. he held a great durbar. There were many who came to pay their respects and present their proposals. Alexander had problems with the shamans in the mountain villages. The tribes there had not changed very much in the thousand years which had passed. About these *brahmans* (called philosophers by the Greeks) Plutarch writes:

> The philosophers gave him no less trouble than the mercenaries, because they reviled the princes who declared for him and encouraged the free states to revolt from his authority. On this account he hanged many of them.

But among those who came to Alexander is said to have been one Chandragupta from Magadha. An ambitious youth. According to most sources, this Chandragupta was of lowly birth. According to some, he was even an untouchable. Other accounts have labelled him *kshatriya*. Jawaharlal Nehru, himself a *brahman*, noted however, that at that time, all sorts of strangers climbed socially and made themselves *kshatriya*. His totem name, Maurya, suggests that he belonged to a peacock totem in a tribe, thus making him free-born, perhaps the son of a headman. But, the Greek tradition, as recorded by Justin, also reports that he 'was born in a humble life.' Accounts have it that this young Chandragupta was accompanied by a learned brahman from Taxila who was hostile towards Dhanananda, King of Magadha. The name of this *brahman* is said to have been Chanakya or Vishnu Gupta, and he is better known as Kautilya. Chandragupta offended Alexander and had to flee for his life. According to some accounts, he advised Alexander to conquer Magadha and when the latter hesitated, Chandragupta insulted him. This may account for Plutarch's remark:

> Sandrocottus himself, who was then but a youth, saw Alexander himself and afterwards used to declare that Alexander could easily have taken possession of the whole country, since the king was hated and despised by his subjects for the wickedness of his disposition and the meanness of his origin.

This tax-collecting realm's reputation for unquenchable royal greed was so entrenched that Hsüan Tsang heard about it a thousand years later when he came to Pataliputra.

It is said that from Taxila Chandragupta escaped with Kautilya back towards Magadha. There he raised his own army. At Kautilya's advice, it was comprised of five different groups: *chora* or *pratirodhaka*—robbers and bandits; *mlechchha*—non-Aryans, strangers; *choragana*—organized bands of robbers; *atavika*—forest people; and *sastropajavi-sreni*—warrior tribes.

In a long and bloody war, begun perhaps before Chandragupta's meeting with Alexander—if he ever did meet with Alexander—a million lives were lost according to some chroniclers. Chandragupta with the aid of the crafty Kautilya succeeded in defeating and killing King Dhanananda. Then, in 317, he proclaimed himself king. He had gained the possession of all of Magadha and also an area in the northwest left by Alexander. In 305 it seems he also took possession of the satrapies west of the Indus as far as Herat from Seleucus Nikator. He also apparently married one of the daughters of Seleucus Nikator at this time and presented his father with five hundred elephants. He was a mighty king, the first of the Maurya dynasty. It was he who, with the aid of his adviser and minister Kautilya, really shaped the state into an all-inclusive, ruling power of a new type.

Justin commented on developments:

> Sandrocottus was the leader who achieved their freedom, but after his victory he forfeited by his tyranny all title to the name of the liberator, for he oppressed with servitude the very people whom he had emancipated from foreign thraldom.

Verily Purana Kassapa could say:

> To him who acts, O king, or causes another to act, to him who mutilates or causes another to mutilate, to him who punishes or causes another to punish, to him who causes grief or torment, to him who trembles or causes others to tremble, to him who kills a living creature, who takes what is not given, who breaks into houses, who commits dacoity, or robbery, or highway robbery, or adultery, or who speaks lies, to him thus acting there is no guilt. . . . In generosity, in self-mastery, in control of the senses, in speaking truth there is neither merit, nor increase of merit.

The rain has stopped. We have passed Bela and left the main road. We now drive along a village road across the plains towards the east. It grows increasingly narrow. We leave habitation behind us. The road is rough from use. It winds between the fields, towards the black mountains. The fields become rocky. Black stones stick out of the ground. The road is cut up by drainage furrows. The car heaves and snorts and the defective clutch slips, but we slowly near the mountains. These are the Barabar Hills. Here Buddha's disciples, fleeing the evils of the world, came to pass the rainy season in tranquillity, two thousand five hundred years ago. The caves they carved out of the gneiss have walls so polished that the stone is totally smooth beneath one's hand.

Is This Suffering Necessary?

The track up to the caves passes through the ravine. Then it turns into a cliffside path. The stones have been worn away by footsteps. Suddenly, it veers off to the left, after skirting a large, black stone slab. The plains drop out of sight behind us and ahead we see a peaceful mountain vale and grazing animals. A shepherd boy sits in the shade, playing for his flock on what appears to be a reed flute. The cows graze in tranquillity and the goats scramble up the bluff above him. Here in the wall of the mountain, we find the first cave. It faces the north, out onto the valley. It is Karan Chaupar, a single, great chamber with an arched ceiling. The air in the room is thick: a curious combination of thousands of years of incense and the stench of bats. The stone has been polished until it gleams. At the entrance, an inscription has been chiselled into the left side of the door frame. It reads that the name of the cave is Supiya, the name of the hill Khalatika, and that the year is the nineteenth in the reign of Asoka, that is, 245 B.C. The doorway is fashioned in a monumental, Egyptian style, with an inward-leaning door frame of stone. Stepping from the cave's stuffiness, all is rural tranquillity.

We walk around the hill. The day has grown warm. These are no mountains. They are stone hills, sticking out of the plain. A knoll of gleaming gneiss. On the other side of this hillock is the cave we have come to see, the Lomas Rishi cave. The layout of the cave is interesting in itself. Like the Sudama cave, located a little to the east in the same knoll of gneiss, the cave's longitudinal direction runs parallel to the cliff wall.

Beyond the outer chamber, which is nearly 10 × 6 metres and the walls of which are highly polished, there is a smaller cell with a crudely chiselled wall so that one can follow the chisel tracks with one's fingers. According to its inscription, the Sudama cave was fashioned for the Ajivika sect in the twelfth year of Asoka's reign (252 B.C.) and was called the "Banyan Tree Cave." The Visa Zopri cave, a thousand metres to the east, also has the same dating, and it, too, was built for the Ajivika sect. The Lomas Rishi cave, however, is not dated. Or, to be more precise, the inscriptions there are from the late Gupta period, the seventh and eighth centuries. Among other things, they say that King Anantavarman had a figure of the god Krishna placed in this cave. At the inauguration ceremonies suggested by this inscription, the earlier inscription from Asoka's time may have been destroyed.

It is possible, even probable, that these rocky hills were sacred long before Chandragupta established his strong state, before the sects appeared and were given places of refuge from the evil of the world by the kings. It is possible that these mountainous knolls were sacred retreats at the time of the *Mahabharata* and earlier. At any rate, the caves were excavated at the time when the strong state was emerging and growing powerful. And it is important to remember, and to see with one's own eyes, how these sanctuaries were then deserted and suffered a change of religion inside of a millenium.

The Lomas Rishi cave is of particular interest for another reason. Its doorway leans Egyptian-fashion and is set into the mountain wall. Above it, a wooden ceiling, replete with beams and bamboo grid, has been chiselled out of the stone. The Lomas Rishi cave is the first in a series of ever larger stone chambers which reproduced sacred rooms built of wood. Thus, we are able to see here, replicated in stone, wooden structures which rotted more than two thousand years ago. In a frieze on the richly carved gable above the monumental doorway walks a procession of wonderfully hewn elephants. They worship at stupas. They are refreshingly, lovingly realistic. It is to see them and this gable from what represents a sacred, Vedic, wooden structure, that we have come to the Barabar Mountains.

These caves were at one time Buddhist. Buddhism was then a mighty religion. Then, at the beginning of India's feudal middle ages, the new Hinduism triumphed, and in the caves where Buddhist monks had passed the rainy seasons, Black Krishna now reigned. But before that, heretical Ajivika sect members had come here a hundred generations ago, seeking refuge from the noise of the world.

Beyond this peaceful mountain vale, with its grazing livestock and dark, young shepherd playing his flute beneath the shade of a tree, a world fell apart. What was it they were pondering, these naked ascetics

who came here under the protection of the king? Their meditation had
yet to become mystical. The questions to which they sought the answers
were very simple: Were the events taking place beyond this peaceful vale
unavoidable? Was this course of events inevitable? Could suffering be
prevented?

They were not followers of Buddha. They considered his teachings
trite. Siddhartha Gautama played games with words instead of giving
real answers. Events around them raised the question of the necessity of
suffering. But Siddhartha Gautama answered them with empty phrases,
what they saw as an evasion.

Of the six schools of thought which rivalled Buddhism, only Jainism
remains a living tradition. The other five, however, still haunt the Buddhist scriptures. *Jataka,* the narratives—the stories of the former incarna-
tions of Buddha—are filled with spiteful outbursts against named leaders
of these sects, as well as the naked ascetics who joined them. Yet, one
can see, "through a glass darkly," how the sages of those sects saw Siddhartha Gautama:

> There is nothing superhuman about the sage Gautama.... He has
> only worked out a system which was the outcome of his own indi-
> vidual thought and study. The ideal for the attainment of which his
> doctrine was preached does not lead to the destruction of sorrow in
> those who follow it.

Three of these sages were quoted, as presented in Buddhist texts, in the
previous chapter. The naked ascetics who sat here, staring out over the
valley 2,225 years ago, were Ajivikas. They were the disciples of Makkali
Gosala. From what we know today, he was the most interesting of contemporary philosophers: the one who posed the relevant questions and
answered them in a straightforward way.

To the question of the inevitability of sorrow, he answered, "human
effort is ineffectual."

According to various accounts, Makkali Gosala was born in a corner of
a cowshed where his mother had taken refuge. Hence the name Gosal
(cowshed). His father may have been a wandering bard. Makkali himself
may have been a runaway slave. Perhaps both of these tales are true. In
any case, he became a wandering singer, musician and dancer, a bard.
Later, he briefly joined Mahavira, Jainism's great prophet. But he broke
away from him. The suffering of this life was too great, and the remedy
that Mahavira's teaching could offer too inadequate. How could one
claim that man was responsible for his own fate? Could he possibly condemn himself, by his *karma,* to these horrors?

It seemed to Makkali Gosala that Siddhartha Gautama and Mahavira tried to talk away this monstrous reality. He wanted to perceive the truth. He wanted to clearly state that man was incapable of changing anything. Fate, *niyati*, decided. Mahavira and Siddhartha Gautama wrapped themselves in veils of illusion. Makkali Gosala ripped these veils apart: space was infinitely black, cold, empty. The brave or cowardly, the industrious or the indolent, the fool or the sage—all like balls of yarn in the hand: throw them and they unwind, each to its own length, long or short.

Makkali Gosala danced in a delirious madness beneath the firmament. During his last fit, when he danced and sang at the home of the potter Halahala, his disciple Ayampula questioned him. But the dancing sage only replied: "Play your vina, my dear, play your vina!"

As Debiprasad Chattopadhyaya, the historian of the materialistic tendency in early Indian philosophy, has remarked, what else could a tribal bard say when everything he valued, his entire existence, crashed down about him, and there was no hope to be found?

Leaving the tranquil valley, we head towards the black ravine. Then the plain opens before us. There in the distance we catch a glimpse of villages and beyond the mist lie the cities. The truth of the matter is that the question of the inevitability of suffering is just as urgent today as it was when Makkali Gosala danced alone beneath the infinitely black, empty sky.

Today, like yesterday, tomorrow, or a thousand, two thousand, two thousand five hundred years ago—when the unarmed untouchables awoke that night, they found five hundred hired murderers surrounding their village, screaming and shouting in the night and firing into the huts inhabited by the *chamar* caste. The members of the *chamar* caste are the most lowly: they work with leather, the women are midwives and the men tanners. And the five hundred leaping murderers threw burning balls of cotton drenched in kerosene at the huts which burst into flame in the night. Thirty huts were burnt down and those fleeing were shot as they rushed out, their black silhouettes starkly visible against the burning huts. And for what reason? The poor had to be taught a lesson. They had gone to the courts and complained that the high caste Hindus had grabbed the property left behind by the Muslim landowners when they had fled at the time of Partition in 1947. Those who tilled the soil had demanded their rights as set down in the laws of the land. And these poor of the *chamar* caste had refused one of the landowners his traditional right to *chamar* women. So they were murdered and burnt. That is what usually happens. It has happened many times in the past and continues to happen no matter who is in power. That is what has been happening for the past two thousand five hundred years in Bihar, and the question is, whether this suffering is really necessary.

As I pass through this dark gorge, away from the tranquil vale over-looked by the caves of the naked ascetics, I am descending into hell. This, of course, is one possible explanation: the man is beaten on the soles of his feet until crippled because of some previous misdeed. The woman has the policeman's lathi, covered with chili powder, shoved up her rectum, and it is her own fault. The child is burnt to death in a hut for his own misdoing. The grandmother who runs out of the burning hut, who is hit in the stomach and rolls on the ground, screaming, suf-fers the consequences of her previous deeds.

This can be interpreted in several ways. They are being punished for what they have done in this life. They are being punished for what they have done in previous lives. It is even possible that the entire earth is but a penal colony of the universe. Thus the guilty from all the inhabited worlds are sent here to endure a human existence. This is as plausible an explanation as any other apologia. For all of these more or less religious explanations are alibis. The house is, in fact, burning. It's been burning for two thousand five hundred years.

At least Makkali Gosala was brave enough to dare face what was hap-pening. What he saw drove him mad.

"Human effort is ineffectual." That is an honest explanation. There is neither meaning nor purpose in this suffering, nor is there any escape. It just *is*.

Debiprasad Chattopadhyaya seems to feel that Siddhartha Gautama served his time better. At least he offered a consoling illusion. Makkali Gosala tried to make the leap out of his historic frame and tried to com-prehend what was taking place about him, when everything was falling apart and the new despotic state was being consolidated. This attempt was naturally futile. It was what the Greeks called *hubris*. Makkali Gosa-la's madness is, therefore, an appropriate punishment. Alone, he ended up in empty space.

I do not agree.

Can it really be that it is only at present, say since about 1847, that it has become possible to see the causal connection behind the monstrous human suffering of which we and our loved ones have continually been the victims?

Why, that is an even worse punishment. In that case, humanity as a whole would be condemned to suffer a couple of millenia of hell before it could deliver itself into a more humane existence. During that time, the issues raised by Makkali Gosala would be without meaning, and people would have to stick to Buddha, Christ and Mahavira, who at least pro-vided a little solace in the misery to which mankind was condemned.

I could, of course, re-write this using Marxist terminology. I would then begin by declaring the whole issue naive, absurd and ideologically faulty. But that would not be very good Marxism, just some theoretical sleight of hand.

Marx, as he has himself noted, was no ox for whom the suffering of others was of no interest. Mao remarked that it was right to rebel. Makkali Gosala posed real questions and was courageous enough to seek answers to them. Unfortunately, he came to the wrong conclusion, finding that blind fate was decisive.

In fact, what was taking place beyond this tranquil valley, was not unavoidable. These events were not inevitable. This suffering might have been prevented.

It was right to rebel, even two thousand five hundred years ago. On occasion, we have succeeded. Then a new situation, with new contradictions, arises. Five hundred years ago, our ancestors in Sweden and Switzerland scored victories in the peasant wars. Since that time, we have been spared some of the suffering endured by those people whose peasant wars were lost.

Of course, victory and defeat have their reasons. But they become clear only later. I have tried to give an account of the cause behind the events here in Bihar. But I don't consider them to have been unavoidable.

What this means is that I see the possibility of another two thousand five hundred years—or, for that matter, many times two thousand five hundred years—of suffering. I think that Debiprasad Chattopadhyaya is wrong. The line of change does not lie at this particular point. There is a line of change, but then it existed even for Makkali Gosala, Siddhartha Gautama and Mahavira, even if they never crossed it; it might still be there in two thousand five hundred years, if we do not manage to leap out of it in our time.

I do not look down upon the naked ascetics and their questions. Their questions are much more to the point than those posed by the academic Marxists who cannot imagine the possibility of a real revolution before the industrial revolution—and who cannot see that the revolution might not occur for yet another thousand years.

The Image of India

Outside, the New Year's Eve celebration in the Travellers' Lodge in Bodhgaya is in progress. The music throbs. People laugh and talk. I sit by the shortwave radio and try to tune in the news. The Russians have just occupied Afghanistan.

Russian policy is consistent and purposeful. Ninety-four years have passed since General Komarov's victory at Kushk, but now they take all of Afghanistan. For a long time now, the British have been out of the running for world domination. And the 1907 treaty between the British Empire and the Russian Empire that divided their spheres of influence and was to keep the Russians out of Afghanistan is no longer even remembered. Yet Afghanistan is in Europe's backyard, as Central America is in the backyard of the U.S. The European powers will let it be known that they disapprove. But that will be all.

The reactions are as lame as I had expected. What Frenchman is willing to die for Kabul? The Americans hope that by shouting a little the Russians will halt before continuing their advance. And the Germans are worried about the future of détente. As for the Swedes, I don't know what they say. No one bothers to report it. But I imagine that they talk of peace, reconciliation and the need for prompt negotiations. I remember what our friend Wang said in Peking a little over a year ago, in a moment of undiplomatic frankness:

"Do you really think that anyone in Europe will dare to fight when Russia threatens to cut off the supply of oil? And do you believe anyone can fight once that supply has been cut?"

No European leader would go to war over Afghanistan. Afghanistan is only an Asian country. Muslim, to boot. Why, at least the Russians are Europeans.

"And don't forget that the Afghans defended themselves in three wars against the British, and won them all," says Gun. "London will never forgive them for that."

Yes, the Afghans—like the Albanians in Europe, incidentally—gained a reputation for being notorious barbarians, cruel and inhuman, since they defended themselves. It was treacherous and underhanded of them to wipe out the British Army during the first Afghan War, and then never to give up even when the British had defeated them according to all the rules of war and international law.

"We were not consulted when you drew up your international law."

Then they drove away the British and upheld their independence. A treacherous, barbaric people. I am convinced that they will also defend themselves against the Russians. But when young, blond boys from Moscow have their throats cut and when the wives and children of the occupiers are treated like alien vermin, the Russians are sure to receive sympathy in Europe. At least the Russians are white, so I am certain that European humanists will soon protest Afghan wrongdoings against Russian troops.

"Why, the Afghans don't take prisoners."

Yes, I believe that racism will continue to be a strong force during the coming decades. "A time of race and religion," as Richard Wright said in 1956.

The empires have fallen and the great realms are gone. Those powers have become economically decrepit states of secondary standing. And yet, the ideas and prejudices, born of the epoch of empires, live on and still maintain their hold on thoughts and emotions.

Racism is irrational. It also runs counter to all the thoughts, ideas and values lending legitimacy to the great revolutions in the Netherlands, England and France, out of which modern Europe developed. It had its origins in the attempt by the French aristocracy to lend scientific legitimacy to its positions in anticipation of the threatened revolt by the Third Estate. But with the rise of the colonial empires in the nineteenth century, this irrationalism became useful in justifying that domination. Just as the British mercenary empire made use of imperial kitsch, decking itself in borrowed uniforms and fabricated titles, the British also fitted themselves with a racism for which they even tried to secure biological support.

I rather tend to agree with those Germans who protest at the fact that it is the Germans and German behavior in the twentieth century that have been portrayed as being the epitome of racism. What the British did in Asia is on par with what the Germans did in Eastern Europe. As for cruelty and the lust to kill, the truth is that I have never read anything in German literature corresponding to the cheerful descriptions of the pleasure of killing, left for posterity by British officers. It seems the German officers considered the killings an oppressive duty, in comparison to a British officer and gentleman like Lieutenant Vivian Dering Majendie of the Royal Artillery:

> Hark to that cheer—a wild Tally-ho! What! is this, then, fox-hunting? No—but not unlike it, only more madly and terribly exciting even than that—it is man-hunting, my friend! and that cheer proclaims that we have "found." Hark! to that quick volley which follows it, with death in its every note! See here and there a flying Sepoy, and here and there a dust-stained, still warm corpse—see, through the trees, the bright-glancing barrels of the deadly rifles as they are raised to deal the fatal blow; see the dark plumes of the Highlanders, and the grey turbans of the Sikhs, and the red coats of our men flitting to and fro—see that soldier fiercely plunging down his bayonet into some object at his feet—see, is it not red as he uplifts it for another blow? Raise yourself in your stirrups and look down and behold that living thing, above which the steel is flashing so mercilessly: is it a dog, or some venomous and loathsome reptile? No—but a human being: it is a man who lies at that soldier's feet—a man disguised with wounds and dust and mortal agony, with blood gurgling from his lips, and with half-uttered curses upon his tongue, who is dying there; and the reeking bayonet is wiped hurriedly upon the grass, and the killer passes on, to drain, in the wild excitement of his triumph, every drop of that cup of blood which this day the God of War holds out to him, and which he sees foaming and brimming over before him. (*Up Among the Pandies*, 1859)

How many died in the Great Bengal Famine of 1943? A million people? Two million? Three million? Three and a half million? And it was completely unnecessary. There was not even any military justification—the Japanese forces were far from strong enough to invade India. No, when it comes to morality, I am unable to see any difference between British and German conduct towards what they considered inferior races. There was a technical difference: gas chambers and crematoria were first developed in the twentieth century. There was also a racial-political difference: Hitler assaulted Europeans.

"If he had limited himself to gypsies and Eastern European Jews, the fuss afterwards would not have been greater than when the Turks did away with the Armenians," says Gun.

"Who remembers that nowadays? But Hitler also did away with as-similated, West European Jews. Since they were Europeans, the indigna-tion will remain in the school books for several generations."

As for the officers in charge of the executions and torture, the British were, as far as I can see from their memoirs of India, by far the less cul-tured. The Germans had not only read the Greek and Latin classics, and Goethe and Schiller, but quite a few could also recite French poetry and appreciate romantic music.

This does not mean that I consider, or considered, it a matter of indif-ference whether it was Hitler or the allies who won the last world war. Hitler was then the greater danger. It is possible that had he won, the world created by Greater Germany would be disintegrating a hundred years later, just as the empire created through British brutality disinte-grated after one hundred years. But we were not alive in either 1842 or 2042, but in 1942, and at that time Hitler was without a doubt the great-est danger for us, this regardless of what the British had been a hundred years earlier, or what Hitler's successors might have become a hundred years after his victory. Nevertheless, any meaningful difference between British imperialism in its rapacious stage, and Germany's brutal attempt at fashioning an empire in the 1940s, is hard to see.

The British empire is now a thing of the past. Here, where they once ruled, their customs are now as obsolete as their sun helmets and cer-emonial dress. That is always something of a consolation. One can be glad that it is not the local contingent of imperial society which is cele-brating the coming of the New Year in strict seclusion. It is the Russian empire which is now on the move. Just as we once wondered anxiously whether the declining British empire would be able to withstand the as-saults of Hitler's aggressive empire-building, today we have cause for concern about whether the declining American empire can resist the Russian expansionists. And yet, we know that at the height of their power, they are all equally bloodthirsty and savage.

But what is even worse, is that fallen worlds continue to govern our thought and formulate problems for us, thereby fixing the confines within which we may search for answers, and shaping the mental frame-work in which we organize the information we acquire. Inevitably this influence produces ideology.

Let us take the study of Sanskrit in Europe for example. The British had all the opportunities. They had conquered the country. Sanskrit was forced on them and they were compelled to study the language in order to run more competently their possession and collect their taxes. With-out access to Sanskrit, they could not gain control of the *brahman's* interpretation of the law. Charles Wilkins was the first Englishman to learn Sanskrit. He achieved this "as a writer in the East India Company's service." When he returned to England in 1786, it was in order to become its librarian. In 1833, he was made Sir Charles Wilkins in acknowledgement of his great contributions to linguistics. Sir William Jones was a renowned Orientalist and a highly qualified jurist when he came to Calcutta—then Fort William—to become a judge at the Supreme Court in 1783.

In January 1784, he founded the Bengal Asiatic Society, together with Charles Wilkins. He immediately began to study Sanskrit so that he could personally read the original texts of Indian law. In 1794, he published *Institutes of Hindu Law, or the Ordinance of Manu*. As a diversion from his work with the legal texts, he translated Kalidasa's *Sakuntala*, as well as various fables, and portions of the Vedas. He was only forty-eight when he died in Calcutta in April 1794. He was succeeded by Henry Thomas Colebrooke, who came to India in the service of the East India Company in 1783, and who made a career as a judge. He took upon himself the task of completing the publication of texts begun by Sir William Jones, and published first *Hindu Law on Contract and Successions* (Calcutta 1798, London 1818) and then *Two Treatises on the Hindu Law on Inheritance* (Calcutta 1810). As a guide to further study, he published his *Sanskrit Grammar* in 1805, and in the same year *Essay on the Vedas*, the by-product of his jurisprudencial studies which was to become the foundation of British Indology.

However—and this is the point I hope to make clearer with this background—the way he perceived the Vedas was shaped, determined and confined by the tax-collecting interests of the East India Company. Despite all his erudition, Thomas Colebrooke, and all the British Orientalists, were unable to see the greatness of their subject. For them, they remained interesting native literature, and Thomas Colebrooke clearly expresses this opinion:

> They are too voluminous for a complete translation of the whole; and what they contain, would hardly reward the labor of the reader; much less, that of the translator.

It was not British but German scholars who were able to make use of the manuscripts collected by the tax-collectors and jurists of the East India Company. In 1816, Franz Boop published *Über das Conjugationssystem der Sanskritsprache (On the System of Inflections in the Sanskrit Language)*, thereby establishing comparative philology. The romanticist Friedrich von Schlegel had shown the way with *Von der Weisheit und Sprache der Inder (On the Wisdom and Language of the Indians)*, 1808. His work was carried on by Christian Lassen, native of Bergen and professor in Bonn, and Theodor Benfey, who in spite of prevailing anti-Semitism became a full professor in Göttingen in 1862 and one of Germany's most renowned Orientalists. It was his translation of the *Panchatantra* in 1859, which opened up the world of mythology and showed how the tales had wandered, proving that what is most local, original and folkloric for us, is a part of mankind's great, commonly-held, cultural heritage. Albert Friedrich Weber, professor in Berlin, laid the groundwork for the study of the history of Indian literature. Rudolph von Roth, professor in Tubingen, dug out the Vedas from under a massive layer of annotations. A long list of other prominent German professors and scholars accomplished in the middle of the nineteenth century the work which British scholars had proved themselves incapable of. The most important work on Indian the literature culture and religion achieved on British soil was that done by Friedrich Max Muller—a German who had moved to England to be near the East India Company's collection of Sanskrit manuscripts. His formation as a scholar was already completed when he came to England.

England ruled India, but that rule produced self-serving ideologies which crippled the scholarly effort. The tremendous advances achieved by German linguistics and Indology during the nineteenth century was only a part of the general scientific upswing that then characterized Germany. The sciences provided the Reich an opportunity to challenge the satiated British empire. One could say that Indology profited from the German bourgeoisie's will to power.

This phenomenon is neither British nor German. It is characteristic of imperialism. The expansion of the Russian Empire provided individuals such as Bartold a chance to make important contributions to research. One could say that Czarism needed its Bartolds, so he was given his opportunity and could also become a democrat. On the other hand, consolidated Russian hegemony over Central Asia produces its own self-preserving ideology. In 1965, when we discussed Turkoman and Uzbek history with Russian representatives in Central Asia, it was discomforting to see how narrow their horizons had grown. The history they read became more falsified every year. They believed this misinformation and contributed more of their own. They had convinced themselves that Russian domination in Asia meant the liberation of the Turkomen and Uzbeks into the great Russian culture, and nothing we said could make them see otherwise. Not even our quoting Bartold, Marx and Lenin. The ideology essential to domination had a stronger hold on their minds than could be shaken by a few sound arguments and quotes from Marxist classics.

"Macht macht dumm," as the Germans say. Might makes stupidity.

We had not come here to Bodhgaya for the sake of the sanctity, nor to see the tree under which Siddhartha Gautama attained enlightenment. We came to see the Mahabodi temple, so often copied and rebuilt, dating from about the third century B.C. Above all we came to get a closer look at the parapet from the second century B.C., where a number of columns are believed to be original. This sandstone parapet depicting a hardwood fence is adorned with scenes from the Jataka. It is through these medallions that I want to peer into the second century B.C. The master masons of that time portrayed the sacred legends with an accurate and richly detailed realism.

From the temple we go to the museum. I run my fingers over the reliefs on the fragments of the original parapet displayed there. But the light is lifeless. In museums, the light in stone dies out. We experience the same phenomenon with these reliefs in Bodhgaya as we did with the reliefs from Barhut in the dusty museum in Calcutta. Even in the well-kept museum in Amaravati, which houses such fantastic reliefs from the excavated sanctuary of the same period, even there the life has gone out of the stone. The masters once chiselled so that sun and shade would bring their forms to life. Now the color is gone and the stones stand in the cold, dead light of the museums.

"It's in Sanchi that the reliefs should be seen," says Gun. "The first time we were there, twenty years ago, I thought it too heavily restored. Especially after I had seen the photographs in Fergusson's *Tree and Serpent Worship* from 1868. But I was wrong. Even if there has been a great deal of restoration and a fragment or two was misplaced, in Sanchi one gets a real picture of how these works of art functioned. Besides sun and light, you need nature and context, too. In spite of everything, Bodhgaya doesn't offer more than Sanchi. There you have reliefs predating Barhut's, and then there is the whole development contemporary with Amaravati, besides."

Yes, Sanchi is one of those monuments where one can spend days at a time and never stop discovering new images, a place to which one returns time and again with undiminished joy. The realism of Sanchi's master masons is by far more inspiring than the more recent court paintings in Ajanta, at least for us.

This period of Indian art has been rather accessible for European art historians of the nineteenth and twentieth centuries. There are reasons for this. As Marx and others noted, one perceives in history and art that which is of necessity in one's own time. To put it in Hegelian terms, one can say that man creates himself and in the process continuously shapes his own history. With a phrase borrowed from Friedrich Schlegel's description of historians, Marx calls David Urquhart in 1855 "a prophet turned backwards." It is wise to remember that it is always a "prophet turned backwards" who speaks of the past and of the art of the past. But it is also this that makes the reception of art—the process in which the past or things remote, are assimilated—into such a fascinating process to observe. It reveals so much about the receiver's relation to his own time. Thus, for example, the text of Ludwig Bachhofer's book on Indian sculpture from 300 B.C. to 200 A.D., *Early Indian Sculpture* (New York, 1929) begins and ends with the same opinionated comment:

> Slowly and hesitatingly the Indian people found itself ready to enter the sphere of high art. The gigantic nation required a long time before it was able to take the first uncertain steps, and it was only in the third century B.C. that the streams of inspiration began to flow. And even then it was not a steady self-development, for foreign-hands had to clear the path and to point the way. (p. 1)
>
> It was only in obedience to the loud call of Asoka that India could venture to abandon the narrow confines of handicraft and of primitive sculpture, and dare to enter the free regions of great art. Lacking in independence and rather embarrassed, the country required at first the encouraging example set by the highly-developed art of the Western Orient. (p. 115)

The factual content of Ludwig Bachhofer's claim—that there is interconnection between Indian and West Asian art—is indisputable. No one has denied it. But it is the ideological content, and the emotional tone of the language, which is of interest. One could say that Bachhofer is in factual agreement, but ideological opposition to what Tegner, from the great age of Swedish poetry, says in his Song, April 5, 1836:

> All culture foreign in the final end, Barbarism alone really patriotic then.

To really understand why Ludwig Bachhofer resorts to this peculiar, keyed-up language, and what he is actually expressing, we must go back to one of his great predecessors, whom Bachhofer refers to—James Fergusson.

Those interested in art and architecture, especially the art and architecture of India, cannot avoid James Fergusson. He is one of the greats. He was born in Ayr in 1806, son of a Scottish surgeon. For a time, he attended a private school, but did not continue his studies. He eventually travelled to Calcutta where he became a partner in a mercantile house and manager of an indigo mill, continuing until he had made his fortune and could live the life of a gentleman of independent means. He attained this position of wealth in a little less than ten years. He then spent the period between 1836 and 1842 travelling in India, visiting temples in various parts of the country. He visited Bhubaneswar, Mahabalipuram, Ajanta, Ellora, Elephanta and many other places. When he published his first book on prehistoric Indian art, *Illustration of the Rock-cut Temples of India* in 1845, he was the first to present a general survey.

In the years until his death in 1886, he wrote the history of world architecture, elaborated on a metaphysical theory of beauty, participated actively in the debate about Greek temples, worked with the Crystal Palace after the World's exhibition in 1851, proved the unsuitability of brickwork for the construction of fortifications, prescribing earthwork and thereby modifying British doctrine on fortification, and took an active part in the ongoing debate on defence. But it was his writing on Indian art and architecture which was to achieve lasting importance: *Tree and Serpent Worship* (1868), *History of Indian and Eastern Architecture* (1876) and the *The Cave Temples of India* (1880), co-authored by James Burgess, to name the most important.

He was among the first art historians who methodically used photography in his work.

> For the purpose of a work such as this, photography has probably done more than anything which has been written.... To discover likeness or discern dissimilarities between objects distant from one another, photographs are almost on an equal to actual personal inspection.... I have in my possession...more than 3,000 photographs of buildings in India.... (*History of Indian and Eastern Architecture*).

By presenting Indian sculpture and architecture from 1864 on in good photographs and precise xylographs based on photographs, he made Indian artistic tradition directly accessible to a broad European public. He possessed great knowledge. Towards the end of his life, he claimed that if anyone were to place before him a photo of any ancient Indian building, he could immediately determine the location—within a range of fifty miles—and the date of construction, give or take fifty years. But he is not just a knowledgeable writer, he is also readable.

Nonetheless, this knowledge is expressed in a thoroughly consistent racist system of thought. Architectural style is a racial characteristic, and the degree of miscegenation can be seen "by the purity with which the distinctive features of the style are carried out in each particular instance" (The Cave Temples of India, p. 9).

The term "Indo-Aryan style" as applied to the Hindu temple architecture of North India is, strictly speaking, incorrect, for no segment of the population carries more than ten per cent of Aryan blood in their veins.

This is proven also by the fact that we cannot "find some trace of external Aryan affinities in their style" (*History of Indian and Eastern Architecture,* p. 408).

The development of Indian architecture can be explained by the fact that the Aryans (who were not builders but poets), after coming to India mingled racially with Dravidians, who were of immigrated, Turanian stock, related to the Finns (*Tree and Serpent Worship,* p. 78). The original native population of India was primitive (*History of Indian and Eastern Architecture,* p. 12).

Indian architecture came into existence at the moment when outside impulses combined with an internal fermentation in the racial mass. Construction in stone was borrowed by India from the Greeks (*Cave Temples of India,* p. 31). The Aryans had lost their racial purity, and as they lost purity and power, their inferiors—who had attained some civilization—attempted to be their equals (*History of Indian and Eastern Architecture,* p. 16). At this point, a unique and original architecture, lacking in any trace of foreign influence, was created. After this, however, Indian art regressed and degenerated. This process of degeneration is typical for India. Bodhgaya and Barhut mark the beginning. This is the peak. Decline is already evident at Sanchi (*History of Indian and Eastern Architecture,* p. 34). Nevertheless, and here Fergusson agreed with Ruskin, Victorian architecture in Europe was a monstrosity, and even contemporary Hindu architecture was a model of elegance and moderation as long as it had not come in contact with "the bad taste of their European rulers" (*History of Indian and Eastern Architecture,* p. 488).

Into this deliberate ideological system, Fergusson has incorporated a wealth of factual information and keen observation. Yet this racist madness is not without reason: it serves to ideologize and legitimize British rule.

In the beginning of the 1880s, a debate broke out over Fergusson's ideological concepts, a debate which was to lay bare their function. In 1868, the secretary of the Asiatic Society, Rajendra Lala Mitra, was appointed to head a group of artists and photographers who were to examine the ancient monuments in Orissa, survey and photograph them, make copies of them and decipher their inscriptions.

Rajendra Lala Mitra was then forty-four years old. He was an Orientalist and a Sanskrit scholar. He had become librarian for the Asiatic Society at the age of twenty-two and had the best of reputations. Upon his return from Orissa, he gave a lecture in January 1871 at the Asiatic Society in Calcutta, where he politely but firmly criticized James Fergusson's ideological concepts. The debate began in earnest in the scholarly journals. In 1875, Rajendra Lala Mitra published the first volume of *Antiquities of Orissa,* and was given an honorary doctorate by the University of

Calcutta.

James Fergusson countered with sarcastic footnotes in *History of Indian and Eastern Architecture* in 1876, but Rajendra Lala Mitra, now Dr Mitra, continued his criticism in *Bodhgaya* (1878), volume two of *Antiquities of Orissa*, (1880), and *IndoAryans* (1881). By this time, the debate had begun to grow acrimonious, and in April 1882 the editor of the journal *Academy* commented. "Into the controversy with Mr. Fergusson about the origin of Indian Architecture, we do not care to enter. There is hardly a third man living who would care to mediate between the two."

As to the important point at issue concerning the origin of Indian architecture, Alexander Cunningham—who in 1870 secured for the second time the establishment of the Archaeological Survey of India and who had again become its head—cautiously took the side of Rajendra Lala Mitra. But on a number of secondary issues and matters of detail, James Fergusson, due to his profound knowledge, had come out on top. Now, he moved in for the kill. But when he struck his blow in 1884, it backfired. *Archaeology in India with Special Reference to the Works of Babu Rajendralala Mitra* clearly reveals the motive force behind James Fergusson's ideological effort.

He now hates Rajendra Lala Mitra. Throughout his book he calls him "the babu," the name the British used for native clerks. He denies that he has education and knowledge, and rather surprisingly, since this is one of the characteristics shared by Rajendra Lala Mitra and James Fergusson, accuses him of being self-taught.

The year before, in 1883, the Englishmen in India had carried out a violent and successful campaign against the Ilbert Bill: the proposal that the law should apply equally to all regardless of race, and that the competence of a magistrate should be determined, not by his race, but by his performance. The Englishman's privilege of being judged only by a magistrate of his own race was to be abolished, and Indians would be able to sit in judgement even on Englishmen. James Fergusson writes:

> The real interest, however, of the volume... will probably be found to reside, in these days of discussions on Ilbert Bills, in the question as to whether the natives of India are to be treated as equal to Europeans in all respects. Under present circumstances it cannot fail to interest many to dissect the writings of one of the most prominent members of the native community, that we may lay bare an his motives and modes of action, and thus ascertain how far Europeans were justified in refusing to submit to the jurisdiction of natives in criminal actions. (*Archaeology in India*, p. VI).

James Fergusson continues:

So little do we understand the nature of the people we have under-
taken to govern, that we petted and pampered the Sepoys till they
thought they were our equals, and that we were afraid of them. Being an army more numerous as ten to one, they believed themselves equal to the task, patriots felt called upon to deliver their
country from the dominion of strangers, and the result was the Mutiny. The present sentimental attempt to place "Young Bengal" on
an equality with ourselves, may not have so prompt and decisive
an answer, but it must lead to one more fatal to our moral influence,
and probably more disastrous to the good government of the country. (p. vii)

When I left India the Mutiny had not occurred to disturb the relations between Europeans and natives, and more than this, the
party usually designated as "Young Bengal" did not then exist.
These are the creation of another age and another state of things,
and are one of the most unsatisfactory results of our attempts to
force our civilization on a people not yet prepared to receive it. One
of the first effects of education set of men beyond anything known
in their own class, and of treating them as equals before they have
acquired any title, morally and intellectually, to be considered as
such, is to inspire them with the most inordinate conceit in themselves. They soon learn to consider themselves not as equal to their
former masters, but as superior, and they turn round and glory in
their own fancied superiority. (p. 3)

No one who has resided long in Bengal, or has been in familiar
intercourse with the educated classes of the natives of that country,
(could have not) been struck with the marvellous facility with
which they acquire our language, and at least a superficial familiar-
ity with the principal features of our arts and sciences. The truth of
the matter is, their powers of memory are prodigious. . . . It is such,
however, as in these days of competitive examinations would enable a native of India to distance an Anglo-Saxon easily in any
struggle for pre-eminence. If a sufficient number of Bengalis could
afford to come to England and reside here for the time required pre-
pare for their examination, the whole of the Civil Service of Bengal
would fall into their hands. In the rarest possible instances could
any Englishman compete with them, and if the selection were fairly
made, as tested by the Civil Service examination, it would be impossible to refuse them any or every appointment. (p. 5)

To my knowledge, no scholar in any scholarly controversy has ever
elucidated more plainly than James Fergusson the underpinnings of his
ideological position. We have thus placed Ludwig Bachhofer's remark-

able words of 1929—a time of growing nationalistic ferment in India—in their correct historical context.

For Rajendra Lala Mitra, and the entire group of Indian intellectuals he represented, this ideological settling of accounts was essential. As Chairman of the Reception Committee, he delivered the opening address at the second session of the Indian National Congress in Calcutta, on December 27, 1886. There he stated:

> We live, not under a national government, but under a foreign bureaucracy; our foreign rulers are foreigners by birth, religion, language, habits, by everything that divides humanity into different sections. They cannot ascertain our wants, our feelings, our aspirations.

Rajendra Lala Mitra, who became Companion of the Indian Empire upon the establishment of that order in 1878, who was elected President of the Asiatic Society in 1883, the first Indian to hold that position, who was granted the title "'raja" in 1888, was no revolutionary. He stood aloof from the struggle of the poor peasants. All the same, James Fergusson was perfectly correct when he warned of the consequences of Rajendra Lala Mitra's and Young Bengal's attack on racist ideology in the realm of the history of architecture and art. It was to have a disastrous effect on British authority.

In the field of archaeology, the ideological conflict grew into a struggle for posts and opportunities for promotion. In 1911, the Indians succeeded in mustering opinion among the Orientalists at the conference in Athens. The British were criticized and censured for monopolizing all the posts in the Archaeological Survey. They were compelled to give in to the demands and the government ruled that even Indians, if qualified, might be appointed to positions of responsibility in the field of Indian archaeology. Nine years later, in 1921, the development James Fergusson warned against had materialized so rapidly that the British authorities decided that 40% of all official posts, even those of the Archaeological Survey, would be reserved for the British. Thirty-five years after Rajendra Lala Mitra attacked James Fergusson, and thirty years after his death, his successors began to occupy the crucial positions of power.

However, the ideological struggle continued to be decisive for the Indian nationalist movement. On the eve of "Independence Day," annually celebrated on January 26 by the Indian National Congress, the Working Committee of the Congress issued a pledge in December 1939, which in part reads:

> The British Government in India has not only deprived the Indian

people of their freedom but has based itself on the exploitation of the masses and has ruined India economically, politically, culturally and spiritually.

During the winter of 1940, this pledge was debated in Calcutta. The rather right-wing, liberal Congressman, Ramananda Chatterjee protested in his journal *Modern Review* in Calcutta. He did not agree that the British had ruined India, except in the case of traditional, native handicrafts. But, of course, he still demanded Indian independence. In the debate that followed, a letter from Dr T. G. P. Spear of Delhi was published which stated:

> These ideas of superiority found an excuse for, though they did not originate, the economic exploitation. . . . The ruin of the Indian piecegoods trade was the work of the Company, when it became profitable to import raw cotton for the new machine mills in the late eighteenth century. . . . The result of all this can be seen in the new attitude towards India, as not only an acquired, but also a conquered country: as not only having an inferior civilization, but as having no civilization at all! This, in its turn, was helped by the wars of conquest, from 1838 onwards, which went on almost continuously for fifteen years; and thus the "annexation" mentality succeeded the "administration" mentality, and the "improving" mentality (as though India was a bit of virgin, cultural soil) succeeded the "conserving" mentality. . . . The Mutiny seems to me to have been the result, rather than the cause, of all this. What it added was *Fear*, which now entered into the English superiority complex itself. (*Modern Review*, February 1940)

Dr. Spear's comments are, of course, an accurate description of the evolution of the ruling ideology. But just as Rajendra Lala Mitra and the other Indian intellectuals of the Bengal Renaissance and "Young Bengal" were incapable of supporting the rebellious peasants, so too had the respectable intellectuals and middle class, those represented by Ramananda Chatterjee, grown incapable of seeing how crucial a question the causes of English racism and the various ideas that gave legitimacy to British rule had become, on the eve of Indian independence. They lost the ability to see this, as their class prepared itself to take over the leadership of the nation.

Suraj was right: these ideological conflicts were no sham battles.

1857

Among the pictures which made a deep impression on me as a child was the illustration in *20,000 Leagues Under the Sea* of Captain Nemo, dark and uncommunicative, standing, his arms across his chest, on the deck of the Nautilus, looking at the ship of evil he is about to sink:

> I am the oppressed and there is the oppressor. Because of him, I have seen everything I loved, cared for, respected—country, wife, children, father, mother, everything—destroyed! There is everything I hate!

What eleven-year old is not an avenger?

Another picture I found in a tattered and torn volume among the junk in the attic at Kvicksta, where I used to spend my childhood summers. It was in August Blanche's *Illustrerad Tidning (The Illustrated Weekly)* from 1857. It was a picture of an English home in India.

The picture is fashioned like a stage setting. A heavy drapery hangs on the right. A young mother is seated on a canape. Besides her, she has a son dressed in a child's frock. He is playing with a puzzle and is holding an ABC book. To her breast she holds a nursing infant. The garden can be seen through an open window behind the canape. In the foreground, a ball is seen lying on the floor. From the left enter two Sepoys. They are barefoot. They have long hair and moustaches. The first one reaches a dark hand toward the boy on the canape. In his other hand he carries a sword. From it drips blood onto the carpet. Behind him stands the other Sepoy. He holds up a burning torch in his right hand. He stares out at the reader with malevolent eyes. The woman looks young, innocent, surprised and immaculate. Above her head hangs a portrait of a uniformed man. The man of the house is away. Years later, I found that picture again. It was published on November 7, 1857. Pictures such as this one shaped opinion about the Indian rebellion of 1857 among the educated and reading middle class.

Yet, in spite of everything, it did not shape my view, for I had read Jules Verne. He gave me my basic view of the Indian war of independence of 1857, the way Mark Twain gave me my basic view of the French "terror" of 1793. Both of them were democrats, republican and anti-imperialist. And just who was this Captain Nemo, that dark revenger of the Atlantic? The answer is to be found in the *Mysterious Island*, chapter 58.

> Captain Nemo was an Indian, the Prince Dakkar, son of a rajah of the then independent Bundelkund and nephew of the hero of India, Tipu Sultan. His father sent him, when ten years of age, to Europe so that he would receive an education in all respects complete, and in the secret hope that he would one day be able to fight with weapons as powerful as those wielded by the oppressors of his country.
>
> From the age of ten to thirty, Prince Dakkar, endowed with the greatest gifts of courage and intellect, accumulated knowledge of every kind and pursued his studies in the sciences and arts.
>
> Prince Dakkar travelled all over Europe. His high birth and great fortune made him sought after but he never felt drawn to the attractions of the world. Young and beautiful he remained serious and sombre with a burning thirst for knowledge and an implacable resentment in his heart.
>
> Prince Dakkar hated. He hated the only country on whose soil he never wanted to tread, the only nation whose advances he rejected: he hated England and this hatred was only increased by his admiration for it for more than one reason.
>
> It was as if this Indian had gathered within himself all the wild hatred of the vanquished for the victor. A son of one of those sovereigns that England had only nominally brought to servitude, this prince from the family of Tipu Sultan had been brought up with the ideas of just claims and revenge. Above all, he was imbued with a fierce love for his poetical country imprisoned in British chains. He refused to tread this soil to him forever damned, to which India owed its servitude.

Prince Dakkar became an artist sensitive to the marvels of art; a *savant* to whom nothing in science was foreign; a statesman formed by the courts of Europe. To the eyes of those who observed him superficially he might have passed for one of those cosmopolitans curious of knowledge but disdaining action, one of those opulent travellers, haughty and detached, who incessantly travel throughout the world and belong to no country.

But he was nothing of the sort. This artist, this *savant* remained an Indian in his heart, an Indian in his thirst for vengeance. He was Indian in his hope of demanding someday his country's rights: to chase away the foreigner, to be restored its independence.

Thus Prince Dakkar returned to Bundelkund in 1849. He was married to a noble Indian woman whose heart bled like his for the misfortunes of the motherland. He had two children he loved. But domestic happiness could never make him forget the slavery of India. He waited for an opportunity. It came.

The English yoke had begun to weigh too heavily on the people of India. Prince Dakkar gave voice to the discontent. He instilled in their hearts all the hatred he felt for the foreigners. He travelled not only in the still independent states of the Indian peninsula but also in those regions that were directly subjected to British administration. He recalled the heroic days of Tipu Sultan who died at Seringapatnam in the defence of the motherland.

In 1857 the great revolt of the Sepoys broke out. Prince Dakkar was the very soul of it. He organized the tremendous uprising. He put his talents and his immense fortune in the service of this cause. He fought in the first line. He risked his life along with the simplest of those heroes who had risen to liberate their country. He was wounded ten times in twenty battles but had not yet found death when the last of the revolutionary soldiers fell to English bullets.

Never had the British power in India been in such danger. If, as they had hoped, the Sepoys had been able to get some outside aid this would have perhaps put an end to the influence and domination of the United Kingdom in Asia.

At that time Prince Dakkar was well-known. The hero did not hide himself but fought openly. There was a price on his head. And though there was not a single traitor who would deliver it, his father, mother, wife and children paid for him with their lives before he knew the danger they ran because of him. . . .

Right had once again fallen to might. But civilization never recedes and it seems it surrenders all right to necessity. The Sepoys were vanquished and the land of the old rajas fell again under the domination of England.

JUSTICE.

Prince Dakkar went back to the mountains of Bundelkund. Now alone in the world, he felt a profound disgust against humanity, hatred and horror for the civilized world. He gathered the remnants of his fortune, assembled a score of his most faithful companions and one day they disappeared.

Where then did Prince Dakkar seek that independence that the inhabited world had refused him? Under the waves, in the depth of the ocean, where none could follow.

This account of the great rebellion which British historians to this day persist in calling a "Mutiny" is more accurate than much of what is claimed to be social science. It is more truthful because Jules Verne took a stand and thus was able to show the greatness and patriotism of the Indian side in this war. But there was no Prince Dakkar who organized the rebellion. Had such strong leadership truly existed between 1857 and 1859, the British would have been expelled from Hindustan. Still, Captain Nemo-Prince Dakkar was no pure figment of the imagination. Behind Jules Verne's character can be seen the outlines of three historical figures: Dhundu Pant, Peshwa Baji Rao II's adopted son, best known as Nana Sahib; his friend and adviser, the European-educated intellectual, Azimullah Khan; and finally, Tantia Topi, the greatest commander on the Indian side during the war of independence.

In 1674, Shivaji had proclaimed himself absolute ruler of Maharashtra in Raigarh. After thirty years of war with the Sultan of Bijapur, the Mughal emperor, the Portuguese in Goa and the pirate chiefs along the coast, an independent Hindu state was established. During the long years of war, he had established a new type of government administration, borrowing and developing traditions from both the Hindu courts and Muslim rule. The Marathas conducted a people's war. Shivaji headed a national movement and in some respects can be considered India's Cromwell or Napoleon.

Following his death, the Maratha state grew increasingly feudal. Various vassals sought independent power. The Marathas became a plundering, military aristocracy which pillaged Western and Central India at the time of the decline of the Mughal empire. For a time, it appeared as though they might succeed the Mughals and establish an Indian nation, but they were unable to rise above their own feudal pettiness. Balaji Baji Rao could not fill the shoes of Shivaji, and never rose to become India's ruler in the 1740s, choosing instead to remain a plundering petty king. This was understandable, but hardly inevitable.

From out of the council of eight ministers established by Shivaji, the peshwa, or prime minister, began to occupy a special position. After 1713, the minister became ruler and the position inheritable. The eighth peshwa, Baji Rao II, was cowardly, slow-witted, perfidious and corrupt. He lost for the Marathas their independence, through incompetence, greed and shortsightedness. In 1818 he began receiving a British pension of 800,000 rupees a year and was allowed to live in Bithur near Cawnpore. Since he was childless, he adopted sons in accordance with Hindu custom. In 1839, Baji Rao left in a written will his title and property to his eldest son, Nana Sahib. However, when Baji Rao died in 1851, the British Governor-General Dalhousie cheated Nana Sahib out of his inheritance. Nana Sahib did not even have enough money to cremate his father with the traditional rites. He was forced to borrow in order to pay for the gifts to be given to *brahmans* at the ruler's funeral. Dalhousie also took away both title and privileges from Nana Sahib. And this was no chance occurrence, but consistent British policy in India.

Dalhousie ruled that adoptions were not recognized and appointed the East India Company sole heir to Indian domains, realms and principalities. Thus, Dalhousie saw to it that the East India Company became the heir to Satara, Jaipur and Sambalpur in 1849, and to Jhansi and Nagpur in 1853. In consultation with London, he deposed the king of Oudh, a state of ten million inhabitants, and added that realm to the possessions of the East India Company in 1856. Nana Sahib's inheritance was a small matter in this context. But Dalhousie was of firm principle and took even that. Nana Sahib was only an adopted son and, what is more, the annuity the British promised Baji Rao II when they added his realm to the East India Company's possessions was, he claimed, only a personal pension. Morland, the British Commissioner in Bithur, took from Nana Sahib the seal of his father. When Nana Sahib had a seal of his own made with the title *peshwa bahadur*, Mr. Morland had that confiscated too. Nana Sahib's hatred was deep, even though he was polite to the British officers who called on him.

It is not clear whether Nana Sahib actually took part in the organization of the rebellion. It is possible that he was one of the instigators. Some sources hold this to be the case. As the war progressed, he became one of the most dangerous adversaries of the British. He was no military genius and was unable to lead the war, but when installed as Peshwa in 1858 he became the legitimate ruler of the Marathas and Hindus, just as the eighty-two year old Bahadur Shah II in Delhi was the legitimate Mughal emperor. It was difficult for the high caste Indians of that time to understand how the British could call troops serving the legitimate rulers mutineers and rebels, when, in fact, it was the foreign usurers and hucksters of the East India Company who were attempting to usurp the authority of the legitimate rulers. It was a question of restoring domestic order and resisting the foreign usurpers and troublemakers.

In April 1859, after the Indian troops had been defeated and the British had captured their strongholds, Nana Sahib crossed the border into Nepal. From there, he addressed the British on the subject of legitimacy:

> What right have you to occupy India and declare me an outlaw? Who gave you the right to rule over India? What! You, firangis, are the Kings, and we, thieves, in this our own country?

Major Richardson wrote to Nana Sahib, proposing that he capitulate and put himself at the mercy of Queen Victoria:

> The Nawab of Farrukhabad, the Nawab of Banda and other great men and rajas in Oudh have laid down their arms and surrendered to the government. The same terms will be offered you and all those who wish to surrender.

But Nana Sahib answered:

> Why should I join you, knowing all the *dagabazi* (miserable treachery) perpetrated by you in Hindoostan? Life must be given up some day. Why then should I die dishonored? There will be war between me and you as long as I have life, whether I be killed or imprisoned or hanged. And whatever I do will be done with the sword only.

After that we lose trace of him. Nana Sahib and his followers slipped into the jungle and became the stuff of legend. At the turn of the century, British intelligence was still searching for him in various countries. British agents turned the words of Jules Verne inside out, thinking that he knew something of his whereabouts. But the fate of Nana Sahib was to remain a mystery.

Azimullah Khan probably really did have a hand in organizing the rebellion. Shortly before its outbreak, he had accompanied Nana Sahib on a journey to North India to the garrison towns. While Nana Sahib was under tight political surveillance, Azimullah Khan was able to make contacts. But whatever his role in the preparations, he was one of the Indians most hated by the British officers. He was the archetype of the uppity nigger, the native who did not know his place. He spoke two European languages, French and English. Later, the British would explain this by saying that he had been a *khidmutgar,* a waiter in an English home, and that it was there he had learned the language. He had then gone to school, become a teacher and finally, *vakil,* envoy, of Nana Sahib. Another account has him an orphan. He and his mother were mercifully saved as they were about to starve to death in the great famine of 1837-1838. The story goes that his mother would not allow him to be baptized a Christian since she was a devout Muslim. He was allowed to attend Cawnpore Free School, where he received a scholarship of three rupees a month. His mother worked as an *ayah*, a maid. After ten years, Azimullah became a teacher at the same school, and two years later he was transferred to Brigadier Scott as *munshi*, a secretary. He was later hounded from that job, accused of corruption.

These stories about him were recorded after the war and his death. His very name was then anathema to the British. He probably came from a very humble background and managed to obtain an education far superior to that of the British officers for whom he worked as secretary. As Nana Sahib's envoy, he travelled to Great Britain to obtain redress for Nana Sahib. This, however, proved impossible. No arguments could loosen the purse-strings of the British politicians. He made many friends in England. He even kept the company of English women. Forty years later, in 1897, Field Marshal Lord Roberts of Kandahar would still remember with distaste the letters he, as a young soldier, had found in Nana Sahib's palace, and about which he wrote to his sister on December 31, 1857:

> We found heaps of letters directed to that fiend "Azimula Khan" by ladies in England, some from Lady—, ending "Your affect. Mother." Others from a young girl at Brighton named—, written in the most lovable manner. Such rubbish I never read, partly in French, which this scoundrel seems to have understood; how English ladies can be so infatuated! Miss—was going to marry Azimula, and I have no doubt, would like to still, although he was the chief instigator in the Cawnpore massacres.

William Howard Russel, *Times* correspondent in India in 1858-1859, described his meeting with Azimullah Khan during the Crimean War. Instead of returning directly to India after having failed to obtain redress for Nana Sahib, he had gone to Constantinople, where Russel met him:

> I went down for a few days to Constantinople, and, whilst stopping at Missirie's Hotel, saw, on several occasions, a handsome slim young man, of dark-olive complexion, dressed in an Oriental costume which was new to me, and covered with rings and finery. He spoke French and English, dined at the table d'hôte, and, as far as I could make out, was an Indian prince, who was on his way back from the prosecution of an unsuccessful claim against the East India Company in London.

Several weeks later, Russel met him again. This time it was in the Crimea, where Azimullah Khan had gone to observe the fighting. He took an interest in the artillery, making rather malicious remarks on the incompetence of the British forces. In a polite but friendly letter signed Azimulla Khan, he thanked Russel for allowing him to put up for the night with him. Russel noted that the visitor did not get a good impression of the morale and competence of the British army.

During the journey Azimullah Khan made with Nana Sahib to the various garrison towns, after returning to India, he reportedly behaved with insolence and arrogance towards the British officers, saying that he and Nana Sahib were making a pilgrimage.

"A Hindoo and Mussulman joined in a holy excursion!" remarks Russel.

He was Nana Sahib's confidant and adviser during the war, and following the defeat he accompanied the routed troops into Nepal. There, in the malarial jungle, he died of fever in October, 1859, at the age of thirty.

The third person contributing to the character of Captain Nemo-Prince Dakkar is Ramachandra Panduranga, known as Tantia Topi. He was a Mahratta-*brahman*. His father belonged to Bija Rao's family, and he was himself Nana Sahib's loyal companion. He was born to serve the peshwa and, for him, Nana Sahib was obviously the legitimate peshwa. It was he who, in June 1858, as the war entered its second year, proclaimed Nana Sahib the rightful peshwa in Gwalior. Like other noblemen of his age who were members of princely families, he had learned to fence and shoot when a boy, but lacked military training. But upon taking command of the troops from Gwalior on November 9, 1857, he proved to be an unusually gifted military commander, possessed of a sure feel for the military utilization of terrain.

As the military superiority of the British became increasingly evident, and the Indian forces suffered repeated defeats, Tantia Topi attempted in the fall of 1858 to move down into the southern Mahratta territories in order to rally the people there to participate in a holy, national war. However, the British controlled the roads and tracks, and he could not get past them. For half a year British troops chased Tantia Topi through the mountains and jungles southwest of Gwalior. He was betrayed in April 1859, by Man Singh, who was willing to sell his friend and comrade-in-arms for the promise of once again becoming Scindia's vassal in Gwalior and a minor feudatory.

On April 15, Tantia Topi was brought before a court martial in Sipri, and accused of insurrection. However, he did not acknowledge British jurisdiction. He was not a British subject. When he was to be hanged on April 18, he demanded the right to go to the gallows a free man, with neither hands tied behind his back nor eyes blindfolded. He also refused to allow the hangman to place the rope around his neck. He positioned the noose himself and took his own life.

Since the hair and fingers of a hanged man were thought to bring good luck, at nightfall the superstitious European soldiers sneaked to the gallows to get talismans.

The uprising began as a military revolt. Attempts have been made, and are still being made, to portray it as a mutiny, or as a last desperate struggle on the part of the old, feudal forces. Such aspects to this great uprising did, in fact, exist. However, what is decisive is that from the beginning, the revolt took on the character of a national, popular uprising. Everything supports the theory that the military revolt was planned. However, if this is true, it was triggered prematurely by the arrogant and churlish provocation of the British officers. One might say that the British were saved by their own incompetence. Had the revolt taken place a few weeks later, simultaneously carried out in the various garrisons, the British would have been lost. This was also the contemporary opinion. When Count Carl Magnus Bjornstjerna, colonel in the regiment of the Crown Prince of Sweden and member of the Academy of Military Science, spoke on "The British in India" at the Stockholm's Officers' Club in 1858, he said:

> Messengers moved swiftly from village to village, showing a piece of bread. No one knows who first set things in motion or why; strangely enough, not much attention was paid in Calcutta: it was thought to be some sort of *brahman* mysticism; and that it was, but of a sort totally different than that imagined. It was probably a signal to prepare for the holy war. It was planned to break out one day in the month of August; they knew, that by then, the Queen would have left England. All the garrisons were to rise simultaneously and massacre the unsuspecting whites: young and old, men and women, without distinction. Could the impatience of the troops have been curbed, thus allowing the uprising to take place on the same day all over the country, India would probably have been lost to England. Luckily, their fervour was all too great; untimely moves woke the government from its slumber, at least permitting Calcutta to be saved...However, in Meerut, things took another, deplorable turn. Meerut, situated northwest of Delhi, is northern India's most important military station. Here were posted an English cavalry regiment, 6 dragoon-guard regiments, the 60th Royal Sharpshooter Regiment, 2 batteries of English mounted artillery, 3 native cavalry units and 11 Sepoy regiments. General Hewitt was in command. It was at this considerable force, at the approaches to Delhi, that the rebels directed their blow. A rumor spread through the camp that

ground cow-bone was mixed in the flour. This was believed and caused great alarm. In addition, there was the matter of the greased cartridges. The ferment grew disquieting. Although there were no new cartridges here, once suspicion had been aroused, it knew no bounds. Even the old cartridges, it was claimed, were produced in England and greased with some waste which would cause defilement. An old prophecy predicted the fall of the British rule after an existence of 100 years. It was called to mind that a bare century had now passed since Plassey. This, too, had its effect. It raised morale. The general decided to nip the insurrection in the bud. The 3rd Bengal Cavalry was ordered out to target practice. 85 men refused to accept their cartridges. The men were jailed; a court martial struck them from the rolls and sentenced them to 6 years' imprisonment at hard labour on the roads. The whole division was drawn up, the Europeans with live ammunition in their guns and rifles. The accused were brought forward, their sentences pronounced; in vain, the criminals beseeched their comrades for help; no hand was lifted. They were stripped of their uniforms, placed in irons and marched off to the nearby stockade. The general believed that he had won, but he was mistaken. On the contrary. For the following day, May 10, a Sunday, while the English troops attended evening services, they were to be attacked and wiped out, and then all the whites were to be murdered. The plan was well-thought-out, and so well kept, that if only they had been able to curb their impatience a few minutes longer, it is probable that not a single Christian would have been spared. As luck would have it, the trumpet signal to mount up was sounded in the native cavalry quarters before the Englishmen had started out for Church. At this unexpected signal, the Sowars were observed mounting up, hurrying to the foot-soldiers, and in loud voices urging them to take up arms. Sepoys rushed out of their billets and the arsenals were broken into. Rifles were loaded—this time without hesitation—with the hated cartridges. Upon learning this, the officers immediately rushed to the troops. With admirable courage, they braved a certain death, in order to bring the men back to their duty. In vain. Most of them were murdered, the rest fled. The rebels then turned partly against the advancing English troops, partly against the stockade which was broken open. Not only the martyrs of the preceding day were set free, but even several hundred criminals. With these in the lead, the frenzied mob rushed to the officers' quarters which soon were in flames. Every white encountered was cut down. As fate would have it, a nearby forest provided an avenue of escape. Then approaching dragoons were heard; at full speed, they fell upon the bloodthirsty, rebel mob; the sharpshooters, too, began to fire; the Sepoys, discouraged, then moved off down the Delhi road.... This city, situated on the right bank of the Jumna, has a population of over 200,000, is resplendent with magnificent buildings, and, despite its decay, is one of India's richest cities, as well as being its gayest. It is India's Paris. The residency of the Great Mughal makes it the capital of the country in the eyes of all true-believers; hence, its occupation carries with it a tremendous moral significance.... Delhi, although not fortified according to modern standards, is encompassed by a strong bastioned wall of ashlar, equipped with trench and heavy artillery. The country's largest arsenal is to be found in the city. Its rabble is the most fanatical in all of India. Over 1,000 Europeans, mainly officers' wives and children, lived there. Displaying inexcusable shortsightedness, the government had left this important center totally bereft of European troops. The garrison was comprised of three regiments of Sepoys and a battalion of artillery. It was commanded by Brigadier General Graves. The outrage in Meerut and the approach of the Sepoys became known in the city early on the 12th. The general drew up the troops, exhorting them to loyalty. They answered with shouts of "hurrah" and asked to be sent out against the rebels. These were discovered not far from the Kashmir gate. They advance, charging cavalry in the lead, and in the very first line, the condemned soldiers, leg-irons still about their ankles. Graves formed a square formation, but his forces fired into the air. The ranks were opened and the comrades were greeted with great shouts of joy. Then the cavalrymen charged up to the unfortunate English officers, shot them at the frontline, without a man lifting a finger to save them. The combined forces then marched into the city where the rabble joined them and looted the bank, as well as all the more affluent shops and homes.... The movement spread like lightning across the country. The nobility called their retainers to arms; Sepoys rose up everywhere. European troops were few or weak, and soon the scenes of bloodshed witnessed at Delhi were repeated all along the Ganges valley. A fit of fury seems to have taken hold of the soldiers. The officers who had led them in battle and who they greatly respected, were mercilessly killed; the battle cry was "death to all whites"! To name the locations where the flag of insurrection was raised, would be to list the military stations of northern India.

When word of the rebellion reached the villages, the peasants began to loot the moneylenders, burn their accountbooks and chase them away. The same thing befell the British tax-collectors. This popular revolt against authority was not planned. The Sepoys, however, were no longer only recruited from the better families. Many now came from lower peasant stock. The peasant uprisings often took the form of the poor peasants uniting with the old, traditional lords, against the new classes which had grown up with British support.

Towards the British troops, the peasants displayed either open hostility or quiet animosity, depending on the balance of forces. Where the British were weak, they were killed or chased away, and only where they were strong, were they grudgingly obeyed.

But when the British administration collapsed in this way in the summer of 1857, in the countryside

> violence and anarchy arose with a suddenness that was quite astounding...great movement from within was beginning to make itself felt upon the surface of rural society, and for a while all traces of British rule were rapidly disappearing from the face of the land....A few days sufficed to sweep away law and order, and to produce a revolution of property, astonishing even to those who were best acquainted with the character and temper of the people. I could not," wrote Mr. Tucker on the 13th, "have believed that the moment the hand of the government was removed there would have been so sudden a rising of landholders to plunder each other and people on the roads. All the large landholders and auction-purchasers are paralysed and dispossessed, their agents being frequently murdered and their property destroyed." To arrest this new danger, which threatened to become a gigantic one, overwhelming, irrepressible, our people had now to put forth all their strength. (John William Kaye, *A History of the Sepoy War in India*, 1857-1859, vol. II, pp. 234-235)

The fact that the Indian masses, tenant farmers and poor peasants began to rise up in this fashion, and that the uprisings in certain villages began to take on the character of a national peasant war, frightened the feudal classes and drove them into the arms of the British.

In 1858, C. Raikes described this process graphically in his *Notes on the Revolt in the North-Western Provinces of India:*

> The *Zamindar* soon found that it was better to pay land-tax and receive protection, than day and night to fight for his possession with every scoundrel in the countryside. And thus, the bulk of the tax-paying agricultural proprietors in Doab, after the fall of Delhi, welcomed their English masters back with unfeigned satisfaction.
> Still more did the moneyed classes, such of them at least as sur-

vived the period of anarchy, rejoice to see the English rule restored. On the retirement of the Magistrate, a furious struggle had commenced at once between the purchasers of land in possession, and the former owners. Native bankers and merchants who had long been investing their savings in land (purchased generally under decrees of court), were either murdered or scared away. The life of a capitalist in possession of land, whether as purchaser or mortgagee, was soon not worth a week's purchase. Old feuds broke out afresh, homicides, affrays, murders by day, by night, gang robberies and arson. Things grew worse and worse, until, as I have said before, every man but the professional robber or dacoit longed for the return of the Magistrate, notwithstanding the fact that he was also the collector of the Government revenue. The robbers joined the straggling Sepoy bands, and to this day are in arms against us, whilst the rest of the people hastened to pay up all arrears of revenue into our treasuries.

Both the British Indian Association and the Muhammedan Association in Calcutta assembled to adopt resolutions against the Sepoys, expressing the hope that they would meet "no sympathy, countenance or support from the bulk of the civil population." The mighty Indian princes such as Scindia, Holkar, Gaekwar, the Nizam of Hyderabad and the ruling houses of Rajasthan, Mysore and Travancore supported the British against the rebels.

When Queen Victoria's proclamation was announced, with the utmost solemn ceremony throughout British-held India, on November 1, 1858, the majority of the feudal rulers openly went over to the British. For, as Colonel Mallesson explains in his *History of the Indian Mutiny:* "The princes and landowners especially regarded it as a charter which would render their possessions secure and their rights...absolutely inviolate."

The British spoke and wrote a great deal about the atrocities committed by the Sepoys. These accounts have since been repeated and incorporated into the history books. Certainly, the Sepoys were brutal. A revolutionary uprising, as Mao Zedong pointed out, is no tea party. They were avenging a century of degradation and exploitation. British ruthlessness during the war resulted in the Sepoys also adopting the practice of liquidating prisoners. Nonetheless, the much publicized victims of Sepoy terror were but a slight fraction of the hecatombs of defenceless Indians slaughtered by the British.

British vengeance was motivated by a raging class-hatred, much similar to that of the French aristocracy following the jacquerie, or of the German nobility after the peasant wars. The British officers relished the causing of pain; they wallowed in sadism. Wherever the British troops advanced, a consistent policy of mass murder was perpetrated against the civilian population. When the British officers and soldiers could not get their hands on other natives, they set upon their own domestics and campfollowers. The British civilians were no better than the officers. I will limit myself to one instance of British terror—and not a very bloody one, at that:

> Volunteer hanging parties went out into the districts, and amateur executioners were not wanting to the occasion. One gentleman boasted of the numbers he had finished off quite "in an artistic manner," with mango-trees for gibbets and elephants for drops, the victims of this wild justice being strung up, as though for pastime, in "the form of a figure of eight."

When it comes to the great uprising in India in 1857, official historiography has functioned in the usual manner. The atrocities committed by the oppressed during the uprising have been magnified, while the terror of the oppressor has been extenuated. British terror in India was like that of the Germans in Poland. In the end, it grew to such proportions that it threatened the economic foundation of the empire and Lord Canning, the Governor-General, made efforts to curb the acts of reprisal. In the proceedings of the Governor-General-in-Council, of December 24, 1857, appeared the following Minute:

> The indiscriminate hanging, not only of persons of all shades of guilt, but of those whose guilt was at the least very doubtful, and the general burning and plunder of villages, whereby the innocent as well as the guilty, without regard to age or sex, were indiscriminately punished, and in some cases, sacrificed, had deeply exasperated large communities not otherwise hostile to the government; that the cessation of agriculture and consequent famine were impending....

This British hatred threatened their domination, and Lord Canning, in the face of the opposition of the amateur hangmen, was forced to check the terror. This terror was not, however, just a manifestation of the fury of certain colonial officials, officers and merchants. It was an expression of the profound fear—to use the words of Percival Spear in *Modern Review*, 1940—which marked the British after 1857. The empire could fall. Domestic popular opinion, as represented by such organs of the establishment as *The Times* and *Punch*, was no less vengeful. Victorian England, which now declared itself the British Empire, was a Christian land and, verily, "the righteous shall rejoice when he seeth the vengeance; he shall wash his feet in the blood of the wicked."

It was only when the raging fury became a threat to their income that the British were able to get a hold of themselves. The Mughal empire had then ceased to exist, the East India Company was abolished and British India was ruled by a viceroy to whom the independent Indian princes stood in a vassal relationship, having shown allegiance to the British Crown.

In Europe and America, opinion was divided. Count Bjornstjerna had striven for an alliance between England and Sweden–Norway during the Crimean War. He viewed the uprising as "the bloody drama...which will probably decide the future, not just of the fabulous Orient, but also of our mighty ally, England."

Consequently, England's struggle was also "the struggle of civilization against barbarism and so must end with a further consolidation of English rule in the Orient....India shall remain for Brittania a source of wealth, power and glory for many more centuries."

Russian Czarism, which had recently suffered defeat in the war with England and France, naturally felt malicious pleasure at the difficulties of its rival. There were also reports—never confirmed or proven—that Russian agents (and also French, corresponding with Azimullah Khan) were in contact with the insurgents. However, the rebellion's increasingly popular orientation brought the rulers together. Against Asia's peasants, Russia's autocrat and England's parliament had common interests to defend, as noted in *Russky Vestnik*.

> We do not sympathize with England's foreign policy; we have points of conflicts with her. But we shall always have the magnanimity and conscientiousness to recognise the unity of our tasks. Both England and Russia are called upon to spread the light of the European way of life in the moral darkness of stagnating Asia. Here we are allies; here there is solidarity between us.

In France, Napoleon III was not averse to using England's difficulties to further his own political aims, but as *L'Illustration's* correspondent noted, "as we are now the brothers of the English, it behooves us to know both the good and the evil which befalls them. At this moment, our allies are in great danger..."

In his *Chronique de la Quinzaine* in the *Revue des Deux Mondes* of July 31, 1857, Charles de Mazade made an analysis of the Indian rebellion. He wrote for the solid bourgeoisie of the second empire:

> Among the problems that are today being debated, there is one

which stands out above all others: it is the unceasing spread of western civilization. This civilization has its weaknesses and terrible crises, but at the same time it advances, it gains ground continually by way of moral proselytism, or, where the moral influence is wanting, by force of arms. It would seem at present, for all peoples who have taken upon themselves the extension of their rule beyond the limits of their national boundaries, that there exists an essay whose parts are known and which one could write daily as dictated by contemporary events. It would be entitled "How to Conquer Empires and How to Hold Them. How the Maintenance of a Conquest can be Shaken or Threatened, even if only Momentarily." Today, the rebellion in India would be the disquieting episode in this essay, while the latest conquest of the Kabyles* its happiest element: not that this is a complete analogy or that the conditions are the same, but in both cases we have a conquest, a permanent labor of assimilation, that a thousand things can temporarily weaken or compromise. In but a few days, the insurrection in India has become England's major preoccupation: it has overshadowed all else. . . . The whole question is whether the uprising signalled by the Sepoys will remain solely a military defection, or if it will have greater ramifications and more extensive roots among the people as a whole.

It was only to be expected that *Le Pays Journal de l'Empire* should claim that "the end of the British Empire in India would signify the triumph of barbarism over civilization."

The brutality and ruthless reprisals of the English shocked all of Liberal Europe. As the Saint-Simonist, Louis-Anne-Xavier Raymond, indignantly wrote in *Journal des Debats* of October 24, 1857:

These transports of fury, equally incompatible with calm reason, high sentiments and the dignity of a great nation, will not elevate England in the esteem and sympathy of Europe. It is several centuries since the wars of extermination are no more, since they have been forgotten by the civilized world; modern people have forgotten the instincts, the conduct and the savage vocabulary of such wars. None has the right nor the power to bring that language, that conduct and those instincts back into practice and honor. No one can raise this hideous, bloody banner without rousing universal reprobation and horror. What opinion will enlightened men be led to form of this empire, the foundations on which it rests, its

---

* The French expedition against the Kabyles during May and June 1857 appeared to have secured Algeria for France.

strength, durability, its stability, its continuance and future, if the
English newspapers continue to declare that British rule can only
be maintained and secured in the Orient through the extermination
of the native population? What hope for humanity! What kind of
effort for progress would this be, indefinitely reduced to relying on
force and terror, on the law of retaliation, on fire and iron, on the
sword, cannon and gallows!

However, he was answered by the liberal political editor of *Journal des
Debats*, Lucien-Anatole Prevost-Paradol, on November 9: "England is our
ally. We must not, therefore, profit by her difficulties at the risk of breaking the alliance."

The prefect of police in Paris took up an official collection for the victims of the bloody events in India—a collection for the British. At that
point, the alliance was important to Napoleon Ill.

A decade had now passed since the great democratic movement in
Europe of 1848, and everywhere the revolutionary liberals of that time
were taking their places in the new, bourgeois Europe which was taking
shape. The Indian rebellion became a watershed for yesterday's liberals
and democrats. Italy stood on the verge of its national unification. But
how was this to be achieved? Who was to lead it? The aristocracy and big
bourgeoisie in alliance with, and intriguing against, the great powers, or
the common people—the republicans from 1848?

There were two factions in the nationalist movement. On the one
hand, the "moderates," Cavour and his supporters. He supported England and France in the Crimean War, but later made a deal with Russia
to provide the Czarist fleet a naval base at Villafranca. He envisioned liberation from Austria as a French war, with England's consent.

The other faction consisted of the "democrats," Mazzini's supporters.
They were republicans. They drew their strength from the urban petty-
bourgeoisie: artisans, small merchants and intellectuals. They were revolutionaries. Their aim: a democratic republic. The moderates feared any
popular movement. They drew their support from the royal house, the
foreign powers and the standing army. However, both camps spoke of
liberation and national unification.

Thus, the moderates' Joseph Massari wrote in *Rivista Contemporanea* in
Turin, July 1857:

Far too many people, confusing races and geography, will imagine
that the Indian rebellion is a bid for independence and an indica-
tion of the aspiration to form an Indian nation. But those who can
think and are familiar with the real state of affairs will not fall into
such gross blunder. The sepoy rebellion is purely an act of military

sedition kindled by the religious fanaticism of the *brahmans:* the desire for independence and liberty has got nothing to do with it.

The revolutionary democrats, however, considered Indian events not from the point of view of the rich and powerful, but from that of—to use a term of the times—little people. *Italia del Popolo* in Genoa supported the uprising from the start, calling it "this first great attempt at emancipation by that unfortunate people." And on September 15, 1857, the paper expressed a political concept, proving just how clear-sighted this European, revolutionary, bourgeois democracy of the common people could be:

> However rapid or slow, complete or partial, may be the restoration of the British Empire in India, this is true forever that the appearance of the spectre of revolution on the banks of the Yellow River and the Ganges is a tremendous event, and in any case an indication of a new élan of the spirit of liberty.

The revolutionary Russian democrats took the same position as Mazzini's democrats in Italy. In *Sovremennik,* Dobroljubov wrote in favor of Indian independence and against the British occupation, on the basis of a political and social analysis. He claimed that the revolt was historically inevitable. He scoffed at the talk of Britain's civilizing duty in India. "England's ultimate aim is state and private profit and not civilization."

In 1857, Karl Marx was the *New York Daily Tribune's* best paid and most highly respected foreign correspondent. In 1857 and 1858, together with Friedrich Engels, he wrote a series of articles in London on the war in India, for North American readers. At that time, the paper was still republican, sympathizing with revolutionary democracy and the nationalist movements. These articles were exemplary newspaper reporting and at the same time they took an unequivocal stand.

On August 28, 1857, Karl Marx wrote a well-documented article on British torture and excesses prior to the outbreak of the revolt. The article appears as an editorial in the September 17, 1859, edition of the *New York Daily Tribune,* and may be said to sum up democratic opinion in Europe and America on the issue of the Sepoys' killing of the British:

> We have here given but a brief and mildly-colored chapter from the real history of British rule in India. In view of such facts, dispassionate and thoughtful men may perhaps be led to ask whether a people are not justified in attempting to expel the foreign conquerors who have so abused their subjects. And if the English could do

these things in cold blood, is it surprising that the insurgent Hindus should be guilty, in the fury of revolt and conflict, of the crimes and cruelties alleged against them?

This is how Mark Twain viewed the terror during the French Revolution; that is how we viewed the settling of accounts with the collaborationists at the end of the second world war. Which was the cruelty? Which the crime? The premeditated, cold-blooded terror which profited and made rich the executors, the terror which allowed them to cash in the victims' blood and tears for honor and wealth...or the short, lightning-like, furious vengeance which destroys the executioners? Who were the victims? The millions of people the British sacrificed for the wealth of the City? Or the handful of Britons and their family members for whom the prefect of police in Paris was instructed to take up a collection?

The Europe of 1848 had gone down in defeat. In England, the growing empire swept along the consumptively poor, worn-out common people, in a chauvinistic trance. Militant Chartism from the thirties and forties was in its final throes. Exhausted and worn, desperately aware of the tide he was bucking, Ernest Jones still continued the struggle for international solidarity between nations. He was the last in England to speak with the urgency of 1848, and his message was clear and unmistakeable:

There ought to be but one opinion throughout Europe on the Revolt of Hindostan. It is one of the most just, noble, and necessary (revolts) ever attempted in the history of the world. We recently analysed and exposed the nature of England's Indian rule. We this week, in another column, give an episode referring to Oudh, and illustrating the nefarious, the infamous, the in-expressible infamous conduct, of British domination. How any can hesitate which side to take, is inconceivable to us. England—the people, the English people—sympathise with liberty. On which side were they when Poland struggled for its freedom against Russia? On the side of Poland. On which side were they, when Hungary struggled for its rights with Austria? On the side of Hungary. On which side are they when Italy struggles for its life against the Germans, the French, the Papist, and the despot? On the side of Italy. Was Poland right? Then so is Hindostan. Was Hungary justified? Then so is Hindostan. Was Italy deserving of support? Then so is Hindostan. For all that Poland, Hungary, or Italy sought to gain, for that the Hindhu strives. Nay, more! The Pole, the Hungarian, the Italian still own their soil. The Hindhu does not. The former have rulers of their own, or a kindred faith, above them. The Hindhu has not.

The former are still ruled by something like law, and by servants responsible to their masters. The Hindhu is not. Naples and France, Lombardy and Poland, Hungary and Rome present no tyranny so hideous as that enacted by the miscreants of Leadenhall Street [Main office of East India Co.] and Whitehall in Hindostan. The wonder is, not that one hundred and seventy millions of people should now rise in part; the wonder is that they should ever have submitted at all. They would not, had they not been betrayed by their own princes, who sold each other to the alien, and the base truckling invader, that with his foul help, they might cut each other's throats. Thus kings, princes, and aristocracies have ever proven the enemies and curses of every land that harbored them, in every age.

We bespeak the sympathy of the English people for their Hindhu brethren. Their cause is yours—their success is, indirectly, yours as well.

However, England's poor had already begun to enlist, soon to be amateur executioners in India. 1848 was a thing of the past, and the great European tragedy had begun. The inability of the British working class to demonstrate international solidarity was indicative of things to come. Not to struggle for India's and Ireland's independence meant, just as Ernest Jones and Karl Marx had warned, to enslave oneself. In the end, rising imperialism would draw the great mass-parties of the working class into a discussion of a "socialist colonial policy" within the Second International.

India's defeat of 1857-1859 had catastrophic consequences for the people of Europe. The opportunity of liberation from 1848 was now over and instead, the road was opened for this "superfluous present" which has led us out into two world wars—so far.

After its defeat India was ruled by a self-glorifying autocratic British bureaucracy. In 1869 the American republican journalist, Charles Carleton Coffin, published the book on which Jules Verne, four years later, would base his *Around the World in 80 Days*. Charles Carleton Coffin reported from India in *Our New Way Around the World* on the behavior of "the master race"—as he put it—and gave his opinion about the way India was being ruled:

> The government now is lodged in the person of the Governor-General and his counselors. Neither natives nor English residents have any voice in making or administering the laws. It is still a close corporation, slow, behind the times, the members impressed with a sense of their importance and dignity. Taxes are imposed, tariffs

made and unmade, laws promulgated, without much importance being paid to the wishes or wants of the natives.

How would the people of the United States relish it if the President were to remove the whole of the executive machinery of government, on the first of May, to some healthy locality among the Alleghanies—secretaries, heads of departments, clerks, printer and all—staying there till October to enjoy the mountain breezes, at a cost to the country of more than a million dollars. Yet Sir John Lawrence, the Governor-General of India has gone to Simla, more than a thousand miles distant, with all the government officials.

The Governor-General has a salary of $10,400 a month, nearly $125,000 per annum—five times that of the President of the United States—-besides $50,000 for entertainment of guests, and also an allowance for servants. His six councillors have each $40,000 per annum. The Lieutenant-Governor has $50,000. There are several secretaries which have each $24,000.

Then come the Governors of the Presidencies and Provinces—Bengal, Madras, Bombay, the Punjab and Northwest Provinces—each of which receive $50,000 per annum. The Governor of the Central Provinces, Oude and Burmah, each receive $25,000. All of these men belong to the Tite Barnacle family (which according to Dickens in *Little Dorrit* administers the Circumlocution Office) and subordinate places are, in a great measure, filled with their nephews and cousins. The sum of nine hundred thousand dollars is paid to twenty-one individuals in salaries.

For educational purposes, for the enlightenment and elevation of one hundred and eighty millions, the amount paid is $3,370,000, and this is set down as unwarranted expenditure by some officials.

The total receipts of the government are nearly two hundred and twenty million dollars and the expenses are the same. The English Church in India is maintained at an expense of $700,000 per annum.

By far the most important article yielding revenue is opium. It is a government monopoly. The poppies from which the opium is manufactured are grown in the valley of the Ganges, near Patna and Dinapore.... There is a sale of the drug at Calcutta on the ninth every month, where there is an excitement equal to that of the New York exchange when gold is on the rise. The trade is mainly in the hands of native merchants, who rush into opium speculation recklessly. Everything about the drug seems to be intoxicating. The sale last year yielded a clear revenue of thirty-five million dollars to the government, and the Minister of Finance, Mr. Massey, with great glee, announces in his budget for 1869 that the sales will yield a profit of forty-one million, seven hundred and fifty thousand dollars.

The success of this splendid bureaucratic government authority, administered by the famous Indian Civil Service, can be seen in the statistics from the nineteenth century. State revenues poured in and poverty increased.

Is Radicalism Only Chic?

It is New Year's Day. By five a.m. the party is over. The last revelers have gone home.

"The civil servants reel home to sleep in the New Year," says Gun. "Governments may come and go, but tax revenues remain and provide for the crew."

Outside, the wind is raw and rain is in the air. Our breakfast is served at six o'clock. We drink strong, sweet tea with buffalo milk. The fat content of the milk is so high that small yellow pearls float in the tea. We eat hard-boiled eggs and warm *chapati*. The eyes of the old man who brings our breakfast are red from lack of sleep.

We discuss 1857. The British did restore order. They demolished native temples and turned Muslim mausoleums into billiard halls to make plain their cultural superiority. They killed people in order to gain respect and systematize their exploitation and tax-gathering.

"You write that and you'll have everyone against you," says Gun. "It's uncouth, dumb and vulgar. You'll have to muffle it a little. Colonialism is becoming respectable again, especially among the Indian middle class."

"They're its children."

"And what do you think your Swedish or American readers are, then? Write refined; be theoretical and erudite, but don't just come right out and say that all this English freedom, British parliamentarism, all that business of a free press, Fabian socialists, societies for the prevention of cruelty to animals—don't just write that all that was paid for by Indian peasants. Lenin once wrote that, but now Leninism itself has become an ideology in the hands of an oligarchy which holds 'communism,' red flags and university chairs as the Victorians kept their Christianity and Church of England. That Church was paid for by Indian peasants; this Communism and Marxism are paid for by Russian, Polish, Turkoman, Cuban peasants and, as far as that goes, by African and Indian peasants, too. Ideologies change, but the profit is still siphoned off. In the past, it was the British and their Indian middle class who were the beneficiaries. Today, the middle class has become independent enough to run the government itself, and the British have been displaced by Americans and Russians. But it is still the poor peasants and coolies who keep the whole thing going and who pay for the pomp, parliament, parties and university debates with their labor."

In 1906, William Jennings Bryan wrote about India. He had gone there to see for himself the British government at work in India. He saw clearly, in a way radicals of a later day have had trouble seeing. Yet he was neither very revolutionary nor very theoretical. He was a farm-state democrat who never became President, who supported the country's war efforts in the world war which he said he opposed, and who died in 1925 after making himself ridiculous in the eyes of the educated world by defending the Bible's literal word against the theory of evolution at the "monkey trial" in Dayton, Tennessee. The government he saw in India weighed on the shoulders of the poor and functioned as a gigantic pump, extracting wealth from out of the poverty.

In proportion to income, the tax-burden was twice as heavy in India as in England. $225,000,000 was squeezed out of that poverty each year. $100,000,000 went to support the army which protected that government from domestic and foreign enemies. No Indian could become an officer in that army. $100,000,000 was paid to the English motherland as compensation for its arduous administrative efforts in India. $15,000,000 was paid in salary to the English civil servants who administered tax-gathering, the courts and the police. Of the total revenues, 40 percent was raised through taxes on agriculture. A grandiose project was drawn up to increase arable land with irrigation works. According to this plan, acreage would increase by about 285,000 hectares, of which 125,000 hectares were to be irrigated. The estimated cost of this project was $45,000,000, that is, half of what the government took in each year from agricultural taxes. Consequently, the plan was shelved due to lack of funds. For education, this tax-gathering apparatus provided $6,500,000. William Jennings Bryan came to the conclusion that British rule in India was even worse than that of the Czar in Russia. He did note, however, that the British had the freedom of speech at home—even if it were sometimes restricted in the colonies. The British immediately banned

Bryan's article in India. An Urdu translation was confiscated by the police and Lala Lajpat Rai noted that "a translator of the American statesman Mr Bryan's article on British rule in India was actually convicted of
sedition and sentenced to a term of imprisonment."

Lala Lajpat Rai wrote this in a pamphlet he published in New York
called *Reflections on the Political Situation in India*. This, too, was immediately banned in India, and in accordance with section 26 of the Indian
Post Office Act and section 19 of the 1878 Sea Customs Act, the authorities ensured that no copies got into India.

However, the state we are now visiting and whose tax-gathering officials partied in the New Year until five a.m. is the same state described by
William Jennings Bryan.

"Except that now only Naxalites write," says Gun. "There is no one today who writes with the straightforwardness and force of an American
bourgeois democrat in 1906 or of an Indian nationalist in 1915. So it's the
Naxalite publications which are confiscated in the mail and the Naxalites
who are assaulted and beaten to death—and who strike back.

They follow a tradition. On October 30, 1928, Lala Lajpat Rai was assaulted at the railroad station in Lahore. He died on November 18. The
Indian nationalists asserted emphatically that it was Mr J. A. Scott, Superintendent of Police, who had beaten and killed him. The police maintained that Lala Lajpat Rai had died a natural death. In August of that
year, the Hindustan Socialist Republican Army had been founded. It
condemned Scott to death. He was to be assassinated on December 17.
But on that day, Mr Saunders, Assistant Superintendent of Police, rode
the red motorcycle of his superior and was mistaken for Scott. Shivram
Rajguru shot Saunders off the red motorcycle and Bhagat Singh went up
to him and put him out of his misery. Posters were then set up in Lahore:

"Saunders is dead, Lalaji is avenged!"

Forty years later, the Naxalites did what Bhagat Singh had done in
!928. They annihilated.

Of course, this assassination-tactic was incorrect. The Naxalites themselves were harmed by it. They became isolated. But I remember when,
in the fall of 1961, our friend Babu—one of the militants during the naval
mutiny in Bombay, 1946—spoke about how Saunders was assassinated. I
asked him, then, if the assassination had served any useful purpose. The
British only made reprisals.

"How did you react when you learned that Heydrich had died?" he
asked.

"I was glad," I replied. "It was a summer's day and my schoolmate
Sten said, 'Now the swine has gone to slaughter.' "

"Well, then you understand how we felt. I was proud to be Indian.
That's one of my earliest political memories. I was walking home from

school and saw one of those officers—a sahib, a gentleman—on his horse. I said to myself: just one shot—bang—and you lie there in the dust, dead."

If I was glad that Heydrich died and considered his punishment deserved, I cannot bemoan Saunders' death.

"And now Babu is an important businessman, a multimillionaire, with connections both in Russia and the United States," says Gun. "During the Emergency, he said nothing about Indira, and now when one asks him about politics he says that he's stopped thinking about such matters. But it's not that simple."

"Yes it is, perhaps even simpler. It is now the Indian middle class that has taken over the administration of this tax-gathering apparatus, so it cannot very well become indignant over what that state did in the past. Lala Lajpat Rai's speech of September 4, 1920, to the Indian National Congress in Calcutta on the conduct of the British government, reads like a description of modern-day India":

> Raliyaram and Abdulla have said that they were forced not only to crawl on their bellies, but, while crawling, were kicked by the soldiers with their boots and struck with the butt-ends of their rifles. L. Kahan Chand, a blind man, told how even he was made to crawl and was kicked. Six boys were flogged in public; one of them, Sunder Singh, became senseless after the fourth stripe, but after some water was poured into his mouth by soldiers, he regained consciousness; flogging was then resumed. He lost his consciousness for the second time, but the flogging never ceased till he was given 20 stripes. . . .Lala Beli Ram Kapur of Hafizabad was arrested and locked up with 23 others in a room measuring 12 by 25, the same room having to be used by all of them for natural purposes also.

This was said in 1920. Twenty-two years later, in 1942, it was reported how the police in Malabar and the British soldiers in Devakottah in South India acted during the demonstrations against British rule in India:

> On the 13th (of) September, the wife of one Muthirulappa Servai and three other women of the village of Vilankattoor were taken in a bus to Thiruvadanai, where, inside the subjail they were subjected to cold-blooded atrocities. . . .Four white sergeants screwed their lathis into their private parts. Blood was flushing out, and these innocent women, unable to bear the torture, smote their heads against the walls and died. What became of their corpses nobody knows. On the 14th (of) September, the above said Muthiru-

lappa Servai, who is aged 55, was shot dead by the Police. On that day, many houses of innocent people were set on fire and burnt to ashes. On the 15th (of) September, one Nagali Nagappan was tortured, mutilated and murdered. On the 29th (of) August, the house of one Ramaswami Servai in Thiruvadanai was burnt to ashes. As he was not to be found, his two sons were arrested by the Police. The houses of Velu Servai, Muthukamakshi Pillai, Shanmugham, Kadiresa Melakkar, Avudai Odhuvar and Nagaswami Pillai were also burnt. The villages of Kakkalathur, Kakkacheri and Muppaiyur, houses and granaries have been burnt by the Police. Most of the houses in the village of Venniyur were also burnt. Three hundred Kalams of paddy were looted and the remainder burnt to ashes. The fields of one Karmegam, who is now in Burma, have been looted and burnt down. His cattle too were shot; five women of this village also suffered terribly at the hands of the Police and were disgraced. In the village of Athangudi, one Velu Thevar and two Pallas were bound hand and foot and they were shoed on their heads and the Police forced them to drink urine.

(*India Ravaged*, Jan. 1943, without printing location, pp. 94-95)

This is part of a long account. Naturally, the book was immediately banned. The war for democracy was in full swing, and the British police tried to track down those who had broken the laws of free speech by reporting how the British were waging that war in India. It was as Lala Lajpat Rai had written in 1915, in his banned publication on the political situation in India:

The highest British Court declared that it was sedition to publish such historical truths as might in any way influence the Indians to think disparagingly of the English. Similarly, it is out of the question for any Indian in India to try to establish by evidence or argument that the statements made by British historians about the Mutiny of 1857 or about the conduct of the mutineers are incorrect. Any attempt to defend the rebels or to speak in admiration of their deeds or in extenuation of the charges laid at their door by biased historians may bring the writer within the clutches of the law and afford ground for a sentence of death or transportation for life. While in India, an Indian can hardly carry on any historical research on British administration as it may easily tend to bring the Government into contempt of hatred.

However, this British state apparatus, which carries out terroristic orgies drenched in blood against the people whenever it feels itself and its tax-gatherers threatened, did change from 1857 to 1919 and 1942. An increasing number of Indians came to occupy high positions. By 1942, the terror used against the Indian people was mainly carried out by Indian civil servants in the service of the British.

This kind of behavior on the part of the state is not especially British. It could just as well be German, Japanese, Russian, Italian or French. The Swedish writer Anders Ehnmark, in his book on Italy, *The Palace*, describes what happened in that country in 1860. The peasants in the south rose in revolt. They believed in Italy and freedom. But the moderates in the north aimed at uniting Italy and establishing their own government to safeguard private property. They wanted the peasants to continue paying taxes and rent:

> Turin sends one army after the other—in the end, two hundred thousand men—to put down the peasants....In Turin, they speak of doing as the English had done in India. The English have just crushed the Sepoy rebellion. Their methods were interesting. Turin sees southern Italy the way London does India. (p. 40)

In order to understand how this state erected by the British really functions, we can look at the shooting in Barahiya in Monghyr district in Bihar on September 1, 1977, when four people died.

On August 31, two notorious goondas abducted a school boy in Barahiya with a homosexual motive. This was immediately reported to the police. When the two goondas heard about their having been reported to the police, they went to the school and beat up several of the students and members of the school management committee. A new police report was filed. The officer on duty was reluctant to discuss the matter, but since the incident was beginning to be noticed, he and a *havildar*—a village constable—went to the school. There, the police were accused of protecting the two goondas. A fight broke out between the police and the students.

That evening the students, teachers, members of the school administration and other concerned citizens met and decided to hold a demonstration the following day, to force the police to take action against the two child-molesters. The inhabitants of Barahiya felt that police action was necessary since the two were terrorizing the village, committing rape, murder, robbery and extortion.

However, the two goondas had more than just good relations with the police. They were also in close association with a member of the provincial government of Bihar. He was a Socialist. But following a 1952 election defeat, he had made a deal with these two criminals and their gang, whereby they acted as his armed forces during electoral campaigns and assured him his victory by taking over the polling places and stuffing the ballot boxes. In return they received various privileges. It was reported that they had, among other things, been awarded the right to collect the toll at the Harohar Bridge. Whereas previous entrepreneurs had paid between 300,000 and 400,000 rupees for this lucrative franchise, they paid a mere 117,000 rupees.

As the people gathered in front of the police station and began to shout, there were a few who threw some stones at the building. The police, who were ready to shoot, were then ordered by the *havildar* to open fire. Between seventy and eighty rounds were fired. Four people died and two others were so seriously wounded that they fell to the ground.

The journalist Arun Sinha, who reported the incident in *The Economic and Political Weekly,* October 1, 1977, recounts that the police continued to fire at the panic-stricken crowd in flight...a crowd comprised of almost half of Barahiya's population: people from both Janata as well as Congress, school boys, teachers, lawyers, peasants, shopkeepers...The shots rang out and people fell on top of one another, screaming, in wild flight away from their government.

This is not classified information. There are brilliant journalists in India who do an excellent job of reporting. There are civil rights groups and committees formed to defend the political rights of citizens. Each time the grip of the censor is loosened and the government withdraws its control over the mass media, report after report is printed. But one can spend a lot of time with intellectuals, educated members of the middle classes and brilliant civil servants in Delhi, Bombay, Madras and other cities, without being more disturbed by these reports than educated people in Sweden are over traffic accidents.

"Ho hum, another accident on the West Bridge."

"Ho hum, more shooting in Bihar."

They talk about Ingmar Bergman. They discuss women's liberation. The servant goes around with small bowls of nuts and snacks. Someone wonders what position Bettelheim will take. An American sociologist explains why the theory of the semi-feudal Indian countryside is so incorrect. The American sociologist has visited the Indian countryside several times over a decade for his institution and has written interesting and fact-filled publications on commodity production in the South Indian countryside. They talk of the latest findings in Soviet parapsychology.

"Why, even China now acknowledges ESP."

A distinguished-looking, older woman with grey-streaked hair and a sober, blue sari with a red stripe has just returned from Geneva. She has represented India there. She has spoken in favor of a new pedagogy.

"The children must discover their natural abilities."

She is very genteel and often appears in the women's magazines of the world.

There are also less intellectual circles. In these, one can drink, laugh, and frequent upper-class brothels or go on spicy outings down Grant Road.

Yes, there are many circles one can frequent. There are also the ones in which we usually spend our time. It might be made up of Santosh, Suraj, Kumar, Hari and Sunanda. We can talk for days on end, travel together and respect one another's work. They might be older intellectuals whose values and religion we may not share, but whom we respect. For all of these people, India is real: an India where even coolies are human beings. An India with 700,000,000 people.

However, for the ruling class—not the class which bears the state on its shoulders, but the one which possesses the state, and which works by and through that state to enrich itself—for that ruling class, India is something different.

"Have you seen the poor?" asked the man with the gold-rimmed glasses. His name is Roy and he is District Magistrate near the Bay of Bengal. It was a warm evening towards the end of winter. We had discussed Tantric philosophy. He was educated, knowledgeable and interested in Tantric tradition. He was also musically inclined.

"Have you seen the poor? They live like pigs. They crawl about in the filth. Have you seen the way they crawl in hovels? Their lives aren't really worth very much. Their brains have been damaged by hunger. It's been scientifically proven. That's why they are unruly and hyperactive. There has been a lot of trouble lately concerning movie tickets. Ticket scalping. I was forced to interfere. There must be some law and order, even in a permissive society such as ours. They assembled, shouted and created a disturbance. The police restored order, but someone suffered a fatal heart attack in the midst of it all. Rightaway, they began to agitate and blame the police, as usual. I tried to talk some sense into them, but it was no use. They just kept shouting. So we restored order, and now everything is calm again.

"We really shouldn't allow things to go on like this. Their lives are without meaning; even to themselves. The children could be cared for and given proper nourishment. But all those who just grub in the gutters. . . .

"Sanjay tried to do something about these problems. All he got was a lot of criticism. He was called elitist and authoritarian. But someone has to do something. At present the politicians always go along with the mob. But an orderly society just can't be run that way. We are much too weak and permissive here in India. That is a positive feature of Hinduism, but it can become a bad trait if it is allowed to take over and dominate society as it has now. Something must be done about the poor."

Roy was well-dressed and educated. We drank whisky in the warm evening air and with a laugh he spoke of European work-habits:

"Tumble out of bed, throw a little water into the eyes, on with the clothes, rush to the garage, the morning traffic-jam to the office, and then work, work, work, over the papers all day long. The soul has hardly struggled out of bed before the body has raced to a lunch of instant coffee and fast food, warmed by microwaves in an automatic oven."

I have heard his kind of talk about the poor before. That they live like pigs. It is to Indian pigs that the poor are then being compared—long-snouted pigs that grub in the gutters, and run to lick up the excrement almost before he who has relieved himself has had time to stand aside. Garbage-eating animals. Animals of filth. Eyes red with fury, blood-thirstily fighting for their sewermouth or their garbage-heap against all the prowling dogs and ambitious young porkers. Only the most wretched of outcastes eat their meat.

Down in the great Indian desert, on the border between India and Pakistan, we stayed in the home of a gentleman in 1967. We had come to his house with a recommendation from a lawyer and Member of Parliament. He had said that this was a colorful character, one we should meet.

Around his pucca house, ran a high wall of rammed earth. It was topped by barbed wire. There was a locked gate in the wall. We were let in. At each corner of the enclosure stood a watch-tower. Armed guards escorted us to our room. The gentleman ate with us. He had huge platters of rice and silver dishes of meat and vegetables. He was fat and had small, beady eyes. He talked right through the meal.

"The trouble with this country," he said, "is that the people work too little. Not enough is produced. People just eat without working. We have too many people. The poor tax the resources of society. They just consume without producing anything. The trouble with us is that we are too indulgent. We allow this waste of our precious resources to go on. The poor constitute a real threat to society. Poverty is parasitic."

We lay awake that night. The search-light swept at regular intervals along the top of the wall, and the chowkidars shouted to each other from tower to tower, so that the master would be sure that they were awake and keeping watch.

The following day, we accompanied him on an excursion. He was going to visit his orchard. We drove in three cars. They pulled up in the courtyard. Then the gates were swung open. The first car carried the guards. They were armed. Then a car with the master and us. It was a pre-war Buick, in good shape. Guards stood on the running boards. They hung on with one hand to the window-posts and in the other they held their weapons. A high wall surrounded the orchard. The chowkidars opened the gates and the three cars drove in. Then the gates were closed. It was a lovely garden: a small paradise. The water in the pond sparkled and the fruit hung down. Peaches. When we sat down to eat, the master took out a small Browning and placed it within reach. The bodyguards stood at a polite distance.

"There are so many evil and envious people around," he said. He was a deeply religious man. We talked of life's brevity and the futility of all human effort. After having napped in the shade by the cool of the water, we got back into the cars. The gates were opened and we drove off at breakneck speed, the desert sand swirling after us. When we arrived at his home, the gates were once more thrown open to allow us in.

We were later informed that he was a notorious dacoit-leader, that he led the smuggling activity across the border and that he had close connections with politicians and the government.

The State is ancient in this subcontinent. For two thousand years, the educated, literate and powerful have lived in terror of what might happen if the bonds burst and the people rise in protest.

"Do you see how the poor crawl into their hovels at night? They're like animals."

The British were supported in 1857 by the feudal lords and the rich, as well as by the intellectuals of the new middle class, because as soon as the British magistrates and tax-gatherers disappeared, the poor again began to surge up from below. Law and order collapsed.

Each time the Indian national struggle against the British gripped the people, each time the poor, the coolies, the untouchables and poor peasants began to stir, the middle class nationalists grew afraid, and Gandhi—who could talk with the poor and for whom the coolies, untouchables and poor peasants had respect—took steps to put a damper on the incipient uprising.

It is not just the feudal gentry and the big capitalists, but also the middle class in its entirety that fears the masses. During the Cultural Revolution in 1967, I spent some time with an old friend in Karachi, Akbar Adil, the economic adviser to President Ayub Khan, and one of the advocates of friendship with China. One evening he said:

"But I wonder what's happening in China. Imagine the same thing happening here. Suddenly the gates would be thrown open and all these Pakistanis would come storming into my yard!"

"Perhaps I shouldn't say this out loud," says Gun, "but I wonder if it is possible to have unity between the middle class and the poor."

"National bourgeoisie, petty bourgeoisie, middle strata, middle peasants, poor peasants, landless agrarian laborers and workers," I reply.

"For the time being, in India, it is enough to talk about the middle class and the people, or about the middle class and the common people, as they did in Europe a hundred years ago," says Gun. "And I wonder if it is possible for them to unite. Democracy and the right to vote are not insignificant rights and the people can benefit from them. The people have also fought for these rights against the British and other authorities. Neither is it unimportant if the laws are obeyed or not. The people want scoundrels like the goondas in Barahiya arrested by the police, tried and thrown in jail. Nor do the people like corruption. Corruption always harms the poor. Nor do they wish to be caught by Indira's spermatic-duct-clipper battalions, to be sterilized by force. If it were up to the people, they would both defend the existing democracy and broaden its scope; everyone would be equal before the law and the laws would be enforced. New and better laws could then be passed. The people are in the majority. The threat does not emanate from them. One must be a totally confused intellectual to assert that a united front is unnecessary, because the people don't need or want democracy, and law and order. But does the middle class want such a front?"

"A hero or two, perhaps. The sort that is strong enough to 'go to the people,' as the saying went in Old Russia. One shouldn't doubt the sincerity of all these journalists and lawyers who talk of democracy and unity against authoritarianism. But does that mean that the Indian middle class has suddenly become different from what it was in the past?"

"When I discussed women in China," said Gun, "with that women's group in Madras, I talked about how they had started day-care centers in China, and how they had set up mills. The members of the women's group talked about emancipation, meaning sexual emancipation, and women's roles, and they wondered why there wasn't full equality between men and women in China. They felt sorry for the Chinese women who worked double—at their jobs and at home. Suddenly it struck me that none of these radical, intellectual women considered even for a moment conditions in the Indian villages. When they talked about women and the lot of women, they were thinking about themselves and those close to them—well-educated, intellectual women from emancipated, high-caste backgrounds. When they talked about people, they were talking about an abstraction. Ninety percent of India's people did not exist in their thoughts. They were invisible like the black-garbed stagehands at a Chinese-theater. How do you think these women would react if democracy and unity were to become a reality? The minute they would have to go and carry buckets of muck, they would become disillusioned by democracy and revolution, and would summon the police or the army, or even foreign troops!

"And what about our Chinese friends? The truth now! Mao felt that they should learn to know their own people and land, and to be one with the masses. They should learn that human excrement was fertilizer and not filth. They should learn where food came from and how much sweat and toil there was in each and every bowl of rice. Many of them went to the countryside. Some were unfit for it and some managed to get out of it. There were some who did what the students of the Delhi School of Social Work did to get practical experience in Rural Welfare in the late '50s. Do you remember that? They went to Koraput to build a road for the villagers up in the jungle. But building a road is hard work. So they paid the villagers to do the digging, carrying and building. Then they returned to Delhi with practical experience and could assume leading government positions. Things like that also happened in China, in the schools for cadres. But some really worked with the pigs and the fertilizer, and really learnt where food comes from. Then Mao died and it was as if a dam had burst: various sorts of intellectuals flooded the cities to become unemployed and disgruntled. They had wasted several long years in the countryside. One of them had even been forced to herd cows.

"Finally," said Gun, "when I got mad at listening to them and told them that I in any case belonged to Tornedalen in the very north of Sweden, from poor-farmer stock and had spent my childhood herding cows, and learning to work, and that I couldn't understand what they were complaining about, they looked at me blankly. But later, an interpreter who had witnessed my outburst, came up to my room and said that he, too, was from the countryside. His father had starved to death and his mother was a poor peasant, and he understood me. He told me that he carried Mao in his heart and was glad that I had said that it didn't hurt a person to work in the countryside. But he didn't say it aloud any more.

"Of course, China needs its intellectuals and needs them in the cities. Industrialization requires an investment in technology and education. But it is equally evident that Mao failed in his attempt at bridging the enormous gap between the urban intellectuals and middle class on the one side, and the millions of poor peasants on the other. He did not even succeed in transforming the intellectuals the way he himself was transformed: to the point of not being ashamed to carry human excrement and get one's hands dirty.

"Do you remember when we were in Cologne in the spring of 1979 and met our revolutionary friends from Berlin? The ones who were so revolutionary that there was nothing militant enough for them. Those who always used to call us lukewarm and right wing bourgeois democrats? They had now left all politics behind them, and talked of house squatting and resistance to nuclear energy instead. Their entire super-militant revolutionary period was just everyday, middle class fantasy. They might just as well have been engaged in parapsychology, vegeto-therapy or advanced philately. And are things any different here? Is this middle class any different than those preceding it since the time of Chandragupta? Although they can use the people against the feudal lords and foreigners, when equality threatens and there's a risk that these people living like pigs in their sties will really pull themselves up and want to share the wealth a little more equitably, then the middle class is prepared to take any steps to prevent them. Then you'll see where the real solidarity is. They'll be solidly united to hold the people—this human-monster—down.

"But it isn't proper to say these things in public. And Hitler was, after all, worse than the Weimar Republic, and Indira Gandhi's Emergency worse than no Emergency. So we'll have to hope that they can hold together to prevent Indira from declaring another Emergency. The Germans were better off unemployed in an inequitable Weimar Republic than dead under Hitler."

At the Roots of the Old State

In the grey, chilly morning the believers pray beneath the Bo tree—the sacred pipal tree under which Gautama attained enlightenment, twenty-five centuries ago. The prayer flags flap in the wind and a Nepalese pilgrim arranges his prayer board as he prepares to pray. No Americans or northern Europeans are here yet. Only a group of Japanese are to be seen.

The Bo tree looks old and decaying. Beneath this sacred pipal tree Siddhartha Gautama was supposed to have sat two thousand five hundred years ago. But the pipal is not a long-lived tree. It cannot live two thousand years like our sacred tree of northern Europe, the oak. This tree in Bodhgaya, in 1980, is exactly ninety-three years old going on ninety-four. The former tree, which eventually toppled in the wind and died in 1876, was old and decayed when Cunningham saw it in 1862, and Buchanan estimated it to be a hardy, hundred year old in 1818. If one tree followed another, this tree with prayer flags in its aerial roots would be seventeen generations removed from the sacred Bo tree under which Siddhartha Gautama attained enlightenment and assumed Buddhahood.

If Siddhartha were a prophet or savior in the Judaeo-Christian tradition, problems and explanations would arise concerning this discrepancy. The faithful would feel the need to constantly defend themselves—as the Christians have had to defend the ruminating rabbit of Leviticus 11.5. What has happened with the sacred relic of Christ's shroud would have happened with the sacred pipal tree. At regular in-

tervals, we would read in the newspapers that a renowned American bi-
ologist, using spectrum analysis, had established that this exceptional pipal tree was, miraculously, many thousands of years old, or that a self
taught Italian, using the carbon-14 variant, has calculated the age of the
tree to be 2687 years, give or take a monsoon or two.

In the Judaeo-Christian tradition, symbols are not allowed to remain
symbols, endowed with contradictions and incongruities; they must be
proven and declared true. Bring on Christ's shroud and all manner of
scholars who corroborate the miracle's authenticity. As if the Son of God,
the supreme mystery of the Trinity could be proven genuine and credible
with a darkroom experiment! This is the most commonplace, vulgar materialism. (Analogous in a non-religious sphere would be the attempts
made to explain Marx' *Capital* with the fact that he suffered from hemor-
rhoids.)

To the Buddhist, the question of the actual age of the pipal tree and
the question of how many generations of trees are genetically dependent
on one another, are not just irrelevant, but, in relation to his faith, totally
meaningless. The stories about how King Sasanka had the tree uprooted
and how King Purnavaram brought it back to life, are edifying legends.

That Siddhartha of the ox-totem in the Sakya tribe meditated on time
and human existence here and attained enlightenment about 528 B.C.,
that he used this enlightenment to preach, and that an order of monks
was established around his person to serve as a refuge from the world—
all this is a plausible, historical narrative. We can speak of this Siddhartha, his activity and words, as we would about people we know (or
believe we know) to have existed. There was such a person. But for the
Buddhist, this, too, is irrelevant and quite unimportant, even if he sup-
poses Buddha did act in this way.

Even as a developed religion with gods, demons, heavens and hells,
Buddhism is characterized by the understanding that only change remains constant. The waves cannot be separated from the sea, but man
sees wave after wave as being individual objects. Individuals, too, appear
as living beings for definite reasons, and, to the ignorant and undiscern-
ing, they appear as one person after another. The phenomenal world has
no real existence; things appear to be real to the ignorant—with enlightenment, causality dissolves and the shadows evaporate. As long as the
various Buddhisms remain in contact with their own past tradition, the
problem of the actual age of the sacred Bo tree will be irrelevant. It cannot be anything but irrelevant as long as Buddhism is still in touch with
the thought of Siddhartha Gautama.

This Buddhist disinterest in matters of the sort which have greatly in-
flamed Jews and Christians represents a genuine and important tradition. The Siddhartha Gautama who materializes in the statements

ascribed to him, is one of the important atheistic philosophers who, around the sixth century B.C., were impelled to free themselves from illusion and assert universal impermanence. In opposition to the priestly conceptions of a soul—even an eternal soul—beyond all change and ruling over thoughts and emotions, Siddhartha Gautama declared that the personality only constituted a summary of ephemeral emotions and bodily functions; when the chain of causality was broken, it too dissolved. Any notion that there is anything permanent, is superstition. The Self, like the world, is only an ever-continuous transformation. An object does not remain unchanged in time, but change forms itself into repeated likenesses that give the uninitiated the illusion of identity.

Like his near contemporary, Heraclitus, Siddhartha Gautama asserts not only becoming as opposed to being, but also the unity of opposites in one constant mutability.

> This world generally proceeds on a duality, of the "it is" and the "it is not." But whoever perceives in truth and wisdom how things originate in the world, in his eyes there is no "it is not" in this world. Whoever perceives in truth and wisdom how things pass away in this world, in his eyes there is no "it is" in this world.

Heraclitus said:

"We step, and we do not step, into the same river. We are and we are not."

The similarity between Siddhartha Gautama's and Heraclitus' statements is not pure coincidence. Both were aristocrats with roots in ancient tribal society, and both lived at a time when their worlds were collapsing around them. Heraclitus experienced the democratic revolution; Siddhartha witnessed the new power of the Magadha kingdom. Greek democracy and the new kingdom in the Gangetic valley were different, and Heraclitus and Siddhartha reflect that difference. But both were slave-owning states which broke ruthlessly with the past. Heraclitus and Siddhartha Gautama were active at a time of new state power, new gods, new 'free-thought' and new terrors.

The period when Siddhartha Gautama lived, and that following his death, when his teaching spread rapidly were times of tremendous expansion and change. In the Gangetic valley, too, humanity took a great leap forward. Out of the old society, shining new cities were built. The population increased. The Indian production of steel was renowned in pre-industrial world trade. Its quality was such that even today the famous iron column in the oldest Delhi at Qutb Minar stands without a trace of rust. It probably came from Bihar, and it is a thousand five hundred years old, perhaps older. Since the end of the seventh century B.C., the weapons produced here by the skilful blacksmiths have been exported. Ancient Patna, Pataliputra, was a center for work in iron. The vast new riches created by agriculture arid handicrafts were channeled in the expanding domestic and foreign trades along the great, royal highways. These were guarded, marked by milestones, and furnished with protected rest areas for merchants and other travellers. Pataliputra was the capital of one of the paramount powers of the day.

In this new state, the iron ploughshare prepared the soil for Buddhism. Buddhism was deeply philosophical speculation for the intellectuals, and its order of monks—with its harking back to the democracy of tribal society and the equality among freemen—was a refuge for the socially displaced. But Buddhism's eightfold path was also well-suited to the new agricultural society:

> Right views...that the world's suffering is caused by greed and desire.
>
> Right aspirations...to neither crave nor become attached; to love others and increase their happiness.
>
> Right speech...to practise truthfulness and mutual friendship.
>
> Right conduct...*ahimsa*, to refrain from killing, stealing, adultery and remunerative activity.
>
> Right mode of livelihood...to not make one's living in an unclean or dishonest way.
>
> Right effort...to practise religious exercises against unclean thoughts.
>
> Right mindfulness...that the human body is composed of unclean matter.
>
> Right rapture...to break the bonds of causality by which the flesh and our desires bind us, and so attain emancipation, deliverance and Nirvana.

This Eightfold Path stood open to all, regardless of social origin.

This was a moral doctrine for an agrarian society. Castes and traditional customs gave way to personal responsibility for one's own salvation; mutual dependence was turned into high morality. The *brahman's* ritual animal sacrifices had become economically devastating for an agrarian society—a society which needed its livestock as droughtanimals. The plough was mightier than the Veda scriptures and the *brahman* gods. One does not kill one's drought-animals. *Ahimsa* prohibits animal sacrifice.

But, at the same time, Buddhism is not absolute. An agrarian society must also eat its animals if its resources are to be properly utilized. Buddhism did not forbid meat-eating—Siddhartha Gautama himself died after a meal of pork—as long as the slaughter was by a Buddhist. Soil-tilling Buddhists could support a thousand people on land which previously had fed only a hundred livestock-herders with singing, brahmanical shamans. Siddhartha Gautama's first disciples included a number of merchants. Nor was Right Livelihood construed to prohibit the taking of interest; even usury was not considered an unclean or dishonest way of making a living. Buddhism was not ill-disposed to the two new phenomena that now appeared in the cities: taverns and brothels. *Brahmans* could not eat with people considered ritually unclean, or consume restaurant food. The *brahmans* also condemned prostitution. But Siddhartha Gautama did not prohibit inter-dining or restaurant food. He himself frequented (purely!) prostitutes, and these women could become nuns in the convents. Buddhism was a doctrine for a new age. Although Buddhism opposed the caste system, it accepted the view that untouchables were below and outside the society of men.

The other sect which gained some popularity in the sixth century B.C. was Jainism. Philosophically, it was quite different from Buddhism. Form is changeable, but matter and the soul are permanent. That which exists or that which does not exist can only be said to exist in a way, or to not exist in a way. More important for the doctrine's social function was the fact that the prohibition against killing was absolute and the requirement of propertylessness was interpreted to mean non-ownership of land; thus, Jainism became a religion for the new townspeople who possessed neither livestock nor land: a doctrine for merchants who could attain wealth but not power, a doctrine for caravan traders and artisans. And its very eclecticism corresponded to both their social circumstances and experience as craftsmen (which is gained in the reshaping of durable matter). Jainism never became a mass religion, but on the other hand, it remains a religious doctrine for businessmen: a minority religion still known for its adaptability and broad views.

It was a vast kingdom that Chandragupta Maurya—of the peacock-totem—and his minister, the learned and cunning *brahman* Kautilya seized from King Dhananda. It continued to expand by means of military expeditions and diplomacy until, in the words of Plutarch, it included "all of India."

Under the rule of Chandragupta's grandson, Asoka, it also took control of Orissa, and the Mauryan empire included almost all of present-day India, with the exception of what is now Tamil Nadu and Kerala, and the northeastern provinces bordering on Burma. Towards the west, the empire had been further expanded when Seleucus Nicator, who had taken over the eastern portion of Alexander the Great's empire and made himself king in 306 B.C., had come to terms with Chandragupta. This peace, sealed with the marriage of one of Seleucus' daughters to Chandragupta, resulted in the provinces east of the Hindu Kush, including what is today Baluchistan, being included in the Mauryan empire. The borders of this empire can be determined approximately, with the aid of the inscriptions in natural rock and pillars which Asoka had engraved. However, it is unclear where the empire's western border lay.

The Maurya dynasty ruled over a rich kingdom. Diodorus Siculus, who during the reign of Augustus attempted to write a comprehensive history of the world, described India's wealth-probably basing his account on the reports of Seleucus Nicator's ambassador to Chandragupta, Megasthenes:

> India has many huge mountains which abound in fruit-trees of every kind, and many vast plains of great fertility, which are remarkable for their beauty, and are supplied with water by a multitude of rivers. The greater part of the soil, moreover, is well watered and consequently bears two crops in the course of the year. It teems at the same time with animals of all sorts—beasts of the field and fowls of the air—of all different degrees of strength and size. It is prolific, besides, in elephants, which are of monstrous bulk, as its soil supplies food in unsparing profusion, making these animals far to exceed in strength those that are bred in Libya. . . . And while the soil bears on its surface all kinds of fruits which are known to cultivation, it has also underground numerous veins of all sorts of metals, for it contains much gold and silver, and copper and iron in no small quantity, and even tin and other metals, which are employed in making articles of use and ornament, as well as the implements and accoutrements of war.

It was on the basis of the reports of Megasthenes and other Greek informants that antiquity formed its view of India. Yet, much of what was reported was preposterous. Strabo, the Greek historian and geographer, born about 63 B.C., noted that Megasthenes was unreliable and fantastic when he described the "strange peoples"—some five fathoms long, some three, some noseless and others with such large ears that they used these to wrap themselves into sleep. That sort of thing is just monstrous. Strabo attempted to sift from these remarkable tales the factual core, and to determine what was plausible. But just as the myths about India remained alive during our entire Middle Ages in spite of Strabo, some of Megasthenes' assertions still turn up in discussion even though they are recognized to be incorrect. In both instances, it is more a matter of misunderstandings about a foreign culture than a question of myths.

One of these misunderstandings concerns the holding of property; the other, the existence of slavery. Diodorus Siculus writes:

The husbandsmen themselves, with their wives and children, live in the country, and entirely avoid going into town. They pay a land-tribute to the king, because all India is the property of the crown, and no private person is permitted to own land. Besides the land-tribute, they pay into the royal treasury a fourth of the produce of the soil.

Strabo relied directly on Megasthenes when, at about the same time, he wrote:

The second caste, he says, is that of the farmers, who are not only the most numerous, but also the most highly respected, because of their exemption from military service and right of freedom in their farming; and they do not approach a city, either because of a public disturbance or on any other business; at any rate, he says, it often happens that at the same time and place some are in battle array and are in peril of their lives against the enemy, while the farmers are ploughing or digging without peril, the latter having the former as defenders. The whole of the country is of royal ownership; and the farmers cultivate it for a rental in addition to paying a fourth part of the produce.

There is some controversy as to whether this last sentence should, in fact, be translated as "the farmers cultivate it for wages, on condition of receiving a fourth part of the produce."

However, with reference to the writing of Diodorus, it is generally taken to mean rent or land-tax, and, in addition, payment of one-fourth of the harvest to the royal treasury. As for the question of slavery, Diodorus writes:

Of several remarkable customs existing among the Indians, there is one prescribed by their ancient philosophers which one may regard as truly admirable: for the law ordains that no one among them shall under any circumstances be a slave, but that, enjoying free-dom, they shall respect the principle of equality in all persons.

A century later, Arrian, writing more specifically, refers to the same as-sertion by Megasthenes:

The same writer tells us further this remarkable fact about India, that all the Indians are free, and not one of them is a slave. The Lakedaimonians and the Indians here so far agree. The Lakedaimo-nians, however, hold the Helots as slaves, and these Helots do servile labor; but the Indians do not even use aliens as slaves, and much less a countryman of their own.

These assertions, which still play a certain role in the general discussion, are incorrect. In part they appear to be ideologically motivated and written for edifying purposes, much as when the Sophist Aelian, in the third century A.D., suddenly asserts in his book *On the Nature of Animals*:

> The Indians neither put out money at usury, nor know how to borrow. It is contrary to established usage for an Indian either to do or suffer a wrong, and therefore they neither make contracts nor require securities.

The slave system was well-developed. At that time, during the centuries before the birth of Christ, widespread slavery existed. The law regulated how a person could be sold into slavery, made a slave for debts or be born a slave. There were house slaves and large landed-estates which were run with slave labor. Slavery was acceptable and in the Jataka narrative of the Videha king Angati, the good slave Bijaka is tempted by the naked sect teacher Kassapa. The latter has asserted that there is no law to right oneself after:

> There is no fruit, good or evil, in following the law; there is no other world, O king—who has ever come back hither from thence? There are no ancestors—how can there be father or mother? There is no teacher—who will tame what cannot be tamed? All beings are equal and alike, there are none who should receive or pay honor; there is no such thing as strength or courage—how can there be vigor or heroism? All beings are predestined, just as the stern-rope must follow the ship.

The slave Bijaka is moved by this democratic doctrine and says:

> I was one Bhavasetthi in the city of Saketa, devoted to virtue, pure, given to alms, and esteemed by *brahmans* and rich men; and I remember no single evil deed that I committed. But when I passed from that life I was conceived in the womb of a poor prostitute, and was born to a miserable life. But miserable as I am I keep my tranquil mind, and I give the half of my food to whosoever desires it. I fast every fourteenth and fifteenth day, and I never hurt living creatures, and I abstain from theft. But all the good deeds which I do produce no fruit; I think that virtue is useless. I lose my game in life

as an unskillful dice-player; I see no door by which I may go to heaven.

When King Angati hears Bijaka's words, he says:

There is no door to heaven: only wait on destiny. Whether thy lot be happiness or misery, it is only gained through destiny.

The king then turned to Kassapa's false doctrine and left the Path, although his daughter tried to dissuade him and the people grumbled. But the Bodhisattva realized that only he could steer the king away from that false path. He succeeded in his aim by demolishing the king's arguments in a heated altercation. He described the tortures of hell for the king and brought him back to virtue and the Noble Path. And—as the Master told his disciples in this life, Bijaka had become Mogallana—one of the two foremost disciples.

It took hard and strong words, and all the authority of a Bodhisattva, to beat down the sectarians' heretical notions about equality among people, that there were none who should receive or pay honor. For the slavery which produced intricate ideologies about its inevitability, and its being a punishment for sins committed in some previous incarnation, also gave rise to rebellion and free-thinking. The slave Bijaka spoke with the experience of all slaves when he said that virtue is meaningless for the slave: he has lost his life. Against him and his brothers and sisters were arrayed divinities and religions, the State and its laws.

The law in force in the Mauryan empire—which Aelian asserts knew neither loan nor security, at a time when Megasthenes reported that there were no slaves—was the law laid down in the provisions of the *Dasa-Kalpa* (Dispositions Concerning Slaves) in the *Arthasastra*:

A *mleccha* (non-Aryan) may sell or mortgage his children. But an Aryan cannot be made a slave. It is, however, permitted to mortgage an Aryan to save the family from prison or (to) save endangered Aryans. When it occurs the members of the family must restore to freedom the child or family member upon obtaining the money. The individual who has been mortgaged, himself becomes forever a slave if he tries to flee. The individual who has been mortgaged by another becomes a slave forever if he flees twice.

The law also ordained that:

A slave or mortgaged individual may not take an issue to court. . . .
On the king's fields ploughed by several ploughshares, the sowing

shall be carried out by slaves, servants and those condemned to penal servitude. . . . Each village will report how many people belong to the four *varnas* (Aryans), how many servants and how many slaves. . . . If the head of the household is not obeyed, slaves, mortgaged persons and relatives shall be punished.

Slavery was an established institution. It was going through changes at this time. In the earlier society, the slave, *dasa,* was totally at the mercy of the master. There were no regulations governing the treatment of slaves. Among other things, the new state-power regulated slavery and established proper laws which governed the treatment of slaves. It differentiated between born-slaves, slaves captured in war and mortgaged individuals.

Wealthy families in Pataliputra owned large landed estates which supplied agricultural products for the market and which were dependent on slave labor. At the same time, there were free laborers and small freeholding peasants. The royal army was comprised mainly of slaves. In addition, there were soldiers recruited from among free men.

Unlike the slave-societies of classical Mediterranean antiquity, there were no intellectuals (teachers, doctors) who were slaves. Nor were artisans or artists of various kinds enslaved. They worked in guilds as free men. Due also to India's vast expanse, rural slave labor was not as prevalent as in Greece or Italy. There was plenty of new land to be cleared. The emancipated slaves in India—unlike those in Greece or Rome—immediately became socially equal; slaves and free men mixed socially during festivals.

Slavery did exist and it was severe, but it was not quite as fully developed or as totally dominant as in Greece or Rome. I believe Dev Raj Chanana offers an accurate explanation in *Slavery in Ancient India* (New Delhi, 1960), when he notes that the difference between the two civilizations is to be sought in the fact that in Greece slavery developed and society was transformed into an iron-age culture within one and the same general material organization of society, whereas in India development was interrupted. The bronze-age cities of the Indus valley were, without doubt, slave societies. When the state was re-established in the valley of the Ganga and the iron ploughshare enabled it to advance economically, the working people took advantage of a thousand-year interregnum. The freedom enjoyed by handicraft production gave the Gangetic culture a swift technological upswing, before state-power could be consolidated. Had the bronze-age society developed into a new state, an iron-age slave society, Indian slavery would have been more similar to the classical Mediterranean variant. However, the slave-owners' disdain for labor and competence also came to dominate India.

Although it seems incomprehensible that Megasthenes could claim that slavery did not exist (he names slave women when describing the royal household), it is more understandable that he could believe that all the land belonged to the kings.

The old villages which had evolved out of the late Aryan tribal society suffered the interference of the state-power only when it came to tax-gathering and matters of state security. Taxes amounted to one-sixth of the harvest. This amount could be reapportioned within the village. In addition, there were various other taxes, and duties to finance the state-constructed irrigation works.

It was the clearing of the new land that Megasthenes had witnessed and described. These areas were expanding, and provided the new state with its vast wealth. Bands of war prisoners, urban slum-dwellers or poor from the old villages, were driven out into the countryside to clear land for farming. A unit was comprised of a village of hundred to five hundred families. The villages were laid out at a distance of five kilometers from one another. For every ten, two hundred, four hundred and eight hundred villages, an administrative body and a garrison was established. Within certain limits, these land-clearers were free men.

He who cleared the land could work it during his lifetime—as long as he paid the taxes. If he was unable to pay the taxes, the land was given to someone else. The taxes were higher than those in the older villages. They went up to one-fifth of the harvest for dry land, and up to one-third, for irrigated land. All forest products and game belonged to the state. If necessary, the minister for state land might permit the cultivation of the land by slaves or prisoners.

There were no collective bodies other than family meetings and common labor for irrigation construction. Members of sects and priests were not admitted. Singers, poets and minstrels were also banned. No building that might be used collectively could be built. A peasant did not have the right to leave the village to settle in an older village.

Kautilya ordained:

> From the helplessness of the villages and the exclusive preoccupation of men with their fields stems the growth of revenue for the royal treasury, of the supply of forced labor, grain, oil and other liquid produce.

This then was the strength of the new state. The new tools and ploughshares of iron had made possible a new agricultural organization for the utilization of the vast, uncleared tracts, and the state became the organization of this effort. A state in which everything could be bought and sold, a new state of steel-like force.

Out of the tremendous struggles of the seventh, sixth and fifth centuries B.C.—when the tribes were destroyed and classes fought, that great time when it was a joy to be alive, when studies flourished, spirits awoke and sect philosophers preached the new truths, when a thousand people could provide for themselves where only a short time before a hundred eked out a living, when the plough opened up new land, when cities grew and handicrafts prospered, when new peasants took the noble Eight-fold Path of Buddha and free-thinking caravan-drivers carried cotton, forgings and handicraft products from the city guilds and cottage industry of the villages—out of these centuries of progress and development a new state had evolved. And this state was hard, sleek and cold, like polished granite that became its distinctive artistic feature. This state still defines India, as the Roman empire still defines Europe. A state which dissolved all values into exchange value and jacked up productivity to the highest it could possibly be at that time. The Mauryan empire is still with us.

The Science of Material Gain

Chandragupta's minister and counselor, the man who helped him seize and consolidate power, the *brahman* Chanakya or Vishnugupta, also known as Kautilya, is thought to have written the *Arthasastra: The Science of Material Gain*. Or at least, the author of the *Arthasastra* claims to be Kautilya, Chandragupta's minister and the man who won him his empire. For centuries this work has been a source of knowledge in the art of statecraft. It was only at the beginning of this century, however, that the text became accessible. Since then, its date of publication has been a subject of controversy. The name Kautilya is in itself remarkable. It means deceitfulness. Would Chandragupta's cunning minister really have gone by such a name? But, then, what is it that Odysseus calls himself when he recounts at the court of King Alkinoos his adventure with the Cyclops:

> I am Laërtes' son, Odysseus.
> Men hold me
> formidable for guile in peace and war:
> this fame has gone abroad to the sky's rim.

Why should not Chandragupta's minister, Chanakya, who taught the art of creating material gain by means of cunning, deceit and violence, not proudly call himself Kautilya? The book contains inconsistencies. Kautilya warns about wooden buildings because of the danger of fire. Megasthenes reports that Chandragupta's cities were built of wood and not of brick. There are references to what might possibly be China, while there is no evidence of contact between India and China before the Han dynasty, which only came to power a hundred years after the death of Chandragupta. The book also contains discrepancies in language and text. But there is nothing that cannot be explained by the interpolations and text alterations of the ages. Collation with other texts places the *Arthasastra* at least as far back in time as the fourth century A.D.

In 149 A.D. the area now known as Gujarat in western India was struck by an awesome storm. This caused the destruction of the huge dam King Chandragupta's viceroy, Pushyagupta, had erected above what is today the city of Junagadh. This was the dam from which Yavanaraja Tushaspa, on the orders of his lord Asoka, had dug canals to irrigate the valley. This catastrophe threatened agriculture, and the peasants called on the ruler, the Grand Satrap Rudradarman I for help. At that time, Scythian satraps of the Kushan empire ruled over western India. The Kushan dynasty was established by the Indo-Aryan speaking people whom the Chinese called yüe-chi and who were expelled from what is today Gansu and Sinkiang by the Huns in the first century B.C. Rudradarman I was the Grand Satrap who made his kingdom independent. From the inscription chiselled in the year 150 A.D. on the natural rock to commemorate the reconstruction of the dam and the saving of agriculture, it is clear that Rudradarman I's officials used legal terminology which Kautilya had elaborated on in the *Arthasastra*. From this we may conclude that Rudradarman I followed Kautilya's precepts in seizing power and securing his independence. This means the treatise would have been compiled before the second century A.D.

Still, it is not sure whether Kautilya was, in fact, Chandragupta's minister or whether the author or the *Arthasastra* merely summed up the statecraft of Chandragupta's time. Through the ages, however, Indian opinion has unanimously attributed the authorship to Chandragupta's minister and counselor. This fact is also worth bearing in mind. The science of material gain taught by Kautilya was always associated with the fashioning of the Mauryan empire. It became the guide for all later rulers and for all those who sought power.

The material gain Kautilya describes is not gain for the individual or group. It is gain for the state. It is not the individual citizen but the state which interests Kautilya. The *Arthasastra* is not held in high esteem in Europe. Just think how much more inspiring the teachings of the Greek philosophers are! Yet, if we were to treat Aristotle and Plato in a Christian manner we should "hew down and cast them into the fire." For if it is "by their fruit ye shall know them," then we should know Socrates and Plato by the nobility and social virtue of Alcibiades; and Aristotle by the justness and concern for the citizens' virtue which made Alexander so renowned. But we need not be so Christian. Suffice to say, in the words of D. D. Kosambi, that Plato's *Republic* and Aristotle's *Politics* make excellent reading, but that the *Arthasastra* showed itself in practice to be a brilliant guide to statecraft. There exists no contradiction between the *Arthasastra's* precepts and the policies adopted by Indian rulers towards their subjects from Chandragupta's time down to our day. That is what makes the *Arthasastra* great. It is the first work of political science which accurately describes the new State's method of working, thus lending itself to use as a guide.

Earthly gain—supreme power over all the inhabited world—is the goal of science; virtue, morality, ethics are secondary. They are derived from the task of gaining power. No means need to shunned. The problems of cruelty, deceit, treachery and violence are practical ones. Does cruelty further one's aims at this time? Well, then cruelty is to be recommended. Can a lie be used in this situation? How can treachery be used most effectively? The state sets its own standards of conduct and the furtherance of State Power is its goal. The book's contents can be summed up in different sections:

The education and chastisement of princes. The qualities of a minister. Various kinds of spies. The King's daily business. The duties of superintendents of the various municipal and state departments. How cities are administered and secured. Handicrafts and rules for prostitution. Civil law. The liquidation of dangerous elements and the penal code. Methods of destroying state enemies and filling the state treasury. Salaries for officials. Warfare. How to win wars and gain popularity in occupied lands. How to concoct pathogenic substances; the political art of poison.

It is a guide in statecraft which provides advice equally useful to he who would attain power and he who would consolidate it.

"Princes, like crabs, are father-eaters."

Yet, if rulers come and go, if sons assassinate their fathers to gain power, if brothers kill each other, and if one dynasty is replaced by another, the state lives on. But that state always needs a ruler. He is the supreme authority. It is the ruler who interprets *dharma* and beneath him, a mighty bureaucracy administers the realm. The state regulates and runs everything. Even the brothels are a government monopoly, and the prostitutes state-property. Every port, every pass, every fording-place is guarded and controlled. No one may travel without a passport. A huge body of functionaries regulate everything. They run the state like one big machine for clearing land and gathering taxes. They are salaried according to rank and the range in the pay-scale is large: from 60 *pana* (a silver coin weighing 3.5 grams of silver) to 48,000 *pana* a year. They are watched over by an all-powerful secret police. Spies see all, hear all, report all. (Still, Kautilya complains that it is as difficult to uncover a swindling official as it is to know how much water the swimming fish drink in the river.)

Analogous methods are used towards neighboring states. The *Arthasastra* is the first work which asserts the necessity of spies and espionage in the pursuit of foreign policy. Small states and surrounding independent tribes should be corrupted and driven to disharmony and internal strife by various methods. This will help to make their annexation possible. This land-clearing machine is to grow larger and larger.

For as its base, this society has the regulated, newly-cleared areas. These are villages where the peasantry is worked hard and is not given a chance to develop strong community ties or other relationships. Everything has been turned into liquid assets, including the peasants.

Out of the collapsing tribal society, this new state consists of its myriad functionaries and its unfeeling power politics. It is a new state. When Kautilya compiled his theory, he did not bother to cloak his thoughts—as Plato and Aristotle did—in concepts such as virtue and justice, shaped in an earlier age of the development of the state. There was no *polis* to be found in the past of the Mauryan empire. Its ideology was its reality.

The Mauryan state borrowed certain features from the Persian empire and the Seleucid kingdom. It has, on occasion, been claimed that Seleucus Nicator was Asoka's great-grandfather. But Asoka did not act like a descendant of one of Alexander's generals. He continued instead to strengthen the new, effectively exploitative state established by Chandragupta. The thousand year interregnum between the bronze-age slave societies in the Indus valley, and the developed, new state of the Gangetic valley, prevented an Indian development similar to the classical Mediterranean stagnating slave society of the Greek-Roman variant. This interruption permitted the establishment of a more productive state-apparatus: a slave society based on an ever-greater expanse of newly-cleared land, worked by an atomized and oppressed class of state-tenants.

When Jawaharlal Nehru was in prison in World War II, he made an analysis of Indian history and had this to say about Kautilya:

> He was a much bigger person in every way, greater in intellect and action. . . . Bold and scheming, proud and revengeful, never forgetting a slight, never forgetting purpose, availing himself of every device to delude and defeat the enemy, he sat with the reins of Empire in his hands and looked upon the Emperor more as a loved pupil than as a master. Simple and austere in his life, uninterested in the

pomp and pageantry of high position. . . .

Nehru wrote this while locked up in Ahmadnagar Fort in the spring of 1944. He wrote by hand what is actually a self-portrait, which he then left for his daughter Indira to emulate. He, too, was a *brahman*, capable of coolly observing the world from above.

Yet, although this state of granite-hard necessity had its own further-ance as its goal, and although lofty free spirits such as Kautilya perceived its stark reality, described and administered it, it, too, needed an ideolog-ical veneer. No exploitation-apparatus in the world of men can function long with the nakedness and straightforwardness described by Kautilya. Virtue, justice and ideals are necessary if the apparatus is to run smoothly and not explode; morals, religion and lofty purpose must dis-guise this wretchedness beyond good and evil. Functionaries, armies, and secret police who watch, check and report everything will not suf-fice.

In 256 B.C., the empire was quite extensive. Within its borders there were many different peoples. But no single group, on its own, was able to rebel. State agents pressed further and further into the forests. They sought out the independent tribes in order to divide and disorganize them. They made use of spies, prostitutes, *brahmans*, sorcerers and swin-dlers of various kinds; they used poison, slander, cunning and bribe. When the tribe had been disorganized through internal conflicts and contradictions, the royal troops arrived to establish order. The tribe members were captured, separated and sent away to the remote new ag-ricultural zones. The tribe's land was then cultivated by land-clearing newcomers sent in from elsewhere, while the agents pushed further into the forests. To the west, the empire bordered on the Seleucid empire. That border area was desert and waste. No danger threatened from that direction. To the north, the realm was protected by high mountains. There were independent lands to the far south, but they posed no threat. However, in the east lay the independent kingdom of Kalinga, the area now known as Orissa. It was a rich land. Its people were independent. The realm was ruled after ancient custom. This was intolerable to the Mauryan empire and its young king, Asoka.

As long as a single festering boil of ancient, popular freedom existed between the two seas, the infection could spread into the empire and everything could be destroyed. Asoka was forced to attack the smaller, much weaker, Kalinga. It was done as a precaution. Asoka was obliged to defend the empire against the danger of spiritual infection from Kalinga's antiquated social order. In the war in which Kalinga was subdued, Aso-ka's armies are reported to have killed 100,000 while another 150,000 were carried away as prisoners. Asoka writes that 100,000 more died. India was now unified under one ruler, and the whole country could be administered according to the same science of material gain.

A new ideology was necessary. Asoka made use of Buddhism, just as Constantine, about six centuries later, would make use of Christianity. In official rock inscriptions around the empire—a custom coming perhaps from the Persian empire—Asoka had solemn, moral sermons chiselled. They preached non-violence, mercy and respect for one's elders. But, above all, they proclaimed the duty of one and all to follow the law, *dharma*. Instead of spies and ambassadors, Asoka sent missionaries to spread the word, and in this peaceful manner, he promoted the power of Patna. To make the words more effective, Asoka built up his navy to serve peace. After having inscribed on rock words about the sorrow and regret Asoka felt after all the killing and misery he had caused in conquering Kalinga, the Beloved of the Gods warned the forest people:

> Despite his repentence the Beloved of the Gods proclaims his might unto them to make them desist and escape being killed.

It is not known whether Asoka himself ever converted to Buddhism; but it is of no more interest than knowing whether Constantine the Great ever became a Christian. In any case, he contributed greatly to the developments through which Siddhartha Gautama's ideas and order of like-minded monks evolved into Buddhism. That *dharma* which Asoka spread to the people through missionaries, the *dharma* which he had chiselled into the rocks and pillars around his empire, was not Siddhartha Gautama's *dharma*. It was a convenient moral doctrine for Asoka. The war-drum had, as Asoka said, been replaced by the *dharma*-drum. Tolerance was to reign and keep the state sound.

Here at Bodhgaya, he had the sacred tree transplanted and a throne of highly-polished granite prepared for Buddha. For it was here that not only Siddhartha Gautama, but also all previous bodhisattvas attained enlightenment. Asoka had stupas erected to commemorate the earlier Buddhas. Siddhartha Gautama's speculations had been made into the Path and The Law.

Kautilya was able, with cunning, deceit and violence, to destroy sixteen kingdoms, nobles and kings included, and he did it with cool calculation. This was a statesman beyond good and evil, uninterested in pomp and pageantry, wishing to retire to a life of contemplation with his mission accomplished. Asoka completed the task, but was obliged to drape his undertaking in morality. The historical personage Siddhartha Gautama, dead not two hundred years, disappeared in a cloud of former and future Buddhas. His words rang out in many halls, becoming great sandstone and marble monuments in the places of worship in the new state.

A pillar was erected in Sarnath. Asoka had many such pillars raised. They were of granite, polished until they shone like metal. That hard, smooth surface is the Mauryan epoch's contribution to Indian tradition, though not its only contribution. The pillars were inspired by Persian monuments to power. Asoka was the Emperor. He was so great that he did not mention that he was King of Kings. There were no minor monarchs to rule over. He stood alone. The pillar in Sarnath bears a lion-capital. With those lions, Asoka still sets his mark on India.

The capital in Sarnath is not an imitation of Persian work. It is an original creation. It is Asoka's. On a bell-shaped lotus which symbolizes the world sits a round abacus. But this abacus in Samath is not only there to act as a supporting bottom-slab. It is a symbolic, heavenly circle with the emblems of the four celestial directions: the lion, elephant, bull and horse. Among the animals sits the wheel of the law—*dharma sastra*. On this heavenly circle stands a four-headed lion, looking out over all creation. The lion is symbol of both Buddha and the ruler. The four addorsed lions once bore up the great wheel of the law.

On January 26, 1950, Jawaharlal Nehru, independent India's first prime minister, made Asoka's capital from Sarnath the new State Emblem. But it was slightly modified. The lions do not bear up the wheel of law. They are free and sovereign. They are no longer the symbols of Buddha and authority. They are merely the lions of the ruling power. They stand on the abacus which has become the socle. Right in the middle is the wheel (*chakra*) between the horse and the bull, directly beneath the lion. But it is not the wheel of law. Buddha passed out of India's history a long time ago. It is thirteen hundred years since the gods returned and this is Vishnu's *chakra*, the discus. This, too, is a symbol of power. He who holds Vishnu's *chakra*—*chakravartin*—is the legitimate ruler of all India. The British saw to it that Queen Victoria became *chakravarti*. Beneath this State Emblem appear in the Devanagari script the words from the *brahman* classic *Mundaka Upanishad: Satyameva jayate*—truth alone triumphs.

Stripping it of its Buddhist embellishment, Nehru took from Asoka's capital at Samath, the essence of the Mauryan state's naked claim to power, and placed it in a *brahman*-Hindu setting. This became independent India's State Emblem.

We drive away from Bodhgaya where few—if any—ask after the historical Siddhartha Gautama of the Sakya tribe. On the way up to the old highway, we drive through Gaya. The British retreated from here on July 31, 1857. At that time, agrarian laborers and tenant-farmers from the sur-

rounding countryside stormed the city. They broke into the British court-
rooms and offices where the tax-records were stored. The administration
had fled and the rampaging masses destroyed the instruments used
against them. Records, documents and promissory notes were put to the
torch. British income from the opium harvest was now threatened, and
on August 16 the authorities retook the city. But it would take a long time
and demand a great deal of cunning and adroitness on the part of the
government officials to subdue the people and restore them to submis-
sion so that production could continue.

The Return of the Gods

Small, odd-looking, black mountains poke out of the plain. The old main road runs towards the northwest under a steel-blue sky. The villages are agglomerations of wretchedness. A worn-out land. The landscape has been shaped by men. An old man turns and stares after us as we drive by. His legs are bare and dark. We are driving through very ancient country. Or are we?

This plain was cleared of forest about two thousand, two thousand two hundred, or two thousand four hundred years ago. It was a time when vast areas of forest land were cleared. This is a social landscape. Not just some abstract social landscape, but an Indian social landscape, and India is talked of as extraordinarily ancient. Ancient Indian civilization is spoken and written about in a very particular way. Indian gods, customs and life-style are made into ancient things, well-nigh eternal. Unlike other ancient civilizations with well-worn landscapes, such as the Greek or Italian, this ancient society is lifted right out of history.

When Karl Marx was in London in 1853 writing reports for the *New York Daily Tribune,* he succinctly formulated this popularly-held view:

> Indian society has no history at all, at least no known history. What we call its history, is but the history of the successive intruders who founded their empires on the passive basis of that unresisting and unchanging society.... However changing the political aspect of India's past must appear, its social condition has remained unal-

tered since its remotest antiquity, until the first decennium of the nineteenth century.... English interference has...thus produced the greatest, and, to speak the truth, the only *social* revolution ever heard of in Asia.

On June 2, 1853, Marx had written to Engels about how he had read Bernier who asserted that the king was the sole landowner in his kingdom, and that cities such as Agra and Delhi were nothing but military camps. And after some quotations, Marx sums up:

Bernier rightly considered the basis of all phenomena in the East— he refers to Turkey, Persia, Hindustan—to be the *absence of private property in land*. This is the real key, even to the Oriental heaven.

Engels lost no time in replying. On June 6, 1853, he writes from Manchester:

The absence of property in land is indeed the key to the whole East. Herein lies its political and religious history. But how does it come about that the Orientals did not arrive at landed property, even in its feudal form? I think it is mainly due to the climate.

None the less, Marx's understanding of Asian history was not based solely on his reading of Bernier and his correspondence with Engels in the spring of 1853. Marx also perceived through concepts, and his conception of Asian history came from the two great inspirational traditions which, together with the French Revolution, formed the basis of his thought and activity: German philosophy and English political economy.

Adam Smith noted in *An Inquiry into the Nature and Causes of the Wealth of Nations* that in China, India and other states the revenues of the ruler were in direct and absolute proportion to agricultural yields, so that the rulers were forced to reinvest a portion of the revenues into agriculture in order to maintain those yields. Hence, investments were made to distribute the waters of the Ganga and the other rivers.

Herder deduced world history from the natural prerequisites, and for Hegel, India was not just without history. These realms, like those of the Far East, were characterized by restless changes which never led to progress but only to ever recurring majestic waves of destruction, waves which did not completely destroy but only repeated themselves: a turbulence of events without any lull and direction.

Marx, then, created an ideology out of this. Engels, in his letter of June 6, 1853, had formulated the idea which Marx adopted as his own.

Marx, while working on his reports for the *New York Daily Tribune*, took this idea and developed it. It has become a theory which shapes our views. It is the Asiatic climate in general, with its aridity, which made necessary the huge, centrally-administered irrigation systems. Only thus could agriculture exist. Villages became small, independent, self-governing units slavishly toiling for thousands of years to produce taxes for the despots who regulated the irrigation systems—and never did there appear a spark of revolt or reason to enlighten and illuminate the dull darkness of this peasant toil. No private ownership of land. No feudalism. No change. Instead of good and bad years, there were good and bad regimes.

The peasants carried on their never-changing chores, and, unconcerned about politics and the warring armies, continued to work their fields. Only when the armies destroyed the irrigation systems, causing famine and bad years, did the peasants lift their brows to view the devastation. The editorials of the *New York Daily Tribune* reflected echoes of Megasthenes and of Engels' unfinished, charming, Heine-inspired travel book, *Von Paris nach Genf* (From Paris to Berne) from the fall of 1848, when Engels avoided the police by walking through the lovely French countryside, describing its wines and women, but, above all, struck by the stupidity of the peasants. The opinion expressed in this revolutionary traveller's tale remains his—and Marx's—to the end:

> But the peasant remains a peasant, and his living conditions never for a moment cease to exert their influence. In spite of all the private virtues of the French peasant, in spite of the fact that he lives under more modern conditions than the peasant east of the Rhine, the French peasant, like his German counterpart, remains the barbarian in the midst of civilization.
>
> The isolation of the peasant in a remote village, with a small population, changed only by the march of generations, the arduous, monotonous labor which, more than any serfdom, ties him to the soil and which remains unchanged from father to son, the narrowness of outlook which makes the family the most important and most decisive social relationship—all this reduces the peasants' outlook to the most narrow of limits possible in a modern society. The great historic changes pass him by, sometimes they carry him along, although he has no idea of the nature of its motive force, of its origins, of its goal.

These comments of an intellectual youth in the revolutionary ferment of 1848 constituted the emotional reserve from which Engels could later draw to develop and assimilate commonplace prejudices about the peasant character which he deduced from the necessity of the climate, thus finding the key to the history of the East.

In the *New York Daily Tribune* it was reported how the Indian peasants carried out their never-changing chores and how the immutability of the villages became the basis for despotism. The peasants spent their lives in drudgery and never-ending narrowminded ignorance, worshipping bestial gods in monstrous ceremonies. Their all-suffering docility became their historical crime. For upon their docility, intruder after intruder could establish his despotism and rule out his time. And while the rulers came and went, the emaciated poor peasants ploughed their fields with eyes lowered to the ground.

I cannot understand how Marx could cling to his notions about the Indian climate through the years. When Bernier wrote about the canal system in the Gangetic valley, he was certainly not describing any huge, centrally-administered irrigation system in the desert, and when he wrote about irrigation in India and Egypt, he presented a picture different from that given by Marx:

> As the ground is seldom tilled otherwise than by compulsion, and as no person is found willing and able to repair the ditches and canals for the conveyance of water, it happens that the whole country is badly cultivated and a great part rendered unproductive from the want of irrigation.

This is a description of the irrigation system recognizable by anyone who has travelled in this arid area, stretching from the Mediterranean to the Ganga. Ditches and canals at the local level were controlled by the feudal lord or the village collectivity, depending on the direction of social struggles.

However, Bernier's entire account of an archaic despotism which hinders progress and compels people to bury their valuables, which turned India into the bottomless pit into which all gold and silver disappears, in which the lack of high lords, parliament and presidual courts—as they then existed in France—hindered trade and handicrafts, and in which the welfare of the individual was stifled, is not just another eyewitness report, but a philosophic exposition in support of mercantilism, written to Jean Baptiste Colbert. Mountstuart Elphinstone noted that when Bernier was not reporting his own direct observations, when he summarized and related the accounts of others, his information could be accepted only with caution.

Bernier's letter to Louis XIV's minister of finance about the government of India, the economic conditions, military expenses and administration are, as stated a hundred years later in *Histoire General des Voyages*, enlightening. The English translator of the second English edition, which appeared in 1826, considered Bernier's description of these conditions a source of understanding for the blessings wrought by the British government in India. From reading Bernier, one clearly saw "the mild and beneficent sway of Great Britain."

The conclusion of Bernier's letter to Colbert clearly shows the bias held by this public proclamation:

> Yes, my Lord, to conclude briefly I must repeat it: take away the right of private property in land, and you introduce, as a sure and necessary consequence, tyranny, slavery, injustice, beggary and barbarism: the ground will cease to be cultivated and become a dreary wilderness; in a word, the road will be opened to the ruin of kings and the destruction of nations. It is the hope by which a man is animated, that he shall retain the fruits of his industry, and transmit them to his descendants.

Bernier's letter to Colbert is both a description of India, but also a radical mercantilist manifesto aimed at directing the attention of the minister of finance and the general public to the urgent necessity of coming to grips with the land question, and the abolition in France of feudal obligations and the corvée of the peasantry. Historical documents, too, must be read in their historical context. Marx—the social scientist—taught this!

Whether the theory Marx and Engels worked out in late May and early June 1853, is correct or not, can only be determined through concrete investigations. A Swedish scholar, Erik af Edholm, has shown in a level-headed, straightforward, and overwhelmingly convincing fashion, that the theory of the hydraulic civilization is incorrect. He has examined thoroughly, on the spot, the irrigation system and its history in one of the most pronounced irrigation-cultures: the Kaveri irrigation area in Tamil Nadu. His investigation, which covered a period from the third century B.C. to the present day and included both literary evidence and field studies, shows that:

> only a small fraction of the volume of water of the Indian rivers is used for agriculture. The requirements for water have been largely met by other means: with reservoirs and, especially in modern times, with wells. These are projects which, generally speaking, have not required a central mobilization of resources organized by the national government.

The Kaveri delta is an extreme case. No other major river is used as intensively. However,

the irrigation system in southern India has evolved over a long period and is primarily a result of the initiative and labor of the villagers
themselves.

Erik af Edholm notes that there were exceptions, as when occasional
efforts were made to build large dams and a general effort was made to
promote irrigated agriculture. His findings, however, show that while
the colonial era meant a heavy tax-burden for the peasantry and little opportunity for the upkeep of the irrigation-systems, which resulted in frequent famines, still

> the colonial era from the middle of the nineteenth century caused a
> development of fluvial irrigation-systems through the construction
> of large dams and flood-control projects. Thus, for example, "the
> new delta" was created. (Erik af Edholm, *Vatten och Makt*. Stock-
> holm, 1977)

Here, Edholm provides us with a truly useful key! The British, in fact,
built extensive irrigation works. They dammed up the whole Indus. And
the consequences were not long in manifesting themselves. In Khairpur,
the earth is so water-logged due to the rising sub-soil water that the Muslims can no longer bury their dead. In the heat, the sub-soil water is
drawn by capillary action to the surface, where it evaporates, leaving behind mineral salts in sterile, white surface-layers. Throughout the Punjab, catastrophes as a result of flooding were a common occurrence. The
irrigation canals of the British cut right across the natural run-offs with
their heavy walls and concrete embankments. In the night, the peasants
got together to destroy the canals and to remove the water from the village fields. There does exist an irrigation system organized by the central
authorities, similar to that described by Marx in 1853. It can be established when a strong, oppressive government has broken up and destroyed peasant opposition. The Mughals attempted to build such a
system; their techniques were better than those of the British, who were
only concerned with quick profits and not long-term considerations of
land-management. The British combined this canal-building with a ruthless destruction of agricultural lands. How this was accomplished and
the economic reasoning behind it was explained in 1853—the same year
that Engels and Marx wrote about irrigation techniques. The former editor of *The Ceylon Examiner*, John Capper, who, for his description of the
rise and progress of the British Indian possessions in *The Three Presidencies of India*, referred to vol xii of the *Calcutta Review* on canal construction
in the northwest, wrote:

Upwards of forty years have elapsed since the attention of the British government was first seriously directed towards the restoration of the canals and tanks of their Mahomedan predecessors. Surveys were ordered, reports and estimates were sent in, a few experimental canal-pieces were opened, and it was soon made apparent, that however slow a road might be in replenishing the treasury of the Company, there was no question as to the profit attaching to water-works for purposes of irrigation, and the executive might look to them for results as brilliant as those of any mining operations. Whatever doubts may have existed in the minds of the authorities in the first instance, as to the propriety of undertaking these truly national works, must have long since vanished; and although much false economy was then practised, to the detriment of these operations, they have, in nearly every case, yielded an annual income equal to the whole sum expended upon them.

At the present time the generality of these canals are in admirable order, and no doubt quite equal to their condition under the Tartar emperors. Some idea may be formed of the extent of these works, and the general efficiency of the arrangements, when it is stated, that on one line, that to the west of the Jamuna, there are not less than 214 masonry and timber bridges, 672 stone outlets for irrigation, 11 mills and 23 mill-bridges, besides an infinity of small cuts and outlets for various purposes.

The extent of land receiving irrigation from this one source was, according to official returns, 1,015 square miles; the population benefiting by it nearly 300,000; and the amount of revenue drawn by government from the land so watered was 93,791 pounds sterling annually, nearly all of which was attributable to the use of the stream.

The chief source of direct revenue from these canals is, of course, the water-rent from the villages partaking of the irrigation; and this rent is levied either on the extent irrigated, according to the nature of the cultivation, or by the area of the aperture for feeding the cross channels; these rates vary from two to four shillings per annum per square inch of the opening, and one to ten shillings per acre per annum. Revenue is also derived from the watering of cattle, for the supply of tanks, from mills erected on the canal worked by the stream, from fines and from transit-dues of goods conveyed on them. In 1828-7 the total revenue from all these sources on this one canal amounted to 4215 pounds sterling. In 1846-7 the income was 30,288 pounds, leaving a net revenue of 12,027 pounds.

To this income, however, must be added the known addition to the land-tax, arising from the increased culture by irrigation; and this in the districts now treated of amounted, a few years since, to not less than 29,691 pounds, which, added to the water-rents, etc. 30,288 pounds, bring up the total to nearly 60,000 pounds; being at the rate of thirty-six percent on the capital originally sunk in the work, after deducting the yearly working expenses.

The entire length of this canal and its branches is 445 miles, exclusive of the main water-courses, for feeding the village sluices. This extensive line is under the control of a superintendent, five deputies, and seven overseers, all Europeans; besides about 113 native clerks, overseers, and artificers, who are divided into separate districts or *zillahs;* and have their regular functions of police, revenue, or labor to perform. In addition to their canal duties, they have also charge of extensive plantations of building trees planted along the banks; and from the sale of the timber thus grown a yearly revenue of fifty per cent on the outlay is derived.

Thus, there are irrigation systems and irrigation systems. It is not the climate, but the class struggle, which determines which system is built.

In the Kaveri delta in South India, Erik af Edholm shows how the state power during the Chola period rested on the feudal support of the local elite groups, and how it allowed them to develop irrigated agriculture. During the Vijayanagara period, when the soil, too, was taken over by the centralized state power based on its military leaders, larger irrigation works were constructed. The soil was then, as in the Mughal empire to the north, formally in the possession of the ruler. Finally, under British rule, the irrigation system was centrally planned and developed, and the local systems decayed with famine as a result.

What Marx and Engels thought to be eternal and ancient, proved to be temporary and new. The social struggle which made possible the establishment of a strong central state bureaucracy on a feudal foundation was able to develop an irrigation system which increased the exploitation of the peasantry to the limit. And the same system engendered forces for such tremendous uprisings as that of 1857 or for the constant peasant rebellions which marked the history of British rule in India, and which, even today, are the motive forces behind the great movement of history!

It should be said that Marx had not read extensively—or especially attentively, for that matter—about India, when he put together his reports for the *New York Daily Tribune* in 1853. Indeed, any old reference-bookworm could prove this today by simply spending a few days in a library, digging into Marx's sources. (Unfortunately, Lenin did quite the opposite when going through the Marx-Engels correspondence. He seized on their remark that the very key to the history of the East is the lack of the right to own property inland.)

Actually, it is not odd that Marx was mistaken. With some effort and a good library anybody can prove how utterly mistaken I am now, how I, too, read with ideologically-tinted glasses. Any text can be pulled apart. Nevertheless, it is unlikely that I will suffer the wretchedness of my works becoming an ideology or that my texts will come spooking about word for word after more than a century. Marx lived long enough to curse the fate of leaving "Marxists" behind him, and Engels long enough to swear about the existence of "raisin shitters" who quoted his letters word for word, unable to distinguish between well-considered texts and casual remarks. More important than establishing the fact that in 1853 Marx had no solid grounds, not even in the works he had read, to support his grand theory, is the reminder that in 1880, when Marx read up on India's history at Mountstuart Elphinstone's and wrote his chronology of East India (for use as a reference for planned, but never completed, works), it was still quite possible to subscribe to the commonplace view of India's history as being "a history without a history." This chronology covers a period from 664 A.D. (forty-four years after the Hegira, as Marx noted) when General Muhallab of Kabul attacked Multan, until August 2, 1858, when:

> Lord Stanley's India Bill [was] passed, and thereby finis of the East India Co. India [became] a province of the empire of the "great" Victoria!

The *Arthasastra* was yet to be published. Forty-two years would elapse before the first remarkable finds from India's great and advanced bronze-age civilization at Mohenjodaro and other Indus valley cities would be discovered and India's history totally re-evaluated. Asoka was still only a shadow-like, legendary emperor, a character in Buddhist narratives. In 1834, some letters in his inscriptions had been deciphered; in 1837 the first text read, but Marx expressed the commonly-held opinion of educated Europe when he, in a parenthesis, wrote:

> (The kingdom of Magadha was a most interesting one. Its Buddhist kings wielded extensive power; they belonged for many years to the *kshatriya* caste, until one of the *sudra* caste—the fourth and lowest of Manu's four castes—named *Chandragupta*—called Sandrocottus by the Greeks—murdered the King and made himself sovereign; he lived in Alexander Magnus' time.)

These notes on Indian history cover one hundred and seventy-two printed pages. Three and a half pages deal with the whole period up to 644 A.D. Three and a half pages are spent on the European traders in In-

dia before 1725. Sixty-three pages are allotted to Indian history from 644
to 1725. One hundred and two pages describe the activities of the East
India Company in India. Such were the proportions of that era's conception of the world and view of history!

All the same, Marx was an anti-imperialist. He condemned English
barbarism in India, as well as in Ireland. There can be no doubt that he
found British colonial rule loathsome and atrocious. But a man can no
more leap out of his time than jump over his shadow. Marx, too, saw
things with the concepts of his time. In an exchange of letters with
Engels in March 1868 on the subject of the legal historian von Maurer's
writings on the history of German land-ownership, Marx notes on
March 25, 1868:

> Human history is like palaeontology. Owing to a certain judicial
> blindness even the best intelligences absolutely fail to see the
> things which lie in front of their noses. Later, when the moment
> has arrived, we are surprised to find traces everywhere of what we
> failed to see. . . . To show how much we are all implicated in this ju-
> dicial blindness: right in *my own* neighborhood, on the *Hunsrücken,*
> the old Germanic system survived up till *the last few years.* I now re-
> member my father talking to me about it from a lawyer's point of
> view.

This antiquated and ancient civilization we visit is neither especially
antiquated nor ancient. It is, in fact, questionable whether it was Islam or
Hinduism which first came to India: Hinduism, the *brahman* doctrines,
the caste system, the villages thought so ancient, and all the customs
which the *brahmans* readily declare to be as old as the hills, are, in fact,
contemporary with Charles Martel; or with Saint Benedict in Europe; or
the Indian Buddhist missionary Padma Sambava who in Tibet fused
Buddhism with traditional beliefs into Lamaism. It is the time of the
Prophet! An age of great religious and social transformation, but hardly
ancient times!

Hinduism certainly does include ancient features which can be linked
with finds from the bronze-age cities of the Indus valley. Other features
can be traced to the Aryans. In a cave painting from the ninth century
B.C., a time when the Aryans were descending towards the Gangetic
valley, a man stands in a war chariot and throws a discus, a *chakra.* That
cave is located in Mirzapur where we passed on the road to Patna. That
discus now sits in the State Emblem.

However, Hinduism's thousands-of-years-old features can, in fact, be
explained like the horns on Michelangelo's Moses in the Julian monument at San Pietro in Vincoli, Rome. Michelangelo started from the

Vulgate's correct translation of how Moses looked when he descended from Mt. Sinai: he was horned—cornuto—and did not just have, as our more modest and dainty Bible translation would have us believe, shining skin. (Exodus 34, 29-35) However, even Michelangelo failed to show Moses descending in the bull-mask after having worshipped the bull god, the god of the new moon, the mountain god. Nonetheless, the distance between the demon, what Archbishop Söderblom called "mountain goblin," and the God of the Christian churches or Jewish synagogues is no greater than that between the discus thrower in Mirzapur and today's Vishnu. The passage from Mohenjodaro is even longer. I carry in my pocket a copy of a seal from Mohenjodaro. The inscription has not been deciphered. But the seal shows a three-faced god as a yogi with his feet drawn up. Perhaps he wears a horned mask. Other seals suggest this is the case. I believe that what I have in my pocket is an early image of Shiva, but even further removed from modern Hinduism than the horned, bull-priest Moses is from today's Baptists.

The Mauryan kingdom where Asoka made Buddhism the State Religion broke apart. Its disintegration followed on the heels, indeed was a part of, its greatness. In 232 B.C., Asoka died. The empire was divided and torn to pieces. The last Mauryan ruler was assassinated by his *brahman* General Pushyamitra Shunga in 180 B.C. (184 B.C.?) In the eastern remnant of the Mauryan kingdom, a new dynasty came to power—the Shun dynasty. The western portions of the empire had already become independent; the Bactrian Greeks advanced in the north-west, and to the south the Andhra dynasty expanded across the Deccan. The mighty Mauryan dynasty was not able to survive its own establishment, and India sank into a morass of warring minor states.

The attempt at organizing agriculture into a rational exploitative apparatus, with the aid of an enormous and constantly expanding bureaucracy, failed. The economy collapsed. When the silver did not suffice for the payment of government salaries—in this state founded on the principle that all services and commodities were liquid and convertible into cash—the state first tried to hide the problem with counterfeit money. Then the cash-principle was abandoned and feudal lords evolved out of the Mauryan bureaucracy. At the same time, the enormous cutting down of forest areas led to catastrophic flooding, and what was supposed to create wealth, instead caused destitution and impoverishment.

The rock inscriptions tell how, in about the first century, the Satavahana rulers in the south enfeoffed the priests with villages. The earliest inscriptions suggest exemption from land-tax, but later inscriptions from the rule of Gautamiputra Satakarni around 125 A.D. suggest a transformation. Not only did they provide exemption from taxes, but the royal officials lost the right to interfere with the administration of these areas.

The central power fell apart, the bureaucracy shrank and, even though Gautamiputra Satakarni was a mighty commander and regent who defeated the Scythians, Bactrian Greeks and Parthians, he lived long enough to see his western possessions lost to Rudradarman—the same Rudradarman to whom the inscription at Junagarh is dedicated.

Agriculture was transformed. Besides the enfeoffed villages, and out of them, rose an independent peasantry. The great law-giver of that time was Manu; not some ancient Manu from the *Rigveda* but the real-life, historical figure who, around the first century A.D., compiled the *Manusmrti* (Manu's laws). This was a man knowledgeable in the law, a contemporary of Julianus Salvius of North Africa, who, in Rome, laid the foundation of Roman law by carefully compiling praetorial edicts. Manu laid down that the field belonged to him who cleared it from the forest; the hind to him who first shot it. The fall of the centralized state was a liberation which opened up new opportunities. (But slavery remained!)

Trade and handicraft production for export continued to expand. Indian traders travelled the Silk Road to China. In the fifth decennium of our epoch, the Greek mariner Hippalus had mastered the art of crossing the seas with the monsoon winds, thus freeing shipping from the protective coasts. Both sea and wind were named in his honor. Merchants from Alexandria, shippers from Arabia and seafarers from distant lands mingled in the coastal cities. The guilds grew stronger. They now played the role of bankers. In Muttra, capital was invested in the millers' guild; the guild made additions to its production apparatus and paid monthly interest on the capital. It was enough to support a hundred *brahmans*. The guilds became powerful enough to mint their own coin.

When the empire was re-established several centuries later by Chandragupta I in 319 A. D., it was a totally different society from the kingdom which had fallen five hundred years before. Chandragupta himself bore a splendid title: *Maharajadhiraja*. This, however, only shows that he pretended to be the great supreme sovereign over all kings, not that he was quite simply the king. The villages were now given in perpetual enfeoffment with all rights and privileges. The monasteries became wealthy feudal institutions. Outright slavery still existed, but the laws of the time mention only house slaves. All the same, the peasantry was bound to the land. The Gupta period was the time of emerging feudalism and serfdom. The independent peasantry sank into servitude. It was no longer the lot of only slaves and bonded laborers to perform unpaid labor: the whole village was organized to carry out unpaid service for the lord, and while new fees and duties burdened the people, the life of the gentry became even more agreeable. The artistically-appreciative and cultured gentleman of the Gupta period made gracious living an art, and just as his inferiors had to provide him with services and produce in kind, so too did they have to satisfy his thirst for pleasure. As early as the third century A. D., the grammarian Patanjali had noted that the serving-girl and *sudra* woman were created to provide for the pleasure of those above. Five or six generations later, Vatsyayana taught through the *Kamasutra* how the man who had become rich by receiving religious offerings, through war or trade, could make use of the available women. The custom whereby the women of the lord were cremated on his funeral pyre—a custom truly belonging to the ancient past—began to be revived and defended by lawmakers and interpreters of the law. The first monument commemorating a suttee is to be found in Eran in Madhya Pradesh, dated 510 A. D.

This period also marked the decline and fall of Buddhism. For a thousand years it had been, in one form or another, society's pre-eminent ideology, but the Chinese travellers now reported that the religion was on the ebb. The monastery at Nalanda was only a shadow of its past. Its monks and sages were divided into ranks; the rich monasteries had become feudal institutions. But the new economy could no longer bear up this vast religious establishment. The Chinese noted that not much money changed hands in India. Instead, barter was now common. The entire monastery system established during the Empire and carried on in the form of large, independent feudalities, now had difficulties supporting itself. At a time when royal armies wandered through the countryside, draining resources, the new feudal classes were in conflict with the monasteries. Buddhism was no longer profitable and its time was past. In marched the gods.

The old *varna* system with its four social groups was now developed into a strict caste system with hereditary social roles. It was during these centuries that the Indian village began to take on its traditional feudal form. The complex rules of caste acted as a safeguard for society against revolts and rebellion. Untouchability was enclosed in extensive purification rites. Poverty was unclean. At the same time, the entire superstructure was transformed. The ancient fertility-myths of the people were merged with the newly ascendant gods. Lingam and yoni now became accepted religious symbols. Instead of the large monasteries, it was the local *brahman* who was the go-between to the supernatural. He also regulated agriculture and decided when to sow and plough in accordance with his knowledge of astronomy and astrology. Animals were no longer sacrificed to the gods, as in Vedic times, nor were great ceremonies held as in the Buddhist monasteries. Religious devotion, *bhakti*, and the individual's support of the *brahman*, were cheaper and more suitable expressions of religious practice.

Temples were now built all over India. The sovereigns made use of the newly-awakened gods in their various apparitions. Buddha became one

of Vishnu's avatars. All of them, including Siddhartha Gautama and the
Black Krishna of the tribal peoples, were incorporated into the new pantheon. Hindu India came into existence around the seventh century
A. D. India's step from antiquity into its Middle Ages came at the time
when Caliph Umar's general raided India in the year 644. Feudalism had
triumphed and a hundred years had elapsed since the last emperor of
the Gupta dynasty had faded out of history. The last attempt at establishing a kingdom of the old sort came to nothing with Harsa-vardhana's
death in 647. The political map of feudal India, like its European counter-
part, was unstable and changing, its realms, states and kings in constantly shifting alliance.

There is, of course, a difference between European and Indian feudalism. But the difference is not that marked. The kings enfeoffed villages
and entire districts, and he who took the enfeoffment could tax and administer it himself—but he was obliged to assist his feudal lord with
troops and money. The King's forces were made up of the troops of his
vassals. From the Gupta period onwards, serfdom had developed into its
specifically Indian variant—still prevalent in large parts of the country.
The feudal lords had more than mere economic power over the villagers:
the law gave him the right to punish and pass judgement. The way out of
this wretchedness was not much longer for the Indian peasant than it
was for the French villain. Neither were the Indian villages more tranquil
than the French. In India, as in contemporary Europe, the entire society
was born out of the arduous toil of the poor peasants and craftsmen. The
sweat from their brows became cities, temples, royal military expeditions
and gracious living. And literature, music, and religion as well. The unclean, sweaty, evil-smelling (Vatsyayana noted that a gentleman should
avoid physical activity and exposure to the heat of the sun) common folk
could only be held down with customs, gods and physical violence. The
Indian caste system proved to be rather more effective than the European
attempt at ideologizing society by setting forth the "natural" functions of
the various estates. Still, if the people rose in protest, the lords killed
them in both societies.

Asoka's attempt at creating the Strong State had not been forgotten.
The lords sat in their palaces, studying the use of treachery and espionage to increase their power. However, the splintered, feudal holdings
they had inherited or captured could not provide them with enough of a
base to rally the force needed for the establishment of an empire.

The Road From Sasaram

We came to Sasaram to see Sher Shah's mausoleum. Or on account of the Indian State. The mausoleum is remarkable. The architect, Aliwal Khan, directed its construction in the sixteenth century for Sher Shah Sur. This Aliwal Khan had learned his craft in Delhi under the sultanate. Here in Sasaram, on the old royal road through North India, lies the most perfect of all the sultanate's monumental edifices.

During his lifetime, Sher Shah Sur fought against Humayun for power over North India. He died at a time when his establishing a dynasty had been a direct possibility. As for the buildings he had constructed, Sher Shah thought that they should be adorned "with such architectural embellishments that friend and foe might render their tribute of applause."

The mausoleum rises out of an excavated tank, the size of a small lake. Originally, the tank was 366 meters by 290 meters. It has silted up and at present extends over an area 340 by 244 meters. But the architectural unity of the mirror of water and the mausoleum's mighty form remains unbroken. From a 74 square meter terrace, the building rises 46 meters. Since nothing—except God—is perfect, this base is not totally aligned with the cardinal points: it is displaced 8°. On this base, with steps leading down into the water, stands, correctly aligned, a foundation, 66 by 65 meters and 7 meters high. These minute, and, for the human eye, subliminal deviations from equilateral perfection provide visual tension and life.

Up on the high terrace stands the grave itself. Above the sepulchral chamber rises the great cupola. It forms a compact, complete totality mirrored in the water. The cupola was once white, with a golden crown, and the heavy sandstone from Chunar was adorned with tile and large geometric designs in red, blue, yellow and white.

I gaze at the building which is mirrored in the water, its structure and its reflection. There was some controversy about whether the embankments of the tank should have been lined with trees. That is Buchanan's opinion when he wrote about the mausoleum, one hundred and seventy years ago. I am not sure. The nakedness makes the building stand out so much more clearly. From the north, a causeway crosses the water, over to the sepulchral island of stone. There used to be a bridge here. But it had already collapsed by 1880. Perhaps Aliwal Khan and Sher Shah had first planned that the grave should only be reached by boat. The landing place suggests this. If this is so, then the land connection which breaks the isolation of the tomb was added during construction.

Sher Shah's grave is situated directly beneath the cupola. The chamber rises 30 meters above him. This is one of the larger cupolas in India, its inner diameter measuring 21.8 meters. Around Sher Shah lie twenty-four of his attendants and officers. The mihrab was once adorned with verses from the Koran. Today, all that remains is a tile or two and well-cut stone.

Leaving the cool tomb chamber, the passage from the room's vast and exalting space out to the heavy stone of the exterior makes for a striking architectural experience. Later, when the whole tremendous building rises out of the water and is reflected in it, I think of Sher Shah Sur's words:

> And may my name be honored on earth until the day of judgement. None of these aspirations has God allowed me to carry into effect, and I shall carry my regrets with me to my grave.

No doubt Aliwal Khan and Sher Shah Sur (who gave the master-builder Aliwal Khan the task of joining the still mass with its glittering, light reflection) will be honored and remembered as long as the building in Sasaram stands.

However, Sher Shah Sur is also important as a statesman. He could have been the founder of the State. Humayun, with whom he fought, was an intruder of a dynasty which had ruled but fourteen years. Babur's expedition might have been no more than a raid into India, and Sher Shah Sur might have become the first emperor of the mighty Sur dynasty.

He died on May 22, 1545, in his seventy-fourth year, during the siege of the rock-fortress at Kalinjar. While he was inspecting the batteries, a powder keg was hit by an enemy shot, and Sher Shah Sur was so severely burnt that he died that evening. By that time, the fortress had been taken, and on hearing this he commended his soul to the Almighty and passed away. He had been emperor of (northern) India since 1539. His descendants ruled with varying degrees of fortune and mutual assassination until 1557. He considered himself a member of the Ghoridian line. His grandfather had come to India seeking his fortune as a soldier. His father was *jagirdar* of Sasaram. This meant that he held Sasaram as his *jagir* and was obliged to field a cavalry of five hundred men.

He was given the name Farid at birth. Sher Shah was his title—Lion King or Tiger King. He was his father's eldest son. But his father had four wives and eight sons and disliked Farid, who left him to join his father's patron Jamal Khan. This lord was captivated by the young Farid, who was not only well-skilled in the use of weapons, but was also widely read, with a deep love of poetry. Jamal Khan ordered Hassan, Farid's father, to make Farid the administrator of Sasaram *jagir*. Farid held that position for twenty-one years. Meanwhile, one of his step-mothers succeeded in conspiring against him, and he was banished. Farid went to Sultan Ibrahim Lodi and demanded his rights, so that on the death of his father, the Sultan turned Sasaram *jagir* over again to Farid. However, his step-brother sought support for his cause with Mohammad Khan Sur of Bihar, and Farid went into the service of Bahar Khan Lohni, the ruler of southern Bihar. It was this ruler who conferred on him the title "Sher Khan," Tiger Prince, after he had gone through the traditional Indian rite of manhood—killing a tiger in single-handed combat. After decades of changing fortune, serving others and as his own master, Sher Khan defeated the Mughal Humayun in 1539 with cunning and military skill, adopted the title Sher Shah as the King of Bihar and Bengal, and became the Sultan of Delhi, ruler of India.

He was an extremely capable general. He was a wise politician, merciful and just when necessary. He sought understanding between Hindus and Muslims, and it was all with the good of the state in mind. He could show magnanimity towards a mortal foe such as Humayun. He treated Humayun's wife and harem with deference and respect, an act which brought him honor among men. But he could also prove himself to be vengefully brutal if the situation called for it. When Sher Shah moved from Mandu against Raisin to capture the fortress and crush Pooran Mal, he was motivated by political necessity—he could not suffer the existence of strongholds within his realm in the hands of others. However, the move was also expedient with regard to religion: Pooran Mal oppressed Muslims and enslaved their womenfolk. When Pooran Mal surrendered, he and his men were massacred; his daughter sold to itinerant minstrels to dance in the bazaars of India and satisfy the lust of men; and his three nephews, who were captured alive, had their testicles crushed and became eunuchs, so that the family line might be extinguished. This put fear into the hearts of the princes: the very reason Sher Shah had it done.

Sher Shah was a ruler like many others in India and Europe at that time. We could name similar sovereigns from Italy or Germany. But Sher Shah was more than a brilliant monarch at a time when the Middle Ages were giving way to modern times. He was a nation-builder, not unlike his contemporaries, Gustav Vasa in Sweden, Henry VIII in England and Suleiman "the Law-Giver" in Turkey. His dynasty was short-lived. His placement between Humayun and Akbar in the list of sovereigns is somewhat problematic. Jawaharlal Nehru describes him as "the ablest among the Afghan rulers. He laid the foundation of a revenue system which was later to be expanded by Akbar."

But Sher Shah was more than this. He shaped the state which Jawaharlal Nehru would take over from the British, four hundred years later. The contributions of Sher Shah were lasting, like those of Gustav Vasa.

The centuries preceding Sher Shah's government reform had been revolutionary. Out of the feudal patchwork, a realm was taking shape. It was the Muslim rulers who served as catalysts for this process. But a social revolution was also in progress across India. Agricultural productivity had risen. Although the major portion of cultivated land was still dependent on the monsoon rains, a growing amount of land was artificially irrigated. The water-wheel had been introduced and in some places the number of harvests had risen from two to three per annum.

The new contacts—the re-established contacts—with the West resulted in an upswing in trade and handicraft production. The craftsman caste began to seek more power and influence. They upset the feudal system. Bazaars multiplied. Cities grew richer. The coin of the Delhi Suitanate found its way along the trade routes towards Europe. At a time when Indian silk and cotton were exported, and domestic trade increased, the land-tax was still generally paid in kind.

While feudal relations between the villagers and the feudal lords remained pretty much unchanged, the new state power took over large tracts of land from those feudal barons who had resisted it and who had been destroyed. This state-owned land was then used partly to pay the cost of government—the ruler now had his own army, independent of his feudal vassals—and partly to be parcelled out in the form of time-bound enfeoffments (such as the Sasaram *jagir* held by Sher Shah's father).

The strong, centralized state apparatus could again begin to take shape, and out of the myriad small feudal principalities, India again began to be forged. A standing army developed side by side with generals, governors and officials who could be appointed and discharged in accordance with the will of the central authority. The thoughts and ideas which formed the basic philosophy used by the sultans to perceive, and, thus, manipulate, the society around them, came partly from Muslim tradition (itself influenced by Persian, Roman, Arabic and Turkish political doctrine), and partly from the tradition surviving from the time of the Mauryan kingdom and Kautilya's *Arthasastra*. The Indian village was still marked to some extent by the brutally thorough-going reforms carried out under the direction of Chandragupta, Bindusara and Asoka. These reforms had been subverted due to their own internal contradictions and had formed the basis of the caste-dominated Indian feudal village. A great deal still remained, though, to form a foundation on which the sultans could build.

But the State which began to be established in the thirteenth century was still lacking in form—like its European counterparts. The feudal lords controlled the city markets and caravan trade. They could set prices and levy taxes. The struggle against these lords was organized in the cities along caste lines. The merchant castes were run democratically, like guilds, and the struggle of the castes was analogous to the struggle of the Third Estate in Europe. But, as in Europe, the struggle between the army of the central power and the forces of the robber barons was carried on at the people's expense.

The feudal lords dominated the country from their strongholds. These fortresses perched, dark and impenetrable, on cliffs and peaks all over western and central India. Standing in one of these fortresses, gazing down over the city, one can hear the murmur of the voices below. The voices of the bazaar rise like a sharp and clear muttering of the people. It was necessary for the sultans to either crush the robber barons, or neutralize them by making them allies and, in time, vassals.

The central power was generous, brutal and unpredictable. Ibn Battuta, the great Moroccan traveller and writer, came to Delhi in 1341. He served Muhammad bin Tughlaq and survived, leaving India as his ambassador to China. He wrote of the Sultan:

> The king is of all men the fondest of making gifts and of shedding blood. His gate is never without some poor man enriched or some living man executed, and stories are current amongst the people of his generosity and courage and of his cruelty and violence towards criminals. For all that, he is of all men the most humble and the readiest to show equity and justice.

He was also one of the most cultivated and learned men ever to rule in

Delhi. He had come to power by having an accident take the life of his father during the latter's entry into Delhi following the defeat of Bengal. Muhammad bin Tughlaq was a philosopher-king, a patron of the arts and sciences, a free thinker who pushed aside the priests and experimented with a new tax system and a new economic policy in order to be able to carry out his plans.

He put down rebellions in the Deccan and Multan, conquered Warangal and other domains, and established the authority of the Sultanate over almost all of India. To pay for his campaigns, he did away with the gold standard and issued his own coinage. It might be said that it was he who first flooded the market with cheap money. His new currency met with strong resistance; it was easy to counterfeit and the result was great economic turmoil in the realm. To fill his coffers, he decided to conquer Persia, and for this purpose assembled a huge army: a cavalry of 370,000 men, according to the chronicler. But before the campaign began, he ran out of money. He could not pay his men, and the soldiers refused to fight for promises. The army disintegrated and the horsemen spread out across the realm in search of loot. It is said that he then decided to conquer China with its boundless wealth, and so sent a 100,000 man army over the Himalayas. That the Indian forces really met a Chinese army is highly doubtful; but as Elphinstone writes:

> When the passage was effected, the Indians found a powerful Chinese army assembled on the frontier, with which theirs, reduced in numbers, and exhausted by fatigue, was unable to cope. Their provisions likewise failed; and the approach of the rainy season did not admit of a moment's delay in falling back.
>
> During their retreat they were harassed by the mountaineers, slaughtered by the pursuing enemy, and worn out by famine. The Chinese were at last checked by the torrents of rain which began to fall, and the Indians, in time, made their way through the mountains; but they now found the low country inundated, and the hills covered with impervious jungle. So terrible were the calamities of their retreat, that at the end of fifteen days scarcely a man was left to tell the tale; and many of those who had been left behind in garrisons, as the army advanced, were put to death by the king, as if they had contributed to the failure of this ill-starred expedition.

Because taxes to cover state expenses grew even more after this, the peasants revolted in many areas against the tax-gatherers. In some places the villages were abandoned and people fled into the jungles. Several cities were also abandoned. Tax revenues fell even further.

Muhammad bin Tughlaq then decided to punish the refractory peas-

antry using exemplary counter measures which would not soon be forgotten. He ordered his entire army into the field. They surrounded one
district after another. The action was planned like a large-scale battle.
The soldiers advanced in a cordon while the drivers scared the game out
of hiding. Everyone found was put to death. This took place in province
after province and the peasantry was beaten down. The cities, too, were
punished in this exemplary fashion. One of these cities was Kanauj, just
south of Aligarh. The result was that the country became even more impoverished and agriculture was ruined in large areas. With the people
dead, the fields lay fallow. No taxes could be collected by the tax-
gatherers. Province after province rose against the Sultan. Governors
and generals attempted to save their fiefdoms, while famine spread. In
1351, Muhammad bin Tughlaq passed away quietly from a fever contracted in the midst of a campaign against the rebels in Sind.

The concentration of power which this new feudal-based bureaucratic
state made possible was despotically and irrationally used by transient
sultans: the instrument was not yet perfected. It oppressed and drove
the peasantry to rebel, and repeated peasant rebellions shook India.
Among the most important was the uprising in Punjab during the time
of Sultan Khizr Khan Sayyid. This ruler, formerly Timur's governor in
Multan, captured Delhi in 1414 from the last Tughlaq. For seven years he
ruled over a Sultanate consisting only of Delhi and the Punjab, in an India once more divided in feudal disunity.

The peasantry in the Punjab had risen against the feudal lords under
the leadership of Sareng. The peasant army was defeated at Sirhing, but
Sareng gathered a new force against the lords. In the end however, the
Sultan's army defeated the peasants. Sareng was captured, taken to
Delhi and executed.

At this time, both in the north and the south, kingdoms which established bureaucratic state power of a new type came into existence. But
Sher Shah's great historical achievement was that out of this emerging
state apparatus, he formed an effective, regulated bureaucratic state
which then lived on under the Mughals, was adopted and transformed
by the British, and which still rules India today, in Sasaram as well as in
Delhi. The fact that he and his dynasty disappeared is of little importance. The individuals he appointed as officials continued to serve under
his successor, Akbar. And the positions still remain. Jawaharlal Nehru
should have shown a little more respect for the predecessor who shaped
the state he inherited in 1947.

What then was Sher Shah's achievement? He had fought his way up
from *jagirdar* to sultan. In the interest of the State, that road had to be
closed. The *jagirdars* were watched closely. They were compelled to
maintain a fixed number of horsemen. The number of horses was

checked and the animals branded so that no *jagirdar* could cheat. The troops had to be in readiness at all times; the *jagirdar's* horsemen could no longer be made up of temporary recruits.

An effective police corps maintained law and order, and also saw to it that the local zamindars remained in constant fear of the sultan. The zamindars were answerable—with their lives if necessary—for the safety of travellers. Abbas Sarwani wrote:

> Travellers and way-farers during the time of Sher Shah's reign were relieved from the trouble of keeping watch, nor did they fear to be robbed in the midst of a desert. They encamped at night at every place, desert or inhabited, without any fear; they placed their goods and property on the plain and turned out their mules to graze and they slept with minds at ease and free from care as if in their own houses, and the zamindars, for fear any mischief should occur to the travellers and that they should suffer to be arrested on account of it, kept watch over them.

Sher Shah's economic reforms have proved long-lived. It was he who established the rupee as the legal tender and fixed its weight. He lowered duties on trade, simplified the lives of merchants, improved roads and way-stations, and established new markets.

However, it is as an organizer of taxation that he made a decisive contribution. So far, the land had not been properly surveyed for taxation purposes. Only estimates had been made. Sher Shah ordered the first land revenue survey. The State share was set at one-third of the harvest. Payment could be made in coin or in kind. It was Sher Shah's opinion that the leniency that should characterize a benevolent rule should manifest itself in the assessment of taxes, and not in their collection—the latter had to be carried out scrupulously so that corruption would not develop. Tax rates were such that those who had good land and good yields paid proportionately less than those owning bad or mediocre land; this meant that the tax system had a tendency to stimulate production. Since agriculture was the ground on which the state stood, the army had orders not to damage any harvest. If, in fact, it did harm some crop, the state was bound to compensate the landowner. It is out of this tax system of Sher Shah's that the Mughal, British and present-day Indian State has evolved.

As for the administration, Sher Shah organized it along regulated, bureaucratic lines. It was he who introduced the system of provinces under civilian, bureaucratic administration. As in his army, promotion was based on competence. All were to be equal under the law. Muslims were tried for civil cases by their own courts and Hindus by caste courts, their panchayat. But criminal cases were tried the same way regardless of religion or social standing. A criminal case which became famous involved the governor of Malva, who had withheld the pay of 2,000 soldiers. Although he did, eventually, pay the money, he was punished—as was said in the bazaar, "as much a governor and as famous as he was." And this is just what Sher Shah wished to be said in the bazaar!

Out of the capricious, but strong despotism made possible by late feudalism, Sher Shah created, through his reforms, an effective, regulated state apparatus he could leave to his successors. It was also a government apparatus which took the most severe and effective measures against any attempt on the part of the taxed peasants—or the *jagirdar's* peasants—to rebel or protest.

Sher Shah divided his realm into tax districts, and then the *jagir* areas where the revenue was paid to the *jagirdar*. The tax-gathering administration he set up in these districts survives to this day. Akbar strengthened the power of the state when he abolished the *jagir* system in 1575, thus subjecting the entire realm to Sher Shah's unified tax system. Akbar also saw to it that the hemp ropes previously used by Sher Shah's surveyors to determine the amount of taxable land were replaced with iron chains. These could not be stretched. However, he retained the *jagirdars* in order to play one off against the other.

The British established their tax-gathering district in 1750 when the East India Company took control of Sutanati, Govindpur and Calcutta. The Mughal's powerful *karori-faujdar* became the British collector. His duties changed over the years. At times the collector—the tax-gatherer—was also judge and chief of police: he played the part of magistrate. In 1793, these duties were split up and a district judge was appointed along with the district collector. But, as early as 1821, the tax-gathering officials were once again judges. Lord Canning followed Sher Shah's principles when he remarked on February 18, 1857:

> As regards the people, the patriarchal form of Government was the most congenial to them, and the best understood by them—and as regards the governing power, the concentration of all responsibility upon one officer cannot fail to keep his attention alive, and to stimulate his energy in every department to the utmost, while it will preclude the growth of those obstructions to good Government which are apt to spring up where two co-ordinate officers divided the authority.

Lord Stanley, Secretary of State for India, endorsed the proposal on April 14, 1859 (the great uprising had only strengthened the need for patriarchal autocracy) and so the system was established in which the role of tax-collector, magistrate and chief of police were combined. This created powerful men who ruled over districts equal in size to the smaller countries of Europe. They formed the steel framework of British administration. This was adopted by Nehru. However, he completed the work of Sher Shah and Akbar by doing away with the princes—the maharajas.

We drive out of Sasaram towards the north, in the direction of Patna. We drive along the narrow-gauge railroad track running from Sasaram to Arrah. Or perhaps it would be more correct to say that we do not drive along it, since it no longer exists. Here and there the rails have been pulled up and carried away. The small railroad stations stand empty and in disrepair. Shacks have already begun to appear on the embankment. Rusty locomotives stand abandoned beside leaky railroad cars. The railroad was a connection between two trunk lines: one over Patna and the other over Sasaram-Gaya. But it was also a tram-line serving the local villages.

"Why is the railroad gone? No one, of course, wanted to pay the fare and the conductors could not force them," says Ashok. He is a reporter from Patna.

"No existing official power was strong enough to protect the railroad."

When the British left, people just stopped paying fares. The line was losing money. So why not shut it down? The politicians had other interests.

Now there are buses, instead. Over-crowded buses.

"Do they pay the fare on the buses?"

"That depends on who's strongest. But the bus-owner generally has strong men on the buses. Besides, the bus-owner has close ties to the local zamindars."

"I thought they no longer existed."

"Well," says Ashok, "they may not exist as zamindars, but they're still around as landowners and power-holders. Almost all the local dacoits are led by sons of zamindars. It's dangerous to refuse to pay one's fare. And the passenger who demands his ticket may as well get off immediately. Tickets are not handed out. For if they were, the company would have to start paying taxes."

"Is there a lot of crime?"

"Not many robberies or assaults. The dacoits collaborate with the local police force, so things are pretty well hushed up. Where can the people turn?"

"Like the mafia?"

"Perhaps. The local landowners, magnates and politicians have adventure-loving sons, and sometimes the police themselves are involved as dacoits or receive their share of the booty afterwards. Sometimes the dacoits are so strong and the police so powerless, that it's safest for them to do and say nothing at all."

We drive along the abandoned railroad. The fields stand dry and scorched. The rain did not break the drought. Half the population here in Bihar suffers from the drought. Once again famine threatens the villages. The irrigation ditches lie dry in the winter sun. But in the main canal, water gurgles and foams past, on its way towards the sea. The wheels of administration have ground to a halt because of the impending election. All functionaries managing the canal have been instructed to do election work. The peasants grumble.

"There's nothing in the papers about this," I say.

"And to think of hearing something like that from you, of all people!" laughs Ashok. "You who worked as a newspaper reporter! The desk editor takes the blue pencil, crosses out and kills all such stories. Life will go on after the election and this scandal is just too big. All the politicians agree that the campaign and the struggle over the reins of power are more important than irrigation. That's why the drought isn't allowed to become an issue in the campaign. Indeed, the drought is a result of campaign work. It's the same humbug as always. I can write that, but it will never be printed. Still, if a new Emergency is declared, I won't even be able to write that for the editor's wastebasket without being jailed. There's the difference between democracy and dictatorship. But the people starve just the same."

All administration will come to a standstill for the sake of democracy. This means that the wheat harvest will be ruined. The water whirls off, doing no good. The officials will not have the time to do their jobs again till January 10th. Then, it is promised, the peasants will get their water.

"But then it's too late," says Ashok.

The canal authorities thunder past in jeeps with large signs saying that they are taking part in the electoral campaign. They laugh and wave.

Politicians now mingle among the villagers. They bring food and home-brewed liquor. They promise everything between heaven and earth, and pledge to support this caste against the other.

Sher Shah is long dead and gone. But although some of its branches have begun to rot, the State he established remains sturdy, sucking up the riches from the soil.

We stop at Maner to visit the grave of Shah Daulat at the large tank. This was Islam's first stronghold in Bihar. It is here that Taj Faqi, a native of Jerusalem, is said to have come with his armed band five hundred and seventy-six years after Hegira—1180 A.D. He was the first of a large family of saints. Almost all Muslim saints in Bihar are of his lineage. His descendents are buried in Biharsharif, Hasanpur Kako and Basar. Many mystics and theologians acquired fame here in Maner.

Shah Daulat is a late saint. His grave dates from the early seventeenth

century. It is known as the finest monument of the Mughal period in Bihar. It is built of sandstone from Chunar. The light touch of the master
masons is evident in the delicately chiselled ornamentation, while the
building's totality gives an impression of Mughal austerity. Ibrahim
Khan had the mausoleum erected. According to some sources, he was
the brother of Jahangir's favorite queen, Nur Jehan. But some think otherwise. In any case, he lies buried to the west of the saint. The building is
said to have been completed in 1619.

Women wash clothing in the green water of the tank. In the past, the
water came from the river Son, but it has been totally dependent on run-
off rain water now for many years. It is getting dark. On the road we see
men carrying guns. They do not look like policemen.

"Sons of landowners?"

"Perhaps. Or maybe campaign workers. Or political activists or just
plain dacoits."

Smoke from the Burnt Villages

There is no denying that Patna is poor and filthy. What is so strange about that? There are reasons why Indian cities resemble those of eighteenth century Europe. Crooked streets, and people pulling, carrying and pushing carts. But there are also cyclists. There were none in eighteenth century Europe. Nor were there cars.

Patna is poor and squalid like eighteenth century Europe for the simple reason that for two hundred years the British drained the country of its wealth and the people of their vigor. Emperors, sultans and Mughals were bad enough. But the English were worse than any sultan. What they took, they took away with them across the seas. Colonialism and imperialism meant that the wealth was transported from here to there. It is that simple.

But aside from that, what is so remarkable about Patna's poverty? The city is not worse off than was the Stockholm described by doctors serving the poor in the 1770s. Besides, the cleanliness of Stockholm is a recent development. As recently as in the middle of the nineteenth century, Stockholm was known for its filth.

When the artist Egron Lundgren was in India, drawing and painting for Queen Victoria in 1858, he got hold of the latest English papers with news of Europe. He wrote anxiously to his cousin Mrs. Laura Maria Grubb, nee Fåhraeus:

In the latest English newspapers I read that cholera has again broken out in Stockholm—and it doesn't surprise me at all. Here in India, it is a well-known fact that the stench from the excrement of the patients is almost the only source of contagion for cholera. I have seen many cities, but none so foul as Stockholm. A beggar is making a mistake in thinking that a fine, foreign piece of cloth is enough to hide his dirty rags—it would be better if he seriously set himself to patching and washing them. Ostentation, filth and disorder are the three witches who seem to get along admirably in Sweden.

The difference between today's Patna and the Stockholm of one hundred and twenty years ago is that, despite everything, Patna is free from cholera. Except to the extent that the illness can now be counted under the all-inclusive and vague term gastro-enteritis. The affluent families let gastro-enteritis breed in their courtyards and servants' quarters the way wealthy European families let cholera breed among the common people. The reason Indian cities are old fashioned in this respect is that colonialism and foreign domination interrupted and distorted Indian development. The fact that European journalists often suffer culture-shock while in India and begin writing about Indian excrement and Indian spiritualism only shows that they are lacking in a sense of history. They would experience the same culture-shock if they were to happen upon their own great-grandfathers.

I do not wish to imply that India is backward. He who would meet a Diderot or converse with a Voltaire today has a greater chance of doing it in Calcutta or Bombay than in Paris. Not to mention Stockholm! To Patna—but hardly to Stockholm—one might travel to meet a Berzelius. Even if Stockholm has become more hygienic since Egron Lundgren's time, it is still a cultural backwater compared to Patna.

That is why it is so important to understand what is happening. This can be done by lifting the veil from one's eyes and beginning to see: by putting aside the ideas of colonialism. India is a rich country. It could, without doubt, feed its population and still more. But the poverty in the half million villages—or, as Gandhi called them, dung piles—has only grown worse during these decades of development. The growth of the poor in India cannot be remedied by condoms or birth control pills or family planning campaigns. International development assistance aids only the international development assistants and their comprador friends and provides them with a reason to exist. Development assistance is a meal ticket, not unlike the curved horn that used to hang in the peasant houses of the past in Sweden, from the tip of which children sucked food. But today it is the development aid worker who does the sucking and who accumulates pension points.

Indian poverty is the poverty of the third world. It is a wretchedness like that of France under the Ancien Régime or of Old Russia. The upper class is feudal and semi-feudal, with feudal customs. It does not invest its money. It squanders and consumes while the poor grow poorer and more numerous. Patna, too, has sent skilled labor to the Arab oil-exporting countries over the past years. This has helped improve the country's exchange balance. But how has the money been spent? I walk to the museum and see the money from Kuwait roar by in the street. Motorcycles for the family. Some land speculation.

What is typically Asian in the Indian mode of production—the thing that distinguishes it from European feudalism—is that the largest portion of the surplus from agriculture went to nonproductive consumption. The British, by systematizing exploitation and by carrying home the surplus, achieved a total impoverishment. In other words, they did not even consume this surplus in a non-productive manner in India, which would at least have created some minor ripple-effect. The only "Asian mode of production" that one can meaningfully speak of is that of Asia exploited by colonialism and imperialism! India's domestic ruling class is trying to live like the colonial masters, administering like the British, but in addition, exporting capital when possible.

As for India's finance capital, "It invests in Malaysia and other profitable countries if it sees an opportunity," says Ashok.

Life, it was said, could never again be quite as agreeable as it had been in pre-1789 Paris. Or, if we are to believe Negley Farson's account, perhaps only in Petrograd, those first happy years of World War I. But, today, he who would live an agreeable life should strive to be rich among the wealthy of India. For most of those with wealth are no tight-fisted capitalists—they still live agreeably and unproductively, without a care. While the misery grows around them.

Indian misery is not a result of any lack of qualified experts. Indian statistics may be wretched, but the Indian statisticians are brilliant. There are many knowledgeable and well-educated people in India. They are exported all over the world. India has gone in for education. Higher education is much more developed than it is in China, for example. The university is an export industry, as there are few positions for the advanced specialists in their own country. It is the agreeable life-style, and not capitalism, which rules the day.

India does host some foreign technical experts. Some of them go to the state owned or private industrial sectors, and some to the arms industry. But that makes a story by itself. The rest belong to the international brotherhood of experts. I have met Norwegian socialists who are on the wrong side of their department superiors and who have been deported to international assistance work, serving as town planning ex-

perts for low-income Indians. I have also encountered Swedish experts
in industrial safety, birth-controllers from the United States, and Czech
puppet-theater specialists. But while the folk minstrels with their complicated tales from the *Mahabharata* and their remarkable puppets are
forced to sell doll-heads to foreign tourists as souvenirs and are crowded
into the slums of beggars and day laborers outside Delhi, the Czech
puppet-theater specialists are driven in black limousines to the reception
at the Ministry of Culture and the ambassador makes speeches about socialism, culture and brotherhood.

But why get upset? The brotherhood of experts means no more for Indian development than did Cagliostro and his kind in eighteenth century Paris for the development of the French chemicotechnical industry.

India is the countryside. India is an agrarian country. The mofussil, as
the world outside the city is called. It is out there that the people live.
The cities could disappear tomorrow and India would not go under.
They have been lost before—Patna has ceased to exist on several occasions. India is dotted with abandoned cities where an upper class once
lived without care, surrounded by their servants, artisans, beggars, wandering minstrels and stationary missionaries. Indian development is decided in the countryside. It is there that one finds the motive force.

The villages are wretched. But this is not for lack of rational development plans. India has brilliant experts, in the field of village-planning as
well. In the fifties, there were great plans for *community development*.
Some of them were not well thought out. But many of them made sense.
Cooperation. Cooperative, small-scale industry. Local initiative. There
was a strong influence of the Chinese *Indusco* movement, from the period of the anti-Japanese war of resistance. Nehru even tried to induce
Rewi Ally, who had inspired the Indusco movement, to come to India to
work with community development.

If it had been possible to put these rational plans into effect, India's
villages today would have been at about the level of the brigades in the
Chinese communes, or perhaps they would even have surpassed them.
At present, many Chinese leaders are not very happy with progress in
the countryside. They talk of poverty and stagnation. Certainly China is
a poor country. I have witnessed its poverty, in the oases past Khotan, in
Shantung (which is said to be rich), in Gansu or northern Shensi. But if
these Chinese politicians and journalists think their poverty is appalling,
they should visit India. Thirty years have now elapsed since China saw
such poverty and in thirty years people have forgotten. But India is poor.
Truly, miserably, wretchedly poor.

However, thirty years ago, India was in a better starting position than
China. If community development programs had then been carried out,
there would have developed by now cooperative, small-scale industry,

functioning health-care and schools, drinking water, housing fit for human beings and a noticeable economic development in the countryside. There might even have been justice for the poor. But it was not possible to put these plans into effect. And so all of India is stuck in its misery and the Indian villages are still, in the words of Gandhi, dunghills for people to live in.

What was it then that stopped the plans? Was it the inveterate conservatism of the people? No! It was the parasites, those who live without working.

The landowners, usurers, their relations among the government officials, and all the scum of the cities who live off the villages—they scuttled the plans and hindered development. Progress in the villages meant an end to their agreeable lifestyle.

Still, they have not been able to prevent all development. Nor was that their desire. They have invested state monies in British style irrigation canals and technical development projects, hoping thus to increase the value of their property and the income from the villages. They had no choice in this, since it seemed to hold out the promise of a still more agreeable life. But in unleashing the water, they have opened the floodgates. There is no stagnation in the Indian countryside. In order to continue their consumption of luxury items, they must promote a modicum of development; but that very development threatens their way of life and existence. Cautiously, they opened the gates of development one tiny crack. But that crack was enough to enable the poor peasants to poke in the points of their shovels and begin to pry.

Here in Bihar, where Siddhartha Gautama once preached, and in Patna, where the ambassador Megasthenes came to Chandragupta's court and reported home, here amid the filth and poverty of this place, rapid change is taking place.

For India too can develop. In the newspapers I read that in Gorakhpur to the northwest, in Buddha's neighborhood, development erupted again last week. The news item was short and tucked away in the paper:

BURNT TO DEATH

LUCKNOW, Feb. 2 (PTI) A Harijan was burnt to death by some persons belonging to a high-caste family near Nautanwa town in Gorakhpur district on Tuesday last, according to a delayed message reaching the state headquarters here.

The report said that as the Harijan got down at Gorakhpur railway station on Tuesday afternoon, he was forcibly detained by some high-caste influential persons of the area.

They sprinkled kerosene oil on his body and set him on fire.

He later died in a hospital. No arrest has so far been made.

Harijan—"God's child"—was the non-name Gandhi used for the untouchables. But the untouchable who was burnt to death might have been uppity. Perhaps he thought himself a citizen. Although many reports are forgotten, and others never arrive, or get pushed aside at editors' desks when more important news comes up, still, if one were to count the number of news items reporting the killing of harijans, the number would be similar to that arrived at by *The Statesman* of September 4, 1972. From 1967 to 1969, 1,100 harijans were killed by landowners. There were, however, no reports of the perpetrators of these crimes having been punished. And things go on like this. In Bihar, the government officially admitted that during the first ten months of 1977, thirty-four harijans had been murdered, one hundred and twenty severely injured and fifty-four harijan women raped. In Bihar at least a thousand persons have been killed by landlords and police in 1977-80. Or to be concrete, take an item which this year managed to appear as a one-column article with a proper headline:

ELEVEN ROASTED ALIVE IN MOB ORGY

PATNA, Feb. 7 (UNI): Twelve persons were killed, 11 of them roasted alive following the worst mob violence and orgy in Parasbigha village under Jehanabad police station of Gaya district last night, according to police headquarters sources here.

The police said armed hired-men of a "zamindar" raided the village and struck terror among the inhabitants at the dead of night by indulging in arson and wanton killing.

Jehanabad Police Station when contacted over telephone told UNI tonight that so far 11 roasted bodies had been recovered.

The police said 14 cattle heads had perished in the fire which razed to the ground at least 32 hutments.

The attack is said to be in "retaliation" for the alleged killing of a landlord named Ramniranjan Sharma in October last year.

Several persons have been arrested in this connection, but the main suspect is said to be absconding. Further details are awaited, according to police.

Here in Bihar, development lies like acrid smoke from burnt villages in the winter mist, and funeral processions wend their way. Here we have progress.

This progress is expressed in caste riots and caste conflicts. High caste and low caste struggle for control of government office and power in the villages. The untouchables are murdered. Their villages are burnt down. Men are massacred and women raped. Low-caste peasants are struck down with hoes in their fields and die kissing their land. Captured untouchables are drenched in kerosene and turned into living, screaming torches. There are daily outbreaks of violence. The fatalities appear, sometimes as small, well-hidden news items.

He died later at the hospital. No arrests have yet been made.

Only when the massacres are sensational do they make the front page. And then they can also be exploited for political ends. Indira visits the victims. Or Indira's opponents visit the victims. They make speeches on the subject of law and order, and traditional Hindu tolerance. Gravefaced and trust-inspiring politicians besides weeping people. Indira usually tries to look maternal. She sighs loud enough to be heard on the radio. And then the petty killing goes on as before, regardless of which government has taken over the official residences, official cars and official privileges.

In Kersserwa village in Sasaram District, the landlords and the police caught four young outcaste men, tied them up, and rode their horses over them and crushed their ribs. The village is poor. People collect firewood in the forest and sell it in the market at Sasaram. The riders were not prosecuted. Because those trampled to death were only destitutes who surely had harbored rebellious thoughts or possibly gone to the extent of committing insubordination or even threatening property and order.

But the truth is that funeral pyres smell of progress and development: the green revolution has made its mark here and agricultural yields have increased. The caste struggles are not about ancient customs or strange traditions. Here, caste is class and these conflicts are signs that something new is taking shape.

Less than three weeks after the assault on Parasbigha, an incident occurred which actually reached the front pages and which inspired commentary and political phrase-mongering: the Pipra incident.

Pipra is a village under Poonpoon police station of Patna district. Twenty-seven families lived there. They were untouchables and belonged to the *chamar* group. Traditionally, these were skinners. They were landless agricultural laborers who worked for the landowner Bhola Singh. He belonged to the *kurmi* caste, a peasant caste, a low caste.

In the fail of 1979 some members of the CPI (ML) party, Naxalites of the Vinod Mishra group, came to the village. They tried to organize the agricultural laborers. For a day's labor, Bhola Singh paid one kg of grain. But the government regulated minimum wage for a day's labor was 6 rupees or 4 kg of grain. The agricultural laborers organized to demand the lawful minimum wage.

Bhola Singh then formed an organization of *kurmi* landowners to defend them against the agricultural laborers. The name of the organization was Kisan Suraksha Samiti. Bhola Singh was the chairman and he collected money from the other *kurmi* farmers. In December 1979, he was murdered.

The landowners in the Kisan Suraksha Samiti responded with reprisals. According to newspaper reports, there were twelve murders from December to February. But the agricultural laborers in Pipra now refused to work for Bhola Singh's family. They planned to leave the area. However, they were worried about the threatening behavior of the landowners. But no one bothered about their worry, just as no one had done anything about the twelve murders. In the village there was a chowkidar from the internal revenue service who supervised the collection of taxes. He did nothing about the landowners' threats. There were police stations located in the area around Pipra. But the police did not bother about the threat from the landowners.

At 10 p.m. on February 25, 1980, the landowners came to teach the untouchables a lesson: to show what happens to agricultural laborers who organize to demand their lawful and guaranteed minimum wages. For six hours, they shot, burnt and plundered. According to official reports, the landowners killed fourteen untouchables—including seven women and four children. This killing was so ruthless that it could not be hidden away in the back pages of some newspaper and forgotten. All the politicians stood up and declared that caste conflicts must stop. Whether from Congress(I) or Janata, they agreed on how unfortunate and bothersome these caste-pogroms were. Indira Gandhi's minister of the interior came to Patna and spoke on the subject of caste. Jagjivan Ram—official spokesman for the harijans—travelled there and talked about caste. But what happened in Pipra was not a matter of caste or religion: it was a struggle on the part of the agricultural laborers for the official minimum wage. Bhola Singh and the other landowners had cheated the agricultural laborers out of 3 kg of grain a day. When the farm workers tried to secure their legal right, the landowners murdered them.

But the politicians spoke about caste and religion, about how necessary spiritualism and Hindu tolerance were in the face of these violent outbreaks of the evil in men's souls. And what was it that had really happened twenty days earlier when the newspapers reported the roasting alive of the eleven people in mob violence?

In the beginning of the thirties, Niranjan Singh of the *bhumiar* caste came to the village of Parasbigha. *Bhumiar* is a land-owning upper caste. Niranjan Singh came from the village of Akuri under Pali police station in Patna district. He was poor. In the late thirties he purchased twenty hectares (eighty *bighas*) from Ganesh Lal Patwari, who had received the land from his lord Tekrai Raja.

Niranjan Singh did not pay for the land. Instead, he pledged to turn over the entire harvest from two hectares (five acres) every year to Ganesh Lal Patwari. As a result of this agreement, the shepherds and share-croppers of the village lost their land.

This, in fact, was a common occurrence. The landlords created by the feudal princes and the British were losing land and power during this period. Niranjan Singh became notorious as a big land-grabber, and succeeded in taking thirteen hectares (fifty-two *bighas*) from the zamindar in Pandui, Jattu Singh. He also managed to grab various other plots belonging to absentee landowners.

He was feared in the area for his fondness for litigation and for cleverness in court. He became the regional leader of the *bhumiar* caste. He was the only member of that caste in Parasbigha. The hundred poor families living there were his subordinates. These families belonged either to lower castes such as the *yadavs* (originally a shepherd caste) and the *koiris* (originally a vegetable-growing caste) or untouchables. He tried to grab the Muslim burial grounds to put it under the plough, but met with strong religious opposition and was forced to give up.

Politically, the *bhumiar* landowners organized themselves through the Congress (I). Niranjan Singh was an active member of Congress (I) and controlled the votes in Parasbigha. It was he who decided how his subordinates would vote. But after the defeat of Congress (I) in 1977 and Indira Gandhi's fall from power, the *yadavs* and *koiris* began to organize politically against the *bhumiar* landowners' Congress (I).

In August 1979, Niranjan Singh claimed two hectares of state-owned land as his personal property. He showed the villagers forged court documents. In reality, some of this state land had been allotted to the untouchables. But Niranjan Singh took it for himself. He destroyed the crops of the untouchables. He stopped them from fetching their water at the deep well the government had dug. The authorities did nothing about either the stolen well or the land.

So the villagers united to resist Niranjan Singh. They defied him and demanded their legal rights. He held the land with forged documents and assembled other *bhumiar* landowners, to carry out a punitive expedition against Parasbigha. The high-caste mob were armed. The houses were looted. People were beaten. In October, seven weeks later, Niranjan Singh was murdered. His head was chopped off. The police arrested thirteen villagers but had no evidence and were forced to release them while the case was being investigated.

In the early hours of February 7, the village was surrounded by a force of a hundred heavily-armed high caste men. Word had it that they were led by Niranjan Singh's son, Madan Mohan, a security officer with the provincial government. The villagers also claimed that it was Mr. Mahendra Prasad, Member of Parliament for Congress (I) in Jehanabad, who had planned and supported the attack. He was of the same caste and a close friend of the assailants. The attacking *bhumiar* landowners burned down forty houses and shot twelve people.

The following day, when those who had survived met with the authorities and lodged their complaints, they specifically demanded, in vain, that the police officer who had been on duty at Jehanabad police station be hanged. He had, on the morning after the massacre, secretly set fire to his own haystack to prove that the villagers had provoked the attack.

When the authorities attempted to calm the villagers, promising an investigation, justice and indemnification, a shout was heard from the crowd:

"A lot of poor people are being killed these days!"

It is clashes such as this one that are called caste conflicts. But it is not a matter of caste conflict—it is the same old class struggle one finds the world over, a struggle which has continuously characterized the violently unstable villages of India. The struggles are bloody because the oppressed are standing up and demanding their rights.

During the great social conflicts of the twenties, thirties and forties in the countryside of Bihar, caste was not in the limelight. The peasants were then fighting against the zamindars, revenue collectors turned into hereditary landowners by the British. They were feudatories. The struggle was over landownership, rent and what the zamindars collected for themselves and the British. It ended in defeat for the zamindars and the end of the zamindars as a feudal class. But caste was not the issue, since the zamindars, as well as the large tenant farmers and rich peasants who opposed and replaced them, were usually high-caste Hindus: *brahmans, bhumiars, rajputs* and *kayastha*—in other words, twice-born.

In the villages, the high-caste Hindus, being landowners, held sway over the lower castes and untouchables. Down at the bottom were the untouchables. The relations between them were of a feudal nature and the villages were characterized by serfdom and serf-like conditions: usury, luxury and misery. The landowner did not follow the plough.

However, the struggle in which the zamindars had been defeated was not over. Instead of investing, the landowning, usurious high castes consumed. On the other hand, the poor peasants, low-caste and despised, pinched their pennies, worked hard and invested hungrily in land and farming equipment. They began sending their children to school.

Meanwhile, the high-caste Hindus manoeuvred for political power, made speeches in parliament, socialized with visiting foreigners, stood in the limelight and captured a growing number of the lucrative political posts. (From having made up 8 percent of Bihar Congress leadership in 1947, they accounted for 29 percent in 1948 and 32 percent in 1954.) But out in the villages from where their income came, the grasping peasants of the lower castes began to take possession of more and more of the land by going without and investing instead of consuming. Their sons had now completed their schooling and began to compete with the *brahmans* for government posts.

Thanks to the green revolution, the lower castes could make the leap from poor peasant to middle peasant. It was at this point that the power struggle in the villages between low and high caste became acute. Today, that struggle is naked and bloody.

The lower castes express themselves in caste terms. They say they are fighting against caste oppression. They say that it should be possible to unite everyone around that. But, in fact, the struggle has to do with land and its yield; here the high castes have already lost the war. They have tried to step into the boots of the zamindars. They have not invested. Their farming methods are not up to date. They are doomed, no matter what the outcome of the various bloody settling of scores.

Yet at the same time, the former poor peasants pushed those who are still poorer further and further down. They wrest from them the small plots of land they have been able to retain. They cheat them out of the land distributed to them by the authorities. They band together to oppose the demands of the landless farm laborers for the legally fixed minimum wage. And while the low castes turn to the untouchables and say that everyone must unite against the tyranny of the high castes and against caste oppression (yes, they have even occasionally spoken of human dignity), the struggle between the lower castes and the untouchables has grown increasingly rancorous. The untouchable farm laborers demand for the minimum wage represents a threat to the investments of the lower castes in the new high-yield agriculture.

But caste does mean something. A member of a high caste can lose social standing without losing his caste. He may become poor. But he will never become a farm laborer. He would rather starve to death. The Hindu high caste landowners of Bihar are doomed. Their fate will be that of the zamindars. Some will try to hold out, maintaining as long as possible their traditional way of life. They will go under and disappear. Some will be spared the ignobility of labor by going in for a life of crime, becoming dacoits or hired guns in the pay of some power holder. Others will die in poverty. But the rest will become like the new peasants of the lower castes: hungrily investing and interested in any method capable of raising yields. In the end, tradition and caste considerations will have to give way. That, or they will perish. Twice-born can already be seen tilling the soil. In order to be able to resist the onslaught of the low caste peasants, the high caste peasants rid themselves of their day laborers and take to work. Social contradictions grow increasingly sharp. In Bihar, semi-feudalism has begun to take on the features of capitalism.

This may mean that caste issues will once again, as during the last generation, become less prominent in political life. But the struggles in the villages of Bihar will not grow less intense with the lower castes' victory over the higher castes: the former poor peasants' advances in the villages have also taken place at the expense of the landless, the untouchables. The new, more profitable farming methods have intensified the struggle for the minimum wage. The fact is that a section of the former ruling caste which accepts the changed conditions and begins to work the soil instead of living parasitically, and the low-caste which has clawed its way up from the poor peasantry to the beginnings of (relative) wealth, now run the villages jointly. But the fact that former rulers join forces with their former inferiors who have struggled their way into leading positions in no way lessens the conflict with the untouchables and agricultural laborers. Modern agriculture in Bihar requires their labor but keeps their income below the poverty line. It cannot give them security or even reduce the number of unemployed and underemployed. If this conflict does not receive a clear political expression, it may well come to be expressed in caste-terms. But the way things are now shaping in North India, it seems evident that progress will carry with it the smell of smoke and burnt bodies for a long time to come.

Conversation in Bihar

"It's hard to say just how class relations stand," says Ashok, who accompanied me to Bihar. "There hasn't been a census here since 1950. Besides, the ruling class control the count themselves. But one can estimate that of one hundred households, fifteen belong to the category of large landowners and rich peasants. The remaining eighty-five are middle peasants, poor peasants and landless. In places where social conflicts have broken out into the open, the lower classes have tended to organize as leftists and to define their situation in political terms. Where the conflicts are not so acute or have just recently broken out, they define themselves in terms of caste and tend to follow their caste leaders, even when this runs in opposition to their class interests. The old landowners were almost exclusively from high castes. The new landowners are from various castes and try to use the caste-issue to sow division among the poor peasants and landless."

"Indira's Congress will win the election," says Bilram Tiwari. He is the head of Congress (I) in Sherpur.

"Why is that? Because kerosene which is supposed to cost Rs 1.60 a litre is no longer available. It has to be bought on the black market where it costs Rs 4 a litre. So the people will vote against the government. Fifty percent of the electorate here belongs to the *yadav* caste. It is one of the higher low castes, and Lok Dal has tried to monopolize its votes. But our candidate is also a *yadav*. So we will win the election, partly because it's impossible to find kerosene, and partly because our candidate is a *yadav."*

"It's out in the villages that the real political struggle is decided," says Ashok. "It is the panchayat, the local government, that is the decisive command post for a class which wants power. Those who control the panchayat, control the food supply and distribute the kerosene and fertilizer. In May and June 1978, elections to the panchayat were held here in Bihar. About sixty people were killed in the bitter struggle for power in the panchayats. But the high castes lost the elections. In Maner, the *yadavs* took 80 percent of the posts."

"The Muslims vote for Janata," says Janata's representative in Maner. "The reason is that the local Janata candidate is a Muslim. We in the Janata are trying to get rid of the reputation of being communalistic, of being a Hindu party. In this area, Muslims are mainly workers, construction workers."

"It isn't certain that the Muslims will vote for Janata just because the candidate is a Muslim," says the man who has come forward to listen to the conversation. "I am a Muslim and a construction worker. Voting has nothing to do with religion. We vote for those who work for a better life. But neither can we say that workers vote for a certain candidate because they are workers. Everyone makes his own decision."

"You see how things have changed," says Ashok. "Twenty years ago, the workers were totally bound to the village they came from. Today, it is more a question of their social standing than of where they work or live. But the working class is still divided and has no stable consciousness of its own class interests. Take the coal miners for instance. They moonlight as peasants. Where do they belong? They are torn in different directions. Religion, too, splits the class. But those who have been workers a long time, or who are second-generation workers, are more politically conscious, while those fresh from their villages are less aware."

"Okay, economic inequality among people exists," says Sitaram Matha, "but it is not that important. Ninety-two percent of the *yadavs* here support Lok Dal. It is the *yadavs'* party, regardless of economic standing. The rich *yadavs* also support Lok Dal. We are the party of the lower castes. Economic contradictions do exist, but votes are cast according to caste and origin, not just money."

"Yes," says Sagar Singh, "things are worse now. Diesel oil, kerosene, sugar and electricity, everything is scarce. But people will vote according to caste. The upper castes will vote for Indira and the low castes against her. The untouchables will vote for her because they are against the lower castes. That's the way it is."

"The elections are a waste of time," says an older man. "I'm a peasant with my own land and what have the politicians done for us? All we've got is words. The politicians are only in the elections for themselves.

The Jami Masjid, great mosque, 1440, Mandu

The Fort, 1459, Jodhpur

Indolent maiden, the Rajarani temple, 12th century, Bhubaneswar

Kerala

Monsoon in Punjab

Southernmost India

Northwestern India, agriculture

Parson Sathaia, in Rapalli village, Jagtial, outside his church

A village barber, Punjab

Porters, Simla

Decorating the cow-dung storage

Prime Minister Jawaharlal Nehru and the then vice-president of India, Sir Sarvepalli Radhakrishnan, at the All-India Writers conference in Bhubaneswar, January 1959

Grandparents attending the beginning of the ceremony of cutting the baby's hair

Members of armed squad in the Western Godavari forest

Prabhakar and his wife Ramak, activists in the Pandiam village *ryotu-kuli-sangham*

Morning in the Gadavari camp

They aren't interested in investing in projects which will benefit the peasants."

"When it comes to irrigation, nothing is happening even though there's a drought and three out of four villages are suffering from famine," says an old harijan.

In the village of Jamunja, a *yadav* peasant says, "The drought has destroyed the rice. The wheat harvest is uncertain. It too is probably destroyed. The government does nothing. There's no kerosene. In the evening, we have to sit in the dark."

"The votes of the poor can be bought," says an older woman.

"No one cares about the peasantry. Not even Lok Dal. The politicians are selfish and corrupt!"

"It's the same with all the parties. They're all alike."

"Here in the village, we voted for Congress until 1977. Then we were told to vote for Janata to improve conditions. But things didn't improve. What'll we do now?"

"Should we support a third party? Lok Dal talks about peasants, but that, too, is just empty talk. But we'll vote for them this year. If they don't do anything either, it'll be for God to judge. We gave all the power to the politicians. If they abuse it, it will be up to God to punish them. But, as for us, we may just stop voting.

"No election has changed anything. We don't even have a school. Before every election they've come here and promised us a school for our children. But it was all just hot air. All we got was a stone. In 1977, a minister came here and laid a cornerstone. Newspaper reporters were here and everyone was glad and promised to put in free labor on the school building. Once the ceremony was over the minister drove off in his car, followed by all the newspaper reporters. Nothing was ever heard about the school again until this election came up. Now everyone's coming here, promising us a new school if we vote for them."

In the village of Bhatheri, a low caste peasant explains, "Indira created differences between peasants and agricultural laborers by raising the issue of the minimum wage. This harmed the unity in the villages. Now the *yadavs* are voting for Lok Dal and the harijans for Indira."

"Not all of them!" shouts a young man. "Some harijans have understood that all the lower classes have common interests. Only 50 percent of the harijans support Indira. The others understand that she is the representative of the upper castes.

"In the past, the struggle was between the landowners and the poor. But now it's between upper and low castes. The upper castes have the authority. They have power. The entire caste system must be abolished. Members of the lower castes no longer stand up when an upper caste member walks by. That's good. It is liberation. The harijans, too, must realize that we must all stand together."

In the CPI's office in Dinapur, Durga Prasad Singh sits in a raw silk shirt and explains the situation. He is a member of the Party Committee of Patna District.

"Our chief adversary is Janata. Not Indira. In the past, Congress was an upper-caste party. Now, the high castes tend to support the Janata. The harijans are leaving Congress (I) to come to us. At the same time, we have formed an alliance with Lok Dal, which is the *yadavs'* party, so we receive the support of the lower castes. The Muslims drop Janata when we point out that Janata is Hindu, so the Muslims, too, come over to us. But people vote primarily to make sure that a hostile caste does not get its representatives elected. Caste considerations are more important than class considerations when it comes to voting."

"Yes, the situation is interesting," says Professor Pradhan H. Prasad in Patna. "The middle peasants elbow the rich peasants out of the economic leadership. The election hinges on caste issues. This is something that has developed over the last few decades. The green revolution enabled the middle peasants to take up the struggle for power, making the whole issue a question of caste. While high caste can generally be equated with the landowners, and low caste with the middle and poor peasants, it is significant that among the middle peasants there are no upper caste members, and that the agricultural laborers are untouchables. There are, however, some poor peasants who are upper caste. We are now witnessing change and stratification. The middle peasants, the lower castes, advances and forces its way in both directions.

"The Naxalites are now organizing the agricultural laborers in this struggle. They are trying to destroy the whole system. To accurately assess their chances, one must take a comprehensive view. The elections are carried out in a feudal manner and they are an expression of semi-feudal relations. I am not referring now to the fact that a village potentate can deliver the votes of his inferiors in a block to the highest bidder, but to booth-capture. What this means is that some armed group takes control of a polling-place, stuffs the boxes with the desired ballots and then drives away the voters. The ballot-boxes can also be captured. In the past, it was the feudal elite in the countryside who, with their armed henchmen, could control the balloting. They are now threatened by the middle peasants. Even if the voting is fictitious under these circumstances, the results do reveal a great deal about the power relationships in the countryside. The class in the weaker position is also unable to succeed in booth-capture. Still, all the parties use these methods.

"The feudal elite supports Indira. But it would be a mistake to regard the Lok Dal leader Charan Singh as a representative of the middle peasants. He has never done anything for them, but suddenly they had clawed their way up and become a social force, so Charan Singh made haste to get into position. Leaders are nothing without followers. Indira, too, must have her supporters. She must agree to toe the line on the peasant question in Bihar. One can say that during the last generation, a shift in power has taken place within the various groups, from the leadership right down to the rank and file. This too is a symptom of the turbulent situation. Nehru was a dictator. Today, there is no such leader, standing above all question. This can be seen as a step forward for democracy. But remember, there isn't a very strong democratic tradition in Congress (I). The fact that the charismatic leaders disappeared and the leadership collapsed does not necessarily represent a democratic advance.

"One should not put too much faith in the press. It is tied to the feudal elite and big business. This is particularly true of the English-language press. It is unable to present an accurate picture of rural development. There are only small glimpses, tucked away in unobtrusive news stories.

"In the fifties, before class differentiation had gone this far in Bihar, one could say that the struggle was between the high and the low. If the old Communist Party had succeeded in splitting at that time, I believe it could have triumphed. That is, if there had then existed a party which had the same goals as the Naxalites today, the carrying out of a new democratic revolution. Because no such party existed to lead political developments, the main contradiction in the sixties became that between the feudal elite and the upwardly mobile middle peasants. The latter could move up within the system through economic—and, now, political— struggle. These middle peasants have been victorious in the villages. Now they want to win politically. This can be brought about with the aid of this or that party, or within this or that organization; the important question is what they want to do with their political power. Can the middle peasants of North India's Hindi area break the semi-feudal relations in the country?

"Big business supports Indira. It supports the semi-feudal stagnation in the rural areas. Indian high finance needs this stagnation. This high finance is trying to break into the international markets. There is a populist element in Indira's image. This was especially evident during emergency rule. But she gets her strength from an alliance between the big capitalists and the feudal elite. This alliance is semi-colonial in nature, and one cannot leave foreign influence out of the picture. The Indian bourgeoisie is dependent while at the same time seeking foreign markets it can dominate or participate in dominating. Together, these interests make up a strong power block supporting Indira.

"In terms of science and technology, India is one of the most advanced countries in the third world. But India remains stagnant and

poor because of its feudal and dependent conditions. Once feudal relations are wiped out, nothing can stop India's development. India will
then become an advanced world power. No imperialist country wants to
see that happen.

"Both the Soviet Union and the United States try to hinder India's development. Both have a stake in trying to maintain the present stagnation, even if they rely on different groups within the ruling elite. When
their interests are threatened, they join forces.

"I have seen this happening at international scientific conferences.
When the third world countries demand that the United States and the
Soviet Union relinquish their monopoly of certain technological fields
and stake their own claim, then suddenly the Soviet Union and its satel-
lites join the United States and its client states to beat back the third
world.

"When they are not able to control the Indian delegation with the
usual political pressure on Delhi, the super powers resort to Machiavel-
lian intrigue. You must remember that many of our officials, including
high officials in the foreign service, are patriotic, and are prepared to take
up the interests of the third world against the Soviet Union and the
United States. That too reflects the advanced state of Indian science and
technology.

"India is a country advanced in science and technology, with a great
growth potential. But feudalism and foreign dependence prevent development, and the key to the widespread stagnation is the semi-feudal relations in the countryside. But what is now taking place in Bihar and the
rest of North India is that the main contradiction is once again manifesting itself in the form of a conflict between high and low, although on a
different level than say thirty years ago. The advance of the peasants
forces the feudal landowners to increase investment in agriculture and to
begin using modern farming methods. Once again, the contradiction is
focused between the landowning exploiters and the landless farm laborers. This raises the possibility of progress.

"There are certain western economists such as Gunnar Myrdal who
assert that our difficulties are due to the fact that we have a soft state.
Among those who speak of the need for a strong state there are some
who consider themselves radicals, and even Marxists. It's true that this
type of government, a strong state—in plain words, a fascist one—offers
the promise of a short period of development. Fascism develops the in-
frastructure. One usually says, like Mussolini or Indira, that the trains
run on time. But past experience shows that fascism is unable to provide
further development, because it is dependent on the support of reactionary classes. Indira is supported by the feudal elite, semi-feudal elements
in the countryside, high finance and the established bureaucracy. There's

a possibility that she might be able to create the strong state some western economists advocate. The trains will run on time. But there will be no development. On the other hand, developments taking place in the Bihar countryside might lead to progress."

"You are, of course, aware that Prasad is very controversial," says Ashok. "There are many 'official' Marxists of various factions whose blood begins to boil when his name is mentioned."

"When discussing the caste issue in Bihar, it is important not to forget history," says one of the students as we drink tea together. "Politics here in Bihar began as caste organization. After 1857, all the feudal elements went over to the British. They considered them invincible. The British made Calcutta a metropolis. Bihar didn't even exist. This was just a remote rural area. The issues were then seen as hostility to the Bengalis. In the 1880s, the students began to raise anti-imperialist demands, but in the form of caste demands. The British encouraged caste contradictions, so that they could play the role of a third arbitrating force.

"In 1912, the *kayastha* caste organized politically. It is an upper caste and twice-born. They formed the *Kayastha Samachar* and demanded an independent Bihar. *Bhumiars, rajputs,* and *brahmans* followed their example. They wanted guaranteed positions for their sons who had now begun their education. Their demands were for an independent Bihar minus the Bengalis!

"They didn't care a jot about those Biharis working in the Calcutta jute industry or on the tea plantations in North Bengal, or in their own fields. It was only after independence that the lower castes formed their own organizations against the upper castes.

"Thus the caste contradictions under British rule and those of the present, have some similar features, but are also of an entirely different nature. And it is only after 1967 that one can talk of a genuinely local elite in Bihar. It was that year that the *yadavs* became the largest caste group in Bihar's Legislative Assembly.

"For a hundred years the struggle for government posts stood between Bengalis and upper-caste Biharis. Who would receive the education that paved the way to these positions? The son of a Bengali babu or the upper-caste youth from Bihar? In this struggle over government jobs, the castes themselves were forced to change. Caste rules are not unchanging. As recently as in the beginning of this century, a *kayastha* who had studied in England had to undergo difficult purification ceremonies before he could be re-admitted into the caste fold. He had journeyed across the dark waters. And remember, outside of the caste, there is nothing! It was Rajendra Prasad and his confederates who worked at that time to change the caste rules. The reform movement meant that one could study in England, that the marriage age was raised, and that women could receive an education. In other words, it meant that the caste qualified itself to serve as civil servants in the British administration.

"Don't forget that British policy was very purposeful. Between 1812 and 1830, there were 100,000 schools. Students from the lower castes also received an education. When the British system was introduced, the low caste children disappeared from the schools. The great educational reform was a disaster for the masses. The British divided to rule. Muslims were given priority in certain government posts. Certain castes were declared to be martial races and could immediately find employment with the police and armed forces. Other castes were branded 'criminal castes' and were barred from all employment. In this way the British established a closely regulated, hierarchical order. It systematized casteism and communalism.

"This they followed up by allotting places in the consultative and legislative councils they established according to religion or caste. The British provided the caste system with both an economic base and a political vehicle. But the economic base remained so simple and clear cut that in 1951, 80 percent of the landowners were *brahmans*, *bhumiars* or *rajputs*, while 75 percent of the tenant-farmers under them were *yadavs*, *kurmis* or *koiris*. What had taken place during the first half of the century were struggles over relative positions in the caste hierarchy. The *bhumiars*, a farming high caste, attempted to adopt the *brahmans'* taboo 'never touch a plough' and, in this way, attain a higher status as well as the position of feudal landowners. *Kayasthas*, originally scribes and book-keepers at temples and such places, went in for British education and civil service positions, and in this way became landowners. During the twenties, *yadavs* and *kurmis* tried to raise their status from upper-low-caste to lower-upper-caste: they made themselves twice-born by using the sacred thread, adopting upper-caste titles and the complicated system of upper caste taboos. At the same time, they stopped performing obsequious ceremonies in the presence of the lower-upper-castes. There were bloody clashes over these issues. *Yadavs* who had begun to wear the sacred thread were beaten to death. But why did the *rajputs* and *bhumiars* kill them? The former were land barons and the *yadavs* tenant-farmers. When the lower castes broke the ceremonial barrier, they were threatening land-ownership. Among the untouchables, the very poorest, the agricultural laborers and others, sanskritization was also taking place. They formed themselves into castes and adopted caste rules. As you can see, these issues of caste are not really all that difficult to understand.

"However, conditions before and after independence are completely different. During the thirties, there seemed to be a peasant movement in this area, in the form of the *Kisan sabha*. The peasants united against the zamindars. The large tenant-farmers opposed the zamindari system. But, on the whole, the zamindars and the more prosperous peasant were of the same caste. When the zamindars disappeared as a feudal class, the tenant-farmers became landowners. Caste issues again came to the fore. And it was then that the low caste, lower-middle peasants elbowed their way up to leading positions by working hard and making use of modern farming methods. These developments also resulted in an increase in the number of landless farm laborers: from 28 percent in 1951 to 39 percent in 1971, or in other words, from 3,100,000 to 6,800,000. These people were untouchables and, to a certain extent, lower caste. In the June 26, 1977, edition of *The Times of India*, Arun Sinha presented official statistics on the consequences of these developments: in 1972, there were 98 cases of assault against harijans and tribal people reported to the police. In 1973, there were 109 such incidents, in 1974, 259. In 1975 almost 300; and from January to September 1976 there were 1,133 cases of assault reported.

"It's one thing that it is the landowners who are attacking agricultural laborers, and that caste coincides with class. But these are not just 'ordinary' landowners. In the village of Rupaspur-Chandwa in Purnea, several agricultural laborers were burnt to death by the former speaker of the Bihari Legislative Assembly. Those who are now beating and burning agricultural laborers to death are less frequently upper-caste members than was the case during the clashes of the twenties; it is now members of the lower castes who are burning the untouchables to death. Or it would be more correct to say that both kinds of killings take place. But the victims are always the low, the poor. And this is Indira's Achilles' heel. She is backed by the elite. It is her own party organizers who use serf-labor, who burn agricultural laborers to death and who stand above the law. Yet, she has also proclaimed Garib Raj, Power and Justice for the Poor! When the authorities and landowners murdered Gambhira Sau, the leader of the poor in Champaran, ten thousand poor villagers demonstrated for Garib Raj. Fascism is no solution; populism creates its own opposition!

"The British endeavored to educate a special class of babus, an intellectual middle class, which would help them govern India. In the beginning it was worthwhile. The intellectuals of the newly-educated Bengali middle class supported the British in 1857. But in 1860, they joined forces with the peasantry against the British plantation owners during the Indigo conflicts. In time, this intellectual middle class also found its interests in conflict with those of its British masters; they became nationalists. This should be borne in mind when one considers developments in Bihar. Prasad's view of the peasant class can be debated. On the whole, I agree with him. But just think what would happen if it develops into something similar to the French freeholding peasantry of the nineteenth century. Consider the possibility of the low-caste middle peasants becoming the popular base of an Indian Napoleon Ill. That is also a possibility.

"No, the number of those without land is continually growing. No stable peasant class of the French or Serbian kind can emerge here in Bihar. But the class struggle in the countryside will grow more intense as agricultural yields increase. The question is what class alliance can be formed between the rural poor and the urban lower classes, those urban classes which, when it comes down to it, really oppose the existing semi-feudal oppression in the villages."

Later, in the street, as we leave behind us the A.N.S. Institute of Social Sciences in its tranquil park setting, the noise and bustle of the crowds are like a tidal wave. Three-wheeled pedal cabs, hand carts, people carrying loads on their heads. Bihar's entire lower class seems to pour past the institute's protective white walls. And that is one way of looking at the situation!

"You ought to read *Agrarian Relations in India* by Arvind N. Das and V. Nilakant; it is just out," says Ashok. "It has quite a lot of material. What you must keep in mind is that during the last decades inequality in the rural areas has increased, the situation of women has deteriorated and female infanticide continues. It is with small girls as with dry cows; nobody kills them, they just die."

We take the road to the right. In front of us lies the *maidan*, but there to the right, west of the *maidan*, stands Golgarh, the round house. This is the most remarkable edifice built by the British in India.

"It can be seen as a symbol of British rule," says Ashok. "It is magnificent, peculiar and non-functional. Like a gigantic bee-hive, it towers above the city. A surrealistic object."

The hive is thirty meters in height. The walls at the base are 3.75 meters thick. The interior diameter is 34 meters. At each of the cardinal points a doorway is situated in the thick wall. The doors now open outwards. When the hive was first built, they opened inwards. On the exterior facade of the hive, two spiral staircases wind around each other up towards the crown of the building. Up on the crown a hole 75 centimeters in diameter leads straight down into the hive. The stairways lead to that hole. A stone now blocks the hole; this is to prevent accidents.

People climb on the stairways. They sit at the base of the hive, talking and smoking. The hive is an attraction to be seen by every villager who visits Patna. Inside one can hear an echo, famous in all of North India. On the hive's northern inner wall sits a plaque:

In part of a general Plan
ordered by the Governor-General and Council

20 of January 1781
For the perpetual prevention of Famines
in these Provinces
THIS GRANARY
Was erected by Captain John Garstin, engineer
completed on this 20 of July 1786
First filled and publicly closed by. . . .

"As you can see the last line is missing. The stone is uncut," says Ashok. "The whole thing was a big mistake. It was never filled. It has never been used."

We walk around it. We climb up and we look at it. A most unusual building. The Indian master masons supervised by John Garstin were the great masters of cupola building. Here they raised what was to be the last great Indian cupola. A building with an opening in the ceiling, like the Pantheon in Rome, and an echo mighty like the one in the great cupola in Bijapur. But a building totally lacking in purpose. Since its construction in 1786, it has served as a gunpowder store and a military depot. Now it is used by the municipality of Patna as a warehouse. And even if it had been possible to fill the granary, seal it and then open the doors when necessary and remove the rice, it still would not have held enough to provide "the province with even a single day's consumption," notes Walter Hamilton in *East-India Gazeteer* in 1828.

"But the famines were real enough," says Ashok. "The famine of 1770 was the first British famine in India, although it wasn't until later, in the nineteenth century, that Indian famines became the topic of conversation in Europe. The number of victims has been a subject of controversy. It is possible that ten million people perished. One third of the fields lay fallow. Children were offered up for sale, but there were few buyers to be found. Cannibalism occurred. Nevertheless, the East India Company continued its tax-gathering. There was a qualitative change in the nature of the famines after the arrival of the British. One can say that the famines during British rule were a function of British efficiency in tax-gathering and administration. The last famine which struck Bengal and Orissa in 1943, caused the death of about 3,500,000 people. Golgarh is an administrative fantasy. A dream-building."

Notes on a Bengali Revolutionary

In the afternoon, I had been down to the railway station to reserve bedding for the night. We were going to Calcutta. This had taken some time and had proven somewhat complicated because I was late; I should actually have made reservations a few days earlier. There was a discussion with the laundryman about whether he could have the sheets ready in time, but, in the end, I was promised that everything possible would be done to help us.

I had already purchased the tickets for the Amritsar Howrah Mail a couple of weeks earlier. The train had left Amritsar the evening before and passed through Ambala, Bareilly, Lucknow and Varanasi. It was due to arrive at 9:43 p.m. and leave for Calcutta at 10:03 p.m. We were down at the station soon after 9 p.m., in time to collect our bedding, check our seat reservations and buy some newspapers. The bedding was waiting for us. A bed-roll containing a sheet, a pillow, a pillow case, a blanket and a towel. I had to make sure that everything was there, sign a pledge to return the bedding to the railroad company upon arrival and pay four rupees per person. The train was running late. We were unable to check our reservation since our seats had not been booked in the direct car from Patna to Calcutta, but in a car coming directly from Amritsar. The station was jammed with people. The Indians are a nation of travellers. But everything worked like clockwork, the way it always does with the Indian railways. When the train pulled in the station and we walked along the row of coaches, the names of those holding reservations was carefully written on a list. Our compartment was waiting. We crammed in our luggage. The conductor made up the beds and we prepared to turn in. Clattering, the train rolled out, the smell of smoke and the sound of voices and train whistles in the distance. I slept.

At about 2 a.m. I woke up. The train had come to a stop. I saw that we had arrived in Jhajha. A middle-aged man in a uniform—a railroad uniform—was getting into our compartment. He took the upper berth and fell asleep immediately. I listened to his snoring. Not even the noise of the wheels and the clatter drowned it out. I lay awake thinking of Kali who had been my father-in-law. In the final years of his life, we had not had much contact with each other. Actually, not since I had returned from China in 1963. He contributed articles to journals such as *Blitz* and in the end, was completely pro-Russian. His opinions coincided with those of Dange, who at that time was on the extreme right of the Communist Party of India. He had also become deeply involved in the Indian-Chinese border dispute. And he was wrong. I knew that right from the start since I had maps with me when we lived in Delhi. But facts made no difference. Just how wrong he was, I could not have known at the time. The grounds of the border dispute—the British forgeries of the thirties under the direction of Olof Caroe—did not become known to a wider audience until the 1970s. It is possible that he would have changed his mind had he lived to see some of the documentation. But the last time we met, when he was in Sweden and visited us at Fagervik, he had committed himself so wholeheartedly to the official Indian standpoint that discussion was impossible.

The last time we really discussed this issue must have been just before we were to leave India for China. The border issue was serious at the time, although no major clashes had taken place yet. It was not before the autumn of that year, 1962, that the border skirmishes flared into a minor war. It was not just that India was in the wrong; the whole war was a total fiasco. A daydream that floundered when exposed to reality. Kali could not forgive China for this. But that was still in the future, that day when he came to visit. It must have been one of the last days before our departure.

Most of the packing had been completed. My book on India was not yet finished. We had some Americans visiting us. They were called Miller, I believe, and they were from the East Coast. Animated academics, and so manifestly Anglo-Saxon that Gun was sure that Miller's father had come from Galicia. She is good at perceiving these significant details. We discussed the caste system and did not agree. I had argued that Americans, with their own peculiar social order involving such strong elements of caste should be able to see that there was absolutely no need to search for strange explanations.

"Indian caste-rules are no more incomprehensible than your American custom of holding your left hand hidden under the table while you eat," I had said to him and the atmosphere had grown a little strained. Sociologists rarely enjoy becoming objects of observation themselves or having their behavior commented on the way they comment on that of others.

It was then that Kali came in. We were not expecting him that day. But he had some extra time on his hands and had stopped by to talk. He was spending a few weeks in Delhi. He used to visit India in the winter. The rest of the year he lived in London.

"It was because of him that I was deported from Dover to Calais as an undesirable alien on February 16, 1950," I said.

"I don't know what the immigration officials found worse," said Kali, "that Jan was my son-in-law or that I was known as a communist. It was probably the combination that they couldn't take."

The Millers fidgeted in their seats. I knew what they were thinking—a Bengali babu—it upset all their American East Coast racial attitudes. Their manners grew painfully polite and they became high-spirited in a strained way. They almost began to pat the two of us on our backs. They really radiated: "We have no prejudices." But, actually, they were two rather shabby East Coast intellectuals next to a London gentleman. Kali had grown almost exaggeratedly British during the thirty years he had lived in London since being deported there. The Millers' behavior was so obviously and typically determined by their North American racism, and—the more I observed them, the more I realized that Gun was right— by the fact that they themselves had passed, had climbed socially. They acted as though they were Anglo-Saxon North Americans, but, in fact, they were from Galicia—Eastern European Jews who hid their backgrounds because they did not live in New York City, but were associated with better universities where Jews were not permitted in the past. Actually, they should have no trouble understanding the Indian caste system. But one could not say this to them. They were as mentally blocked as the *yadavs* of Bihar who wore the sacred thread and called themselves twice-born.

Kali visited us in the summer of 1950. I was then living in Kaffatorp, a little post-station in Goinge Forest in South Sweden. It has since been shut down. That happened so long ago that it is not even listed among the changed offices in the catalogue. I was renting a small farm, no longer being worked: Lilla Byrona. There I had my library and study. It was in the early autumn and we walked in the beech forest. I asked him about communalism in India and about the Partition, developments I did not understand.

"Religious contradictions are actually political or social in nature," he said. "When it comes down to it, there is a historical explanation for the religious divisions. It is a consequence of Indian feudalism. The ruling dynasties and their administration were Muslim, and, at the same time, Islam provided some of the poorest and most oppressed an opportunity to escape their wretched lot. But the contradictions that have emerged during the decades preceding independence, and now during the partition, are a consequence of a determined policy on the part of the British. Whether they desired these results or not is a moot point. They believed that by using the tactic of 'divide and rule' they could maintain their sway. And what happened to them was what happens to others who play with fire. The same thing is taking place in Palestine.

"What happened to us in Bengal was that the British created a religious conflict. Before 1909, there were no religious riots. The first years after the British partitioned Bengal, attempts were made to maintain unity right across the border. On the one side there was now a Muslim majority, and on the other a Hindu one. Certainly, the large province of Bengal could have been partitioned. It should have been partitioned. The speakers of the Oriya language should have been united in one administrative unit, the Hindi speakers in another, and those of us who spoke Bengali in another. But it wasn't done that way. The Bengalis were divided. In the area which became the new Bengal, those who spoke Bengali were a minority. There were, for example, seventeen million who spoke Bengali as opposed to twenty million who spoke Hindi. East Bengal became a Bengal where religion, Islam, was decisive. If the British had merely sought effective administrative units, then they would have established a unified Bengal for all those who spoke Bengali. Look at the map! Bengal constitutes an economic entity. After the partition, my family found itself in East Bengal.

"In this manner, the British were able to turn the contradictions into religious issues. In 1905, after all other forms of political activity had proven useless, and the British refused to listen to reason, the boycott movement was initiated. The idea came from China. A boycott of American goods had begun there to end the racial discrimination suffered by the Chinese in the United States. The Chinese were treated like bonded labor and were deported as soon as they were no longer of use. This campaign against British goods would unite fifty million Bengalis in opposition to the British and would hit them where it hurt most: in their wallets. At the same time, it would be beneficial to the development of domestic industry. Everyone participated in the *Swadeshi* movement, from zamindars to washermen. Those who persisted in buying British products or serving the British were ostracized. It was in a sense the caste system which put its stamp on the social boycott. This, incidentally, is one of the tactics of the British working class. In Britain they call it to 'send to Coventry.' So this business of caste shouldn't be taken too seriously. He who violated the swadeshi movement was punished in such a way that no one ate with him, no one bought anything from him or sold him anything, no one married him, no barber shaved him and no children played or spoke with his children. The British could do a great deal to aid those serving them, but no government can break a social boycott like this. In a small town, it was enough to drive a man mad if he and his family became the object of this boycott. Man is, as Aristotle said, a social animal.

"But the British had a weapon. Religion. In 1905, 1906 and 1907, the swadeshi movement grew. But it was the Hindu middle class which led it and profited from it. The nationalist movement was also dominated by well-educated, well-to-do Hindus of the new middle class—and, to some degree, from the zamindar families. So the British put through a series of minor reforms in 1909. They gave the Muslims a greater representation on religious grounds; they received more posts within the administration. They were given various personal privileges. You see then how caste, class, religion and nationality are woven together into a complicated snare. At first, Hindus and Muslims had demonstrated side by side for a unified Bengal. The crowds had shouted 'Alla ho Akbar' and 'Bande Mataram' in turn. But with British assistance, the class contradiction between the poor masses and the usurers who exploited them was transformed into a contradiction between Muslims and Hindus. The agents of the British political police incited the Hindu and Muslim fanatics. On March 4, 1907, their efforts bore fruit. On that day in Comilla, in what is now East Pakistan, the first real pogrom took place. 'Communal riot' is our name for it. But in Europe you say pogrom. It is the same: looting, arson, rape and persecution. The authorities did nothing. The pogroms were in their interest just as they were in contemporary Czarist Russia. The British government and the Czar's black hundreds pursued the same policy. If Jews are turned against gentiles, and Muslims against Hindus, it is easier for the rulers to oppress them all. Once religious strife flares up, it takes on a life of its own. That is obvious when you see what has happened in our country, or in Ireland, or in Palestine. the British start the fire, but are then unable to put it out.

"But naturally, we are influenced by our culture. We are—or, at least, were in our generation—trained in introspection and analysis. Europeans often believe that Hinduism is a strange, mystic ritualism. That's completely wrong. I am not religious, but I am naturally fascinated by the *Upanishads*. I was brought up to be. One needn't believe in a god to be a good Hindu. The *Upanishads* demand an uncompromising intellectualism. That is, if one is of a philosophic nature or if one is, at all, a product of the intellectual tradition and its castes. For others, the *Up-*

anishads can naturally play the part of a Bible for the worst kind of hea-
thenism. But for us, Hinduism is not what it seems to be to the European.

"Although I am bound by neither religion nor caste, I know that I am
influenced by Hinduism, that I am Hindu. For better or worse. We
Bengalis are known for the 'worse.' The intellectual training we receive in
studying the *Upanishads* leads also to hairsplitting which can pervert
both sense and reason. First one is drawn into rational arguments, and
then one argues so smoothly, so cleverly, so dialectically—that, in the
end, one finds oneself stuck in a metaphysical quagmire. That is a deep-
rooted tradition. The whole tradition of introverted speculation that
lures men and women into sterile meditation, self-abnegation and passivity, is a dangerous temptation. I myself have felt it. Many of our best
minds have fallen victim to it. It is a scourge among Bengalis. Our great
tradition has both its good and bad elements. But it is our very own."

That evening he looked at my books. He asked what I had on India. It
was not much: *Bhagavad Gita* translated by Nino Runeberg, the Penguin
edition of *Coolie* by Mulk Raj Anand, Tagore's *My Reminiscences*, and
something else, *The Little Clay Cart*, I believe.

"*Gita* can be read in different ways," he said. "But for those of us who
were nationalists, it was a call to patriotic action. It is still a revolutionary
work, a revolutionary poem, for the Indian people. It's just a matter of
interpreting it along those lines. Towards the end of the twenties, when
all our leaders sat in jail, many of us in Jugantar and Anushilan, the
western and eastern sections of the nationalist party in Bengal, believed
that the time of terrorism was past. We were well-settled. Many party
members, including myself, believed that we lived in a peaceful age. India would not be troubled by turmoil, we would not be summoned to
action, there would not be an uprising before the next world war—and
that seemed far off. There were even those among us who believed in
Gandhi and civil disobedience, who thought that would lead to Indian
independence, and who felt that we would write off our goal of armed
insurrection. When our leaders in jail heard this, they became worried.
They felt that we were in the process of being lost to India. So they sent
us a message which said, 'the age of Gita is not yet past; we must pre-
pare ourselves for selfless karma, or action.' We had no difficulty understanding the message, and immediately changed course and prepared
for the armed struggle."

I was not aware that the *Bhagvad Gita* could be interpreted in that way.
But after having spoken with Kali, I re-read it in a new light:

So consider the welfare of the world
And carry out the actions duty bids!

Whatever a great man does
Ordinary people will imitate
They will follow his example. (III, 19-20-21)

If the age of the *Gita* was not yet past, this meant that someone had to come forward to kill the arrogant British so that the people might see that they could be defeated.

"Terrorism must be considered in a historical context. It is not enough to hold a moral judgement on it. It was the same for us as for the nineteenth century Russian revolutionaries. We lived under total oppression and we felt that the inertia too, was total. The idea was not to terrorize the people, but to awaken them with a courageous, liberating deed. I am aware of what Marx, Lenin and Stalin said on this subject, but I must also say that I, with my own eyes, have seen that the courage and self-sacrifices of a few individuals can really rouse the masses. As long as it was only a question of civil disobedience, India could seethe with unrest, but the British were calm. They were on top of the situation. They made use of the non-violent character of the movement. But when we initiated terrorist actions against the oppressor, and the British saw that they couldn't stop us with arrests, torture, deportations or even hangings, they became afraid. They put up screens on their windows. The high officials travelled with bodyguards. Civil servants began to carry guns, grew distrustful and were afraid to meet unknown young Indians even in their own offices. The entire nation saw that they were not invulnerable. Indians then stopped crawling before the sahibs. It gave them self-respect. Terrorism was—and I still believe this—a step in the development of the mass movement.

"Of course, it was characteristic of middle class revolutionaries. But can the middle class just be ignored? All of us, and Jawaharlal Nehru and Bose, were from middle class backgrounds, and we developed in different directions. Some moved to the right and became fascists—even if it did take a while to see where they were going—and others moved to the left. Some of us went all the way to the Communist Party. When considering developments, one can no more remove middle class revolutionaries from Bengal than one can from nineteenth century Russia. Under certain conditions, when repression is severe, a small group of self-sacrificing individuals must take up the cudgels for the whole nation. A handful of heroes must breach the wall so that the masses can follow. That's why it was so important for us that our jailed leaders reminded us of *Gita* and of the inevitability of action."

Kali was right. There is a tradition of terrorism in India as there was in nineteenth century Russia. But so that it will not be confused with the criminal demi-monde that calls itself revolutionary-terrorist in Western Europe, one should see clearly the difference between Russia and India, and Western Europe. To quote from a banned nationalist text from 1925:

> The Indian revolutionaries are neither terrorists nor anarchists. They never aim at spreading anarchy in the land, and therefore they can never properly be called anarchists. Terrorism is never their object and they cannot be called terrorists. They do not believe that terrorism alone can bring independence and they do not want terrorism for terrorism's sake, although they may at times resort to this method as a very effective means of retaliation. The present government exists solely because the foreigners have successfully been able to terrorize the Indian people. The Indian people do not love their English masters, they do not want them to be here; but they do help the Britishers simply because they are terribly afraid of them; and this very fear resists the Indians from extending their helping hands to the revolutionaries, not that they do not love them.
>
> This official terrorism is surely to be met by counter terrorism. A spirit of utter helplessness pervades every stratum of our society and terrorism is an effective means of restoring the proper spirits in the society without which progress will be difficult.

Five years later another banned text stated:

> We have been taken to task for our Terroristic Policy. Our answer is that terrorism is never the object of revolutionaries, nor do they believe that terrorism alone can bring independence. No doubt the revolutionaries think, and rightly, that it is only by resorting to terrorism alone that they can find a most effective means of retaliation.

The arguments against these views were to the point and clearly formulated. Take, for example, the open letters written in July 1925 by the Communist Youth International to the Bengal Revolutionary Organization of Youth:

> Individual terror cannot serve as a means of emancipating the Indian people, for the reasons: (1) a terrorist act directed against an individual does not remove the whole system: in place of the one who has been removed the British imperialists will appoint another; one official merely takes the place of another, but the system of oppression remains intact; (2) terror demands a tremendous expenditure of effort and diverts attention from the fundamental tasks of rallying, organizing and revolutionarily educating the masses.

Individual terror is the usual method of fighting adopted by groups of intellectuals who do not understand the significance of mass fighting (who have no confidence in the possibilities of this form of fighting) and who believe that a small group of intellectuals is able to bring about the revolution without the active participation of the masses of the toilers.

Instead of sacrificing our best forces on acts of terror, these should go right in among the masses of the people, in order to rouse them for the fight. All your efforts should be directed towards organizing the masses for the fight; the whole experience of Russia and of other countries, and your own experience, teaches this. Lenin's elder brother was a terrorist and was executed for his attempt to assassinate the tsar. On the death of his brother, Lenin vowed to fight to the end for the same cause, but by other and more certain methods. He did not take up the method of single combat adopted by the intellectuals. He set to work to rally the masses for the heroic struggle for liberty, and he led the masses of the toilers to victory.

It was M. N. Roy who was given the task of writing this letter by the Executive Committee of the Communist Youth International. He was then India's representative in the Comintern leadership and he knew what he spoke about on the subject of individual terrorism.

In 1905, a young *brahman* student from Changripota in Bengal, Narendranath Bhattacharya, received a warning from his school principal. Bhattacharya had been reading books about Garibaldi and had been seen at political meetings in Calcutta. Narendranath countered by organizing a public meeting in front of the school when class was not in session. The authorities took measures. Narendranath and seven others were expelled from school. He was eighteen at the time.

During the next decade he became one of the leading members of the Bengali terrorist movement. He was a militant nationalist. He developed the technique of knocking down British soldiers with a single well-aimed blow behind the ear. The club was concealed under the clothing and emerged only at the very moment the blow was delivered. By the time the soldier sank to the ground, the assailant would have already disappeared into the crowd. He carried on subversive activity in the Tenth Jat regiment. The British were forced to disband it. Disguised as a holy man to get away from the British informers, he wandered throughout India to visit the survivors from 1857 and to learn from their experience. He took a leading part in confiscations and bank robberies.

At the time Narendra Bhattacharya—later known as Roy—led this activity in Bengal, the young Koba, later known as Stalin, led his Party's

confiscations and bank robberies in the Caucasus. Roy planned and carried out the first motorized hold-up in India: the theft of 18,000 rupees
from Bird & Company to finance party work. His friends and comrades
from that time describe him as being thoroughly political. If he killed, it
was not because of emotional motives, but only out of political necessity.
In the organization, it was also he who most seriously attempted to
transform terrorism into guerrilla warfare as the only road to liberation.
While others still talked about gods and feelings, he discussed methods
for disintegrating the British Army through revolutionary terror.

In 1914, with the outbreak of World War I, the British educated lawyer,
Mohandas Karamchand, better known as Gandhi, promised the British
total support. The Bengali *brahman* Narendranath Bhattacharya, however, was given the task of negotiating with the Germans in order to pro-
cure weapons and ammunition for the armed struggle against the British
in India.

After many adventures, some quite involved, he landed in San Francisco, California, disguised as Father Martin, a young theologian on his
way to Europe for further studies. On disembarking, he became M. N.
Roy, the name he kept until his death. Together with the Ghadar Party
he was to obtain weapons to be used in the national liberation struggle of
India.

In time, Roy found himself with Lenin and the Comintern in Moscow.
For a period, he was the Comintern's chief representative for activity in
the colonial and dependent countries. He was sent to China, failed, and
clashed with Mao Zedong who, in his talks in northern Shensi in 1936,
scornfully dismissed Roy as incompetent. Roy returned to Moscow, dis-
agreed with Stalin, quit the Comintern, returned to India, was jailed by
the British, tried to establish his own party and, later, his own political
philosophy: radical humanism. He died in 1954. He is one of this century's most remarkable figures. A nationalist, more nationalist than anyone. On reading Marx in 1916, within a span of a few years, he was a
leading world revolutionary. He made a break with the Comintern—or,
rather, the Comintern broke with him—after the Sixth World Congress in
1928. He returned to India and was imprisoned by the British. He
worked in the Congress, but broke with them in 1940 as an anti-fascist
who saw Hitler as the main enemy. He defended and made excuses for
Stalin who had expelled him. He wrote brilliant books. It was he who
both developed the theory of terrorism and combated terrorism with intellectual arguments. But towards the end of his life, he wrote in his (unfinished) autobiography:

> Those reflections drove me to the conclusion that only the tradition
> of an older, more spontaneous, less conventional culture could en-

able one to reject the artificialities and vulgarities of the bourgeois
social order, and look beyond for a richer pattern and higher ideals
of human culture which will not be constricted by any class prejudice. Concretely, I felt that an aristocrat, intellectually emancipated
from the prejudices of his class, might be a more disinterested and
culturally more Dionysian social revolutionary than the most pas-
sionately class-conscious proletarian. In other words, intellectual
aristocracy, being a common human heritage, could alone lay down
the foundation of a really new social order.

Kali never spoke thus. But he did speak once of his struggle against
the temptations presented by anarchistic individual intellectualism and
of his love for Aldous Huxley. While his loyalty to the socialist ideals
turned into loyalty to Russia, he maintained his sympathy for Bengali
terrorism as he once knew it. In many ways, Roy and Kali explained each
other—and the Bengali intellectual—for me.

What I was not to learn for many years and did not have confirmed before I saw in Bombay in 1974 what P. Sundarayya had published, was
that six months after Kali had spoken to me of terrorism, depressed by
the constant dissent among the Indian communists, Josef Stalin had criticized the Indian communists for their ambiguous attitude concerning
the use of individual terror.

The ever-divided Communist Party of India was, at this point, more
divided than ever. While a peasant war was taking place in Telengana,
the party had ceased to function as a unified organization. Various
groups and factions operated independently. The divisions ran along political lines, as well as regional and individual lines; various leaders de-
tested one another. Unable to reach any kind of unity, the central
committee decided to adjourn and for the time being send a delegation
to Moscow to get directives from the Soviet party. The delegation of the
central committee of the Communist Party of India was made up of its
General Secretary C. Rajeswar Rao, M. Basavapunniah, and the representatives of the Bombay opposition, S. A. Dange and Ajoy Kumar
Ghosh. The central committee of the Soviet party had established a commission on Indian affairs headed by its General Secretary J. V. Stalin, including G. M. Malenkov, V. M. Molotov and M. A. Suslov as members.
At the meetings in Moscow, the party program which was submitted to
the congress of the Communist Party of India in 1951 was drawn up.
Guidelines were formulated for political work in India, the party's general secretary was dismissed and other changes in party leadership were
made. I will return to this subject. But first I want to point out that there
was no legal way that the central committee of the Communist Party of
India could delegate its responsibility in this fashion to J. V. Stalin, G. M.

Malenkov, V. M. Molotov, and M. A. Suslov. The Comintern had been out of business for almost eight years.

To the best of my knowledge, these commission meetings were the last time that Stalin appeared in the role he had played in the Comintern's various commissions during the twenties. Mao Zedong's revolution had triumphed in China only a year before. For Stalin it was a matter of consolidating his reputation as a leader of partisans. At the same time it was important for Stalin—who as Koba in 1907 had borne the political responsibility for the robberies in Tiflis and Baku—to now reiterate Marxist theoretical condemnation of individual terror:

SOME QUESTIONS RELATING TO PARTISAN WAR AND INDIVIDUAL TERRORISM

Question: Is it correct to resort to partisan war in one particular area where the conditions are ripe for it, even though other rural areas are not ripe for it, and the workers are not ready to support it with mass actions?

Answer: Yes, you can and should resort to it. To start or not, does not depend on us. It depends on the organizational state of the masses and their mood. If the masses are ready, you must start it.

Question: Have we to take up partisan struggle only when the peasant struggle for partial demands reaches the stage of land distribution and establishing of village peasant committees? Or can we take it up when the movement is still in the stage of struggle for partial demands, for example, rent reduction?

Answer: The partisan struggle also has stages. It starts with smaller demands—let us say, reduction of rent. It is not yet a partisan struggle. If the enemy refuses to grant the demands and the peasant is eager to win it by force, then partisan struggles can start. True, it is not the struggle for seizure of land but only for a reduction of rent, still it will be partisan struggle. Hence, it does not depend on us. If the masses are ready and eager, we should assist them.

Question: Can partisan warfare even of the most elementary type be developed in areas where communications are well-developed?

Answer: Yes, when encirclement occurs, transfer the best forces to another area. Lead out the armed forces so as to join it with the armed forces in another area, so as to create a liberation army of your own.

Question: The aim of the partisan struggle must be liquidation of the enemy's armed forces with the active assistance of the masses of peasants. To kill individual oppressors with a view to terrorizing all the other oppressors and making them renounce their oppression is terrorism. But I cannot understand the complete banning of any individual action against any oppressor landlord, notorious official or a spy, as a matter of principle, under the name of terrorism. In my opinion, at times, it becomes necessary in the earlier phase of the partisan struggle, to organize individual actions against some notorious oppressors, not in order to terrorize other oppressors into renouncing their oppression but to guard the safety of the partisan squads. I am unable to understand how such actions make the people passive. As I understand international literature, such individual actions were conducted by partisans against German and Japanese fascists in the occupied countries during the anti-fascist war, and they are being done even now in Asian countries where partisan warfare is going on—Malaya, Burma, Indo-China, etc. If I remember rightly, such actions were not only not banned by Lenin in his article on partisan warfare but, on the other hand, he severely criticized the Mensheviks who condemned them as anarchism. I seek clarification on this point.

Answer: The comrade says he cannot understand why individual terrorism should slow down the action of the masses. Individual terrorism is so called not merely because it is directed against individual oppressors but also because it is carried out by individuals or groups irrespective of the masses. Individual terrorism creates the illusion that the main evil is not the regime but individuals; that if only a few more are destroyed, the regime will be finished off. What conclusions will the masses draw? That with the help of terrorism of this type, it is possible to destroy the regime after a long struggle. And if such conclusions are drawn by the peasants, they will say, 'no use developing the struggle against the regime. Our glorious terrorist will do the job.' Such sentiment weakens the onslaught of the masses against the regime. Therefore, it is harmful and dangerous.

Individual terrorism creates the belief that the main force lies in the heroic terrorists and not in the masses. The role of the masses becomes to watch and applaud. That means to cultivate passivity. Marx and Engels taught that the liberation of the masses has to be won by the masses themselves. That is what you ought to tell them. Different results follow from individual terrorism. The masses look to the terrorist as heroes and liberators.

The comrade's reference to Lenin is without foundation. We can give him articles by Lenin directed against individual terrorism.

You must know how hard Lenin hit the Mensheviks when the revolution was at an ebb and they took to terror.

The theory of individual terrorism comes to the front when the revolution recedes. It is a reflection of the weakness of the movement. Whenever the revolutionary movement is rising and the masses themselves rise, the theory of individual terrorism disappears from the horizon. The comrade must bear that in mind.

P. Sundarayya had, of course, his own reasons for publishing this in December 1972: it can partly be explained by the fact that he—as a leader of that sector of the old communist party that calls itself the Communist Party of India (M)—wanted to damage C. Rajeswar Rao and S. A. Dange, who belonged to the leadership of the totally pro-Russian, rightist communist party, the Communist Party of India; and partly by the fact that he wanted to get at the peasant revolutionaries and Naxalites in the Communist Party of India (Marxist-Leninist) and closely affiliated groups, trying to make use of Stalin's authority against those who were trying to use Mao Zedong's.

Yet, more important than all that, more important than Stalin's statement of his views on individual terrorism (which as far as I can see, is not an answer to the comrade's question) is the light these talks throw on the miserable state of the political left in India: its lack of national responsibility and of the understanding that it is the masses, and not a few heroes—not even J. V. Stalin or V. M. Molotov—who, relying on their own forces, must liberate themselves. Just as India suffers from the existence of a comprador bourgeoisie, so, too, did India suffer—and still suffers—from the existence of comprador revolutionaries and comprador communists! The revolutionaries act like Calcutta's intellectuals of the nineteenth century: they turn away from the masses and travel across the oceans in search of an authoritative gospel in a guiding metropolis.

The acute dissension among India's communists had been caused by the party's General Secretary B. T. Ranadive in 1948, when in connection with an attack on the peasant movement in Telengana, he had criticized Mao Zedong and "the so-called theory of the new democracy alleged to be propounded by Mao (as) a new addition to Marxism." B. T. Ranadive condemned Mao's theories, calling to mind Tito and Browder, and declared that "Marx, Engels, Lenin and Stalin (are) the authoritative sources of Marxism. It has not discovered new sources for Marxism beyond these."

Besides the fact that B. T. Ranadive's statement is an expression of a dogmatic theology completely alien to Marx (a Marxism in the tradition of Marx cannot have its "source" in some authoritative texts), it is worth bearing in mind that this report to the Political Bureau and Central Com-

mittee was adopted by the Political Bureau as the party's official standpoint in December 1948, probably at the behest of the Russians. It is inconceivable that General Secretary Ranadive would attack by name the
chairman of China's Communist Party as being a revisionist without having the assurance of Moscow. Ten months later, Mao's armies were victorious, while even now, thirty-two years later, the official Indian
communists are weak, disunited, mired in parliamentary intrigue and
widespread corruption. A guerrilla war is in progress in the forests, but
the Indian peasant masses still remain in deep poverty and under an oppression similar to that of China in the twenties.

Where does the difference lie between India and China? I do not believe that it is a matter of more or less correctly, grasped theory. I own
several running meters of revolutionary documents from both countries.
In these texts there is much wisdom and much that has proved to be fool-
ishness. Nor are the Chinese masses by nature more revolutionary. In India, the poor peasants and untouchables take up the struggle whenever
possible, and they make use of the slogans, organizations and banners
which seem appropriate. Neither were the Chinese leaders so much
more knowledgeable or competent. Mao became a leader of world stature, but he achieved that rank by standing in the forefront of the peasants' struggles. He was not a born genius who suddenly appeared in
China.

The decisive difference in the development of India and China is that
the Indian revolutionaries were never able to emancipate themselves
from European authority. In China, they learnt from the Comintern and
its representatives, and then went their own way. The errors and mistakes they made were their own, errors which they could correct themselves.

As long as Roy held chief responsibility for Indian affairs within the
Comintern, there was a natural link. But when Roy, during the intriguing in the Comintern (to a large part due to the fact that Roy was in opposition to Pjatnitsky, who managed the Comintern's finances and who
preferred easily corrupted foreign comrades to the aristocratic Roy), lost
responsibility for work in India, and when India's communists were put
under the authority of the Communist Party of Great Britain, the prevention of the Indian revolution became a purely routine affair for the police.
The idea that the British communists, who had certainly been unable to
influence developments in their own country, should be able to lead India's millions on the road to social revolution, was a fine colonial
thought. It also led to such catastrophic consequences for India that one
is forced to ask oneself if even back in the twenties Moscow really
wished to see genuine revolutionaries in foreign countries. In any case,
revolution and the nation did not come to be merged in India. Also the

communist leaders remained brown sahibs...regardless of the fact that most of them were *brahmans*!

Kali was not a *brahman*, but almost: he was a *kulin kayastha*, and when he was looking at Tagore's *Reminiscences*, I said:

"That's what I know about growing up in India."

"We weren't that rich," Kali responded.

He came from a zamindar family from near Khulna in what is now Bangladesh, about 150 kilometers from Calcutta. In 1793, the British had transformed the feudal revenue gatherers in the Bengal they occupied into zamindars: hereditary landowners with the obligation of paying tax to the British, but also with the right to wring what they could from their subordinates. Kali's father was a lawyer in the city of Khulna. His household was large. It was not unlike a Victorian English upper middle class household with its many servants. The fact is that the existence of a great number of servants in Indian households is something introduced by the British. In the traditional Bengali household, the women of the house attend to all the indoor chores. Possibly, there was a *brahman* cook who prepared food that everybody could eat. Like so many other things considered typically Indian, the household with a great number of servants, each performing one of a vast number of specialized tasks, is a product of the independent feudal innovation in a Mughal setting of the British colonists.

A steady stream of poor peasants visited the house with gifts and services. That is what is called in Bengal *vate* or *veth*, and in Andhra Pradesh *vetti*. It is forced labor, forced service, unpaid; it was given to the zamindar and his family as *pranami*, obeisance before the lord. It could be fish, eggs, chicken, lambs, fruit, vegetables and even cows with calves. It was this that was necessary when the tenant-farmers, who in reality were serfs, were to negotiate with the lord.

Agents conducted the gathering of rents. The methods used were heavy handed. The tenant-farmers payed 50 percent in rent. During Kali's childhood, they carried on a struggle to lower it to 30 percent. The tenant-farmers tasted the milk, eggs and meat they produced only at weddings and funerals. To pay for these ceremonies, they borrowed money at an annual interest rate of 75 percent. They were always in debt. At harvest, the tenant-farmers paid 50 percent of the harvest to the lord, beside having to repay him the grain borrowed to keep the family alive. They had to support the family on anything that was left over.

Some of the tenant-farmers were obliged to work certain days on the land of the lord; some served thus ten or fifteen days in a year. Others—washermen, shoemakers, potters, barbers, chairbearers and people of similar occupations—were expected to serve whenever they were called upon. In exchange, they had the right to cultivate a plot of land. The priests, too, belonged to this category, although they were treated with respect. At the village markets and similar festivals, the sellers had to pay the zamindar two paisa per booth every day. Whoever protested was beaten. One tenant-farmer who had not paid on time was punished by being made to stand naked in the courtyard in the sun with a brick in each hand. He hanged himself later. This, however, was not one of Kali's father's tenants. Among the zamindars themselves, several battles occurred. On the state-owned land down in the Ganga's delta, Sundarbans, Kali's family had thousands of acres of rice paddy. Bloody conflicts took place with other landowners over these fields, conflicts in which, naturally, only subordinates and tenant-farmers could be hurt. But his father was a good, popular and well-respected man. When he died, the family moved back to the village of Senhati, across from Daulatpur, a little above Khulna.

There they lived in the traditional fashion of the extended family. Kali's uncles managed the business affairs. As for Kali, he attended school, and read the classics and novels such as Bankimchandra's *Anandamath*. This novel has been tremendously influential. For generations, young Bengalis have followed the example of the heroes of this novel, joining secret patriotic societies like the sanyasins, who in this novel admit no God other than the motherland and who were willing to sacrifice everything for it. The hymn 'Bande Mataram' (Hail Mother!) is part of this book. For long periods, this was the song of the independence movement. Bankimchandra Chatterjee can be considered Bengal's Walter Scott. The theme of the novel has been taken from the Sanyasi Rebellion in 1772-1774. A sanyasi—in Europe we might say holy beggar—gathered around him other beggars and starving peasants during the great famine. In 1773, near Rangpur, they succeeded in defeating a sepoy detachment commanded by Captain Thomas. The rebels were, however, eventually put down by regular British forces.

The novel is about a group which calls itself *santan*—that is, children, children of their native land. They live in an abandoned temple, called Ananda Math—abode of supreme happiness. They are initiated into the order with a ceremony in which they promise to forego home and friends "until Mother is rescued," Mother being their native land. They swear to deny themselves pleasure, renounce all wealth and property, resist their desires and give everything to the order. All caste differences are also to be abandoned: "All children belong to one caste; we do not make any distinction between *brahman* and *sudra* in this great mission."

They greeted each other with the phrase "Bande Mataram"—Hail Mother (Motherland). Those who became Children gave up their former names and took new ones. For Kali and his friends, *Anandamath* was the first great political inspiration. It was the same for almost all Bengali youth. The initiation ceremony for the militant, underground nationalist party, Anushilan—of which Kali was a part—was taken straight out of *Anandamath.*

Just as the *Upanishads* became philosophy and not mythology, and intellectual youths like Kali emancipated their minds from blind faith, they also struggled against superstition. He spent many a full-mooned night at the cremation-site down by the river. There he sat alone through the night, partly to show that the talk of ghosts and specters was just superstition, and partly to contend with the feelings the stories had stirred up in him, and to steel himself in the service of Mother.

The countryside was being transformed during these war years, when Kali and his friends trained themselves with lathis for the liberation of their homeland, when they founded their secret society to serve their Mother. A shortage of manpower was developing. Work could be found in the cities' textile mills, and the cities were not far away. In the village the workers could earn between 5 and 6 annas (16 annas to the rupee) for ten to twelve hours of hard labor in the fields. In the cities, they could earn between 12 annas to a rupee for eight hours of work in the textile mills. The war effort gave a boost to India's industrialization.

It was during the agitation in connection with the first world war that Kali became politically aware and joined the underground nationalist party. It took a long time after he first came into contact with the party before he could become a member. He eventually realized the reason. He was from a zamindar family. In Congress there were many zamindar families, but not in the underground movement. He had to prove his dependability before being accepted despite his social background.

In 1920, Congress organizers came to the village. By then Gandhi's movement had grown. Congress had officially adopted Gandhi's line. Members of the party joined Congress and made use of it as a legal front organization. In 1921, Kali became a member of the village Congress committee. That year, the party opened an ashram in Daulatpur. It was called Satyashram—the home of truth. Kiron Mukerjee was in charge. It was said of him that if he ran his hand across the forehead of a boy, that boy would forever be devoted to the revolution. Once when the police had surrounded the house he was in, he stripped naked, covered himself in ashes and wandered out, disguised as a holy man, without anyone noticing or recognizing him. Other revolutionaries such as Charu Ghosh and Kuntal Chakravarty—both poets and both taken early by tuberculosis—also stayed at this ashram. To this place came great men such as Bhupendra Kumar Dutt who could talk all night long about revolutionary theory and Party policy in a straightforward, crystal-clear way. He also came to this ashram to personally care for the two tuberculosis patients. He had just been released after serving five years in prison and would soon be jailed again for another six years, and then jailed yet again. Satish Chakravarti and Jiban Chatterjee hid from the police in this ashram. The remarkable thing about all these revolutionaries—men whose very names were feared by the police, men who were hunted all over Bengal—what was remarkable was their gentle and mellow patience, and the pains they took in talking to and teaching Kali and the other young members.

In 1921, Gandhi had been given dictatorial powers by Congress. He led the non-cooperation movement and promised *swaraj* within the year. No one explained exactly what *swaraj* was, whether it was dominion status within the British Commonwealth or total independence. All the same, he promised it. The Party worked within Congress, and with Congress as a front for this *swaraj*, while holding as its strategic goal total independence. Among themselves, Party members could joke about Gandhi's sanctity and the whole movement's sanctimoniousness, but in public and while working openly, they had to keep up appearances. In 1921, Gandhi came to Khulna where Kali met him. Had it not been for Kali's revolutionary consciousness, he would have been captivated by his gentle personality. He was, however, a vegetarian for several years following his encounter with Gandhi. In the summer of that year, Congress held its provincial conference for Bengal in Hessore. At first it was very impressive. But it was all just empty talk. Shyam Sundar Chakravarty spoke for two hours without saying anything of political interest. It was all just rhetoric. There was no debate within Congress, only oration.

In 1922, Gandhi called a halt to the movement. Just when it started to have an effect, he suspended it. All the Congress activists were left to face the government's brutal reprisals. The nation was shaken when this happened. It was treachery. Tens of thousands of activists had risked their lives and liberty, thousands had been beaten bloody and senseless, or had been shot. The Indian troops of the British had begun to waver, to go over to the side of the people, to turn against their foreign officers, and to refuse to fire on defenseless people. With final victory in sight, India lost everything.

"A single man put to nothing the sacrifices and efforts of millions."

In January 1924, the British arrested the nationalist leaders. That year, the provincial Congress conference was scheduled to be held in Seragunj. Kali was a delegate. It was decided that something should be done to put an end to the demoralization then widely felt. Gopinath Saha, a young political terrorist whom Kali had met in Calcutta and whom he knew to be a wise and sensitive individual, had decided to shoot a British officer, a man especially notorious as a torturer of political prisoners. He had not submitted his decision to the Party for approval. He also happened to shoot the wrong person. When he realized this, he immediately turned himself in to the police and expressed profound sorrow over his mistake. He proferred his deep regrets to the family of the victim, but at the same time emphasized that the torturer had to die and that he should be executed as soon as possible.

The Party delegates succeeded in having the provincial Congress conference adopt a resolution in which the conference paid tribute to Gopinath Saha and his patriotism. This was a slap in the face for Gandhi and the entire ideology of non-violence. It was also a direct challenge to the British: it was the first time in India that anyone ever applauded the terrorists' courage publicly. This aimed at unifying public opinion and radicalizing the struggle. The result was described in the Intelligence Bureau's secret report, "Terrorism in India 1917-1936":

> In June 1924, the Bengal Provincial Congress at their meeting at Seragunj passed a resolution expressing admiration for the spirit of self-sacrifice exhibited by Gopi Mohan Saha. The effects of the resolution were electrical. It became by far the most potent instrument for organization, and a perpetual incitement to the youth of Bengal to take to violent ways.

Later, Kali worked as an organizer at Daulatpur Hindu Academy and organized a student strike. He took part in the discussion on the need to resume the armed struggle, moved to Calcutta in 1928 and began studying law. In villages and schools all over Bengal, youth and student organizations were established. Elected delegates from these organizations were to form the Calcutta and Bengal Youth Association and Bengal Students' Association. Kali was elected member of the executive committee of the Students' Association. Out of about twenty committee members, there were only three or four who did not belong to the underground Nationalist Party. That was how effectively the organizational work had been carried out. The movement now possessed a good front, a legal organization with an office and newspaper.

At the same time, discussions were held about the long term goals of the movement. Some contact had been made with the communists, and during these discussions which were held underground (they met and talked informally so that it would not appear that they were holding a meeting), the leadership issued new directives. The Congress was not revolutionary. The Party must remain intact and maintain its independence. The members had to be trained in guerrilla warfare. A parallel underground organization must be set up clandestinely in the event that the police destroyed the first. The leadership also felt that socialism could not be ruled out in independent India. The minimum program, however, called for an independent and democratic India. The leaders had been released from prison and had begun to organize the Party along stricter lines. These new directives meant that the conditional support Gandhi had been given since 1919 was now withdrawn. No regular guerrilla training had taken place for ten years. Now preparations were made for the armed struggle. Laboratories were set up for the production of explosives. This was done by a group of medicine and engineering students under the direction of a young doctor who directed a research institute.

Kali was active in Congress with propaganda work. He was second in command. The group's task was to make contact with individuals of social and economic influence, who were not to be recruited into the Party but were only to be made sympathetic towards revolutionary ideas and be ready to participate in legal activities when necessary. He was also a member of the Bengal Provincial Congress Committee, and of the Indian League for Independence, whose guidelines had been drawn up by Bhupendra Kumar Dutt and which had Subash Chandra Bose as its president. He was then secretary of the National Congress. Jawaharlal Nehru, who was president of Congress, as well as labor leaders not belonging to Congress, were also members of the League.

In December 1928, the Indian National Congress was held in Calcutta. The Party was the driving force in the establishment of the volunteer corps. It was called Bengal Volunteers, and its members wore khaki uniforms and trained with lathis. The drill book was the same as that used by the British Army. Subash Chandra Bose was given the title General Officer Commanding, according to British custom. His uniform was impressive. Kali was treasurer.

Gandhi did not approve. He spoke of comic-opera soldiers and held the suspicion that the Party was involved although he could not prove anything. The police hated it. Suddenly, the entire underground army was openly demonstrating in the streets of Calcutta and calling themselves door-keepers. However, the police were careful not to make things more difficult for Gandhi in holding down the radical opposition. Except for Bose and a few others, the whole organization came from Jugantar or Anushilan. The organization functioned for about six months before it was officially disbanded in March 1929. But as for the Congress meeting, it was a step backward. Gandhi opposed the resolution on independence. Jawaharlal Nehru, who had pledged to speak in its favor, went back on his promise a few hours before the meeting. It took two hours for Kali and the other cadres from the Party to talk Subash Chandra Bose into speaking in opposition to Gandhi. He finally agreed to do it. But although Motilal and Jawaharlal Nehru beat Bose, their victory was weak. They drove through a compromise resolution which threatened the British that if they did not turn India into a dominion within a year's time,

Congress would demand total independence. But it would make this demand in a non-violent manner. At the same time, both the elder and younger Nehru were frightened by the strength of the radical opposition.

The year 1928 was also the first time that the working class appeared before Congress. Twelve thousand workers marched in a demonstration to the meeting to hear Gandhi speak. Congress had felt that it did not have the time to hear the workers. The time was strictly apportioned. In any case, when the demonstration arrived, negotiations were in progress between police representatives and Congress leadership about whether the workers' demonstration was to be stopped by the police. The police were ready to step in against the workers the moment Congress leadership requested assistance. Both the Congress voluntary infantry and cavalry were made ready for action. The motorcycle brigade was also prepared. The workers' demonstration advanced. Confidently, the workers shouted nationalist slogans. At the last moment, Congress decided to receive the workers' delegation. Gandhi and other Congress leaders made speeches to them.

In March 1929, Kali went to work on the weekly publication *Swadhinata* (Freedom). At that time it had a circulation of between ten and twelve thousand copies and was the leading revolutionary paper. Every week the police raided the paper. Since the penalty for seditious writing was approximately two years in jail, there was always a group of volunteers ready to go to jail for the Party. Bhupendra Kumar Dutt and Arun Guha wrote the editorial articles and Kali shared the editing duties with Jotish Bhowmick.

That year, thirty-two members of the Worker and Peasant Party had been placed on trial charged with high treason. The British held the trial in Meerut to avoid the jury they would have been forced to deal with in Bombay or Calcutta. A jury, according to the administrators of justice, would have difficulty in taking a judicial view of the case. This trial pushed the nationalists closer to the communists. The gulf between the communists and nationalists was otherwise deep. The nationalists felt that while the communists did think as rebels, it was also a question of acting as rebels. Now that the communists were on trial, many nationalists felt that they had proven that they also lived as rebels.

In 1930, the situation grew more charged. Congress began the non-cooperation movement and in Chittagong the nationalists seized the arsenal on April 18. This was the sharpest blow to strike the British since 1857. Mass arrests followed immediately. *Swadhinata* decided to publish an editorial entitled "Bravo Chittagong!" The paper was bound to be shut down by the British in any case, and it was better to go out with an article praising the armed insurrection than to just disappear with a whimper. The British made a final attempt. They contacted Hari Kumar Chakravarty and promised 500 rupees a month from the Intelligence Bureau in Calcutta if the publication from that time on would express positive opinions on the recommendations of the Simon Commission. Otherwise, they threatened, the consequences would be grave.

But *Swadhinata* published the article "Bravo Chittagong!" and the Party went totally underground. The British introduced censorship and special laws which suspended the normal rule of law.

After the Party had gone underground, Motilal Nehru made contact with it. He wanted to put some force behind Congress' struggle. He arranged that the Party would cut the telegraph lines in Bengal. Motilal Nehru had the money to pay for the operation handed over to Kali. But Motilal Nehru did not understand that covert operations demand absolute secrecy. He had allowed word of his plan to leak out. The Party found itself in a difficult situation. Because the British had been warned by Motilal Nehru's indiscretion, the operation became very dangerous. But it was also an act that was politically appropriate, and politically correct to cooperate with Motilal Nehru who up till then had been so cautious. Since most of the leaders were now in prison, the operations were led by Manoranjan Gupta, Rashik Das and Kali. Kali was the liaison man between headquarters and the operational field groups. Thanks to proper planning, the Party was able to cut the telegraph lines at the same time in almost every district in Bengal, and in only two cases were the saboteurs caught.

While the organization was hard pressed by the need to provide safe houses for all those who had gone underground and those who had fled into Calcutta, the group led by Dr. Narayan Roy, which was to produce explosives, had finished their work. They had produced large quantities of amatol and aluminium powder with detonators and all that was necessary. However, they still did not have adequate bomb-casings. Experiments were carried out using brass and iron. The results were splendid, but the bombs were difficult to hide in clothing.

Together with a metallurgist and an industrial chemist, Kali developed a suitable brass and aluminium alloy. Tests proved that bombs cased in this alloy were ideal. Later, it became known that the British considered these aluminium bombs to be of the highest professional quality.

Weapons were hard to come by. They were smuggled in but the British had tightened their surveillance of the ports. The criminal element and the organized gangsters were also hostile. The British had threatened them against cooperating with the nationalists, and they had sided with the British in order to be able to carry on with their regular criminal activities. The first bombs were ready in July 1930. The plans were also drawn up. Suitable targets had been selected in Calcutta for a hard-hitting concentrated operation that would hurt the British ten times worse than Chittagong. But there were not enough small arms. Means of transport and money were also in short supply. At the same time, many of those in hiding were becoming increasingly uneasy and nervous. They wanted action. Any action.

Ganesh Ghosh proposed that one city block, any block in Central Calcutta, should be liberated in such a way that the British could only get to it through aerial bombardment or artillery. The Indian flag would be raised there. This would be a total challenge that would be seen and heard throughout the world. The plan was adopted.

However, on August 25, the assassination attempt on the life of the police chief of Calcutta failed. Anuja Sen and Dinesh Mazumdar threw two bombs at his car. He got away but Anuja Sen and Dinesh Mazumdar were arrested by the British. Anuja Sen was a skilful bomber. He was not killed by the bomb. He was arrested and executed by the British police in the same way the Indian police execute political prisoners who do not reveal useful information. During the day that followed, the police carried out raid after raid. The entire communication system of the Party was destroyed. The various groups now began to act on their own. The leadership no longer had control over developments. Through great effort the organization was re-established and on August 27 and 28 the headquarters began to function once more. But out in the provinces, communications were still broken. On the 29th, the chiefs of police of both Bengal and Dacca districts were shot. The former died. On the 30th, a bomb was thrown into the home of the police inspector in Mymensingh. But it was hoped that developments could be brought back under control so that a broad coordinated attack could be mounted. But on August 31, 1930, Kali was arrested by the Special Branch of the Intelligence Department in Calcutta.

What followed is not atypical. Interrogation and prison, and more interrogation. But the head of the Intelligence Bureau was a relative, a cousin, and he told Kali:

"You are disgracing the family."

Three thousand people had been jailed, and British methods were harsh. Kali's cousin threatened him with a stay in prison of not less than five years. Perhaps seven. But considering the family connection, he did have a way out. Kali could leave the country, he could agree to be deported. Fourteen days after this conversation with his cousin, Kali sat on a train to Bombay in the company of a police inspector and a plainclothesman. In the spring of 1931, Kali sailed from India for London.

Many of his friends were dead. Others were in prison.

Verdict on the Dead

In Calcutta, I live in the past. The hotel is typical of the turn of the century. The room is spacious. This is a hotel for missionaries, plantation owners and big shopowning Parsis from Bombay. Outside the main door, the servants sit on the ground, leaning against the wall.

I have received a letter from Mr A. Datta. He is P.A. to the Deputy Commissioner in Mokochung, Nagaland. He is upset with me. He is reading *China Notebook, 1975–1978* which has just appeared in English. In it, I have compared Shanghai with Calcutta. I wrote that Shanghai before 1949 was as repulsive as Calcutta.

> I have not much knowledge of Shanghai, but what makes you write that Calcutta is a repulsive city? A non-Calcuttan must read the pulse of Calcutta, then only will he find the charm of the city. You have damaged the image of our city by making such a comment. I wish you to drop this line from the next edition.

He is right, of course.

I can excuse myself on the grounds that I meant to write that the poverty, slums and oppression in Calcutta are similar to that of Old Shanghai. But that is not what is written in the book. Thus I committed the very error I have attacked so many others for making: I adopted the commonplace European, standard image of Asian poverty. The grovelling beggars, Mother Theresa, dying children. That was a mistake. For while all these things do exist, that is not the truth about Calcutta. Calcutta is a tremendous intellectual and financial power center. Just how is it that I spent my time in Calcutta? I visited museums, bought books, met friends, frequented editorial offices, discussed issues.

The truth about Calcutta—and about Old Shanghai or Paris of the 1830s—is that it is a fantastic metropolis, a seething revolutionary center where new ideas and new solutions spring forth out of the great social conflicts. It is also a fascinating city in many ways, and A. Datta is entirely correct when he writes that a foreigner who comes to Calcutta must be ready to read the pulse of the city. The wretchedness is there. It is over this very wretchedness that the conflicts rage.

"And do you imagine that we could solve Calcutta's problems even twenty years after a revolution?" I am asked.

I see the statue of Bose. The great leftist, nationalist leader of the thirties became the German-Japanese agent of the forties. Or was that not the case?

One could say that Bose did during the second world war what Roy tried to do during the first: free his country with the aid of the enemies of his enemies. The fact is, however, that the first and second world wars were not really the same kind of war. There was a difference between the Kaiser and Hitler. The Indian National Army which was led by Bose was an auxiliary to Japanese fascism, just as Ustaja's Croatian Army was an auxiliary to Hitler. If I had been asked in 1944, my answer would have been plain and simple:

"Bose is a fascist."

Perhaps he was. It was, as Kali remarked, often difficult to see which way nationalism would develop. As far back as 1934, Bose, who was still the darling of the left and who still talked of a socialist India, wrote *The Indian Struggle*, an expression of nationalism leaning towards fascism. But to admire Mussolini in the India of 1934 was not unusual. Anti-imperialism was stronger than anti-fascism. The presence of British imperialism obscured the threat of fascism.

There are other ambiguities. According to the Russo-German negotiations of 1940, India was to fall to Moscow upon the defeat of the British. It is not clear just who was deceiving whom during these talks. When Bose fled from India, it was with the aid of the Communist Party of India. He escaped by way of Afghanistan and the Soviet Union to Germany. But Hitler did not wish to receive him. Moscow might not have liked it. At the same time, the underground apparatus of the Communist Party of India was linked up to German and Italian intelligence in Kabul. Certain parts of this apparatus remained tied to the Germans (for anti-imperialist reasons), even after the Party as a whole swung over to support the British war effort in late-autumn 1941. It took the Party leadership a few months to move from a policy which, in fact, represented support for the axis-powers, to a line which stood for almost total support for the British. But in taking this new position, they had also put the Party in conflict with the nationalist interests of the Indian people. The Quit-India Campaign of 1942 was a true national movement. But just as Bose and his supporters had used nationalism to serve the axis powers, so had the communists used their social revolution to serve the interest of the Soviet Foreign Office. The national uprising was denied genuine leadership. I believe that both Bose and the communists thus betrayed the Indian people.

Although the situation was complicated, this treachery was not inevitable. Pyotr Parfenovich Vladimirov was sent in May 1942 as the Comintern's representative to the Central Committee of China's Communist Party in Yenan. When the Comintern was disbanded, he remained in Yenan until November 1945 as a Tass correspondent. He died in Moscow in 1953. In 1974, the notes he left behind were published. They are of course edited both by Soviet intelligence and propaganda experts. I had this book with me when I was in China in 1976, and because I had loaned it to some Chinese friends, I did not get it back until 1978. My friends were of the opinion that, although some details were incorrect or altered for propaganda purposes, the factual content concerning Soviet-Chinese relations during the war was accurate. Mao refused to sacrifice the interests of the Chinese people to aid Soviet foreign policy. The Chinese stood in solidarity, but they did not subordinate themselves. The anti-Sovietism reported home to Stalin by Vladimirov was, in fact, the responsibility towards their own people that made it possible for the leadership in Yenan to later become the leadership for the whole country.

Is it possible though that the matter of Bose is not that clear cut? He travelled by submarine from Germany to Japan in 1943. He had been unsuccessful in Germany. Upon his arrival in 1940, Hitler had refused to meet him both out of consideration for Stalin's interest in India and because Hitler as a racist disliked the very idea of independence for Indians—people of a lower race. Even after Germany's attack on the Soviet Union, Hitler did not change his mind. Hitler refused to sign any Free India declaration. He was in fact deeply worried about the agitation against the British in India. If the deterioration of Britain's prestige continued they would no longer be strong enough to act as the dominant race, as he put it in his table talk on April 23, 1942.

Bose succeeded in getting the Japanese and Mussolini to go along with the idea of a declaration of Indian independence. He also had the strong support of Hitler's foreign minister Von Ribbentrop for such a declaration to be announced simultaneously in Berlin, Rome and Tokyo. But Hitler refused. The legion Bose established, composed of captured

Indian soldiers from the British Army, was forced to swear allegiance to Hitler. So Bose left Germany.

There are still other questions. Bose had travelled to Germany by way of the Soviet Union. He tried to keep his lines open to Moscow during the war. On May 25, 1945, he spoke on the radio from Bangkok. He directed his words to Moscow and repeated that his Free India had one—and only one—principle when it came to foreign policy:

"The fundamental principle of our foreign policy has been and will be—Britain's enemy is India's friend."

The Japanese tried in every way to hinder his attempt at making contact with Moscow. On August 15, 1945, when Japan surrendered, Bose issued his last order of the day as commander of the free Indian forces:

> Comrades: In our struggle to liberate our native country, we have now been overwhelmed by a crisis we could not have dreamt of. You perhaps feel as though we have failed in our attempt at liberating India. But allow me to say to you that this failure is but of a temporary nature...There are many roads that lead to Delhi, and Delhi is still our goal....

From Bangkok, Bose and his closest adviser, Habib-ur-Rahman, flew towards Dairen. They were to make contact with the Russians. The Japanese authorities were unable to provide more room in the plane for his followers. At 14:30 on August 18, Bose's plane is thought to have crashed while taking off from Taihoku in Taiwan. It is said that Bose was killed and never reached Soviet territory. Although there are many people who claim that he survived the crash, he probably did die in that accident.

I do not agree with those who simply label Bose a fascist. But neither do I agree with the Communist Party which holds power in Calcutta— the so-called Marxists. They honor Bose as a great hero. They consider him to be one of their forerunners. At the same time, they are obsequiously loyal to Moscow's foreign policy. They defend Vietnam's invasion of Kampuchea and the Russian invasion of Afghanistan.

Bose was neither a traitor nor an agent. But, at the same time, he is proof that it is impossible to liberate one's country with foreign power. The means transform the end. It is not enough to have a long-handled spoon when eating soup with the devil.

During the war, when I was a teenager, I was forced to think a lot about Bose, about what was right and what was wrong. The questions of the war years, about what was correct anti-imperialism, were not nearly as easily answered as they may now appear. The reports produced afterwards do not tally with the picture we got then. Even the individual born in the thirties, a person who did not participate in a consciously political way in the events of the war years, probably has a hard time understanding just how important this issue of Bose is today. These people may even believe that the real-life German Nazis actually acted like the Hollywood Nazis of the sixties and seventies. They are mistaken. If one believes that, then it is impossible to understand why Bose did what he did, and one may fall into the same trap as Bose, the same trap the so-called Marxists in Calcutta fall into when they further Russian interest in the hope of being anti-imperialist.

At that time, there existed German propaganda about India for internal German consumption. I did not, and could not, know about it. It was the internal education that took place within the Wehrmacht. What I have in mind are publications such as Vörenbach's *India* from October 1942, in which sixty-four information-packed pages provided the soldiers with a good deal of knowledge. The assessment was objective and sober, although 1857 was seen as a mere mutiny and the British Indian Civil Service was described with admiration...but then these opinions were consistent with the general reactionary view on the State and dominion. This was before Stalingrad. An advance towards India still seemed possible. Hitler had rejected the proposal to support Indian independence and German soldiers were given basic instruction in Indian politics. For the Germans, Nehru was then a good Indian nationalist who had not yet dared to make a complete break with the British world of ideas; Gandhi was the real leader of the Indian people.

The German propaganda on India which reached me in neutral Sweden consisted partly of the objective geographic textbooks I could purchase at Nordiska Bokhandeln, books such as Dr. Hermann Lufft's *Die Wirtschaf Indiens (The Economy of India)* and Mukund Vyas' *Männer und Mächte in Indien (Personalities and Political Forces in India)*. They were, of course, ideologically-biased—as were the British or French standard works—and their ideology was Nazism. But they were also extremely well-written and informative. Also available was literature on political education, books such as Hans Walter Gaebert's *In Sachen Indien genen London: Die Geschichte des Indischen Freiheitskampfes (The Case of India Against London: The Story of the Indian Struggle for Freedom)*. They were scholarly but extremely biased...although, here, Nehru and Gandhi seem to be allied with the so-called "New Europe." One could also find the pure propaganda of Reinhard Frank's *British Tyranny in India* (which also appeared in a Swedish translation entitled *England och Indien*). And finally, there was material such as A. Paul Weber's artistically unrivalled propaganda in *Signal*. His pictures of British oppression and decadence and of American war hysteria, made a profound visual impression. (The fact that this anti-Semitic, anti-democratic graphic artist was called fascist, humanist and artist of the resistance in post-war West Germany, I consider to be an expression of black humor.)

At times, the style was bombastic, but just what else was wrong with what Reinhard Frank wrote?

> A *colony of slaves*, that is the status to which India has been degraded by British leadership and "trusteeship." That is the truth about the work performed by England in India for 200 years. But India and the world will not forever let themselves be deceived by what happened here.
>
> *The day of India's liberation must come!*
>
> It will be the day of liberation for the whole world from the base and selfish policy of exploitation adopted by the ruthless British rulers. For the masses in England—this also must be mentioned here—have never been allowed to benefit from the British world power. Exactly as in former years—now in the form of so-called democracy instead of monarchy—the small class of British oligarchy and plutocracy, *the ruling class of the rich cliques,* have, in the guise of a honeyed hypocrisy, consistently and with insatiable greed and love of power, plundered their own people and the peoples of the Empire.

And if I, who was very American after having attended school in New York, wished to be in touch with radical American tradition, it was Hitler's Germany which helped out with a new edition of Scott Nearing's classic *Dollar Diplomacy,* published in Leipzig in 1943.

In the allied countries there were perhaps those who sided with their own country—right or wrong: Russians who, despite everything, fought for holy Russia, Americans who fought for God's own country, Englishmen who fought for the Empire. Perhaps there were also those who took a stand for Good against Evil, Democracy against Dictatorship. But that kind of black-and-white choice was not very obvious. It demanded that one overlook Katyn, the Bengal Famine and all the atrocities. Generally speaking, the German charges against the British Empire, dollar diplomacy and Stalin's foreign policy were valid. Nonetheless, it was necessary to destroy Hitler. German Hitlerism was a worse evil. But that stand-point is not nearly as self-evident as it may now appear to be.

The statue of Bose symbolizes the dichotomy of radical nationalism. It is a dichotomy we must learn to recognize: both because it marks the entire era from the French Revolution up until the present when nations liberate themselves (how else will we be able to understand how the Vietnamese heroes we applauded yesterday have become today's executioners of Laotians and Kampucheans, and understand that it was correct both to support them wholeheartedly and to condemn them wholeheartedly); and so that we ourselves will be able to do the right thing in this era when empires struggle for hegemony and we, willy-nilly, must fight for the continued existence of our nations, so that we will not be absorbed into the British Empire, Hitler's Neuropa, Japan's Co-prosperity Sphere, America's Free World, or Russia's Socialist Community of Nations. The very nature of this era is dichotomous.

In 1975, in a used bookstore in Paris, I found a cloth bound brown book with gold print. It was in English. It was on the subject of 1857 and was written by someone who merely called himself "An Indian Nationalist." The book indicates neither place nor year of publication. But it does provide a key.

In 1907, a twenty-three year old Indian student sat working on a manuscript. His name was Vinayak Damodar Savarkar and he was from Bhajur, near Nasik, outside Bombay. His father was a minor landowner and money lender. The student wrote in Marathi. The title of the manuscript was *The Indian War of Independence of 1857*. He explained:

> The nation that has no consciousness of its past has no future. Equally true it is that a nation must develop its capacity not only of claiming a past but also of knowing how to use it for the furtherance of its future. The nation ought to be the master and not the slave of its own history. For it is absolutely unwise to try to do certain things now irrespective of special considerations, simply because they had been once acted in the past. The feeling of hatred against the Mahomedans was just and necessary in the times of Shivaji—but, such a feeling would be unjust and foolish if nursed now, simply because it was the dominant feeling of the Hindus then.

His intention, he explained in a later article, was to write a factually correct history which would inspire the people to rise once more and with armed struggle free their native land from the intruders.

The declared purpose of his book was to make the people aware of the necessity for armed insurrection and to demoralize the British Army. Savarkar felt that if the Indian soldiers understood their plight, learnt the lessons of 1857 and rebelled against their officers, British rule in India would be overthrown. That rule relied on bayonets and the bayonets had to be turned against the oppressors.

Those who claim that this theory is wrong, that the British quit India for other reasons, are correct in the sense that the Empire returned less and less of a profit as an apparatus of exploitation, that the British were driven from the world markets by competition, and that Great Britain turned into Little England during the Second World War. Yet, what finally decided the British was that the facility with which Bose had been able to recruit the Indian soldiers of the British Army to his Free Indian Army suggested that they could no longer rely on their armed forces—a suspicion confirmed by the 1946 mutiny of the fleet. Had the British not decamped in 1947, they would have been thrown out by force...and in that case, neither the foreign investments, the bureaucratic apparatus nor the Indian ruling class could have been maintained intact.

The book written by the young student in London in 1907 is brilliant. It is written with blazing fervor, its style sharp and ruthless. Much of the material which should have been included in any account of 1857 was unavailable to Savarkar. The question of the popular uprisings in 1857 and of class struggle in the countryside had not yet been properly investigated. At times, Savarkar read too much into his material. It was, in fact, his intention to write a memorial to his nation's heroes. But compared to British academic historians, Savarkar is scholarly. Hatred for the oppressors makes, for he who seeks historical veracity, a more fruitful point of departure than does the apologia for that oppression. Even today, those historians—Indian or otherwise—who defend the established order of things seek to depict 1857 merely as a mutiny, a military rebellion or a feudal insurrection. The sharper the contradictions within Indian society grow, the more apologetic the official Indian scholars tend to become.

Even before the manuscript had been completed, two chapters disappeared. They had been stolen by detectives from Scotland Yard. The British authorities suspected Savarkar of carrying on subversive intellectual activity and they kept him under close surveillance. The empire over which the sun never set (and on which the blood never dried, as Ernest Jones said) feared the written word.

The manuscript was smuggled into India despite efforts by the British authorities to prevent this. The British immediately conducted police raids against the leading printing houses in Maharashtra. But the British could not trust their own police. A patriotic police officer warned the shop where the book was being printed just before the raid was to take place. The British did not find the manuscript. Since the British now had the printing shops under surveillance, the manuscript was smuggled back to Europe. The young student recovered his manuscript in Paris. An unsuccessful attempt was made at having it printed in Germany. Finally, it was decided to have the manuscript translated into English and printed in that language.

However, the British police were on guard. The book was banned. In an open letter, Savarkar asked the authorities:

How does the Government know that the book is going to be so dangerously seditious as to get it proscribed before its publication, or even before it was printed? The Government either possess a copy of the manuscript or do not. If they have a copy, then why did they not prosecute me...if they have no copy of the manuscript how could they be so cocksure of the seditious nature of a book of which they do not know anything beyond some vague, partial and unauthenticated reports?

No British printer dared to print the book. The Intelligence Department was in contact with their colleagues in France and threatened the French printers; no French printing house dared do the work. But a Dutch printer was found who secretly printed an edition. These copies were smuggled into France. From there they found their way into India. The copies sent to India were fitted with false covers, disguised as respectable novels such as Dickens' *Pickwick Papers*.

In 1910, the British carried out one of their periodic mopping-up operations in India. They attempted to crush the resistance movement. They hanged a few and jailed others. Savarkar was arrested in London on March 13, 1910, and conveyed to India. In December 1910, he was sentenced to deportation for life and conducted to the British "Devil's Island" in the Andaman Islands. But the book survived. And in surviving, this book came to play a major role in the Indian struggle for independence.

In 1910, there were thirty thousand Indian immigrants on the American west coast, from Vancouver to San Francisco. Most of them were from Punjab. Although they were the victims of racial discrimination and economic exploitation, they benefited from political and civil liberties unthinkable under British rule. They constituted the base for the Ghadar Party. "Ghadar" means rebellion. They had taken the name from the rebellion of 1857. Their goal was

to overthrow imperialism's "Raj" (rule) in India, and in its place establish a national republic based on liberty and equality. This goal can only be attained through armed national rebellion. Every member of the Ghadar Party is duty bound to take part in the struggle against slavery no matter where in the world it is taking place.

In order to finance their activities and to spread the message of the Rebellion, they published an edition of Savarkar's book in the United States. Their efforts led to the second real threat against the British in India. The British took revenge. Two hundred and fifty patriots were hanged. The Ghadar Party had made use of the contradiction between the British and German imperialists during the first world war. But they were not—as the British and their historians claimed—German agents. In the agreement reached between the German government and the Indian revolutionary committee, the Indian representatives declared:

> The economic assistance provided by the German government will be regarded by the Indian revolutionaries as a national loan to be repaid when India becomes independent. German military forces do not have the right to set foot on Indian territory. The right and authority to rule over Independent India lies totally in Indian hands. Germany shall provide the Indian revolutionary movement with assistance in the form of money, weapons and ammunition, and by sending German specialists to train Bengali revolutionaries.

Two additional conditions for cooperation between the Central Powers and the Indian revolutionaries were spelt out by the Indians during the 1914 negotiations in Berlin:

> If our revolution is victorious we aim to establish a Socialist and Democratic regime. The Austrian-German governments will in no way hinder this.

And even more clearly:

> There are many mighty princes in India. If any among them attempts to establish a monarchy in all or any part of India, the Austrian-German governments will not assist him, but instead assist us in establishing a republic as is our wish.

It was to these Indian patriots in San Francisco that Father Martin—Narendranath Bhattacharya—M.N. Roy travelled. And when, during the debates with Lala Lajpat Rai, he repudiated nationalism and took the position that the proletarian revolution, the world revolution, was the answer for the Indian people, he also came to change his opinion about 1857. Socialism seemed to require of him that he renounce his former nationalism to the point where 1857 became for him "the last death throes of dying feudalism...a military mutiny...objectively, of a reactionary character."

When his book *India* appeared in 1922, published by the Comintern (*Indien*, Verlag der Kommunistischen Internationale, Hamburg 1922), he summed up—with a side-long glance towards Savarkar:

> Orthodox nationalists of later years interpret the rebellion of 1857 as

a great struggle for national independence. This tendency shows up the serious reactionary danger inherent to religion-based nationalism. No Indian nationalist who stands for the social progress of his people and who, to further that goal, fights for national independence, has the right—if he does not wish to go astray—to associate himself with the ideas which were behind the rebellion of 1857, in which we are not to see merely a military struggle to overthrow foreign rule. The foremost cause of the rebellion was a spirit of raging social reaction. It was not a revolt against the British government as such, but against the progressive social and political concepts it represented—concepts shared by the intellectuals of the Indian bourgeoisie which was materially ready for them, and who would have developed them if the foreign conquerors had not introduced them into the country. (Translated from the German edition pp. 120–121.)

Roy's standpoint—as he has himself observed, had its roots in the Bengali Renaissance and in the activity of the nineteenth century Bengali intellectuals. This led him into an incipient conflict with Lenin in the Comintern and into a direct clash with Mao, when Roy, as Stalin's representative, was sent to guide the Chinese in making revolution. It also eventually placed him in a peculiarly isolated position within Indian politics. Still worse was the fact that this standpoint was adopted by the leadership of Indian communism. The social struggle thus came to be disconnected from the national struggle, and the communists were made subordinate to Moscow's short-term foreign policy interests. Eventually, the leadership of the official communist party became agents for Russian imperialism, as the Bengali renaissance intellectuals before them had become agents for British imperialism against the Indian people.

In 1944, a new edition of Savarkar's book was published, this time in Japan. It was Rash Behari Bose, the man who had once thrown a bomb at Lord Hardinge, who lived as a political refugee in Japan and organized resistance to the British, who together with Subash Chandra Bose published the book on 1857 to guide the soldiers in their Indian National Army.

Subash Chandra Bose tried to do the same thing the Ghadar Party tried during the first world war. The Indian soldiers who fought against the British under Japanese command carried Savarkar's book with them. This book, banned by the British in India, was their inspiration. It was also to this book that Bose referred in his last order of the day before his plane crashed on its flight to Dairen, where he was going in search of Russian support for his Indian nationalism, after German support had proved impossible to attain and Japanese aid had been halted.

Many roads lead to Delhi.

Nationalism, too, ended up in the pay of imperialism. The circle seemed closed.

It is necessary to take two steps backward, in order to get a perspective on the future:

When Vinayak Damodar Savarkar was fifteen years old, the Chapekar brothers were hanged. They had shot two British officers who were on their way home from the government building in Poona, where they had taken part in the celebration of Queen Victoria's diamond jubilee. The Chapekar brothers were hanged and Vinayak Damodar Savarkar swore to avenge their deaths by fighting to drive the British intruders out of India.

When he was seventeen he founded his first political organization. Its goal was India's political independence, the method, armed rebellion. Mazzini's Young Italy served as its source of inspiration.

However, both Mussolini and Gramsci derived from Mazzini; both fascists and partisans traced their roots to Young Italy. Savarkar himself took the road of fanatic, black Hindu reaction. He was released from prison in 1937, but was unable to cooperate with official nationalism which stood too far to the left for his tastes. He contributed to the ideological groundwork for the massacre of the Muslims at the time of Partition. In 1948, he was suspected of having a hand in the assassination of Gandhi. He was tried and acquitted. Thereafter, he quit politics. In 1962, however, he advised Nehru to march against Peking, to settle the border issue in a large scale, victorious war. He died in 1966. But his book lives on.

The statue of Bose is a symbol of a great defeat. But, actually, there should be two statues where there is one: M.N. Roy should stand next to Bose. They were both Bengalis and both revolutionaries. They took positions on the same issues, but came to different conclusions. Objective developments proved both Roy's revolution without national roots, and Bose's nationalism without social roots, to be self-destructive; they grew self-consuming and destructive. The young nationalist who wrote so glowingly on the great uprising of 1857—the Indian War of Independence—became a reactionary fanatic causing severe damage to Indian independence. But the book written by the twenty-three year old Savarkar is still important and worth reading. It is still necessary to take a stand for 1857. The party in India which is able to take this positive stand, to continue the tradition from 1857 and Ghadar, and able to unite the tradition from both the Bengali Renaissance and the sepoys, the rebellious peasants and the militant untouchables, will succeed in establishing the free, democratic and socialist India that Bose and Roy believed themselves to be working for.

Polluted Air

A taste of metal in the mouth. The air is thick. It is difficult to breathe. This is winter smog.

"No wonder you cough," says Gun. "Six hundred and seventy tons of pollutants are released into the air here every day. I read that in the papers. Twenty-five percent of the students in Calcutta have, or have had, tuberculosis. People sneeze, sniffle, have headaches and break out in rashes. The laws concerning the emission of air-pollution date from 1905, and the newspapers write with real local patriotism that conditions here are worse than anywhere else in India. Even worse than Bombay. The problem caused by automobile exhausts is also most severe here in the center of town. A mere 6 percent of the built-up area is used for roads. The traffic is jammed and hisses in the sun. And the Hooghly River is an out-and-out sewer."

The radio carries the news of the triumph of Indira's Congress. They speak of a "landslide" victory. But it is the kind of parliamentary landslide that occurs in systems based on single-member constituencies. Only 56.8 percent of those eligible to vote have actually cast a ballot. At least in 1977, the year Indira Gandhi was swept from office, 60.5 percent voted. Actually, her landslide victory boils down to no more than the fact that she, using every means of persuasion, has been able to get, not quite every fourth eligible voter, to support her. And a large part of the votes, both those cast against her as well as those cast in her favor, are openly bought, rigged, or cast by voters who vote the way they are told to by landowners and political bosses who support the highest paying candidates.

In 1977, when she was swept out of office with a crash, she received the support of 21 percent of the eligible voters. In 1980, the year she made her much vaunted come-back, she was supported by 24 percent of the voters. I wonder how large the rigging and cheating margin is: 10 percent, 20 percent? Indira's return to power is a political reality, but Indira's landslide victory among the people is just a product of the mass media. If the electoral system had been based on proportional representation, it is doubtful that she could have formed a government. But the single-member constituencies turn politics into a lottery. The inhabitants of Uttar Pradesh were so tired of political corruption and bickering that a mere 45 percent of the eligible voters went to the polls. Out of this 45 percent, Congress (I) received 35.4 percent, or in other words sixteen votes from a hundred eligible voters. This gave them 51 seats out of 85. It was Sanjay's people who were now assuming power. Goonda-politicians. People without opinion or profile. Of members of Sanjay's version of the Society of December 10:

> Alongside decayed *roués* with dubious means of subsistence and of dubious origin, alongside ruined and adventurous offshoots of the bourgeoisie, were vagabonds, discharged soldiers, discharged jail-birds, escaped galley slaves, swindlers, mounte-banks, *lazzaroni*, pickpockets, tricksters, gamblers, maquereaus, brothel keepers, porters, *literati*, organ-grinders, rag-pickers, knife grinders, tinkers, beggars—in short, the whole indefinite, disintegrated mass, thrown hither and thither which...felt the need of benefiting themselves at the expense of the laboring nation. (Karl Marx, *The Eighteenth Brumaire of Louis Bonaparte*)

For a time following the election, it appeared that this mass, under the direction of Sanjay, would form the picked troops of a new Congress of brutality. But Sanjay killed himself in an airplane crash. His death was not due to a Russian assassination or to a conspiracy on the part of his enemies, but logical and in perfect accordance with his general personality: he flew a plane too advanced for his capability, dressed in unsuitable clothes, and attempted to perform stunts disregarding all rules of safety. In other words, he was killed by his own bad character, and although official India stood at his graveside, tearful and full of fine-sounding phrases, on the sly they all tittered happily and talked like the senior Indian official who told me:

"Nothing but good for the dead, but we are all so happy that Sanjay has escaped from his earthly prison."

Sanjay's lumpen gang fell apart after his death, and Indira's hope of passing on a dynasty to India was temporarily dashed. But I am not sure whether it is very significant one way or the other. Sanjay was not much more brutal than other Indian politicians. Nor was he much more corrupt. He was just a little less of a hypocrite. Or perhaps, as Saxena in Delhi said, he was not even refined enough to be hypocritical.

However, on this day in Calcutta when the air tastes acrid and moist against the palate, Sanjay's death is still in the future. We listen to the roar of Indira's triumph on the radio and our friends, who come to drink tea and talk, are dejected:

"We shall see if she begins arresting people again," says Biplal. He is a Naxalite.

"You're type who will be accused of making revolution in prison so that twenty guards will have to beat you to a pulp with their lathis," says Rabi.

They joke, but the jokes have a bitter taste to them. They were released from prison when Indira fell in 1977. According to the official count, 17,000 political prisoners of the left were jailed during that time in West Bengal. Two of them were beaten to death in the prisons. And some were shot. Indira had decided that the peasant revolutionaries, the Naxalites, should be wiped out. This she had decided even before her Emergency. She had given the police a free hand.

"It's hard to say how many were executed. Most of the executions were never reported. They were arrested and tortured, and then shot or beaten to death. Sometimes it was reported that they had clashed with the police, sometimes that they had been shot while attempting to escape and sometimes that they had died of natural causes. But for the most part, nothing was said at all.

"Torture has always occurred in our prisons. Torture is carried on as it was under British rule. But when Indira really went in for crushing her opponents during the Emergency, torture became prevalent. Of course, she knew of it. Everyone knew about it, although not many really cared. Indira does know how to read.

"In Europe and America, there was a great deal of talk about the Shah of Iran and his Savak, and about Pinochet and his police, but very little was heard about Indira and her methods. But she was at least as loathsome as the Shah. Perhaps even worse. There are degrees in hell. But in Europe, her actions were disregarded."

"Amnesty's report had some effect."

"That's true. Some books were also written about it. But your Social Democrats or British Labor or the various Eurocommunists who call themselves radicals did not care about the torture. Instead, they all praised Indira."

In England, Labor's traditional left wing assembled to congratulate Indira. Michael Foot declared that he considered Indira Gandhi's victory to be a victory for democratic traditions and democratic rule in India, and Aneurin Bevan's widow, Mrs Jenny Lee, applauded. In France, radical feminists declared that Indira Gandhi's victory represented a defeat of the phallocrats.

The person Indira Gandhi is not very important. She is slow in forgetting or forgiving a slight, vindictive and scheming, but hardly really intelligent.

But her lust for power, on the other hand, is of consequence. She comes from a totally secular family. Jawaharlal Nehru kept his distance from religion and religious ceremonies, and wanted India to be a secular state. He attempted to bridge the gulf between Muslims and Hindus. But Indira Gandhi uses religion as she uses everything else. She visits the temples. She requests the benediction of the priests. She fosters holy men of various sorts if she can benefit by it. She lets people know that she spends time praying to the goddess Padmavathi Devi, wife of Venkateshwara, and in Tirupati she makes it known that it is thanks to her having asked the god Venkateshwara to bless her that she won the election. This cynical use of religion is not without its dangers for the Indian people. Indira and her Congress make use of religious contradictions, like everything else, in order to guarantee their power, and Jawaharlal Nehru's attempt at establishing a secular India is brought to nought amidst arson and plunder. For in this way, the poor can be made to fight against each other, and divided in their struggle against their oppressors.

Here are the statistics for the twenty years between 1960 and 1979:

year	religious riots
1960	26
1961	92
1964	1070
1965	676
1967	198
1968	346
1969	519
1970	521
1971	321
1972	240
1973	242
1975-1976 (Emergency)	374
after April 1977	400

These religious riots have resulted in fatalities ranging from a hundred and fifty in 1967 to three thousand in 1969, according to the report "Six Parliaments and Democratic Rights" from the People's Union for Civil Liberties and Democratic Rights, from which these figures have been taken. During this period, the religious rioting has also spread to areas where it was previously unknown. Indira's cynicism is paid for in blood.

"Haven't you thought about the way she dresses?" asks Gun. "Widow-white here, in costume there. She "kisses ass" as the Americans say, by dressing like a Bhil-woman when among the Bhils, and dancing with the Madhya Pradesh women like one of them if she can gain by it. But at home she wears specially designed saris. She's like Jiang Qing—everything from the kerchief to the hypocrisy. In a way, I feel almost as sorry for Jawaharlal Nehru as I do for Mao. Do you remember the way Indira put on an act for her father when she played hostess for him? Like Jiang Qing serving bowls of peanuts for Mao. There are women who really are as false as the male chauvinists say. Jiang Qing and Indira Gandhi are two of them."

One can wonder about the class background of Indira Gandhi's regime. One way of approaching an answer is to examine the strikes and lockouts that took place around the time of the Emergency. This has been done by Ruddar Datt of the University of Delhi. During the entire period from 1961 onward, the number of days a striking worker was off the job remained almost unchanged, while the number of days a worker was locked out quintupled. The Emergency strengthened this tendency. In 1976, the number of strike days fell to five per striking worker, while the number of days of lockout rose to fifty-three per locked-out worker. Of the total number of workdays lost due to labor disputes, 78 percent were due to lockouts. The number of successful strikes for the working class has been between 29 percent and 37 percent during this twenty year period, with the exception of the economically prosperous year 1976 when Indira Gandhi's Emergency was in force. That year the percentage of successful strikes slumped to a record low of 20.5 percent.

An analysis of the conflicts which were preceded or followed by strikes shows that management now is able to hit back harder than the working class. For every strike day, management now answers with 1.76 days of lockout. Only where the working class has been able to organize properly—as in West Bengal—do the number of lockout days sink in relation to strike days. The situation was worst in Maharashtra, where in 16 such conflicts management had responded with 562,000 days of lockout against the working class' 310 days of strike.

From 1974, when Indira crushed the railway workers' strike, and on through the Emergency, the capitalist class grew stronger and the fighting ability of the working class was reduced. At the same time, India's rate of growth remained low—about 3.5 percent per annum—while the entire decade of Indira's rule was characterized by inflation, growing poverty and unemployment, and the rapid concentration of land and capital in the hands of even fewer people.

Such was the class character of the regime which had the political support of India's pro-Moscow communists and their fellow travellers, the regime which sought support in Europe among British Labor's left wing and Sweden's Social Democrats, the regime which tried to pass itself off among the feminists as being the adversary of the phallocrats and which cultivated contacts both in SIDA and the U.N. bureaucracy.

"Now that Indira is back in power, the situation in South Asia will become more dangerous," said Singh. In her foreign policy, Indira will support the Soviet Union and its client-states. Indira will support Viet Nam's occupation of Kampuchea and the Russian occupation of Afghanistan. The former regime attempted to reach some kind of agreement with China, Pakistan, Nepal, Bangladesh and Sri Lanka. Indira will continue her policy of expansion. We can expect conflicts with all our neighbors—maybe even war—and an increased oppression here at home.

"Indira will give the Russians a lot of assistance and do them favors in the international arena. But this has nothing whatsoever to do with ideology. It can be explained in part by the Russian economic interests and their immediate influence within the government apparatus; our *government* has never been independent. It was first the British, then the Americans took over and now it is the Russians. However, part of the explanation is the fact that Indira is naive enough to believe that by supporting the Russians, she in turn will receive their support for her own expansion. It's not just a question of Bhutan. It might mean that she will attempt to divide Pakistan between herself and the Russians. She is stupid enough to play Poland's role when Hitler carved up Czechoslovakia.

"It is this that represents the great danger posed by Indira. She is ready to further Russian interests in Afghanistan and Southeast Asia, and for this policy she has the support of the more chauvinistic circles of India. I don't know if she'll come to terms with China. She actually may do so, since nowadays that conflict no longer makes any political sense.

"She is no Russian puppet. She's far worse. She considers herself clever enough to obtain some advantage by helping the Russians over the Hindu Kush to Bolan and Khyber, and by aiding the Vietnamese to dig in west of the Mekong."

Indira fell in 1977 because she had succeeded in uniting against her both right and left. They had all had a taste of her prisons. She had turned the legal system into a bad joke and had institutionalized arbitrary rule. The State that had grown up was not so much classically fascist as typically Third World Caesarism. Politics had become contract-work. As for the contractors, they cared little if the profit came from new production or from speculation. Sanjay's car deals are typical. Indira fell from power because although this policy did mean a violent suppression (police terror, torture, arrests, suspension of civil rights, covert police censorship) of the mass struggle and an attempt at stifling the class struggle thereby contributing to an increase in profits, it had also hindered capitalism and harmed conservative and reactionary social groups and political currents. Members of the RSS shared prison cells with Naxalites, while Socialists found themselves in the same prison as bourgeois intellectuals who honestly believed in phrases such as "rule of law" and "civil rights."

For a while, after her fall, these diverse groups were held together by the events experienced during the Emergency, and by their commonly held hatred for Indira and Sanjay. Then this unity was disrupted by their mutual incompatibility.

The question is whether Indira will again challenge all these groups in the same way, thus creating a united opposition to her rule—that is, if, in the aftermath of her rule and the following period of corruption and decay, a liberal bourgeoisie still exists. What kind of state governed by law is there to defend when the state itself has abandoned legality?

Just what is the nature of this Indian State? Indira has her support among its bureaucrats. A parasitic organism whose interests she expresses. By means of nepotism and corruption, a growing number of the middle class can retire into idleness and uselessness within a swelling bureaucracy. The cities become swollen hang-outs for this bureaucracy, for speculators, landowners and a whole array of middle strata who live like parasites off the labor of the villagers. And around this bloated, unproductive middle class mass, swarm tens of thousands, millions of lumpen proletariat, beggars and all kinds of servants, who, when it comes right down to it, also need this parasitism to continue. Is this not an accurate description of her actual political base? And is it possible to imagine some kind of rebellion against this rule by this bloated middle class and these swarms of lumpen proletariat? Is it not rather the case that they can only oppose Indira the individual or go against the new Nehru dynasty she is trying to set up—for this or that caste, clique or community?

"You forget," says Gun, "that prices continue to rise. Desperation grows. Up until now the only manifestation of that desperation is to be seen in the disintegration and destruction of the legal system, guaranteed civil rights and rule of law adopted from the British by India, and in the fact that violence, corruption, stealing and nepotism appear blatantly right in the heart of society. Are these grounds to build on for the establishment of unity in the defence of democracy and the rule of law?"

"I don't know. But some sort of unity should be possible in opposition to torture, rape and organized brutality. And then she would fall. In any case, one must act as though it were possible."

Notes on Democracy, 1959

All India Writers' Conference, Bhubaneswar

January 4, 1959. Visit to Konarka:

We drive towards Konarka in fourteen black limousines. First comes Nehru. Then the dignitaries. We, too, have become dignitaries. Radha Kumud Mookerji has been allotted a vehicle by the provincial government. This is the last of the fourteen. He herds Gun and myself into it. This amuses him. Far behind, the general mass of writers bump along in two old green buses. The dust flies around the limousines. Children stand along the roadway. They wave. They are school children who have been ordered out to cheer the nation, according to Mookerji. Young girls hold up bunches of flowers. Young boys wave paper flags. We stop. The children cheer. Nehru climbs out of the car. We all get out. Nehru gives a speech about equality. He pats a child. All the children cheer again. They wave their flags. The limousines drive on. As I turn and look out of the back window, I catch a glimpse of the children in the swirling white dust. In the far distance I can see the two green buses.

We walk around the temple. Radhakrishnan sits on a peg chair with his back to the wheel of life. When he sees me, he points to the wheel and says: "In those days they had no inhibitions." Then he looks straight in front of him and talks about spiritualism. As he talks, he swings his leg. He wears socks of black silk and English sock-suspenders. An educator from Bengal declares that one must purify the realm of base ideas belonging to the common people. When collecting folklore "one has one's responsibility as an intellectual. The people express themselves in such a filthy fashion.... One must pan the spiritual gold out from among their dirty thoughts."

It is only then that the green buses carrying the mass of writers arrive. All of us dignitaries, together with Nehru, Radhakrishnan, the governor and provincial ministers, hurry to the fenced-in tea garden up by the rest house. The soldiers watch over us. They make sure that we are not forced to mingle with the rabble. Here we now stand with our tea cups in hand, and everything is just culture and equality. I can hear Nehru talking about India in the world. India is respected. Around him, people make sounds of agreement in their throats. Out there stand the two busloads of Indian writers. They gaze at us with respect, as we parade ourselves culturally under military protection, and as we drink our tea, eat biscuits and talk about culture. Radha Kumud Mookerji chuckles all along.

"Do you remember what I said in Puri?" he whispers to Gun. "They are all crooks!"

We march back to our fourteen black limousines. The writing-rabble will have to get home as best they can in their two old green buses. Perhaps they will stop and look at the sun temple more closely. Who knows.

Twenty-one years later, we are back again. Out of all the dignitaries from that occasion, Gun and I might be the only ones still alive. But Indian society is unchanged. This time we are in Konarka to see the temple. We stay in the newly-built tourist hotel. In the afternoon, we go swimming in the ocean. The next morning, we watch the sun rise over the temple.

The Witches' Ring

Late in the afternoon, we arrive in the village of Hirapur. It is located approximately twenty kilometers east of Bhubaneswar. Coming from Puri, one turns right just before the bridge over the Bhargavi River. The cloudless sky is steel-blue. The village is small, the road leading there hard to find. We have to ask for directions repeatedly and take village roads which grow increasingly narrow. Hirapur is not mentioned in the tourist guide. But it can be found in the archaeological books. For here is one of India's most remarkable temples.

The temple is a ring-wall, open towards the sky. But it is not just a place of worship. It is a temple-building. And that in itself is remarkable. Temples open to the sky, hypaethral temples, were described by Vitruvius in his treatise on architecture in the first century. But whether such buildings actually existed in classical antiquity is in dispute. There are, however, a few here in India.

The most ancient temple at Khajuraho, built before the year 900, is a hypaethral temple of massive grey granite. The roofless chamber measuring 31 meters by 18 meters is surrounded by a wall with 65 inches. But nearly all the stone beings who once gazed into the chamber are gone. The chamber has a gloomy air about it. There are two such temples here in Orissa. One is near the villages of Ranipur and Jharial, 30 kilometers east of Titlagarh, a railroad junction in western Orissa. There 64 similar, dancing female figures stand along the inside of a round stone wall and in the center, a dancing Shiva, with *urdhva-linga* (erect penis). That temple, too, like the one in Hirapur is known as "Chaunsat Yogini" (the sixty-four yoginis). But it is the temple here in Hirapur that is perfect and beautiful.

The ring stands closed upon itself under the steely sky. The wall is actually not very high. If I were to stretch, I would be able to brush the top of the wall with my fingertips. Neither is the body of the temple large. Nine female figures look in my direction from out of the exterior wall. It is hard to say who they are. Above them sit the royal parasols. They hold, or rather hold out, bowls. Their breasts are taut. The bowls are for milk or wine.

In Ranipur-Jharial, the entrance is only an aperture in the wall. But in this place, the doorway is narrow. It is like a dark tunnel leading into the chamber. On either side there are figures of men. Naked ascetics, garland-decked. They march in with great strides on both sides, and they are waited on by small figurines.

This is a remarkable chamber that gives one the impression of enormous space. The walls swing out before one's eyes, and above there is only the empty sky. The world has disappeared. Here in Hirapur, space plays tricks with perspective. Infinite space rests directly upon the stone floor. I stand in the well of the world. The experience is stark and unsettling, like that in the heavy Romanesque or soaring Gothic church chambers. But this is different. It has the shape of the stupa. I have penetrated it and find myself inside it. The globe has a completely solid form above me, while at the same time, it is clear—open against space and the steely sky.

Figurines of women stand around the walls. They have not all been created by the same hand. Some of them can be included among the most fascinating portraits of women I have ever seen. All of them are masterful. They are thought to date from the ninth century. "Chaunsat Yogini" in Hirapur is older than the one in Ranipur-Jharial or in Khajuraho. The figures are not erotic in the same sense as the ornamentation on many temples in Bhubaneswar and Khajuraho are thought to be. But they do emanate a strong force. Some of them have demon-like faces on lovely bodies. There stands also the woman of destruction, dancing, a garland of human skulls about her head. She holds the severed heads of her victims in her hands. I do not name her since this figure is older.

These are sacred images. They are rubbed with *ghee* until they shine. I cannot determine whether the stone itself is black, or whether it has obtained its luster and blackness from the sacrifices of a millenium. This temple has never been plundered. It was a while before it was written up, but once described, it was also made into a protected temple. Its statues never fell into the hands of the British officers, and never turned up on the world market. One may wonder why this particular temple is not included in the otherwise exhaustive tourist guides. It was, after all, known.

But then there is not much written about this temple or this category of temples—of which there are four in all of India—in the major standard works on art history. The hypaethral temples might be mentioned, but only in passing. Nor do the yoginis usually rate many lines.

The temple looks totally different from the usual Hindu temple. The entire idea behind it is different. It is not just another way of building, it is another way of thinking about spatial form. The difference is as great as that between Stonehenge and a Christian cathedral. That is why I do not give a name to the yoginis. These sixty-four yoginis probably have something to do with Kali the goddess. But the texts do not deal with these yoginis, just as art history does not deal with these temples. There are names for them, a lot of names, lists of names; but there is no information about who they are. Nor is there a text which describes how one should worship these yoginis.

It would naturally be simplest to translate yogini to witch; to "Kali's witches" or simply "the sixty-four witches." That is what Charles Fabri did, and it was he who first brought us to this place. He is the person who has written most about Hirapur. We met him a couple of times in Delhi, in the late fifties and early sixties. But it was his book *Discovering Indian Sculpture*, published posthumously in 1970, that brought us here. In this book he presented a picture of a "smiling yogini." When Gun saw the picture she said, "We must go there."

Later, at the museum in Bhubaneswar, we had got hold of Charles Fabri's *History of the Art of Orissa* written in 1974. This of course was also posthumously published. In this book he wrote a great deal about Hirapur. Of less obvious worth was Nik Douglas' *Tantra Yoga* (1971), in which the yoginis appear. He takes them seriously in such a way that he mixes all the periods and all religions into one big Tantric mishmash. For him, it is witchery, significant witchery, worthy of imitation.

Fabri refers to the story of the witch Kalaratri in the *Katha sarit-sagara (Ocean of stories)*, Somadeva's enormous collection of tales dating from the eleventh century. Kalaratri is one of the famous yoginis. She also appears in another of the stories in that very form. But, according to Fabri, the witch stories provide the key to understanding the cult. I believe that he is correct in his assumption. The story describes how King Aditya-prabha comes home unexpectedly and finds one of his queens, Kuvalay-avali, stark naked, praying to the gods with her hair standing straight out, her eyes half-closed and a large vermilion mark on her forehead, in the center of a large circle made of different colored powders: she was just completing the sacrifice of blood, wine and human flesh. When she saw the king she became confused and grabbed her clothes. After she begged his forgiveness for what she had done, she told him that the sacrifice had only been for the sake of his prosperity.

She told him how she had been enticed into becoming a witch by some friends while she still lived in her father's house. They could fly through the air and had told her that it was witches' spells and the partaking of human flesh that had given them the ability. They had also told her that they had been taught these things by a *brahman* woman named Kalaratri. The queen then described the loathsome appearance of this Kalaratri, how Kalaratri had undressed her and how she had been able to fly through the air after having eaten human flesh which had been sacrificed to the gods.

"Thus," said the queen, "even as a girl I became a witch and during our gatherings we ate the bodies of many men."

Kalaratri now stands in her niche here in Hirapur, staring at us. And if this is actually a witches' ring (in Swedish, the word "witch" is related to the words enclosure and fence), then this image of the female death-dancer with the severed heads is not all that innocent.

What the cult was like in the ninth century when the temple in Hirapur was erected is hard to say. Somadeva's description two hundred years later would certainly have been thought biased by the practitioners. There is a great deal to be written about the "left way." The various Tantric schools that preached in the already long established iron age (Kali's age) that the way to personal liberation was by way of meat, wine and sex. In India, as in China (Taoism), there also existed involved speculation about how life could be prolonged if the life energy, the sperm, could be held back and could be made to mount through the body to the head; orgasm was the "little death." Conversely, the woman could suck life into herself.

Many such beliefs are still with us, both among those intellectuals who have abandoned reason, put their faith in personal feelings as arguments, and lie in boxes, screaming; as well as among readers of men's magazines who are given advice on how the yoga technique will help them postpone ejaculation.

However, these speculations and sexual techniques are relatively harmless, even if they are silly. (Retained sperm does not mount to the head at all, but is passed with the urine.) However, the fact that this witches' ring makes possible rituals of wine and sex which were supposed to prolong life and bring happiness (to where the naked ascetic wanders) becomes something less than harmless when Kalaratri stands there staring at us.

Hirapur was a place of human sacrifice. The salvation offered here in Hirapur was accompanied not just by meat but by human flesh. It gave force. It was the ritual consumption of this meat that held the faith together. The temple in Hirapur opens itself not only up towards the heavens, but also towards evil folk tales. These had their basis in reality.

The belief in witchcraft still exists. Barrenness is treated with the blood of girls not yet sexually mature. Children thrown into the concrete of bridge foundations offer protection against collapse. Untouchables and the very poor keep out of sight when work is about to commence on the construction of a new hydroelectric dam.

I do not think much of Europe's so-called leftist-intellectuals' flirtation with Tantrism and witchcraft. When I read about how radical young women in Stockholm give birth at home in order to bloody up their own homes, and how they save the placenta in the freezer, later to take it out, dice it, fry it and serve it to their friends at a real birthday party, I am definitely not amused. Witchcraft is not progressive. The fact that it is necessary to write this in Europe in 1980, however, is rather appalling.

When the headless corpse of a six-year old was found in Midnapore, it merited only a well-hidden short news item about a suspected human sacrifice. The "left way" breaks taboo. The reason we do not sacrifice two-year olds to gain fertility is because of taboo. . . and reason. The flirtation of American and European feminism with blood myths, witchcraft and ritual cannibalism is as dangerous as was Reactionary Europe's flirtation with blood-mysticism and *Männerbund* during the last generation. The taboos that are broken are those which most effectively preserve society.

The witches' ring in Hirapur is great architecture and beautiful art. The sculpture there is among the best of its age. But Hirapur is not a holy spot for women's liberation. It is only when one has realized this that one can also enjoy this beauty.

Is Woman Human?

Small heads, long legs and slenderly swelling shapes. Certainly, the maidens are attractive. That is why they are there. They protrude, strutting and clinging in the nooks. They are famous. The Rajarani temple from the eleventh century is adorned with probably the most beautiful maidens of the entire Bhubaneswar group. They are as beautiful as their contemporaries in Khajuraho. Some of them are also as lustful in their indolence.

India is full of indolent maidens. They are made of stone. For a thousand years the various types of *alasa-kanya* (indolent maidens) have been carefully catalogued in the ancient manuals of architecture. This is the way a *mugdha* (innocent girl) is formed, and in this way a *manini* (a wronged girl) and a *nartaki* (dancer). The navel this way and the hips that, and the lips pouted in *lasyabhava* (desire for love).

"Because, like a home without a wife or a celebration without girls, a monument without statues of women is incomplete and sterile."

Those are the words of the classic *Silpa Prakasa* from Orissa, and from temple walls, indolent maidens have pouted at visitors for more than a thousand years.

A great deal has been written about these figures and about the portrayal of women in the religious art of India. It has been claimed that they are the ancient religious symbols of the common people. Mothers, tree goddesses, the eternal annual fertility, death and rebirth of the earth. There is certainly a coherence in culture. We still put our hand to our mouth when we yawn; we decorate with greenery for death, even if we are not aware of it (and have forgotten the term once used); a line runs from our European Christmas celebrations back to paleolithic ceremonies of fire and feast held at about the time of the winter solstice. But there is not a great deal that survives. And if one is searching for an explanation for our twentieth century consumer-Christmases, one will not find it at Altamira.

There is a connection between the clay mother-figurines, pre-dating the Indus civilization, and the stone maidens in Bhubaneswar and Khajuraho. But the more this connection is emphasized, the more misleading the total picture becomes. The clay figurines are actually related to the local goddesses and places of worship of the villages. These religious gifts are still offered up to the Mother; the agricultural fertility rites are related to the past. But the maidens of Rajarani temple are not mothers.

Naturally, they can be arranged in a series. The tree goddesses become heavenly brides. The yakshis from Sanchi, the erotic female figures from Bhutesar and the yoginis in Hirapur belong in one category. Mystical magical women dance and strut from the thirteenth century down to our day, portrayed in stone, clay and paint on the temple walls. It is possible to place the women in Bhubaneswar and Khajuraho in this series. However, these representations of women from the eleventh century differ markedly from those coming before and after. In Hirapur and later in Palampet, for example, the sculpture is the portrayal of women.

The thing that sets these female figures in Bhubaneswar and Khajuraho apart is not that they are—or form a part of—erotic subjects. In India, too, there exists a great deal of art with erotic motive, religious images with erotic form, as well as erotic mysteries and erotic symbolism. What is interesting about the maidens in Bhubaneswar is that they are erotic in a different—and, actually, rather incoherent—way. If one examines the Rajarani maidens closely one can see that these celestial brides belong to the ethereal world in the sense that they lack musculature and skeletal structure. They are pumped up with spirit as a bicycle tire is filled with air. They are pneumatic. Fantasy images of girls for one's pleasure. Objects of pleasure. These temples are the monuments of triumphant feudalism. The female beauty exhibited here is the beauty desired by those who had commissioned the building. Indolently pouting maidens.

Real-life girls look different, even in India. Girls like those of the Rajarani temple I have never seen in real life. (On the other hand, the beauties from the Konarka Temple, celestial musicians and the love-making women, with their forceful facial expressions can be seen in Orissa, Bengal and Bihar.) I suspect that women have never looked like the dream-visions of the feudal lords, the visions that materialized in Bhubaneswar and Khajuraho. The struggle the women of the real world are involved in is to avoid being mere objects of pleasure.

For the pleasure of the eleventh century is like that of the present day—reserved for the few. The girls are from the lower classes and castes, and they are without human dignity. They may be rather indolent, pretty and enticingly plump to squeeze when they are still young. Later, they are just something that can be used to work in the fields. Feudal society creates both ideal and practice. The feudal ideal of beauty can be seen on the temple walls and corresponds to the feudal sexual repression in the villages. In Bihar, it is the landowners of the *bhumiar* and *rajput* castes who have the right to spend the first night with the low-caste bride. Before she may enter into her low-caste marriage, the high-caste lord has her by right.

In contemporary discussions, the vast erotic scenes from the reliefs at Khajuraho and the lustful pictures in Bhubaneswar are sometimes interpreted as expressions of interest in sensuality or sexual emancipation. They are sometimes interpreted tantrically and, on occasion, are even said to derive from the mother-cult. These views are mistaken. These scenes have nothing to do with the fertility cults and mother-images of the villages. Nor are they tantric as in Hirapur. They are the visions of the feudal lords, turned into figures of stone. They are as lacking in sensuality as the brothel scenes in the turn-of-the-century barber shop magazine. In India, there does exist rustic fertility art, tantric mystic art and erotic art of various types, but this is feudalism's view of women in which the procured female object is used as long as it is young. The fact that it is just this sort of art that later began to be viewed as emancipated in Europe tells us something about the nature of this European emancipation.

The tenet which has here been made into stone, the view that the women of the lower classes, the untouchables and those of the lower castes, lack human dignity and can be made use of when the need arises, is deeply engrained. It has characterized the views of the upper class and high castes in an Indian society where feudalism is still a living reality. Just how deeply engrained this view really is among upper class men can be seen in how the Justices of the Supreme Court dealt with the Mathura case.

Mathura was of a low caste. She came from a poor peasant family in Nagpur district in the state of Maharashtra. In 1972, when she was about fourteen and had just become sexually mature, she worked as a serving girl. On March 26, 1972, Ashok, the nephew of the master of the house, abducted her. Her brother, Gama, an agricultural laborer, immediately reported to the police that Mathura, a minor, had been abducted. She was found later that day. The interrogations of those involved began at 9 p.m. at the Desaiganj police station near Chandrapore. At 10:30 p.m. the interrogations were completed and everyone was asked to leave. But as Mathura was on her way out, Police Constable Gupta grabbed her and pulled her back into the station.

She was forced into the latrine. There was a cot in the room. With the assistance of Police Sergeant Tukaram, Constable Ganpat raped her. Then it was Police Sergeant Tukaram's turn, but being too drunk to have intercourse, he had to settle for abusing her in various ways.

In the meantime, a crowd of people had gathered in front of the police station. Tukaram then came out of the latrine and said that the girl had gone home and that everything was in order. But just as he was saying this, Mathura broke lose and shouted to her brother and to the whole crowd that Constable Ganpat had raped her. The crowd grew very agitated. In order to save the police station from being burnt down and Constable Ganpat and Sergeant Tukaram from being beaten to death, the chief of the police station agreed to allow the police to be reported. Eventually, they were sentenced by the Bombay High Court. Ganpat was given a sentence of five years and Tukaram one year.

However, when the case reached the Supreme Court the police were acquitted. Not because what had taken place was substantially different from what was described by the prosecutor. But the three learned judges, Justice Jaswant Singh, Justice Dailasham and Justice Koshal, made a lot of the fact that the girl was not a virgin. She had done that kind of thing before. And among learned judges, it was no secret what girls of that sort were.

There is an interesting juridicial finesse here: Mathura was about fourteen or fifteen. But she had not yet turned sixteen. It was to protect her state as a minor that her brother first turned to the police for help. According to current Indian law (Indian Penal Code, Section 375 [e]) sexual relations with a person under the age of sixteen is punishable regardless of whether it takes place with or without the consent of the person concerned.

When the police dragged Mathura into the latrine, she should have been able to stop them had she really wished to. In fact, she went along with it. The artistic image of the indolent maiden, and the learned judges' speculations about whether a fourteen–fifteen year old, locked in a stinking latrine, is not carried away by irresistible lust and thinks it pleasant when two unknown and drunk men in uniform hold her down and show her their penises, these are both reflections—one in art and the other in law—of the same brutal, feudal reality.

This judicial decision did not create a stir. But a year later, when it appeared together with other cases in an anthology, it came to the attention of lawyers in Delhi and Poona, greatly disturbing them. It was obvious that this was a case in which basic human rights were violated with the aid of legal artifice. Those who took an interest in this case were university professors, including Lotika Sarkar, the first female member of the faculty of law at Delhi University.

In September, 1979, a year after the verdict, they published an open letter to Chief Justice Chandrachaud. Thus began a campaign which brought together intellectual middle class women with poor and untouchable women. What they oppose is not an occasional expression of male chauvinism or lack of equality. They are fighting against being objects, against being indolent maidens. They are struggling against the feudal oppression of women which is so customary that it hardly shows.

Like this one-column news-item:

Young Woman Raped by 3 Policemen

Banda Feb. 20 (PTI) Three policemen allegedly raped a young woman in Sarah village 50 kms from here yesterday.

According to a report lodged with the Banda police the policemen knocked at the door of her house. When her husband opened the door they beat him up and tied him with a rope. After that they raped the woman.

Yet another case of rape was reported from Hinaihua village. The victim burnt herself alive after the incident.

It was this feudalistic, male outlook of the learned justices of the Supreme Court, their view of young low caste women as objects to be made use of as one sees fit, that acted as a catalyst. At meetings and conferences, organizations and pressure-groups were formed with the demands for new legislation, and an end the molestation of women and real human dignity for women. Pressured by an extensive and powerful campaign, the politicians were forced to begin to take steps through legislation to provide women with greater protection from rape and to ensure extra severe punishment to policemen who rape while on duty.

Nevertheless, in a semi-feudal India, rape is still what untouchable and poor girls can expect when they near puberty. Rape is still a form of punishment persons in authority can make use of when they wish to restore respect for law, privilege and property, when they quite simply wish to punish insubordinate elements, or when they want to feel the thrill of power.

The fact that sexual issues are, ultimately, class questions, and that there exists no solidarity among women superseding class interest and political association, can be corroborated daily in the newspaper stories appearing in Indira Gandhi's India.

I read the report on the Baghpat case by Amiya Rao. On July 18, 1980, Maya Tyagi, together with her husband Rajbala and two friends, arrived by car in Bhagpat. They had rented the car and were on their way to the wedding of Maya Tyagi's niece. They were of a peasant family. They were not numbered among the poorest families. Maya's husband, Rajbala, worked at a dairy and her brother, whose daughter was getting married, was a member of the Indian Army.

The car had a flat tire in Bhagpat. While the men were busy trying to repair the inner tube, a man approached the car and tried to grab Maya's necklace. She screamed and her husband and two friends stepped in to protect her. The man who had tried to steal her necklace withdrew after a short fight. He soon returned with armed policemen. They immediately shot Rajbala and his two friends. Then they ripped off Maya's sari, stripped her naked and took her jewelry. Then, to humiliate her, they beat her with their shoes. Following this, they paraded her back and forth through Baghpat's bazaar and then the police took her to the station house where seven of them raped her (she knew three of them). When she asked if she could have something to drink they gave her urine to drink.

At the gynecological ward of the hospital, Maya was given six stitches. Her husband was shot. Her two friends were shot. She was defiled. All her jewelry had been stolen. All the family's presents to the niece who was getting married had been stolen. The police issued a report that some dacoits had been killed in a clash. There was a news item about it and everything seemed forgotten.

However, journalists began to look into the incident. At first, Minister for Home Affairs Zail Singh (now President of India) seemed willing to investigate the matter. Then pressure was brought to bear on him from above and he backed out. Prime Minister Indira Gandhi was not interested in the fate of the girl. She might have been promiscuous. When asked if promiscuous girls really ought to be stripped naked in public and raped, she merely muttered something about how it was wrong that the police had been given the right to establish labor unions.

The police in Uttar Pradesh are protected against unwarranted lawsuits. Hence, Maya's brother cannot take legal action. The ongoing investigation is expected to take four months, and organizers from Youth Congress (I) have gone around Bhagpat together with members of Parliament and police officials from Meerut. They have threatened the people. The person who witnesses against the authorities will be punished.

For it was none other than Indira Gandhi's dead son Sanjay who appointed the police officers in Baghpat, and that police force forms a part of Indira's political apparatus. In the face of that, justice means little. That some French feminists consider Indira Gandhi's policies a triumph over the phallocrats would probably be seen by the seven rapist-policemen as just more proof of the inferiority and stupidity of women.

Confronting these conditions, the Indian movement has raised the demand for protection against rape. The demands they put forward—that the victim shall not be stigmatized, that consent attained through improper means shall not be considered consent, that women who file complaints that they have been raped shall have the right to be attended by a policewoman, and that women shall not be made to answer questions before the Court concerning previous sexual experience—these demands are not very different from those raised by women in Sweden or the United States. But there is no comparison between the unbearable feudal oppression suffered by the Indian women and the conditions in our own countries.

We can take the burning of brides, for example. In order to marry off his daughter, the father must give a dowry. Without a dowry, the girl cannot marry. If the father cannot deliver what he has promised, the girl's life can be sheer hell. Or she can be burnt and done away with. While it is mainly untouchable and extremely poor women who are raped, it is the girls from the middle class who are burnt. Every day, one can read in the papers short news items on the burning of brides.

> New Delhi 23 February: Shri Munna Lal, in a complaint filed with the Lahori Gate police station has alleged that his daughter, Mrs Shanti Devi, 24, resident of Kara Neel, who was admitted to the J. P. hospital yesterday for burn injuries and who died this morning, had been burnt to death by her husband Ashok and his brother.

> New Delhi 24 February: Mrs Pushpa, 20, wife of a Delhi Police constable, Vinod, was yesterday allegedly burnt to death by her husband and her father-in-law, Head Constable Naubat Ram, because of a dispute over dowry in her Kingsway Camp house. The police registered a case of murder following a complaint lodged by the victim's father, Mr Laxmi Chand of Meerut.

These are two out of a great many news items about women from the lower middle class. From time to time, a case is investigated. But most of them are hushed up. The police and the relatives agree to write off the burnings as an accident at the stove. According to official statistics, 149 women burned to death at their stoves in Delhi in 1979. Most of them were middle class brides of about twenty.

However, women are not just burnt to death (or beaten to death or drowned in the well, as is common in the country-side): untouchable girls, tribal girls, girls from the mountain villages are abducted to broth-els around India. Girls living under conditions of serfdom do not even have to be abducted. They can be sold directly. These girls are sold at a good profit to the brothel-keepers in the big cities. They are sold from one city to another. They are usually illiterate, often sold to an area where they cannot speak the language.

The red light district is owned by members of the upper class. Among them are politicians and senior government officials. The fine lady who receives foreign guests and talks about her fine values over a cup of tea, who dabbles in decorative arts and international understanding, has built her house from the profits provided by the child-brothels down on Grant Road.

In the winter of 1961, one of my friends took measures because the daughter of his sweeper had been abducted. She had not even reached puberty. The police thought it strange that anyone should bother about such a matter. But since he was an influential foreigner, they felt them-selves obliged to take some action. They located the girl in a child-brothel in Madras—and placed her in a reformatory for fallen women.

In Vishakhapatnam in Andhra Pradesh, a male nurse working at a hospital fell in love with a prostitute, a girl. When the girl's owner no-ticed that she was trying to escape, he transferred her to another brothel. The male nurse went to the revolutionary students for help. They searched all the brothels and finally found her in a luxury hotel for tour-ists which also served as a brothel—an upper class brothel for govern-ment officials. The students went to the owner and threatened him with the police. He laughed in their faces. He was himself a police officer and one of Vishakapatnam's important citizens. But with the help of large street demonstrations in which students, workers and untouchables par-ticipated, they did succeed in getting the girl released. They placed her in an institution for juveniles in Hyderabad. The couple was to be mar-ried. The students were proud of themselves. They held meetings and declared that the 'serve-the-people' attitude had scored a victory. Ten days later, the matron of the institution had sold the girl south, no one knew where. And since the girl did not know how to write, she could not inform them of her whereabouts.

This is not something out of nineteenth century *Mysteries of Paris*. It is but a part of the normal, dreadful shamefulness of everyday life.

Torture is a common occurrence in India. The Indian police stations and prisons are among the worst in the world. As far as I can tell, Indira's police were—and still are—far worse than those of the Shah of Iran or of Pinochet in Chile. Indira's friends in the world press have shielded her regime from criticism. But while torture is a common occurrence and fe-male prisoners are beaten and abused sexually, the treatment of female political prisoners is particularly atrocious. I will limit myself to but one case. It is well-documented and did not occur during the Emergency. Those who testified were political opponents of the victim. On May 3, 1974, two hundred and fifty women were arrested for agitating against the rise in prices. They were transported to Presidency Jail in Calcutta. There they came into contact with a group of seven female Naxalite prisoners. The prison was only built to hold 2,200 inmates but at that time housed 3,100, conditions which made it possible to break the isolation and make contact with the Naxalite women. These women had not been put on trial. They were to be *broken*. Once a month they were conveyed to Lalbazar police station. They were questioned and the police regularly used methods of torture:

> The women are completely stripped and laid on a table. To begin (with) they are burnt with cigarettes on their throat, chest, abdomen and all tender parts of the body to the accompaniment of insults and obscene suggestions. If the women still refuse to answer, an iron rod is inserted into their rectum. Screaming with pain they become unconscious. The unconscious body is dumped back in jail and allowed 20–22 days to recover before being called again to Lalbazar. As a result of the repeated insertion of the iron rod, the membrane between the rectum and the vagina has been ruptured in most of these women and their rectum and vagina have become one.
>
> The democratic and self-respecting women of India will not tolerate this indignity. They will demand of the government an immediate end to this jungle law.

Signed   Shukla Das
                                Gita Sengupta
                                Bani Mazumdar
                                Nupur Dey

But Indira Gandhi continued and conditions similar to those in Lalbazar police station continue to prevail in those areas where her underlings have direct influence...nor did the other politicians do much to change conditions. Political adversaries were fair game, and, what is more, when it came to female political adversaries, lower caste policemen could treat high caste women anyway they wanted.

As for the untouchable women and those from the lowest castes, the way they were treated did not change. They are not only sold for domestic use, but attractive girls are also bought by travelling agents to be exported. The authorities are aware of this commerce. Why, it is their own caste brothers, friends and relatives who are involved. As recently as in the early sixties, Indian girls were still quite cheap. But now the price may be as high as 2,000 rupees (about 200 U.S. dollars at the official rate of exchange) for the delivery of a young Indian girl for export. That is a lot of money for a family subsisting at starvation point. It is not for lack of morals or a sense of family that the poor sell their daughters.

Organized rape in India seldom has anything to do with sexuality. It is a meting out of punishment. In 1974, the railroad workers demanded higher pay. The strike that followed threatened the government of Indira Gandhi. The authorities swung into action. The wives of the railroad workers were the victims of mass-rape. The same thing befell the wives of the untouchables in Maharashtra in 1977, when they grew very militant. They refused to call themselves "harijans" (children of God) and began to title themselves "panthers." Their wives were raped en masse to make them see their place.

Wherever one travels in India's villages and poor quarters, one hears the same appalling tales. Late at night on February 18, we came to the village of Kothapeta in Karimnagar. This was an area that was off-limits—a disturbed area—and we had to be careful since the police were after us to get us out of there. They did not want any witnesses. There in the village of Kothapeta, we met the fifty year old woman Rajakka and her son. They had come to this place to tell their story. She had taken part in the women's movement. The chairwoman was one Kankamma. It was she who had been the driving spirit. It was Kankamma who had made the statement quoted by Professor Aswini K. Ray in *Mainstream* (January 13, 1979):

> We grew up with the knowledge (that) we would be raped after puberty. It was the reality of our experience. We never talked about it; now we do.... Women are determined to ensure a life for their daughters that they can at least call their own, not just "flesh and blood for the dora's pleasures."

Now Kankamma, too, was on the run. Rajakka had taken part in the women's movement. She had stood up to the authorities. She had been among those who had demanded a halt to the rape of women. That was, by the way, at the time when the landowner still called himself a communist. Now he is a member of Indira Gandhi's Congress Party, but then he belonged to the CPI, the party most loyal to Moscow.

On October 29, 1978, the landowner's goondas came to her house. They were drunk. They had just looted the house of one of the woman activists. Now they came to Rajakka. She was at home. Her husband was bedridden. He was sick. Her son was also at home. But her grandchildren were away. The landowner's men beat up her husband and then tied him to the bed. They beat her son until he lost consciousness. Then, one by one, they raped the fifty-year old Rajakka. She speaks their names one after the other and her voice is ice-cold with hate:

> Muthegala Kondaiah, Suddala Narasaia, Macha Banaiha, Katrepaka Nampelly, Puntegala Venkati, Bongoni Shankaraiah, Bongoni Lingaiah.

When she tried to file a complaint, the police did not want to accept it. The landowner offered her five hundred rupees if she would forget the incident. The police advised her to take the money.

"That man is divinely generous," said the police.

She has now fled from her village. The landowner's men are after her. Four other women have also fled. Her son talks about the village. Then he says, "I, too, am being hunted. They say I am dangerous. They say I have threatened the men who raped my mother."

Do you want to hear more?

Up in the coal-mining district, Indira's men wanted to break a union organizer. Four of them raped his wife. Then they stuffed her vagina full of gravel.

In the city of Kootgudem, I hear another story. There was a notorious goonda whom even the police feared. He had run his village for the landowner for twenty years. He raped a washer-girl and she drowned herself in a well for shame. Four students from Warangal were in town. They called him out to the bazaar. He came. He was foolhardy and feared no one since he was confident of his power and strength, and since no one had dared stand up to him in 20 years.

When he arrived at the bazaar, the students caught him with a lasso and tied him up. Then they cut off his hands and nailed them to the shop wall. Above the severed hands they placed a sign which read: "This is what happens to those who lay hands on the people's women."

When they saw this, the people in the bazaar drew back in horror. They stood there in total silence and gave the four students plenty of room when they left. Their emotions were mixed with fear. But now the incident has become the subject of a song.

Well, What about Capitalism?

"India," said Shailesh Chandra Jain, "India must move fast just to stay at the same place. During the past sixty years, tremendous industrial development has taken place. The number of industrial workers has doubled. According to the 1971 census, there were 22.37 million industrial workers. However, at the same time everything has remained just as it was. The percentage of the population working in agriculture has remained constant at 73 percent. In fact, between 1921 and 1971, we experienced a negative tendency, if anything. The percentage employed in the agricultural sector increased from 73 percent in 1921 to 73.8 percent in 1971.

"In other words, mass poverty is on the rise. Unemployment and underemployment grow more predominant from year to year. One development plan follows another, and since 1971 the number of registered unemployed has risen 12 percent each year. But it is not those totally lacking employment who are the problem, since the individual without income the year round does not have much chance of surviving at all. It is underemployment that is our problem. And if a country has more than 30 percent of its population employed in the agricultural sector, seasonal unemployment is unavoidable. India has 70 percent of its population employed—or rather, underemployed—in the agricultural sector. Add to them the 20 percent of the population working in antiquated cottage industry, bazaar commerce, small, old-fashioned operations, and various service occupations. When one speaks of Indian development,

one is talking about the remaining 10 percent of the population. They are
the ones who are living in modern times. The other 90 percent don't.
And they are growing poorer."

S. C. Jain sits at his desk and talks. He heads J. K. Paper Mills in
Orissa. He is forty-five. A technician with an M. S. in chemistry, he sits
on a number of boards of directors and committees. He is a typical Indian business executive: knowledgeable in his branch, with a good all-
round education, effective and hardworking. He is not in the same class
as the *dora*, the landed gentry in the villages of the south. They do not
even belong to the same era. S. C. Jain represents capitalism. J. K. Paper
Mills is part of the J. K. Singhaina group which is India's fourth largest in
size, after Birlas, Tatas and Mafatlal. Its net assets amount to roughly 2.5
billion rupees. Birlas is five times as large.

J. K. Paper Mills is located in the city of Jaykaypur. (This would be
equivalent to Jaykaytown in England or America.) A company town,
newly-built in the jungles of Koraput. It is well-planned and neat. The
company management is well aware of its social responsibility. It was, for
example, the management that went to the Therbali temple in the jungle
and found that the statues there were important and interesting. They
saw to it that an archaeological survey was carried out in the area and
then turned directly to the government to have the temple declared a
protected monument. Surrounded by its town, the mill lies there like a
small oasis of development. Everything is model-perfect: the roads,
parks, the various residential quarters. Eighty percent of the workers'
children attend school. They march to their classrooms in straight lines.
They are drilled and coached, and 90 percent of them graduate. The
daily schedule of the workers' children is fixed and supervised:

0600-0645	getting up, washing, morning prayer
0700-0800	individual study of mathematics
0800-1000	study hall
1000-1800	school day
1800-2000	leisure, evening prayer, dinner
2000-2200	study hall
2200-0600	sleep

The students are alert, clever and knowledgeable. They have a far
greater store of general knowledge than do their Swedish contemporaries. They are also more self-assured. They speak more clearly and give
direct answers.

"Children from homes not conducive to study may remain in school
after class is over for supplementary instruction. Those with learning
problems are given remedial teaching. We do not hold anyone back. All

the pupils are prepared for their examination."

Each school day has its motto. Today's is: "Rest means rust." The weak are to be helped towards strength and success. The school shines like a puritannical jewel in an ordered world, like one of Robert Owens' model-societies of the 1830s. But once outside the city limits, India is still the same: the villages resemble dunghills, and conditions of serfdom and feudalism still hold sway.

The leap from the village to the mill is a long one. The income of the industrial workers is four or five times that of the villagers. On top of that, there are the social benefits and the security provided by the mill. Only the most unskilled positions are filled by inhabitants of the surrounding villages. Out of 2,000 employees, 800 are skilled workers. They have gone to school and come from far away. But to fill even the unskilled positions, management prefers workers with at least three or four years of schooling. They have an easier time understanding the work process. The influence of this new, sparkling town does not reach many feet beyond the city limits.

In the fifties, it was thought that India would experience a tremendous demand for paper, spurred to a large degree by the explosion in popular education. In 1958, the mill was moved to this primitive, out-of-the-way part of Orissa. Here in this backward state was to be found the raw material—bamboo. Cheap electricity would be supplied, there was sufficient water and there was a railroad.

The railroad is working. For the last two years there is a through-train to New Delhi. But there is an energy problem. Several plants have been forced to shut down for lack of power. A lack of raw materials is also beginning to be felt. Today, one would not build a paper mill which depended entirely on a local supply of bamboo.

The provincial government owns the timber land. They leave it to contractors to supply the bamboo. These are interested only in quick profits. They are not concerned about renewing the forests. The contractors ruthlessly denude the hills. They have their six-month contracts, and the day their contract ends so too does their responsibility. But regrowth takes between six and seven years. The reckless cutting of timber creates serious problems of erosion. The J. K. group has asked the government to do something about this problem. Either the government should take responsibility for reforestation and forest conservation, or the forests should be sold or leased on a long-term basis to the paper mills which can care for them. But up until now, neither the central government nor the provincial government has done anything about this problem. That is how industry sees the problem. There are, at this very time, big strikes in progress up in the woods. The bamboo-cutters are on strike against the contractors for better pay. They claim that the forestry officials are corrupt and that in order to secure bribes and income these officials work together with the contractors in destructive deforestation.

The facts presented by the government of Orissa to the J. K. group at the time of the mill's establishment in the state have proven to be incorrect. The water supply is running short. Either the mill will be forced to shut down three months of the year or the plans for expansion will have to be shelved. But in that case the mill will remain a size which places in doubt its long-term profitability. Nor is subsoil water available in any great quantity. A filthy sewer now stands where, according to plan, a river should be flowing. The factory uses all available water. Even the beautifully landscaped botanical garden has begun to wither away. The Robert Owens-perfection surrounding the mill is peeling off, because as the forests are destroyed, the water shortage grows more acute. And there is no political solution in sight. J. K. Paper Mills is rationalizing production and experimenting with combining bamboo and other raw materials, and saving water while increasing production. The 2,000 people who work bear up the 20,000 who are indirectly dependent on the mill for their livelihood. This is the fifth largest industrial enterprise in Orissa; it is second largest private company.

"It has proven difficult to get skilled and truly qualified workers to come out here," says S. C. Jain. "The worker with a sound technical background prefers to look for a somewhat lower-paying job in, or near, the big cities. Even if they are unemployed, they would rather not move to a remote part of the country such as Koraput in Orissa. They feel that it is also a matter of their children's future. We do have an excellent school here. We have to. Those with schooling realize the importance of education, and they prefer to live in the cities so as to be able to enroll their children in good schools and give them a headstart in life.

"Looking at the situation for those outside the 9 percent or 10 percent employed in the industrial sector, the picture is different. The 75 percent of the population employed in the agricultural sector have work fifty, perhaps a hundred, days per year. Perhaps they demand improvement in their economic situation. But if one turns to the tribal peoples, those who live on an even more primitive level, they do not even make demands. Suppose a man from a tribe receives four rupees for an eight-hour workday. There is a struggle to raise wages, and wage negotiations are held. His earnings increase say to eight rupees for an eight-hour day. He will work four hours and then go home with his four rupees. They are even untouched by rising expectations.

"What is more, the demand for paper has not grown as had been anticipated. Today we place our hope for the future in the growth of the packaging industry. The market in that branch is expanding swiftly. It meets the needs of the cities. As for paper used for printing, it depends on how the educational sector is influenced by population growth."

About a month later, I discuss the Indian economy with journalist friends in New Delhi. Mother Theresa has been to Europe, and Western publications are filled with pictures of starving Indians. Indeed, the export of human skeletons is also one of India's sources of hard currency. For the budget year 1978-'79, India earned three million rupees on the export of skeletons. They are sent to teaching institutions in Europe and North America.

At about the same time, however, on February 22, the Indian Minister of Trade and Steel then, Pranab Mukherjee (now Finance Minister), had announced that Hindustan Steelworks Construction Limited had put up a tender to the Soviet authorities for the construction of a steel mill in Nigeria and a nuclear power plant in Libya.

"What have they written about that in the Swedish newspapers?"

"Why, nothing, as far as I know. They are busy playing songs on their guitars about their longing for sun, wind and hedgehogs."

For the fact is that in Sweden, where the fires of the nuclear debate have raged, India's bid to build nuclear power plants in Libya for the Soviet Union was never an important news item. In Sweden, Mother Theresa was the big news story about India. The export of skeletons would have been considered newsworthy if the story had reached Europe; the announcement by the Indian minister, however, was of no interest to the news media. Little wonder then that friends in New Delhi scoffed at the European radicals and the leftists in the news media.

The picture of India must be double-exposed. India is a poor country, but it is not pitiful. In industrial capacity, it ranks fourteenth or fifteenth in the world. With an annual capacity of 11.4 million tons, its steel industry exceeds that of Spain, and with its plans for expansion, India's production may top that of France.

In Southeast Asia, the Middle East and Africa, Western industrial nations have already felt the competition from a knowledgeable and aggressive Indian export industry, seeking to capture important contracts. Indian construction methods are among the most modern, and Indian experts meet international standards. Already India is working with major investments in third world countries alongside countries such as Brazil, Venezuela, South Korea and Mexico. At present, India is involved in a hundred and four joint ventures in various third world countries. Birla AG with its headquarters in Switzerland is building textile mills in South Korea. Birla is investing in Kenya, Malaysia, Indonesia, Thailand, Nigeria and Philippines. In Singapore, the name Tata is as important as Mitshubishi.

In the last few years, India has also been collaborating with the increasingly powerful, Soviet-based multinational companies. The Libyan nuclear power plant project is no isolated case. Indian state owned industries linked to Russian interests have grown strong and are rapacious on the world market. Bharat Heavy Electricals Ltd., Indian Oil Ltd. and Engineering Projects Ltd. are all on the list of the world's two hundred largest firms.

Meanwhile, India grows poorer year by year. The World Bank notes that India now no longer belongs to the third world, but to the even poorer fourth world, together with countries such as Uganda and Bangladesh. India is headed towards the bottom. It is estimated that in the year 2,000, India will have 54.8 percent of the world's illiterates in the age group of fifteen to nineteen. Of the world's illiterates, 500 million will be in India. 75,000 of India's villages do not have a school. Girls, especially, are denied schooling, and 62 percent of school-age girls in India do not go to school.

Only 10 percent of the Indian work force can read. In the Philippines, the corresponding number is 83 percent and in South Korea 55 percent. Only 29 percent of all Indian adults can read. This is not due to chance. The class which controls the Indian government and economy, and which determines policy (regardless of what the politicians may wish to believe) allot the least amount of money possible to general education. The resources are used to educate their own children so that they can be exported as specialists, thus becoming a source of hard currency.

In 1970, India exported 3,141 medical doctors and scientists to the United States. They had all been educated in India at Indian expense. Up until 1971, the Indian government educated approximately 30,000 scientists, scholars and engineers, 5,000 of whom had taken a doctor's degree. Out of what is left over after educating their own children, they provide youth the literacy necessary to work in the industrial sector. Ten percent of the gainfully employed work in industry and 10 percent of the gainfully employed are taught to read.

This has nothing to do with the question of child labor. Advanced Indian industry cannot use children as labor. Child labor is to be found in small-scale industry and rural industry. Those branches of the economy employ India's backward 90 percent. In order to survive the competition, they must use the cheapest labor possible. And that is small, quick children.

Approximately half of India's population live below the poverty level (40 percent in the countryside, 50 percent in the cities) and lack both human and political rights. The poverty is growing. If one defines poverty in a slightly different way, statistics show that over a twenty year period, poverty has increased from 30 percent to 70 percent of the population.

The fact is that since the eighteenth century, when direct British plunder began, the people of India have become poorer and poorer. The country witnesses a *deindustrialization* during the entire nineteenth century. From 1809-1813 to 1901, for example, the number of people employed in cottage industry decreased from 19 percent to 8.5 percent in five districts investigated in Bihar. During the same period, only one industry was established there: a railway workshop in Jamalpur. From 1881 to the present, the number of persons employed in industry has decreased rather than increased. This is not so strange when it is remembered that the plunder of India continued over the period of British rule of India. The annual tribute paid to Britain by the Indian people during the interwar years amounted to 150,000,000 pounds. That was equal to three pounds a year per inhabitant of Great Britain for the entire period. The loot, of course, was not divided equally among the classes of the mother country. Still, if it rains on the hen, the chicks too get wet. The English working man, too, received something from colonial plunder. Indeed, it was this that kept him peaceful and democratic.

To understand post-independence development in India, one must remember that the feudal class which cooperated with the British because the British guaranteed their right to exploit their own peasants, remained a power after 1947. The class established by the British to administer Great Britain's plundering, now desired to keep this plunder going for its own benefit, with the aid of the government apparatus created by the British for that purpose.

Little wonder then that while India grows strong, mighty and richer, India is also sinking further and further towards the bottom. Industry develops, but does not even require the labor of those born in its own company residential quarters. From 1962 to 1976, 8,000,000 workers were passed from the cities into the agricultural sector—agriculture which cannot even support half of its own, and where those lacking land grow in number and job opportunities decrease.

During the four five-year plans from 1951 to 1974, the number of the officially-registered unemployed has risen from 3,300,000 to 22,900,000. Economic growth projected at 5.1 percent per annum was from 1960 to 1976 only 1.2 percent. And if one looks at Indira Gandhi's record years, 1970-1976, with the Emergency laws in operation, Soviet assistance and such, the annual rate of growth is 0.5 percent.

This kind of development is not inevitable. China's point of departure was even worse than India's. China has its own problems and makes its own mistakes. China seems now to have ended up repeating India's development model. It serves the needs of what Mao called the bourgeoisie in the party—the new class. If we compare what Mao's political line meant for China and India's and China's economic development from 1950 to 1978, before the December 1978 plenum of the Central Committee of the Communist Party of China that abrogated Mao's line the picture is clear:

	1950		1978	
	India	*China*	*India*	*China*
coal million tons	35	49	102	618
crude oil million tons	0.3	0.3	11	104
electricity billion KWH	6	6	101	257
cement million tons	3	2	20	65
steel million tons	2	1	10	32
fertilizer million tons	0.02	0.02	2.7	8.7
bicycles thousands	114	45	2464	8540
grain million tons	56	139	114	305
cotton million tons	0.5	0.9	1.3	2.2
jute million tons	0.7	0.2	1.5	1
railways thousand kms	35	23	61	59

In China, the masses were mobilized—in all their hundreds of millions. But the hundreds of millions of people cannot be organized for labor unless the entire, shameful old society is destroyed. In India, the trend has been in the opposite direction. At least 50 percent—perhaps 70 percent—of the population has become superfluous. At the same time, big business has grown even bigger. The nationalization of the banking industry—proposed as a means of restricting capitalism—has, in fact, only aided in its concentration. Birla's assets totalled 2,829 million rupees in 1963-'64; 4,469 million in 1966-'67; 7,258 million in 1972-'73; and 10,646 million in 1975-'76. And this trend continues.

That government administration and defence spending are the areas which have witnessed the most rapid growth is perhaps not as surprising as the fact that 60 percent of industrial capital is owned by the State. The state sector consists mainly of heavy industry. But one cannot call this socialism. The company structure is the usual one. In other words, only a simple decision need be made to sell the companies entirely or in part, and thus make them privately owned. The companies are also led and managed exactly like any other enterprise of a comparable size. The social make-up and background of senior management within the state-sector are also similar to those in the private sector. Investments are financed primarily through domestic and foreign borrowing, and the profit goes to those who have advanced the capital. This state-ownership is just the type of enterprise system that the ruling class in India has found to be the most suitable.

Following Indira Gandhi's election victory, the populist slogans have been played down. Instead, her government has decided to ease credit restrictions for large loans. Congress (I) has promised a better "climate of investment for the private sector," and both the Vice President and the Minister of Commerce have welcomed a greater participation by the multinational corporations in India. They have also stressed—as the Minister of Commerce did at the 1980 World Marketing Congress—the importance of Indian cooperation with the multinational corporations on the export markets.

In the agricultural sector, India has, over the last fifteen years, invested growing amounts of money to develop that segment of agriculture which is capable of producing for the market and which can concentrate on the world market.

We might say then what the feudal dacoit leader in the desert along the Indo-Pakistani border said:

"The poor are parasites. They eat but don't produce." Or, like the senior official in Orissa, one might say:

"Have you seen how the poor live like swine in the filth, how they creep into their hovels like pigs into pigsties? Their lives can't be of much value."

India is no failure. India is capitalism's most successful development model. It is just that there are 500,000,000 superfluous Indian parasites living like swine in their poverty. Perhaps they could be sprayed away? Or something could be put in the well-water? Perhaps SIDA could lend a hand?

The Artist as Imperialist

While travelling in India a great portion of our time has been spent in dead abandoned capital cities, in the run-down palaces and empty forts of once-mighty kingdoms, or in fortified towns and the fortresses of robber barons far out in the desert or mountains. Part of the reason also explains why we travel to the bastides in France and search out wooden architecture in the streets of Finland's Osterbotten: we are interested in architecture and the spatiality of townscapes. Cities such as Fatepur Sikri, Jaisalmer, Jodhpur, Daulatabad and Gwalior are something to behold.

Part of the explanation is to be found in the fascination for magnificent technical achievements. The Roman aquaducts are not beautiful, but the Pont du Gard delights the eye like the finest autobahn bridge or the dam at Liuchia on the upper reaches of the Yellow River. One is filled with elation on seeing the clear-cut dome above the grave of Muhammed Adil Shah in Bijapur. It was built in 1659. Grandiose and sharp in contour, it carries no superfluous ostentation. There is no need to conceal the dome in quantities of stone and mortar, as the Pantheon is, because it threatens to burst apart. It is suspended there on its own weight, at rest, a concrete dome built of brick-reinforced cement. The contour displays itself. The technical solution is so magnificent that it evokes a deep feeling of joy. The vast space does not weigh upon the viewer. Michelangelo's dome over St. Peters is slightly larger. But although it is wrong to compare great things with one another, the fact is that the mausoleum of Mohammed Adil Shah is a more beautiful, better solution. It was not until the end of the nineteenth century that European architects, making use of this building material, were able to carry on and develop the inspiration of the dome in Bijapur. (The Taj Mahal in Agra is also worth seeing, although it has been prettified.) Seventeenth century India was in no way "backward," "underdeveloped" or "untechnical" in comparison to Europe. It took Europeans two hundred years and the introduction of Portland cement to catch up with the creators of Bijapur in 1850. The dome rises above an open area measuring 1,700 square meters.

It is here, at these crossroads, that our visits to Vijayanagar (City of Victory) and Bijapur (City of Victory) are of such interest. Both these "Cities of Victory," both these capital cities, are located north of Kamataka, the state previously known as Mysore. From the fourteenth to the sixteenth centuries, Vijayanagar was the capital of the mighty feudal kingdom of southern India. Today, it is just a vast field of ruins. It lies just beyond Hospet, not far from where the River Tungabhadra has been dammed as part of one of modern India's largest irrigation projects.

Bijapur is a remote and sleepy district capital. In 1883, the British made it an administrative center and moved their departments here. They established an unusual city right in the midst of the great monuments. The building style of the British era might best be termed Brighton architecture, a sort of nineteenth century pier and amusement park style planted in this dry city of the Deccan. The city is poor and rundown. Seldom have I encountered such rapacious gutter-pigs as those in Bijapur. Hairy, black beasts that zealously guard their sewers against any threatening dog or human. The pigs rule in this city of Islam. Once this had been the pearl of the south, capital of the Muslim kingdom of Bijapur. It had been the seat of government from 1489, when the governor, Mahmud Sawan's Turkish slave, Yusef Khan, made himself sovereign, until 1888, when Aurangzeb captured the city from the last Adil Shah, Sikander.

The cities are worth visiting for the sake of their architecture and townscapes alone. The dome in Bijapur is such that I have spent entire evenings listening to Professor Elias Cornell expound on it. It is indeed a masterpiece of engineering. However, the thing that makes this all so interesting is that here we are visiting the known, described world.

If I lift my gaze from the typewriter at this moment, I can see Gripsholms Castle across the water. Heavy masses of red brick. It is part of our time. Both Vijayanagar and Bijapur are described for me in the published accounts of various travellers. People have visited and written about them. Commentators from the fifteenth, sixteenth and seventeenth centuries, in particular, present us with a picture of normalcy. When in the 1580s, Ralph Fitch, an adventurous gentleman and mer-

chant, travelled to India, it was but another foreign country he was visiting. As a foreigner, he would have had a more difficult time of it had he
attempted to travel across Sweden and Finland in 1584. He would
scarcely have been able to record that "their houses are of stone, very
faire and high."

Like other contemporary travellers, Ralph Fitch visited foreign countries, not an alien world.

How was it then that India and the rest of Asia came to be thought of
as exotic and different? When Egron Lundgren wrote home to Mrs.
Laura Grubb from Calcutta on April 21, 1858, Indians had become different, strange and alien, as they had not been for Fitch:

> The other day was the Indian New Year and on that occasion reli-
> gious celebrations took place at their temples. I was out and wit-
> nessed one of these heathen ceremonies held at an ancient temple
> half a mile from here, in a place where roads and paths cross under
> high, verdant trees, superb bamboo and palms. There we found a
> great crowd of people, men and women with their children, all
> dark Hindus, half-naked, with silver rings around their ankles,
> with strands of pearls and ornaments, and rings in their noses, in
> their upper earlobes and on their toes. In addition, they had
> painted marks on their foreheads and noses, while many of the
> women had tattooed inscriptions on their upper arms. Besides me
> and my companion, there were very few whites present, but the In-
> dians possess such a healthy fear of their masters the English that
> there is really no danger going out among this mass of black peo-
> ple.

Almost a hundred years later, the liberal, radical, freethinking philosopher Bertrand Russell wrote his autobiography. In it he describes the
pushy newspaper photographers in Yokohama in 1921. He fears that his
wife will have a miscarriage. And then he writes something quite
strange:

> I felt at that moment the same type of passion as must have been
> felt by Anglo-Indians during the Mutiny, or by white men sur-
> rounded by a rebel colored population. I realized then that the de-
> sire to protect one's family from injury at the hands of an alien race
> is probably the wildest and most passionate feeling of which man is
> capable.

Yet this feeling that Bertrand Russell, in *The Middle Years 1914-1944*,
claims to be the most passionate of which man is capable, was something

completely unknown to Ralph Fitch (who, unlike Bertrand Russell, really did meet with misfortune during his travels).

Strictly speaking, Russell experiences the same thing as Egron Lundgren. The free-thinking artist and the free-thinking philosopher both reason along socially determined lines and see that which is socially acceptable. How is it then that they see?

The image of the lone English family surrounded by a sea of rebellious Indians can be exchanged for the picture of the lone SS family living in the midst of a sea of rebellious Polish concentration-camp prisoners, say in March 1945. The reason Bertrand Russell (and probably the great majority of his European readers) can empathize with the racist sentiments of the Anglo-Indian family, but not with those of the SS officer, obviously cannot be found in some well-considered or principled belief that it is right to dominate and kill Indians and Asians, but that it is wrong to dominate and kill Europeans.

This prevalent attitude is but the product of historical circumstance. Had Halifax succeeded in ousting Churchill in the spring of 1940 and obtained peace in Europe, or had Hitler succeeded in the creation of his New Europe, having avoided the ill-conceived invasion of Russia, then we might have seen some future German "Rüssler." This would have been a famous philosopher of a time when the exploitation of the occupied countries had resulted in a mild, mature administration replete with ancient Germanic liberties for the ruling people who also benefited from the plunder. Some such free-thinking German Rüssler might allude to the widespread fear of a sub-human rebellion capable of overwhelming the lone SS officers in their strongholds out on the desolate frontiers of the Reich.

If this analogy is not valid, why not?

For me (and I suppose for many others of my generation who hated Hitler-fascism), this problem began to take on a grave significance during the war. After 1958, it became the decisive issue in my writing and travel. The question was how to break with this programmed attitude and how to achieve a consciously aware one. I tried various models: an account written from another horizon (*Gates to Asia*); an account in which the characters through their narratives convey the reader into another reality (*Report from a Chinese Village*); an account which, by making use of personal emotion, guilt and anguish, cuts through to the heart of the programmed attitude (*Confessions of a Disloyal European*); and an account in which the characters reveal themselves to the point where the readers choke on their laughter (the feature film *Myglaren*). But art lies with style, while there is, in fact, an objective reality. Several editions of my writings were published, and I was translated and read. I do not know if I was able to crack the programmed attitude of my readers. I doubt it.

In 1970, we drove to India. We had several reasons for going. There was work to do. There were many things to see. We also had a clearly formulated goal for our journey: we were going back to Mandu. But above all, we needed time to think through and discuss several questions. We stayed in Mandu. The weather was still hot. The sound of our footsteps echoed through the enormous monuments of stone. Beneath the vaults, the light was ice-blue and aqua green. Our first visit to Mandu was in 1958. Since then we have often returned, to rediscover the strictest, most austere Muslim architecture in India. During the fifteenth and sixteenth centuries, it was the home of rulers.

> From thence we went to Mandoway, which is a very strong towne. It was besieged twelve years by Zelabdim Echebar before he could winne it. It standeth upon a very great high rocke, as most part of their castles doe, and was of very great circuite.

Thus wrote Ralph Fitch about his visit in 1584. However, the statement about Zelabdim Echebar (the Mughal emperor Akbar) besieging Mandu for twelve years is a myth.

We stayed at the tourist hostel. We wandered about in this desolate Mandu, now little more than a small market town scattered about the feet of the Jama Masjid from 1454. In the evening we read and talked. I was also working on this book. Our discussions centered around the need to find genres capable of depicting reality in a way that would cut through literary artifice: argumentation, descriptions, flashbacks, ruthless personal attacks, the use of romantic irony to demolish any and every attempt at academic dissimulation, and direct reports on the horrendous degradation of humankind. The need to oppose the conception of the world held by the cultured, Beethoven-playing, SS officer, with the humble truths that all through history it has been right to rebel, and that the mightiest lord can be overthrown.

For art, left to be art, lied with style, the same way that documentaries and science lied with objectivity. During those hot afternoons in Mandu, we read publicists of the Empire, the rightists as well as those who considered themselves otherwise.

At 4:30 p.m. on April 13, 1919, the British empire, its subjects states and protectorates, covered one fourth of the earth's land surface. One fourth of the world's population lived within the confines of this empire. It was at this time that Brigadier General Dyer came to Jallianwalla Bagh near Amritsar in Punjab. A public meeting was in progress. Those present opposed British rule. The audience numbered 8,000, or perhaps 10,000. Brigadier General Dyer arrived with armored cars and fifty riflemen. He deployed his troops on the slope facing the area where the meeting was taking place. The general had not warned the assembly. He had not even tried to prevent it from taking place. He had allowed the people to gather and then placed his men in firing position. When everything was set, the general gave the order to fire into the crowd. The soldiers fired from a distance of about 60 meters. As he later observed, Brigadier General Dyer had the intention of spreading terror all over Punjab. One thousand six hundred and fifty shots were fired. It took ten minutes. The crowd screamed and tried to run. While the Brigadier General watched events unfold, the Punjabis screamed, jumped and ran. Small children howled. The rebellious crowd clambered all over itself like trapped rats since there were few avenues of escape. Shot after shot rang out, and the bullets lodged in Punjabi flesh.

Later, the British claimed that only five hundred died, but more reliable informants put the number of victims at a thousand or more. Brigadier General Dyer certainly spread terror over Punjab. He put fear into all of India. But if he believed that fear would demoralize the people, he was mistaken. Instead, the massacre at Jallianwalla Bagh became the start of a new phase in India's struggle for independence. On April 15, martial law was imposed on Amritsar. A public platform on which natives were to be whipped was erected near the fort. Indians were beaten in the streets. On the street where natives had dared to assault a white man, the Brigadier General issued a "crawl-order." Every non-European who used that street had to crawl on his stomach.

In Kasur, Captain Doveton required the natives to touch their foreheads to the ground before him, the representative of British authority. He was the one who thought of a way to use the long noses of the Punjabis. Instead of a brush, they had to dip their noses into white paint and use them to draw white lines in the road. It was also he who whitewashed Indians from top to toe and then placed them out in the sun to dry. The Punjabi sun is the hottest in the world. Doveton also had a barred cage built. He filled it with a hundred and seven Punjabis, and had them stand in the sun to warm up. As the sun struck their heads, they could not stand it and began to piss and shit, crowded in the cage.

These were not isolated acts of cruelty. Lieutenant Governor Sir Michael O'Dwyer discovered in Punjab that the airplane could be used against the mob. Lieutenant Dodkins of the. R.A.F. flew against twenty peasants working in the fields and rattled them down. Major Carberry of the R.A.F. caught sight of a crowd and dropped a bomb in their midst. When the crowd dispersed in panic, he picked them off with his machine gun. He flew over the village at an altitude of 70 meters, certain that it was not in the people's best interest to assemble. By killing a few villagers, he produced "a moral effect."

These British officers and gentlemen were fighting for high ideals.

They had their salaries and they had their Empire. And what about the SS officers? While famine and pestilence spread through the realms, the metropolises of the masters grew rich, cultured and luxurious. The British ruled so long that they could afford democracy and Oxford at home. Had the SS ruled long enough...well, luckily they did not.

For reasons of diplomacy (the British had suffered defeat in their war against Afghanistan, and the anti-colonial movement spread across Asia and Africa), the British government was to take exception to Brigadier General Dyer's massacre in Amritsar. Their disapproval was, however, both mild and genteel. He was relieved of active duty. But it was only with reluctance that the House of Commons agreed to such action against a British hero. The vote was 232 votes for the government proposal and 131 in favor of Brigadier General Dyer's acquittal. As for the House of Lords, it voted 129 to 89 in favor of Dyer and regretted that he had been forced to resign. To console the brave general, a sum of 20,000 pounds was collected for him.

From that time on, the history of South Asia is the story of how Punjabis, Bengalis, all the hundreds of millions of inhabitants of that empire, rose in revolt. During the 1920s and '30s, the people of British India proved that they were not rats but human beings. They revolted against oppression.

It is a matter of interest to see how British writers and artists depicted this epic-making struggle of mankind against servitude.

The answer to the question is quite simple. They did not depict it. They did not see it.

As far as I know, no writer (including those writers who called themselves leftists) wrote about this struggle from an antiimperialist position. In this English literature, there exist no Asian men or women, only servile domestics, native clerks, westernized Oriental gentlemen, indolent maidens to be made use of as "sleeping dictionaries," scheming half-breeds, unreliable Hindus, big dumb Muslims, and honest—but blood-thirsty and stubborn—men from the northwest frontier. The picture of South Asia as portrayed in English literature was developed as a caricature at the clubs of the Empire, clubs reserved for Europeans.

Let us take, for example, the famous modern classic *A Passage to India* by E. M. Forster. It has sold over 1,000,000 copies since 1924. But read it! Professor Godbole is a typically racist caricature of an intellectual Hindu.

English intellectuals (and European intellectuals in general) do not like to hear this sort of thing. When I noted this fact at the PEN meeting in Stockholm in 1973, the fine English liberals frowned. I was being rude and boorish. They were genteel and lettered. They spoke of freedom of the spirit. And in their company were free spirits from all over the world. Later, they came up to me quite upset. It was not true that Brigadier General Dyer was some kind of a blackguard. He was a fine man. My answer was that General Governor Hans Frank was also a fine man and, as far as I knew, better educated than Dyer, yet that had not kept him from the gallows in Nörnberg. At this, all these travelling stipendiaries of the spirit, these conference-publicists in the free speech association were shocked: I was uncultured! Then the revolutionary Enzensberger shouted:

"Let's go out onto the lawn and talk about poetry."

The cowardly evasion into literature.

Yet, no matter what the fine critics write, Forster's best-seller represents the sale of a million polemics against Indian national independence. Forster furnished imperialism with a cultural fig-leaf. He ends his novel with these words:

> "Why can't we be friends now?" said the other, holding him affectionately. "It's what I want. It's what you want."
>
> But the horses didn't want it—they swerved apart; the earth didn't want it, sending up rocks through which riders must pass single file; the temples, the tank, the jail, the palace, the birds, the carrion, the Guest House, that came into view as they issued from the gap and saw Mau beneath: they didn't want it, they said in their hundred voices, "No, not yet," and the sky said, "No, not there."
>
> Weybridge, 1924

Forster can go take a flying leap! Kipling, at least, was honest.

What was it, in fact, that kept men such as Aziz and Fielding apart in 1924? Was it the sky? The buildings? The earth? The horses? Fate? At that time, hundreds of patriots sat jailed without a trial all over India. They had been arrested and deported by the authorities with the help of various statutes. (In Bengal, the old Statute III proved invaluable.) All over India people protested against this system of arrest, detention and deportation of political activists without a trial. The representatives of British democracy in India listened attentively to the complaints, while the British Labor government in London studied the many depositions about the torture and repression. Just before being given its walking papers, this first Labor government in the history of Great Britain struck a blow at the Indian people with its remaining strength. On October 25, 1924, the Governor General promulgated the Bengal Criminal Law Amendment Ordinance which gave the government authorities almost unlimited power to deal with the dissidents. The imperial machinery extracted three pounds annually from India for each and every inhabitant of Great Britain. Three pounds for every man, woman and child. So that even if the plunder was divided unequally, the workers represented by the Labor government did receive some crumbs of the cake, and wished to preserve them.

Or, let us take another example: *Burmese Days*, by George Orwell. He was a leftist. He describes the astute Oriental magistrate, U Po Kyin, who was fat in that peculiar, Burmese way:

> for the Burmese do not sag and bulge like white men, but grow fat symmetrically, like fruits swelling.

The native mistress has that rare and inscrutable way of showing her sexuality:

> Ma Hla continued to stroke Flory's shoulder. She had never learned the wisdom of leaving him alone at these times. She believed that lechery was a form of witchcraft. . . .

The educated Indian is the obsequious Dr Veraswami:

> The fact iss, my friend, there iss a most unpleasant business afoot. You will perhaps laugh—it sounds nothing—but I am in serious trouble. Or rather, I am in danger of trouble. It iss an underground business. You Europeans will never hear of it directly. In this place—he waved a hand towards the bazaar—there iss perpetual conspiracies and plottings of which you do not hear. But to us they mean much.

These caricatures are racist, not racial. Dr Veraswami speaks and behaves in a strangely familiar fashion. Observe:

> You goyim vill never hear of it right straight off. In this here place— he waved a hand towards the ghetto—perpetually der iss conspiracies and plottings vich you vill not hear of. But to uss, dey mean much.

This is the Eastern European Jew from countless anecdotes. Orwell even makes his character speak that strange language heard only in books and anecdotes. Real Yiddish, like the real English language of India, is not half as funny.

We see then what this novel really is. The girl, Ma Hla May, is not Burmese. She is a gypsy-girl from Galicia. Or rather the caricature of a gypsy-girl in that kind of novel. Not even a brilliant young communist writer like Ralph Fox was able to write differently. When first writing about Asia, it was Lawrence of Arabia who determined his style. Fox's

Conversation with a Lama belongs to the modern imperialist literary genre: the psychology of the Oriental. His book *Genghis Khan* (London, 1938) is a strange kind of racist interpretation of history; the Marxist variant. It is filled with assertions such as:

> To understand the peculiar character of Asiatic history, the causes of its political instability, the real root of that Asiatic pessimism, miscalled fatalism, which has placed such a distinguishing mark on the civilization of the continent, we must go deeper than a mere description of the political divisions in the period which interests us. The very idea of change, in the form of enrichment, of concentration (in the chemical sense) which is the basis of the Western view of life, is foreign and incomprehensible to the Asiatic. (pp. 22—23)

And racist lore such as:

> We do know, however, that this part of the world was once inhabited by a race which conquered China, exterminating its aboriginal population, a race with white skins and fair hair, which later mixed with the original Turko-Mongol peoples. (p. 35)

European Marxism of the thirties!

I have chosen to use these three examples since they are considered uncontroversial: Forster in literary circles, Orwell among intellectuals of the New Left, and Fox because he, in fact, became a martyr and a model for the communists, the entire left in the Europe of the forties. He died defending Europe's people against the fascist assault on Lopera in Andalusia in January, 1937.

English fiction writers wrote loyally. They had to. There were however, political publicists who did otherwise. They were not numerous, but they did exist. (Even if Hyndman turned so utterly chauvinist during World War I that he was expelled from the labor movement he had helped found, his valiant efforts for the Indian people should not be forgotten. Read, for example, *The Ruin of India by British Rule from 1907*.) Many British officials were so disturbed by what they had seen that they made public what they knew. J. S. Furnivall worked for the British colonial administration in Burma at the time Orwell was there. Both wrote books meant to portray Burma. But *An Introduction to the Political Economy of Burma* by J. S. Fumivall, I.C.S. (published by the Burma Book Club, Ltd., in 1931) differs from *Burmese Days* by Orwell in 1934, in its realistic description of the situation in the country:

> Burma has become a workplace rather than a country, and Burma's

people and land are seen as workers and machines in a factory, as a means for the creation of wealth rather than those for whom that wealth has been created.... Considering this, the nationalism so evident in Burma in recent years is an expression of a healthy instinct working in the people's economic interest.

This book helped the Burmese people. It could be used by those struggling for national independence. It is not the color of a person's skin that determines his ideology. There were scientists, researchers and even government officials who in their writings actually took a clear cut anti-imperialist stand. There were politicians who stood up for fundamental principles. But, to the best of my knowledge, from 1857 to 1947, there was not one English writer of fiction who was able to portray a Hindu as a human being.

Even more interesting is the fact that the same Bertrand Russell who was able to clearly show British rule in India to consist of terrorism and war crimes, to be similar to that of Germany's in Belgium, slipped over into racist, imperialist thinking when, as in Yokohama, he allowed his emotions to get the upper hand. And the same Ralph Fox who was able to make a lucid theoretical analysis of imperialism, who understood the importance of the national and colonial questions, and who died for the sake of his correct analysis, carried the delusions of imperialism and racism in the back of his head, so that when he let himself go, let himself become artistic, he allowed those misconceptions to shape his words.

This loyalty was more important for the continued survival of the British empire than the thousand six hundred and fifty shots fired into the crowd at Amritsar at the orders of Brigadier General Dyer. That loyalty arose out of two historic defeats: 1848 and 1857. In 1848, the sole truly broad-based, popular, democratic movement in England, the Chartist movement, suffered defeat. Across Europe, democracy was dealt a decisive blow. In 1857, the British succeeded in crushing the first great Indian uprising. From the middle of the nineteenth century, the ruling class in London was able to keep its own people in servitude by making them prison-keepers for the Irish, Punjabis, Burmese and others. These British prison-keepers were not a prosperous lot. To them fell only a small portion of the plunder. But they were as confined in the imperial prison as were those they stood guard over. Prior to their defeat, the Chartists had been able to see this. Afterwards, only a very few people such as Ernest Jones were capable of seeing the monstrosity of this fate. Not even World War I, when the people of Europe trampled each other into mass graves, nor World War II, when they marched into the gas chambers, could make them reject this attitude imposed on them. Not even then could they lift their sights, look around and liberate themselves. At present, the poor, downtrodden Russian people stand guard over the oppressed nations in that prison of nations that is the Soviet Union, sending themselves to the Gulag when they find themselves grumbling.

But the chain breaks at its weakest link. The downtrodden of the third world liberate themselves and, in the process, topple the entire structure. Only when the European people are freed from their imperialism will they shake off their fetters.

The charge of art (whether modernistic, traditional, popular, elitist, leftist, rightist, Hollywood, Broadway soap operas, or the most intimate lyricism) is to support and reinforce this prisonkeeper role. In the back of one's mind, art sits with prejudice, emotion and metaphor, steering one's thoughts so that the exploitation may go on. It makes no difference whether it adopts the guise of a porno magazine or that of a sonnet.

This is not inevitable. Other traditions do exist. Mark Twain was no prisoner. Strindberg was able to formulate an image of the upper class' invisible shackles, making them visible for the victims. It is possible to raise one's gaze and yet not see reality through one's eyes. It is right to rebel; the emperor can be overthrown from his high horse.

This is what we discussed in Mandu in 1970 as we walked through the vast stone room, once the abode of power. We had only been in Sweden a few months before we drove south towards Mandu. During those months we had worked on the material we had gathered in China. We had returned to Sweden from a China undergoing a cultural revolution.

The Cultural Revolution in China had formulated the right problems. It was not able to solve them. It had met with many difficulties. In some instances, it had gone wrong. A few careerists and intriguers surfaced on its waves. But this does not take away from the fact that the Cultural Revolution had posed the important, decisive questions. Now, as I write this, there are many people trying to forget this fact. But these questions changed the face of China so completely that it would be as impossible to return to the times before the Cultural Revolution as it would for France to return to the year 1788. It also posed new questions. Questions which will take us the next century to answer.

The Cultural Revolution took art seriously. Through the discussion of the questions it posed, it was possible to understand and explain why writers such as Forster, Orwell, Fox and Russell acted as they did when they permitted themselves to be led by emotion. The Cultural Revolution also took up the struggle for the ideas sitting in the back of one's mind. It made a complete break with Stalin's position on art which spread fine art and literature without ever looking into just what that "fineness" conveyed.

Above the Jaha Mahal, the air shimmered with heat. When Sir Thomas Roe, ambassador of James I to Jahangir, came to Mandu, he was nothing more than an ambassador to a foreign court. His successful embassy marked the beginning of a process which during the nineteenth century was to completely enslave Europe, and which was to force the people of India into a condition of famine and misery. But when the poorest and most downtrodden rise, we shall be freed from our prison-keeper role.

> Débout! les damnés de la terre!
> Débout! les forçats de la faim!

These are the words of the song "The International" by Eugene Poitier.

> Arise, you wretched of the earth!
> Arise, you prisoners of starvation!

To understand the true meaning of the Cultural Revolution one should also ponder over the next line:
"For justice thunders condemnation!"

Are You Thinking About Your Christ Now?

Pastor Sathaia is the head of a congregation of fifty families in Rapalli village, Jagtial taluk. They belong to the unified Protestant Church of South India: the Church of South India.

The village has two thousand inhabitants. It lies in Karimnagar district in North Andhra Pradesh, and the authorities would rather not have us here. A state of emergency has been in effect in Jagtial taluk since autumn 1978. It has been declared a "disturbed area" by the state government. The Christians are poor people.

"I was arrested in September, 1979," says Pastor Sathaia. "I was on my way out of the village to perform a funeral service. An old woman in the congregation had died. Police Sergeant Dasarath grabbed me. He took my Bible and threw it away. He forced me to walk back to the village. I was then taken to the police station in Jagtial. Inspector Rajveli interrogated me. He asked me if I had given food to Naxalites. They had again shown up in the village. With a clear conscience, I was able to tell him that I hadn't been in the village at that time.

"Because I couldn't tell them anything, Inspector Rajveli ordered Police Sergeant Dasarath and Constables Ashok and Afzal to beat me. They used a leather belt. Inspector Rajveli also beat me. They kept asking me questions, and I couldn't answer, they struck me."

It is early in the day, and we are standing beneath the banyan tree in the center of the village. Now, as Pastor Sathaia tells his story, he begins to cry. People around him show how they, too, have been beaten. His mother comes forward. She interrupts her son, saying: "They beat and beat and beat him."

Actually, we had not come to Rapalli to meet Pastor Sathaia. We were supposed to meet the leader of the local peasant movement, the leader of the *ryotu-kuli-sangham* (Peasant Workers' Association) in this area. But when we got to the village, he and the other cadres were gone. The police had been there, so they had to hide. We lay hidden in our jeep for half an hour. But the heat beneath the tarpaulin was unbearable and, on being informed that for the moment the police had left the village, we took a chance and asked to be driven into Rapalli, even though our contact person was no longer there. We stood under the banyan tree and asked the villagers about life there. A crowd soon gathered around us. They told us their stories. Some of the Christians went to get their congregation leader, and that is how we met Pastor Sathaia.

"For all their beating, they learnt nothing from me. I had nothing to tell. Then they forced me to the ground, my face to the floor. They placed a cudgel in the hollow of my knees and bent them forward. I was forced to hold the cudgel in the hollow of my knees. Sergeant Dasarath then stood on my legs and jumped up and down. "Are you thinking about your Christ now?" he said. Actually, my mind was focused on the suffering of our Savior. Then I passed out."

"When I came to, I had been carried out onto the verandah. Inspector Rajveli was now personally handling the interrogation. He beat me with his lathi and again I lost consciousness. When I became aware of my surroundings again, Inspector M. D. Rajveli told me that since I was so uncooperative, they were obliged to interrogate my wife instead. He ordered Constables Ashok and Afzial to bring in my wife for questioning. In order to save her, I decided to tell a lie. I told them that Naxalites had come to my house received food from me that day.

"I was released after five days. I was also instructed to report to them if any Naxalites entered the village. Then I spent fourteen days in the hospital."

People tell of atrocities. They show their scars. Bathini Lachaia was whipped until he vomited blood. They show us his scars. Merugu Thirupathi was beaten with lathis till he lost consciousness. There seems to be no end to these stories.

"Didn't you report these acts of police brutality?" I ask. "Torture is against the law in India."

"There are no investigations. Who would make them? Who listens to us?"

A woman, self-assured and voluble, says, "The people here know nothing of courts or laws. They are ignorant. That's why there are no papers documenting landownership. When people find out that they have rights and begin to make demands, they are labelled Naxalites. When they attempt to set up organizations in order to defend their legal rights, the police step in."

She herself is from a land-owning family. At the heart of the struggles are questions concerning land and power in the village. The village *dora*, the landlord, is Venkateshwar Rao. He is a member of the *vellama* caste, a land-owning caste. There are approximately fifty *vellamas* in the village who serve their *dora*. There is nothing particularly strange about caste. Caste is clan and class. The woman who tells us about the way the courts and police function is not untouchable, Christian or poor. For her, the issue is a disputed field. Her name is Jogini Vella Chilakamma.

"I, too, am a *vellama*. I inherited the field from my husband's father, but my husband's brothers claimed it belonged to them. The case is in the courts now. On October 29, 1979, as I was on my way to the field, four men attacked me. J. Venkateshwar Rao led them. With him he had J. Narsing Rao and my husband's brothers J. Ganga Rao and J. Rama Rao. They grabbed me and pulled off my sari. They used it to tie me up while insulting me with obscene language. I lay tied on the headland as they ploughed the field. Thinking I was dead, they took me away on an ox-cart. They dumped me behind my house. But of course, I wasn't dead. I filed a complaint with Inspector Rajveli, but he refused to acknowledge it. Now I am accused of being a Naxalite."

While we stand there talking, a young man arrives on a motorcycle. He is wearing dark glasses, a white shirt and grey trousers. He stops and looks at us. Then he drives on.

"All those who protest are called Naxalites. Last winter, before the parliamentary elections, Inspector Rajveli came here in a jeep. He said that if Naxalites were seen here before the elections, or if anyone cast his ballot for the Naxalite symbol, a burning torch, he would personally hang us one by one from this banyan tree."

"I think it's best that you come along with me," said Pastor Sathaia.

He led us to his church, a rather large, two-roomed building. In the outer room lay two charpoys, and on the walls hung pictures of Christ. It was here that the people assembled for church services. We sat in the inner room. It soon filled with people around us. There were Christians as well as other poor people, untouchables and low castes. We were served food and tea with milk. We sat facing each other on the floor and ate. On the wall above the Pastor hung a framed, brightly colored Indian print of Christ in agony. The people around us tried to explain what had happened in the village and why a state of emergency was in effect here.

"The *dora* owns 120 hectares and, in addition, holds large tracts of land illegally. Of the fifty *vellamas* in the village, only two are really big landowners. The rest are middle peasants. But they stick together with their caste-leader. They are his henchmen. They carry out his orders."

"We used to have the custom of *vefti chakiri*. That meant that everyone in the village had to work for the dora for nothing. The barber had to shave him. The peasant had to plough his land."

"At all the great festivals, the village had to make gifts of animals to the *dora*. He took sheep when he needed them."

"When someone had a request to make or was called to the *dora*, he always had to bring a gift with him."

"The wage for a day's work here in this district Is at least four rupees. But those who worked for the *dora* were only paid two rupees.

"Anyone who disobeyed the *dora* was driven out of town. The *dora's* men beat him until he left."

"He tied the untouchable women to special poles in the bam, and had them whipped if they didn't do what he wanted." (While I remained where I was, taking notes, Gun was taken to see the whipping-posts. Half the village seemed to go along, and they demonstrated how the punishment had been inflicted.)

"In this district, a *dora* thinks it is his right to have any woman he desires. It is said: "No matter in which hut the hen begins to cackle she'll end up in the *dora's* pot.'"

"The *dora* was master here. We had the custom of *panchayat mamul*. This confers upon the *dora*, as master of the village, the right to arbitrate and adjudicate all conflicts arising in the village. It also awards him all the fines he has levied."

"As a result of the growing peasant movement, a *ryotu-kuli-sangham* was organized here after the fall of Indira Gandhi and the repeal of the Emergency Powers Act in 1977. The *dora* was then made the object of a social boycott. No one would work for him. No one would serve him as a domestic. And no one would talk to him. All the villagers had recorded what they had been forced to pay him in fines. All together, it was found that he had illegally extorted thirteen thousand rupees from the villagers. The people surrounded his house. He was terrified and quickly repaid the money. Four hectares of state land, stolen by the *dora* from the untouchables, were also now taken back. All *vetti chakiri*, all sexual slavery and the *dora's* right to *mamul* were abolished. The leaders of the different castes formed a mediation committee with the task of settling disputes."

"After returning the money, he fled to Hyderabad."

"We also put an end to usury and abolished debtors' slavery."

"However, the *vellamas* have tried to create conflicts between the Christians and other poorer castes. They have tried to win over the Christians in order to mount a joint attack on the toddy-tapper caste, the *gowda*. But they have not succeeded."

"The Christians too are part of the peasant movement."

"Since they tortured me," says Pastor Sathaia, "the *dora* has suggested three times that I join forces with him. The first time, I really believed that he wanted a reconciliation. I was still in the hospital then. Two *vellamas* came to me, saying that the problems of the village should be solved peacefully. I was glad. So twenty *vellamas* and twenty Christians met in my hospital room and arrived at an amicable settlement. But when I returned to the village, the entire Christian congregation stood waiting for me outside the town. They told me that the police had come searching houses and beating people.

"I asked the *dora* why he had again called in the police. He replied that they hadn't come for us Christians but for the *gowdas*. I understood then that it had only been a ploy on the part of the *dora*. He had made peace with one part of the village so as to be able to bring in the police and strike a hard blow against another. That was October 1979. We had been a "disturbed area" then for one year.

"I am no politician. I have kept away from all political activity since tortured. But the policemen who tortured me have not been punished. No one can file a complaint against them and no one can bring legal action against them."

Before we have had time to finish our meal, someone comes in and reports that the police are back in the village. The Special Branch has come. Two men. They have begun to question the villagers about us. The young motorcyclist, the one who had stopped to get a better look at us as we stood beneath the banyan tree talking to people, was a *vellama*. He went to the police in Jagtial and alerted them. But the villagers play dumb when questioned by the police.

"What? Foreigners? There may have been some. No, they weren't foreigners, they were from Karimnagar. Yes, they were Punjabis. Or perhaps they were from Kashmir. That is, if they weren't from Bengal. There were two of them. No, there were five. All men. Some might have been women. Hard to say how many there were. I think there might only have been one. He was from Karimnagar. Or was that yesterday?"

They kept interrupting each other like that, pointing in different directions. But no one told them that we were in the church.

We end our talk, leave the church and get into the jeep. The tarpaulin is fastened carefully over us. When word comes that the police are moving through the village in the opposite direction, we take off with a tearing start out of the churchyard, slide up onto the roadway and bounce along in a cloud of dust. We make a detour across some fields to avoid the police cordon, and the driver drives fast to spirit us away.

But What About The Law?

The villagers in Rapalli demanded their legal rights. The police were then sent out to restore order. Which order? What law?

This requires a brief explanation.

There is no serfdom in India. The British had the first law against serfdom promulgated in 1843. But anyone who has ever lived in India knows that the Indian government's construction work in Delhi is carried out with the help of bonded laborers. The Indian government is equally aware of this fact. In Mehrauli, three hundred and fifty untouchable families work in these conditions with stone masonry. They have been slaving there for fifteen years. Their contractor brought them from Rajasthan. On June 2, 1980, when Premila Lewis went to see them, she was assaulted by goondas working for the powerful. She was there representing Action India, a welfare organization active among the most downtrodden women. Such is serfdom in the Indian capital. The individual who demands that the laws be obeyed can come to as much grief as an abolitionist in Alabama in the 1850s.

Undisguised serfdom is so glaring that it is possible to gather statistics on it. A study of seventeen states in 1977-1978, "India's Agrarlan Situation," by Nitish R. De (in *Agrarian Relations in India*, New Delhi, 1979) showed the existence of 825,239 serfs and bonded laborers, and estimated the total for all of India at twice that number. According to an unpublished report, 10,000 serfs have been identified here in Telengana where the village of Rapalli is located.

Yet the type of serfdom prevalent in Telengana has been specifically, and for the umpteenth time, forbidden in the law of 1976. The law is titled: "Government of Andhra Pradesh, the Bonded Labor System (abolition) Act 1976 (Central Act No. 19 of 1976); Government Central Press, Hyderabad 1976."

This act makes it the duty of the police-judges to administer the law. But the public official who zealously performs his duty and tries to obey the law is transferred, according to an unpublished report made at Kakatiya University in Warangal. When the peasants demand that the law be obeyed, the police are sent to deal with them. A report from Maharashtra, in the spring of 1977, says:

> If a bonded laborer runs away from the village, the local police not only bring him back to the village but subject him to severe beatings and torture. Evidently, whatever the law, the local police consider it one of their duties to look after the interest of the money-lenders. (Husain Dalwai, "Bonded Labor Continues," *Economic and Political Weekly*, vol. X, p. 869)

After Indira Gandhi's fall in the spring of 1977, democratic and civil rights were officially reinstated. One of these was the right to organize. Among the villagers in Andhra Pradesh, there spread a movement for law and order, against serfdom and oppression. *Ryotu-kuli-sanghams* were set up as a means of enforcing the legal minimum wage, implementing the lawful prohibition against serfdom, and combating unlawful usury. The demands pressed by these organizations, in accordance with their declared goals, were to remain strictly within the confines of existing laws.

In the political situation existing in Andhra Pradesh, the Congress Party (Indira's Congress) had been in power since 1947, and the various official communists, after winning fame in the peasant rebellion of 1948-1951, have become corrupt, well-to-do, and blessed with their own close contacts with the landowners. Against this background, it was the Naxalites, cadres from the various Marxist-Leninist organizations, who went to the countryside to agitate in the villages, to inform the people of their rights and to build up mass organizations.

As a result, seventy powerful landowners requested a meeting with the chief minister of Andhra Pradesh and demanded that the state government do something. The government's response came on October 20, 1978, when Sircilla and Jagtial taluks were declared "disturbed areas." By means of massive police actions, the government restored the unconstitutional and illegal state of affairs prevailing in the villages, conditions which violated the peasants' human rights. They did their best to create conditions which would allow the *doras* to return and re-establish their feudal power.

The law used by the government to achieve its purposes is almost unique. So unique that I want to reproduce its text. Paragraphs 5 and 6, especially, need careful reading.

THE ANDHRA PRADESH SUPPRESSION OF DISTURBANCES ACT (Act No. Ill of 1948)

An act to make better provision for the Suppression of disorder in the State of[1] (Andhra Pradesh)

Whereas it is expedient to make better provision for the suppression of disorder in the (state of Andhra Pradesh), it is hereby enacted as follows:

1. Short title, extent and commencement:
i) This act may be called the[1] (Andhra Pradesh Suppression of Disturbances Act, 1948)
ii) It extends to the whole of the State of[1] (Andhra Pradesh)
iii) It shall come into force at once.

2. Definitions: In this Act, "Disturbed Area" means an area for the time being declared to be disturbed area by a notification under Section 3.

3. Power to declare areas to be disturbed areas: The State Government, by notification in the official Gazette:
a) declare that the whole of the State or any part thereof specified in the notification is a disturbed area; and
b) add to, amend, vary or rescind any such declaration.

4. Certain offences to be punishable with death in disturbed areas:
i) Whoever in a disturbed area commits any offence punishable under any of the following sections of the Indian Penal Code, namely, 307, 363, 364, 365, 366, 367, 368, 376, 392, 394, 395, 397, 398, and 436, may in lieu of the punishment to which he is liable under that code, be punished with death.
ii) Whoever in a disturbed area attempts to commit or abets the commission of, any offence punishable under any section of the Indian Penal Code referred to in sub-section (i) may, notwithstanding

---

[1] Substituted to 1st version of Andra Pradesh Act nr XI, 1961.

anything contained in that Code, be punished with death or with the punishment provided in that section for the offence.

5. Power to fire upon persons contravening certain orders in disturbed areas: Any Magistrate, any Police Officer not below the rank of Sub-Inspector, may, if in his opinion it is necessary to do so for restoring or maintaining public order, after giving such warning, if any, as he may consider necessary, fire upon, order to fire to be opened or otherwise use force, even to the causing of death, against any person who in a disturbed area is acting in contravention of any law or order for the time being in force, in such area, prohibiting the assembly of five or more persons or the carrying of weapons or of things capable of being used as weapons.

6. Protection of persons acting under section 5: No prosecution suit or other legal proceeding shall be instituted, except with the previous sanction of the State Government, against any person in respect of anything done or purporting to be done in exercise of the powers conferred by Section 5.

This act is a legal prop for violence and murder. It is a unique law, with its fifth and sixth paragraphs close to the note D'Artagnan presents the Cardinal after he and his companions have murdered Mylady:

> December 3, 1827
> It is by order and for the good of the State that the bearer of this note has done what has been done.
> Richelieu

However, this time these are not some words from a romantic tale of adventure. These words form part of a legal text which has meant, and means, torture and agonizing death for the poor peasants who demanded their lawful rights.

Peasant Struggle

The village of Lathnoor in Jagtial taluk, Andhra Pradesh, is famous. Bloody clashes have taken place here. Just before our arrival, a police patrol has been asking about us. The police snoop about, but the people say nothing or give misleading answers. At night we stay in the villages and small towns. We stay in the homes of peasants, teachers and doctors. Unseen, we come to them at dusk. They keep us hidden. If the family has two charpoys, the sleeping children are placed on the floor and the adults sleep out in the yard. Anything for the guests. If there is only one charpoy, they leave it for us.

"You are our guests."

The entire area is off-limits to outsiders. Police troops can be seen everywhere. We drive cross-country, guided by the peasants, so that we will not get caught in a police roadblock. If the police catch us, not much would happen to Gun and me. We would spend a while in prison, nothing more. But our friends and guides would not get off so lightly. They would be beaten, tortured, assaulted. Most of our friends have already experienced this kind of treatment. Because it is the second time, the police might just shoot them or beat them to death.

Shot while trying to escape. Killed during an encounter. Or the police might quite simply allow them to disappear.

Careful planning is required to ensure our safe travel within the quarantined "disturbed areas". The civil rights movement, the peasant movement and student movement help to make our visit possible. The police have learnt that we are in the area. But they do not know our names. They do not know how we got here or where we are. We are expected in the village of Lathnoor. But the police have not been able to find out anything about us. The villagers want the outside world to know what has happened in Lathnoor.

The people have drawn up a detailed report. The peasant Koppala Mallesham has written it down and each villager has put his thumbprint on the report to confirm its accuracy.

Land reform has been in effect since 1951, but it has not altered the structure of landownership.

150 families of the village own the land:

acres	number of families
200—300	1
25—50	4
10—25	20
3—10	35
less than 3	80
no land	30

(1 acre = 0.4 hectares)

The name of the *dora* is Jagga Rao. He is the one who owns 250 acres. In addition, he has occupied state owned land. He also receives the estate of those who die without heirs. Rightfully, this should go to the government.

The people own 150 ploughs. They must use them to plough the *dora's* fields, free of charge. The fifty sheep-owning families must each present him with a sheep at the Dassera festival in October. They must also present a sheep each at the *dora's* festivities. The families must give him *ghee* (clarified butter) and he can also demand use of their ox-carts to transport it.

Koppala Mallesham reads out article after article of this deposition, and the people around us murmur agreement with what is being said. The list of goods and services the *dora* is entitled to is long.

Washer-women and barbers must serve him free of charge. The barber must massage the *dora's* feet at night, if that is the dora's pleasure. Every year the villagers must repair the dora's large house.

Group after group of villagers has described the *dora's* demands. But there is more to the story. The government distributes a ration of eggs, milk and cooking oil among the school children. The *dora* takes half of it. The government appropriated land from a peasant for the construction of the new canal. The *dora* signed for 1,620 rupees in compensation and kept the money. His son, Sagar Rao, contracted to build a road. He let the villagers build it for him. He ordered them out and promised to pay them. But he took the money and did not pay the 4,220 rupees he had promised them. The villagers tell all. They know to the very last paisa how much has been stolen from them. They have forgotten nothing.

To sit there on the charpoy in the midday heat, surrounded by a hundred villagers, and listen to this enumeration, is like finding oneself back in eighteenth century France, listening to the grievances of the peasants.

Here in Lathnoor, the peasants refused to continue serving the *dora*. They demanded their legal rights. Here, too, the *dora* responded by calling for the police. The police came to the *dora's* house and ate and drank. When the washers refused to do the dishes, the sub-inspector became violent. He ran out of the *dora's* house and began to beat people. Some fled. Others were obstinate and spoke their minds. Sub-inspector Chilwakuddu has eaten and drunk well. He fell in the mud, and then the police constable began to shoot. Lakkam Pochaia was killed.

People come up to show their scars. Many in the village have gun-shot wounds. One-legged Bhomula Rajam says the police were reinforced that evening. They were then led by the *dora's* son on a punitive expedition against the village. Sagar Rao grabbed the crutch from Bhomula Rajam and beat him with it until it broke. Later, the police had searched his home and had stolen the five hundred rupees he had managed to save. He had gone to the police, but when the sub-inspector heard about the report, he had come to him and said: "If you try to pursue this, or talk about it to anyone, I will personally cut off your other leg and I will grease my lathi with chili powder and screw it up your rectum."

This was no empty threat. It is standard procedure with the police. It is a popular method of torture. It is employed in Tihar Jail in Delhi. A British method. There was a small scandal in 1909 when Ghulam Bano was strung up by her feet to the ceiling so that the superintendent and two police sergeants could stick greased with green chili powder into her rectum. Word got out when the doctor, Dr. More, witnessed about what he had seen. Everything repeats itself.

"In the evening, the police sat in the *dora's* house drinking. They downed 18 liters of arrack."

The village is now subject to the Act on Disturbed Areas. The *dora* has fled to the city, but villagers get together in order to have their complaints properly recorded. They know—and are not afraid to say it—that if things were as they should be and if the laws were observed, the police and judges would not be in the *dora's* house stuffing their faces, but would, in accordance with the laws, take from him the illegal power and wealth which he has stolen from the village.

In village after village, the stories are the same. On occasion, new information surfaces. In the village of Shekala, we are told about how the *dora*, Raghavendra Rao, is fighting back with prosecution suit and legal proceedings. The legal cases inch through the judicial machinery.

Twenty-three peasants are accused of:

> grazing their livestock on the *dora's* land;
> resisting the police;
> building houses on the *dora's* property;
> having been present in Lathnoor during the clashes which took place there.

Initially, the struggle was over one and a half hectares of land belonging to the untouchables, which the *dora* had grabbed. Then the peasant movement agitated against the system of police bribery, and serfdom, and for the minimum wage. The first time the police came at the behest of the *dora*, they meant to arrest eight untouchables. But the villagers surrounded the police. Only when the collector came and promised that the untouchables' land would not be taken by the *dora*, did the villagers release the police. Two months later, the police struck. Twenty-three villagers were taken to the police station. There they were beaten. The *dora* initiated legal proceedings against them. The cases have now reached the Karimnagar District Court. Time after time, the peasants have tried to get the police to take action on their complaints, too.

"The *dora* and the police are friends. The police arrest us whenever he asks them to. How can we complain through the police?"

Rowtu Lachi tells us that she bought a hectare from the *dora* ten years ago. She paid 2,800 rupees for it.

"In 1976, the *dora* came and said that the government was going to take the land. He would take care of it for me, for a price. I gave him 1,800 rupees. When I bought the land it was arid. Now the government has built irrigation works and I can get water. That's why he wanted to take it back.

The *dora* was powerful. He had those who stood up to him whipped. He fined the peasants. Then students from the Radical Youth League came here. They agitated and we understood our rights and established a *ryotu-kuli-sangham*. Then the *dora* gave back the 1,800 rupees. But now, with the aid of the police, he has initiated legal proceedings against the peasants.

"I still have my land because the *ryotu-kuli-sangham* remains united against the *dora* and the police. The rich oppress the poor. The rich have the power. The rich have the police. Today we are telling you about our situation. Tomorrow the police may come and ask us what we told you. Every time we talk to an outsider and complain about the *dora*, the police show up. Some have come from the city to hear our story. The day after their visit the police come to beat us.

"Before the elections, the Naxalites held a campaign meeting here.

People came to listen. They were interested in what was being said. The next day, Sub-Inspector Chilwakuda and seven policemen came in a jeep. They beat people with their lathis till they fell on their knees and begged for mercy. Then they drove to the *dora's* house and had a drinking bout.

"The *dora* is still in the village and the police come around to make raids. They go from house to house, beating people. Then they sit down with the *dora* and drink. But the *dora* cannot do much since the *ryotu-kuli-sangham* remains united. No longer is he able to have work done for nothing, We have abolished serfdom and his right to levy fines. He has lost the war. All he is trying to do now is to initiate legal proceedings.

"The police are corrupt. When the *dora* took me to court and I was arrested but released on bail, I went to the police station because the court had asked me to. Constable Pochaiah told me that if I gave him two hundred rupees, he would see to it that all the documents against me were lost."

In the village of Maddunoor, the people are wary. We can only come at night. There is a police bivouac in the village. Fifty of the villagers are on trial, accused of conspiracy. All of them have been severely beaten. Sub-Inspector Mogilai, in particular, enjoys beating up people. When the villagers set up the peasant association, members of the Andhra Pradesh Special Police came in five trucks. They jumped down from the trucks, surrounded the village and proceeded to attack. The peasant association was crushed.

"Still, we have not yet been totally defeated. The *dora*, J. Rajeshwar Rao, had illegally occupied twenty hectares of state owned land. This land had been allocated to the untouchables. He has since been forced to flee the village, and the untouchables have taken back almost all of it. The *dora* had a private jailhouse in the village. When the toddy tappers tried to sell their toddy on their own instead of handing it over to the *dora*, he arrested ten toddy tappers. He had them beaten and thrown into his jail. It isn't possible to hold the *dora* accountable in a court of law for this kind of thing. He is friendly with the police and a relative of the judges. But his jail is no longer there since the *dora* has run away.

"A *patel* (a village sheriff) and two goondas tried to rape some women, but they were stopped. Now, those who prevented the rapes are accused of being Naxalites and are in jail.

"The Naxalites put up posters here, urging us to boycott the elections. The police tore them down. Three days before the elections, some police officials came here and said that if there was any boycott, that if anyone didn't vote, we would be battered to a pulp. Everyone voted. Every time there is a disturbance somewhere, the police come from their bivouac and beat us. We live in constant fear here, and if they learn that you have been here they will beat us."

The Naxalites they are talking about belong to various organizations. On some issues, their politics are different. For example, some of them take part in the elections despite everything, while some do not. At the grassroots level, violent conflicts among these organizations do take place sometimes. But, in general, they work in the same way to build the peasant movement, to make it into an association of lower middle peasants (and sometimes middle peasants), poor peasants and the landless. This endeavour is not always problem free.

The landowners have their own private armies. These are recruited from among the lumpen proletariat and degenerate elements. In the village of Kistampet, it consists of thirty men. It is led by a former communist from the period of 1947-1948, a man who later went over to the landlords. His name is Amukth Lal Shukla from Nimapally. The struggle is fierce here. When the Emergency was lifted, many landowners banded together and made use of Nersivu Rao's goondas.

"They really hurt the people. It was so bad that people rose against him and killed him. Twenty-two people were arrested, accused of murder. One hundred more have been indicted on various charges. One hundred and twenty people are now in jail.

"Daplu Ramoo was an activist in the *ryotu-kuli-sangham*. When the police arrested him and beat him, he could not stand it. He began to name his friends and comrades. When the police released him, he could not come back; he had become an informer. So now he is a goonda.

"Another person who became an informer was Medari Puddulu. The police strung him up, beating him and saying all the while: "Where are your great leaders now? Do you think they can help you now?" He finally could not take it any more. He, too, succumbed and became an informer."

The village of Chekapalli is under strict surveillance. The Andhra Pradesh Special Police are there. We must be very cautious. The sup-inspector has his own extortion racket going. A couple who want to marry must pay him fifty rupees. The people must keep the police supplied with chickens. The *dora* sees to it that the village landowners are organized through the Congress (I). His wife has been appointed village leader. The Member of Parliament, Satyanarayan Rao, comes from here. It is said that he shields the *dora* and the police. The peasant association is completely clandestine. The police have been brutal in their repression of its members. Police Inspector Abdul Pasha has let it be known that anyone who joins the peasant association will be killed. They shall be shot down like curs. When torturing, he pinches the victim's larynx between his thumb and fingers, while his subordinates use their lathis on the soles of the feet and phalanxes. He squeezes hard. Those released from jail are forbidden to speak about the torture. The villagers are forbidden to speak with outsiders. Sub-Inspector Narsinga Reddy has beaten about a dozen people for talking too much. Anyone caught giving food to a villager who is escaping from the village may be fined five hundred rupees. There are four known informers in the village. All of them are alcoholics. They do it for the liquor the *dora* gives them.

This is normalcy in a semi-feudal state like India. I notice one morning that the sign which stands outside Jagtial reads: LIONS CLUB WELCOMES YOU TO JAGTIAL.

During the time we spent visiting these "disturbed areas", police activity escalated. New police batallions were called in. During the spring of 1980, 11,000 men were recruited into the Criminal Investigation Department in Karimnagar, and divisions of the Central Reserve Police were brought in from Srikakulam. Several of our friends have been arrested. As for some of those who have gone underground, the police have taken action against their families. In some cases, mothers and wives have been tortured. The last letter I received from India reports that the mother of one of my friends has been arrested. She was pregnant and the police kicked her in the stomach till she aborted.

Special police patrols from Andhra Pradesh have been sent to other parts of the country to uncover contacts of the peasant movement. Two such contacts in Bombay were arrested, only to disappear. They have apparently been returned to Andhra Pradesh which in all probability means death.

The peasant association has carried out three executions: those of a *brahman* usurer, an informer, and a goonda. I cannot say whether these executions were politically right or wrong. But I am convinced that these three did receive their just deserts. Here in Andhra Pradesh (as in Bihar, West Bengal, Kerala, Haryana, Punjab, and the rest of India), the class struggle is grim and merciless. The poor peasants are literally fighting for their lives.

Peasant rebellions and uprisings have taken place all over India. Rebellion lies smouldering in every village. It might be a month, a year, a generation or more before it erupts into flames. Everywhere there are memories of uprisings and the knowledge of the way authority (regardless of whether it is the Raja, Sultan, Mughal, Englishman or the Congress) ruthlessly and brutally strike against the poor peasants attempting to regain their human dignity. Every bloody defeat has, despite everything, been a triumph, in the sense that those in power were forced to give in on some issue.

An uprising took place in 1948-1951 here in Telengana. A great Indian peasant war in modern times. Initially, it was directed against the Nizam of Hyderabad, and against his vassals. Then it opposed feudalism and repression in the interest of land and freedom, and then also fought the large number of Indian troops sent in by Nehru and Sardar Patel to capture Hyderabad and put down the peasants. Both aims were of equal importance to them.

The war went on for five years. Step by step, it grew into a war of liberation for the poor peasants. The land was divided. The political power of the peasants was established. For eighteen months, 3,000 villages with a total population of 3,000,000 were controlled by this new power. Some 400,000 hectares of gentry-owned land was redistributed. Power was held by local village councils which were elected democratically. Out of the local militias grew armed forces increasingly well-trained, and able to develop their own officers. Against them ranged the entire force of Nehru's India. It cost Nehru more to fight the peasants of Hyderabad than to conduct his first war against Pakistan.

The uprising and war were led by local communists. The Communist Party in Andhra Pradesh (then the Hyderabad of the Nizam), had come of age in the struggle against feudalism and in the national struggle. It was well rooted in the area, and was able to lead the struggle. These communists had also studied Mao Zedong.

However, the Indian Communist Party was deeply divided. The leadership could not relate to popular uprisings. At the onset of World War II, it had slipped over into a position of aiding Germany and Italy. After December 1941, it began to work for Great Britain. It lacked a nationality of its own. At the time of the uprising in Telengana, it was unable to unitedly support the peasant movement. With Russian help, leading theoreticians pondered over whether what was happening in Hyderabad was not actually an outbreak of class collaboration. Were they not trying to unite the poor and middle peasants?

Hence, there was never any organized support from the Communist Party of India for the movement in Andhra Pradesh. Instead, party leadership helped Nehru to keep the peasant movement isolated from the urban proletariat.

Moscow had no use for an independent peasant movement. Nor did it like the peasant guerrillas in Telengana reading Mao Zedong. Moscow saw to it that no international solidarity movement gained strength. Three million Indian peasants who had liberated themselves, who held 40,000 square kilometers in Telengana (an area as big as Denmark), and who had carried out land reform, established a new democracy and defended themselves with their own armed forces. This was not a movement to which Moscow wanted to provide the support of international solidarity. The leadership of this peasant movement was not dependent on Moscow and had Telengana been allowed to continue, India might have become some new Yugoslavia or China, countries where the revolution stood on its own two feet.

It was the leadership of the Communist Party which eventually set-
tled Telengana's fate. This it was able to do because such a large portion
of local leadership was of upper caste and upper-middle peasant background. Individuals who could survive this defeat, go over to the side of
the new landlords, and establish their own economic apparatus. The
communists who led the uprising in Telengana have gone into business,
just as the communists of 1948 who were active in the struggle of the forties for a progressive culture came to dominate the Madras film industry.
Their economic base in Andhra Pradesh is not confined to publishing
companies and newspapers, but also includes the hotel trade, the textile
industry, the cultivation of tobacco and the sugar refineries. It is not
merely a question of individuals, but of the entire Party policy of going
over to the bourgeoisie. It is no more than natural that the support
among the masses for these parties is waning.

Yet, even this defeat in 1951, even this defeat which snatched back
from the poor peasants the land they had just liberated was not a victory
for the mighty gentry. They had been crushed by the peasant movement.
Today, large investments are being made here in Telengana. Investments
in irrigation works and the production of energy. This means that the
land, which was till recently almost worthless, has suddenly become
very desirable. Arid ground has been turned into irrigated farmland. The
landowners and their associates determine investments through their
government administration. The question is who will reap the benefits.

The villagers of Lathnoor have, so far, remained united against their
dora. But both they and the dora are aware of what is now happening to
the value of the land. United, the villagers will try to drive away the dora
to free the new farming methods from the stranglehold of feudal custom.
In this struggle, both the villagers who can be considered affluent, and
the landless farm laborers, are united, and struggle side by side in their
ryotu-kuli-sangham.

The dora, together with all his patrons and friends, will be swept into
the dustbin of history, no matter how mighty they are. The large land-
holding interest which direct their investments into irrigation works,
have no patience with low productivity and unprofitable feudalism. The
villagers, too, demand their rights, and irrigated land. It may be a while
and it may see the spilling of some blood, but for the toddy-drinking dora
who has the village girls brought to him, and who has the village barber
to massage his feet at night when he cannot sleep, his time is past. These
parasites fill no function in a modern system of agriculture.

The question is what will happen after that, and under what circumstances this transformation will take place. The cooperative alternative—
a genuine "community development" of small-scale industry, focused

on the villagers' ability to change through cooperative effort—that alternative is still open. It is a democratic solution that people talk about, and that many desire. If the *ryotu-kuli-sanghams* can now win against the hordes of police troops, this solution is both possible and probable.

But if the police troops are able to suppress the peasant movement again this time, the power of the landlords will be restored, and class differences will develop amidst the ruins of the *ryotu-kuli-sanghams*. So that a raging, bloody struggle over the land between the new landowners and the landless farm laborers is also a possibility. When the *dora* has disappeared, like the zamindar before him, perhaps the peasant Koppala Mallesham will face the one-legged Bhoomula Rajam in the next struggle for land and a minimum wage.

Perhaps, in twenty years, the villagers of Lathnoor who piled their sorrows in the midday heat of summer 1980 will be working together in some kind of democratic cooperative movement....Or, then again perhaps they will be tying in ambush, trying to kill each other, locked in their struggle over the irrigated land.

The peasants determine the shape of their future. If the peasants succeed in the raging and bloody struggle they are now waging, one of these alternatives opens before them—the democratic one. If they suffer defeat, they face the other.

Today, the situation can be compared to that in France before the Revolution took final shape. As yet, the question of the future still stands open.

For A People's Culture

It was a month earlier. We had come down from Koraput and Srikakulam. We, were now in Vishakapatnam on the Bay of Bengal.

"Spiritualism," said Professor Venkateswarlu from Andhra University, "that special Indian spiritualism, is a fabrication. When you were visiting the Simhachalam Temple, did you listen to the pilgrims' songs? Did you find out what they were singing about? Those songs are more secular than religious in nature. The pilgrims sing about their troubles with drought and about how the wild animals trample their fields. They sing to each other, and while they walk, they make up new verses.

"The temple is actually no different than any other place of pilgrimage. About a thousand families are dependent in one way or another on the temple. It is a large economic apparatus. The economic influence of the temple spreads in a ripple effect. The temple is a focal point. People come here from many places. It also serves as a market.

"Society's traditional economic surplus goes to religious music and dance. But there is also another tradition. This we see when the pilgrims come singing. It is the tradition of folk dance and folk music. It is not as well known among outsiders, but it runs deep and strong, perhaps deeper and stronger than the formal religious music.

"In many ways, it is the picture of India itself that has been distorted. Asoka is described as gentle, while Chin Shih-Huang in China is portrayed as cruel. But they have played an amazingly similar role in history. At roughly the same time, they carried out approximately the same, equally inevitable, task of national unification. But in both cases (and this is generally not mentioned) they did it on the basis of a highly advanced technology. Since this early advanced technology is not dealt with, the unifying work of Asoka and Chin Shih-Huang is impossible to understand correctly. Asoka becomes the embodiment of Indian gentleness and Chin Shih-Huang that of Chinese cruelty.

"Abroad, those who have mentioned India, have spoken and written of her gentleness and spirituality. During the entire nineteenth century, Indian tradition was made to seem more and more spiritual. The British encouraged this. "You Indians don't understand machines and material things," they said. "You are so full of soul." Many Indian intellectuals were led astray by this. They ignored our genuine tradition. The spiritual metaphysics depended on a firm foundation of highly-developed agricultural techniques, world-renowned metal work, and an extensive trade. But the British had their reasons for wishing to restrict us to the spiritual spheres. They left us the spiritual realm, while taking the material world for themselves.

"Even those Indians who came to represent India abroad, such as Vivekananda, emphasized only India's spirituality."

"That kind of thing can be turned around, and still remain the same," said Gun. "In Calcutta, I met revolutionaries who claimed that the difference between Indians and other people was that other people thought about food, while Indians thought about revolution."

A few days later, Professor Venugopala Rao drove us from Vijayawada to the Buddhist monuments in Amaravati.

"India will make rapid progress," he said "once it has aroused itself. People have been forced to develop an incredible ingenuity just to stay alive. Once the social impediments which keep the masses in misery are gone, tremendous human resources will be liberated. Intellectuals may come and go from the various social movements. They may become disappointed. They may tire of it all. They may find something else to do. But the downtrodden masses have nowhere else to go. They cannot quit. They cannot tire and find something else to do. They desire change. They desire rapid change. The so-called stagnation of the countryside is only that the masses are held down by severe repression. As soon as that repression begins to weaken, they surge forward. In a short time, they can create a new, many-sided India."

In Vijayawada, we stayed at the State Guest House. At night, Sitarama, a poet and a revolutionary cadre, comes to visit. We sit on the lawn and talk. He is on his way to Hyderabad. He has been out in the villages organizing.

"They use carrot-and-stick tactics. The government promises to pay each village 2,000 rupees, if it elects only government-approved candidates to the panchayats. That's a lot of money for the village, but a small amount for the government to spend and be spared of troublesome opposition. If the villages elect Naxalites, the police come. The choice is theirs! People aren't so dumb that they don't see that.

"We capture an area and build up an organization. Then the police move in and go to work. There is hell to pay. We have to make sure that the organization can survive even if the cadres are forced to disappear for a time. Otherwise, we must begin again at the beginning. Songs help us in our work. We sing a lot in Andhra.

"When I first became active in the student movement in the sixties, I did not have too clear a picture of how things stood. But my understanding increased during my first years in jail. I shared a cell with a girijan, one of the mountain tribes. He had been a guerrilla fighter. He was illiterate. I taught him how to read. He called me 'guru,' although I asked him not to. He was very diligent. He would copy page after page from the newspaper to practice. In the end, he could read and write properly. He could even read books.

"Some rightist intellectuals in the prison derided us Naxalites for our educational work with the prisoners. 'You and your serve-the-people! What do you think you're accomplishing with the masses?' they said. 'Your cellmate is still religious!' They went to him and asked, 'Do you believe in God?' 'Yes, I do', he responded. 'See!' the rightist intellectuals crowed. 'The people are stupid, no matter what you do. Who is your God?' they asked the girijan. 'Vempatapu Satyam!' he replied, looking them right in the eye. That shut them up, and I began to understand our movement better.

Vempatapu Satyanarayana is Srikakulam's great hero. He and Adibhatla Kailasam began to work in 1955 among the poorest, most oppressed tribes in the mountains around Srikakulam. He was a teacher and a charismatic leader. The poor peasants of the mountains were totally devoted to him. They followed him in everything. He helped them rise up against the oppressors and demand their rights. He was the one who in 1968 declared that it was necessary to take up armed struggle. He led the uprising.

"He joined CPI(ML) in 1969, and led the Party in Srikakulam. There were various opposing views among the members, but that is another story. He was able to lead because he was respected. My cellmate told me a story about him. He had summoned all the leading comrades (and that meant all the leaders since outside of the Party there were only the men of the police and exploiters) to a conference. Even among the tribal peoples there exists a kind of caste system. They do not all eat together. You know how caste is in India. That kind of custom is deeply ingrained. But Vempatapu Satyanarayana said, 'Let us now, once and for all, be done with caste. From now on we shall be like brothers and sisters! Let us eat together, men and women, paying no mind to caste or prohibitions!' My cellmate said that a sound passed through the people assembled. It felt like a wind on the body, and one's hair stood on end. Then all, all of them, followed Vempatapu Satyanarayana's example. They broke with everything that had made up the very basis of society, everything that they had been raised to follow even before they had learned to talk. Without hesitation, and in a body, they put aside those customs as if they were a worn-out raincoat of leaves. They never took them back. Vempatapu Satyanarayana was such a man, and that was the reason that the rightist intellectuals gave a start when my cellmate looked them in the eye and said his name."

In July 1970, Vempatapu Satyanarayana and Adibhatla Kailasam were shot by the police in the Bori Mountains near Parvatipuram. They were not killed in battle. They were executed. Later, the Minister of the Interior of Andhra Pradesh, K. Vengal Rao, claimed that this meant the end of the Naxalite movement in that state.

Sitarama began to sing. His voice was soft, the rhythm of his song intense.

"Telugu veraratnama Vempatapu Satyam Adibhatla Kailasam...." This song is sung in the villages; it is sung across Andhra Pradesh and southwestern Orissa.

"Oh, Telugu's jewels! Heroes! Vempatapu Satyam, Adibhatla Kailasam, hear our homage!"

"Our first step in organizing a village is to send in our song troupe," Sitaram said later. "We now have hundreds of song groups. As soon as the organization is on its feet, a local song group is established and in this way the songs spread from village to village. There are both old songs and new ones in their repertoire. There are the creations of our great poets and songs made up by the villagers themselves. It's really something. One song gives rise to another. It's like a great tree. The people are constantly creating new songs. And when we arrive to talk about the peasant movement and the future, and begin with songs such as the one about our heroes, 'Telugu's Jewels,' the entire village assembles. There isn't a person who doesn't know and cherish the memory of Vempatapu Satyanarayana. He is like the Joe Hill in the American song: he is dead, but still organizing, still with us in every battle. It was only after my cellmate taught me this that I understood our movement and could begin my work. We are the blood of the people's blood, and we are the words of the people's songs."

Culture does not stand isolated from politics and society in Andhra Pradesh. Indeed, the authorities themselves see to it that the writers understand their responsibility for what they write.

In May 1974, the railroad worker and poet, Sayam, published a poem in the Telugu literary journal *Srujana*. The title of the poem was "Can the Prisons Run the Trains?" It was about the great Indian railroad strike.

The journal was published by Sahitee Mitrulu (Friends of Literature). The editor was the poet Varavara Rao. He had been arrested for his writings in October 1973, but released in November of the same year, and not arrested again until May 1974. Upon his arrest in 1973, his wife Hemalatha had assumed responsibility for the journal's publication.

The railroad worker's poem was viewed as a challenge to government authority, and the journal was confiscated. The trials began and continued for three years. The judge who sentenced Hemalatha to prison for two years said: "The fact that the defendant is the mother of three is grounds for clemency. But since she shows no signs of remorse, justice demands that she be dealt with firmly."

In October 1977, when it appeared that Indira Gandhi could not make a political comeback, and when the courts began to be more cautious in political trials, Hemalatha was acquitted by the High Court in Hyderabad.

In order to understand the struggle for a people's culture in Andhra Pradesh, it is necessary to bear in mind that for a thousand years a struggle went on in the realm of literature between Sanskrit and popular writing. The ruling class used Sanskrit. Popular literature organized itself around the cult of Siva. It was at the Siva temple in Warangal that Palhwa Samatadh turned to the people with literature written in the vernacular. The religious struggle during the late middle ages between Vedic orthodoxy and Siva worship was also an expression of the class struggle. In lyric poetry, Siva stood for revolt.

Until the nineteenth century, literature meant poetry. Even scientific works were written in verse. This resulted in the creation of a profound, lyrical tradition, also among the people. The nineteenth century witnessed the blossoming of the new Telugu Renaissance. Veerasalingam Panthulu is the pioneer of that movement. Modern revolutionary poetry was shaped by Sri Sri from 1934 to 1944. It was he who fashioned both the new language and the new ideas. Throughout the entire Telengana uprising, it was this tradition that was developed in popular song. Sri Sri also initiated the progressive literary movement in the 1930s. When the other leading figures of this movement faded in the fifties, Sri Sri continued to develop his art. The others became commercialized. They wrote bad film scripts. They lost their artistic touch. But Sri Sri maintained both art and revolution. His work drew its inspiration from the traditions of both Shaivite lyricism in the vernacular as well as contemporary folk songs.

Sri Sri is a great and beloved poet with a following that numbers in the millions. The language in which he writes is spoken by as many people as those who speak French; and those who speak it, even those who cannot read and write, possess a literary background in its lyrical traditions and potential. Although the peasants are poor and unable to read a book, they do know their lyric poetry.

The state government of Andhra Pradesh tried to cash in on his greatness. It wanted to pass itself off as a lover of lyric poetry and a champion of the Telugu language. On his sixtieth birthday, the government tried to arrange a tribute to him. But Sri Sri was a poet of the people and he refused to have anything to do with a corrupt government's tribute. Instead, he spent that evening taking part in the founding of Viplava Rachayitya Sangham (Revolutionary Writers' Union). His poems castigated corrupt officialdom. The government responded by seizing the poems and jailing Sri Sri, the living classic of the Telugu language.

The Congress Party, which was in power in Andhra Pradesh for the last generation, has taken a continuing interest in culture. The most popular plays have been banned for the past generation. Both *Ma Bhumi* and *Mundaou* are about the peasant movement. When the state government declared Sircilla and Jagtial "disturbed areas" in 1978, one of the accusations against the people was that they had performed banned plays in the villages.

Over a span of ten years, the government has banned a total of eighteen anthologies of lyric poetry and short stories. These include some of the best works written in Telugu during that period. But before the police have had time to do anything or to hunt down every copy of the anthologies, they have already found their way to the people. Lyric poetry has grown into a popular movement. This has resulted in increasingly harsh measures on the part of the government. Publishers have been jailed, and writers repeatedly arrested. They have been tortured. Some have even been murdered. Especially disturbing to the authorities is that proletarian writers have begun to appear in Telugu. These were not only lyricists who can be considered part of the popular lyric tradition, but also writers of prose. It is significant that it was against a railroad worker-poet that the government chose to take action, when it attempted to shut down the journal *Srujana*.

The sugar mill employee Allam Rajaiah is another such writer. He has used the Telengana dialect to write his prose. But this popular language cannot be read and understood by the intellectuals from the coastal districts. The issue of popular language or book-language has, through realistic prose writers like Allam Rajaiah, become as crucial in Andhra Pradesh as in Norway. When the realism becomes strong and clear the government hits back with censorship and police.

The government hatred of literature is deep. Telugu poetry is not about beauty or soulfulness. It is not even lewd—though of course it includes love and passion. It is about the life and struggle and honor of living people—and thus a conspiracy in the eyes of the government.

G. Alfred has clearly expressed the attitude of the government to this literature. He was the Deputy Superintendent of Police on special duty who wrote the charge sheet of August 19th, 1974, in that mass trial of writers that never seems to end:

> 7) In pursuance of the ideology of Naxalites to overthrow the Government by violent means, a body of persons claiming to be Revolutionary Writers known as VIRASAM (Viplava Rachayithala Sangham) consisting of A24 from Warangal, A25, A26 and A28 from Hyderabad, A27 from Nellore and A29 from Tirupathi and others was formed in October 1970 in Khammam Town. In furtherance of objects of this association A24 to A29 resorted to writing and publishing inflammatory and seditious and objectionable writings in order to incite the youth, students and educated people who are prone to violence to join the movement and to intensify the armed struggle programme. They wrote and published Revolutionary writings of highly objectionable and inflammatory nature calculated to bring the Government into hatred and contempt and to excite disaffection towards the Government; and prejudicial to the maintenance of harmony inciting the people to take up arms to bring about armed revolt and to overthrow the Government established by law as envisaged by the Naxalites. These accused published such objectionable and inflammatory writings in magazines captioned as *Srujana, Pilupu, Erra Pidikili, Viplavam Vardhillali, Rakta Ganam, Red Army, Ippudu Veestunna Gali, Viplava Shankaravam, March, Jhanjha, Telangana Poratalu, Uregimpu* etc. at regular intervals from different places in the state and also by circulating unauthorised pamphlets.

The jailed writers Tripuraneni Madhusudhana Rao, K. V. Ramana Reddy, M. Ranganatham, Cherabanda Raju, M. T. Khan and Varavara Rao replied in court on August 13, 1974, by declaring that while the police considered literature to be a conspiracy, it was, in fact, the ruling class which for hundreds of years had been conspiring against the people. It was up to the writers to expose this conspiracy and that was why the people loved their poems and why they defended their writers from those in power.

The trial is pending. The defence asked for investigation reports on the (fabricated) accusations, but these were not available. A stay order has now been issued on the case.

The authorities have decided to destroy the new vernacular Telugu literature. In 1980 the accused writers were out of jail on bail but the government was planning new legal attacks. For the fact is that this new literature does represent a danger to the government. This literature has carried on the thousand-year Shaivite tradition of radical works in the vernacular with its barbs aimed at the rulers. And with the guidance of Sri Sri, it developed this tradition into a vigorous literary weapon. It has taken a stand for a people's culture.

The poets have learned from the vernacular and the rich treasure house of popular song. They have adapted and further developed this vast store of folk songs, and have also developed the great, national stylistic tradition, while making concrete the demands for democracy and land in their poems. All over Andhra Pradesh we met poets and troubadours. Not all of them are members of the same organization. Some belong to the Revolutionary Writers' Union, some do not. At the temple in Palampet, J. Sitaram sings, or recites his poems, concealing himself behind the names of his works. He sings of the new world. In Vishakapatanam, we meet Jana Natya Mandali, a song and poetry group, the members of which are workers and clerks from the shipyard. In Hyderabad, we are visited in our hotel room by Gaddar, Cherabanda Raju and Rama Rao. Each is a great artist and different from the other. Everywhere we met poets who recite and sing their poems and discuss the meaning of lyric poetry and the new life of the language.

Gaddar sang his ballad of the four martyred student leaders— Janardhan Rao, Murali Mohan Reddy, Sudhakar and Ananda Rao, murdered by the police in Giraipally in 1975. He sang only part of it since the whole thing takes two hours to perform.

"It is in the traditional Telengana-style. I sing the ballad. Two speakers stand beside me. One delivers the dramatic and comic comments that are interspersed with the tragic account. The other is there to draw conclusions and point out the lessons to be learnt from the events portrayed. It's like a play."

Gaddar sings and plays the drums even while talking. He is of untouchable origin. His songs follow this tradition. He now works in a bank. He is also one of Andhra Pradesh's most beloved artists.

The traditional popular style—or rather, the traditional popular styles, since they are numerous—now adopted by the poets and troubadours are neither banal nor stereotyped. They allow for a genuine social realism which, in a Shakespearean sense, encompass profound tragedy, burlesque antics, and the insight which makes possible conscious action. Popular realism is rich and many-sided.

Yet, if the poets have turned to popular tradition, they have also shouldered a great responsibility towards the people. Cherabanda Raju began as an innovator of style. At that time he wrote what was known as the new, naked poetry. But in writing, he was forced to take the side of the people, democracy and the agrarian revolution. When things got rough, he had to choose between writing praise of the powerful, and treading the more difficult path of naked poetry: writing for the people. During the 1970s when Indira Gandhi cracked down on the people and the prisons were filled with political prisoners (thirty-five writers were in prison for "poetic crimes" at the same time in Andhra Pradesh, among them Cherabanda Raju), the political prisoners used to sing Cherabanda Raju's "Padutam Padutam" when entering the courtroom. Bound by iron chains, they beat out the rhythm of the slow, wistful melody with their fetters.

> We sing
> we sing
> that the people are our leaders
> that people's power is truimphant
> ...We sing the songs of liberation
> Naxalbari has written them
> We sing, We sing.

And outside the prison, people gathered in thousands and sang the night through, keeping time to the rhythm with their clapping. The prisoners heard them and sang back, keeping time with their chains. The prison guards were unable to silence this song.

It was also Cherabanda Raju who wrote the song about Kistagowda and Bhoomiah, the two peasant leaders who were sentenced to death in Andhra Pradesh. Their execution, however, had to be postponed due to widespread protests. It was not until after Indira Gandhi declared the Emergency that the government was able to carry out the sentence. Then, too, the whole prison sang. The singing continued all night long, and when the two men went to their death, a thousand prisoners around them sang:

> Lal Salam!
> Communist Kistagowda, Comrade Bhoomiah
> Lal Salam!

The words "Lal Salam" are words understood throughout the length and breadth of India. They mean "Revolutionary Greetings!"

A song I heard both in the villages and up in the mountains was "Ye Kulamurabbi". It was composed to unite the people. Written to a bitterly lamenting folk melody from Telengana, it is almost Andalusian in tone.

It poses the question: "What is your caste? What is your religion? When you take clay, make bricks and build a house brick by brick for others, what then is your caste? What then is your religion? When you've dug your way through all the mineshafts, and coughed up your lungs in black phlegm, what then is your religion?" And the long song concludes "Your legends are now antiquated and your triumphant chariots have been destroyed, for the people are united."

In 1972, when Indira Gandhi led the hunt for the Naxalites and urged the police to exterminate them, regardless of the laws, the violence of the police resulted in a bloodbath. Captured activists or suspected sympathizers were first tortured and some were taken into the woods to be shot. This was common knowledge. It was known that the police held thirty to forty thousand prisoners who had not been properly tried, and that those executed without having been charged or without even having been recorded as being arrested, numbered in the thousands. While in prison, Cherabanda Raju wrote "Ma Loni Manishive!" (You Are One of Us!).

This poem was addressed to the police:

You are one of us, you belong with us
You became a policeman to earn a living
Why do you shoot at your brothers and sisters?
Why do you shoot at your old parents?
Don't you see their emaciated legs?
Don't you see their collapsed bodies?
Brothers, dear brothers, you are doing wrong
You are one of us, you belong with us
Some people live in luxury and wealth
Hunger and sickness is the fate of the masses
You are one of the poor ones
They want you to join them
To be a man means to want to do something with one's life
You aren't allowed to say what you think
Brother, dear brother, you are doing wrong now
You are one of us, you belong with us.

This song is still controversial among some leftists who are being hunted and tortured.

Cherabanda Raju criticized the political line which held that revolutionaries must see every policeman as a class enemy. He felt that anger should not cloud one's perception of actual class relations. Some of my friends still cannot agree about that song. But Cherabanda Raju felt that now, after a period of five years, actual experience had proven who was right and who was wrong. On several occasions in different places, the police have protested against their miserable working conditions. The government has had to call in military troops against them. Then, the police too sang Cherabanda Raju's Song.

One evening, he sat in our hotel room in Hyderabad, and sang. He was a sick man and to die soon after. From time to time, his voice faltered. He sang:

"Yes, it's true, it is true, this our fertile Telengana/has always borne/ the songs of heroes."

The government had tried to break him down through starvation. It had suspended him from his teaching job. Funds were collected all over India because he was incurably ill and in pain. But up to the very end the authorities feared and persecuted him. An aura of clarity surrounded him as he sang:

"Darkness in every home/tears in every eye/to whom does power belong, O Rajanna?/To whom happiness?/For whom is this land milked?/ so that some starve and others reap bounty?"

Down in the hotel lobby, a plainclothes policeman sat recording the names of all those who visited me. Cherabanda Raju shrugged his shoulders. For nine years he had been arrested constantly. At the moment he was out on bail.

This great poet finally died in July 1982. But to the government he was nothing short of a criminal. His crime was his song, a crime severely punished in Andhra Pradesh.

In Warangal, I met the twenty-five year old Jnaneswar Keerti. He was a member of the Revolutionary Writers' Union and belonged to the circle around *Srujana* which had invited me there. He had taken part in our nocturnal discussions about a people's culture, the tasks of poetry, the false left, and the development of literature in Telugu and the European languages. He had also attended the lectures I gave at Kakatiya University.

On the evening of January 22, I was to speak to an evening class about village problems in China. The audience was made up for the most part of elementary school teachers from the countryside and petty clerks. The room was on the second floor. There was standing room only. But the RSS, a Hindu extremist organization, and Indira Gandhi's Youth Congress had joined forces to break up the meeting. Led by their most prominent goondas, they mounted their joint attack. Two hundred students and faculty members held them at bay on the stairway, permitting me to complete my lecture and the discussion that followed. For two hours, the Youth Congress and RSS banged and shouted without breaking through. Jnaneswar Keerti was one of those who organized the defence of the stairway.

I was back in Warangal on February 16. My return to the city coincided with a solar eclipse. I was unable to get in touch with my friends since I intended to visit the "disturbed areas." The police did not know that I was in Andhra Pradesh and I was forced to lie low. I also carefully refrained from contacting my writer friends at this time so that they would not later be accused of having illegal contacts.

In Warangal, there were posters about Jnaneswar Keerti on the walls. He was dead. Dead for a week. He had died at the hospital on the morning of February 9, surrounded by the local poets and members of the Revolutionary Writers' Union. He was thought to be a promising young poet.

He was of a poor family of tailors. He had his shop behind a "student-factory" in Warangal. It was poetry that had made him politically aware. Through his knowledge of older Telugu poetry, he had come to love Sri Sri's poems. In time, he had become acquainted with Varavara Rao and other poets in Warangal, and had himself begun to write. Some of his poems had been published. He joined the Revolutionary Writers' Union.

Every day from his workbench in the shop, he saw how the student-factory was run. There is a saying that goes: "If you want to get rich in Andhra Pradesh, open a student-factory." This is a place where those who cannot attend a normal school are forced to study. And this is also where the upper class sends its good-for-nothings to have them licked into shape. The manager of this particular student-factory was named Kondaya. He was closely allied with the local leaders of Congress (I) and had friends in the state government.

The teachers are supposed to receive a monthly salary of about seven hundred rupees. But because of the unemployment among intellectuals, the student-factories officially pay only four hundred or five hundred. However, in Andhra Pradesh, unemployment among intellectuals is so widespread that teachers and journalists can be had for almost nothing. Kondaya employed women. They cost the least. He paid them one hundred rupees a month for five hours of work per day. Their reasoning is that women are more easily intimidated than men. The women do not dare complain since they have such poor prospects on the job market.

Kondaya exploited the women. He also exploited them sexually. If they did not agree to sleep with him, he fired them and they lost the hundred rupees a month they otherwise took home to their families. They did not dare report him. They were afraid. They were also afraid of being disgraced.

However, when Kondaya raped one of the young teachers, Jnaneswar Keerti felt things had gone too far. He went to Kondaya and told him that he intended to take up the matter with the authorities and various orga-

nizations so that Kondaya would be forced to pay normal wages and be-
have properly towards his female employees.

Late in the night on February 8, 1980, Jnaneswar Keerti was sleeping
out in his courtyard, as most people do in summer. Suddenly he was
awakened by an icy-cold feeling against his body. He smelt gasoline.
Matches were lit and in their light he saw the face of Kondaya. Kondaya
and another man threw the matches, and Jnaneswar's body immediately
burst into flames. He screamed and tried to chase them. He rolled on the
ground. The neighbors arrived and he was taken to the hospital. His
friends came. They sat by his side.

He told the policeman who had been summoned to his bedside what
had happened. But the policeman refused to record the testimony of the
dying man. He refused to put on paper the dying man's claim that the
crime was of a political nature.

"You're no poet." he said to Jnaneswar Keerti, "you are just a tailor!"

Jnaneswar Keerti explained that he took action against Kondaya pre-
cisely because poetry had made him politically aware: there are limits to
how one may abuse another human being. But the policeman departed
without recording Jnaneswar Keerti's dying declaration because Kondaya is an influential member of the Congress (I). According to the police
report, Jnaneswar Keerti lay there dying from the consequences of a
midnight row sparked by a personal grudge. This would allow Kondaya
to get off without severe punishment. If he had to serve any time at all
for such a trifling matter, he would soon be released to continue with his
student-factory.

But the poets who gathered around the hospital bed of Jnaneswar
Keerti recorded the dying man's last words:

"I am a poet and a member of the Revolutionary Writers' Union. As a
member, I have become aware of how society functions. Because I am socially aware, I reacted to the way the manager of the student factory behaved, and the manner in which he used his power against those weaker
than himself. I told him that I would not watch silently the abuses he
committed. So tonight he poured gasoline on me and set me on fire."

The last thing Jnaneswar Keerti said before he died was: "I don't want
to die. I want to live. There is so much left for me to do."

The Armed Squads

High up in the Eastern Ghats, west of the Godavari River in Polavaram taluk, the path had become totally impassable. The jeep could go no further. The jungle was thick, but toward the northwest, the valley opened out beneath us. In the distance, the mountains appeared dark against the sky, for dusk had come. As we pitched camp, night fell, and across the black sky, the stars seemed to come crashing down upon us.

He had come from the forests of Warangal and Khammam, and had spent the previous night in the home of a union man in the coal-mining town Kottagudem. In the morning, we had packed ourselves into the jeep. It was vintage World War II, and had seen service in Burma. Under the tarpaulin, it was unbearably hot and stuffy, but since we were to drive right across the lowlands, it was best that we keep out of sight. The police should not be given any reason to ask questions.

But the jeep broke down in Koyyalagudem. We were stuck four hours while the driver and some mechanics from the village made the necessary repairs. When we finally reached our rendezvous, high up in the mountains where the trail forked, there was no one there to meet us. The bamboo-cutters said that two couriers had been waiting since that morning. But they had left at about five o'clock.

A boy from the village thought he might know where the camp was located. He jumped onto the jeep and took us to where the trail came to an end. He and one of our companions proceeded on foot. We sat around the campfire and waited for them. Bashgaranna told us about the first time he had been arrested.

"It was in Adilabad. Three of us were captured. I had gone out into the forest in June, 1973, when I was seventeen. But we managed to escape. That is why they wanted to shoot me immediately the second time. I had a price of 10,000 rupees on my head. But the arresting officers did not get any of it. Inspector Mathabra took the money for himself. He has advanced in his career since then. At that time, they beat me on the soles of my feet until I lost consciousness. That is why I have trouble walking. They wanted me to tell them where the Party Secretary for Maharashtra was. I had been working as an organizer in that area. By then I had spent five years out in the forests. But I didn't tell them where they could find Lakshmi Pagar.

"Later, they captured Lakshmi Pagar anyway. They tortured him. When they realized that no matter what they did, he would say nothing, they cut off his tongue. Then they took him to Warangal where he was shot.

"After having been beaten and held prisoner for six months, I was brought to trial. They said that I had been captured carrying a gun in Adilabad's forest five days earlier. That's what they always do. That's how people disappear. They said nothing about the six months I had spent locked up by the Special Branch in Hyderabad.

"I am out on bail now. But I've been ordered to go into hiding. That's the right thing to do. The Party cannot afford to repeat the mistake it made during the Emergency. At that time, we were too trusting. It cost us 2,000 comrades, many of them leading cadres whom we badly need now."

Gun gathered some sticks. The fire sent up sparks, and flamed skyward. Footsteps were heard in the darkness. Four men stepped into the firelight. They were armed and dressed in khaki. They had come for us. Two of them went down into the valley to look for our companion and the boy from the village. The other two jumped into the jeep. We drove back to the village and then turned off in another direction. After a moment, we got out of the jeep and began to walk.

It was a long march. One of the armed men carried a case of Gold Spot, a sweetened orange drink, on his head.

"The guests must be comfortable," he said and laughed.

When we reached the camp, we found soft beds prepared for us. A thick layer of dry leaves had been spread under our ground sheets. We were served hot, strong tea with milk. We were given washed sugar sacks to use as blankets.

In the deep of the night we heard the changing of those on guard duty. Sentries were posted around the camp. They were relieved on the hour. As morning approached it grew cooler, and just before dawn the dewdrops fell pattering against the bamboo leaves. Heavy drops.

A conference was taking place here. The entire leadership for the Khamman and Western Godavari districts had assembled. Some of the participants had travelled a week to get here. There were representatives from all the armed squads. Cadres had come from the leading bodies of the Party. During a five day period, the international and domestic political situations were discussed. The conference also heard a report from the latest Central Committee meeting and about existing political differences within the Party. Reports on the work being done in different taluks were made. Mistakes in the work were also discussed and the political line corrected. In the evenings there were cultural presentations. As dusk falls, Yellanna sang Agade Chenniah's elegy for Party Secretary Ramanarasaiah. In Hyderabad, Rama Rao had sung this song for us. Now, it was sung here in the bamboo forest. It is a song of such fantastic pain and beauty that it excels anything I know. It far surpasses the Russian song "The Revolutionaries' Funeral March." It is simpler, more direct. The mood changes as another song begins: "Palle, palle, gudisa naduma" ("From village to village/and hut to hut/a bridge of moonlight/ Let village strike sparks against village/sparks which grow into a fire/into a raging fire.").

The armed struggle has now been going on for more than ten years here in the forests of Andhra Pradesh. Many times, the government has declared that it has been crushed. Yet, here we are, conveyed safely by the armed squads through the jungles from squad to squad, from village to village. Although it is not yet India's Yenan, it is one of the many hotbeds which may set off the prairie fire. It is perhaps one of India's Chingkang Mountains.

Several days earlier, outside the village of Pandiam, we had been visiting a squad when Doranna, the district organizer, dropped in. He was already an active member of the movement at the time of the Telengana uprising. He was now fifty-five years old and had been wounded many times. He had fought from 1948 to 1951. Towards the end of the uprising, he had been captured when the village he was in was suddenly surrounded by three hundred soldiers. He spent three years in prison. The illiterate prisoners were taught to read. They helped each other, and he learned to read. At first, he worked in the CPI. When it split, he joined CPI(M). But the leadership was bad. In 1967, the revolutionaries began to organize. They worked using legal methods until 1969, the year he went out into the forest. Everything he owned had been confiscated. In 1969, the government burnt down his house, worth 70,000 rupees, and expropriated his four hectares of irrigated land. A reward of 30,000 rupees is offered for his capture. He is wanted *dead or alive*.

"We have made some errors in the past. On occasion, our squads stole from the landowners. We called this confiscation. It was wrong. It strengthened the enemy while weakening and isolating us. Our other error was that we neglected legal forms of activity while concentrating solely on illegal forms: We did not quickly set about developing activity among the masses. Mistakes like these cannot be avoided in the beginning. But even then, our primary task was to organize the masses for resistance.

"We are totally dependent on the masses. They provide us with shelter. They provide us with food. They supply us with information. And we protect the masses."

Yes, the long guerrilla war is a reality. Its roots run deep among the people here in the forest areas. In the village stood a stupa—a whitewashed monument with a hammer and sickle on it. It had been built in memory of squad member Papanu (whose real name was Lakshmi Narayan), who had been shot by the police in April, 1974, in Konapura village. A police informer had pointed him out. The informer received five hundred rupees. The stupa also commemorates Tati Mutanna who was shot in Mitapalli village, Yellandy taluk, in 1972. The stupa stands outside the childhood home of Papanu and was inaugurated in a solemn ceremony in September 1978.

I asked Papanu's father what had happened to the informer. He stood silent for a moment and then said, "He was killed."

This is no student movement; its roots run deep in the local culture. Stupas are to be found in many villages. The food-collectors who go around the villages remind one of apprentice monks. Two by two, they collect food for the squads. Squad members do not address each other as "comrade." Comrade Subba becomes "Subanna" (elder brother Subba), comrade. Nirmala becomes "Nirmalakka" (elder sister Nirmala), comrade Party Secretary becomes "pedana" (the eldest). The warmth in the Party, the mutual respect and love among these brothers and sisters who have lived for many years in the forests with a price on their heads, working to organize the villagers and protecting them all from the police, is a love that reminds one of primitive Christianity. There are many Europeans and Americans who are unable to understand this. They would be puzzled over things like stupas, food collectors, "elder brother" and "elder sister." They think that revolutionary movements are born in theses and grow with resolutions, that they take their symbols from some kind of central supply depot. And they are mistaken.

There are quite a number of women in these armed squads. Many of them are married. The ceremony is solemn and comradely. The couple swear faith and respect to each other and to a common struggle for the liberation of all humankind. When the women are about to give birth, they return to their villages. Later, they come back.

No member of the armed squads ever touches toddy, let alone beer or any other liquor.

"Liquor is a plague on the people. The exploiters, traders and forestry officials use liquor to hold the forest villagers down. That's why we never touch it. Not even if he were starving to death would a member of the armed squads—a person the people rely on—have the right to let a drop of toddy pass his lips. It's as unthinkable as someone raping a woman or using foul language to the people."

Here in the forest, we were with the armed squads of the CPI (ML) led by Chandrapulla Reddy. There are other parties and organizations. We are familiar with the various groups and parties and have seen them work in different parts of India. There are historical reasons for their diversity and proliferation. They also have differing views on various political issues. But they are all Naxalites, and they speak of each other as comrades. (There are also groups who are not comrades, but that is a different story.)

As a foreigner I have no right to say who is correct and who is not. That is for the Indian masses to decide. Under the cloak of anti-imperialist solidarity, many Europeans and North Americans go around telling third world revolutionaries what to do and what not to do. That is as colonial as the British communists directing communist activity in India!

I do not intend to tell the story of the Naxalites. Nor do I intend to discuss their differences. I am especially not about to throw myself in from the outside and bluster and reject. What is important and what some of these revolutionaries do sometimes forget is the fact that the Naxalites represent India's first genuinely native revolutionaries. It is true that they are often called "'Maoists," and that they have learnt from Mao Zedong. And they, or at least some of them, once said "China's road is our road, and China's Chairman is our Chairman." However, this was at the very beginning of the movement. Today they have grown independent. It will, possibly, be these Naxalites who will give India her future. Heterogeneous as these groups are, they form the first revolutionary current to unite national and revolutionary necessity, the first movement able to learn from the experience and theory of other countries while still maintaining its Indian roots.

Many people in Europe and America think this is a small scale movement. However, a movement which can have 40,000 of its cadres in jail; and 5,000 of its leading members executed; and that still continues to grow all over India despite massive campaigns of repression; and that grows increasingly adept at the business of political organization, while maintaining and strengthening its austere morals, this hardly amounts to any "little"—or, for the powers that be, innocuous—movement.

Indira Gandhi attempted to drown the Naxalites in blood. She failed. Had she remembered the words of Thomas Jefferson addressed to W. S. Smith on November 13, 1787, she would have understood why she was doomed to fail.

"The tree of liberty must be refreshed from time to time with the blood of patriots and tyrants. It is its natural manure."

And if she does not repress them? Then village will strike spark against village, and soon all India will be ablaze! The people will break free, and the India of Indira and the powers that be, will disappear forever like the Ancien Régime in France before it.

However, there is no people's war in progress in India. In a few places, guerrilla warfare is taking place. But nowhere has it taken the leap to people's war. The agrarian revolution is considered by the various Naxalite groups to be the decisive element in India's transformation, but the fire is still smouldering in India's half million villages.

Strictly speaking, there are no liberated areas or consolidated revolutionary base areas. But for a week we accompanied the armed squads through forest tracts where a state of emergency has been in effect for the past ten years, and where a police force of 20,000 men has been engaged to restore order. We spend the nights in villages in perfect safety. The squads are kept fully informed of police movements by the people, who, on the other hand, never breathe a word to the police of the squads' whereabouts. In these nine taluks, law and order reigns, but it is a law and order different from what the police are attempting to impose.

At the present time, the bamboo-cutters are involved in a labor conflict. They are now about to win their latest strike against Birlas' cellulose factories. In 1972, they were paid between seven and ten rupees per hundred 3 × 10 foot panels. Since then the price has been increased to forty-five rupees and in some places to sixty rupees. Today, they are struggling for hundred rupees.

The bamboo-cutters live in forest camps. When a strike is called, they choose their representatives. The armed squads coordinate and lead the strike for the entire district. When the police come to the camp of the bamboo-cutters and order them to work, they reply:

"No pay, no work!"

When the lumber company hires strikebreakers and sends them into the forest, the armed squads explain the dictates of solidarity to them.

"There have been no strikebreakers here. As soon as they are informed of the situation, they leave."

The armed squads organize sympathy actions. The transport workers have shown solidarity. Timber is no longer transported. Nor are vehicles able to travel in the bamboo forests. The road workers also show solidarity. To drive here, one needs the permission of the strikers.

The armed squads are political organizers, not anarchists or bandits. They do not plunder. They do not commit isolated acts of individualistic terrorism. Here in the forest, the form adopted for political organization is the armed group. This is not because of any romantic attitude towards armed struggle. Neither is it because of a desire for illegality. The mass organizations being developed are legal. As far as possible, the work is done openly and within the law. The struggle for democratic rights is considered to be the principal task for the present. But here in the forests live the poorest of the poor, those most lacking in legal rights, the most downtrodden people of India. These are the tribal people. They are the same people who live in the rest of Andhra Pradesh. It is hard to see any difference between a Konda Reddi, or a Koya, and a farm laborer from the lowlands. But the tribal people are even more oppressed than the untouchables on the lowlands. The people in the jungles live in dire poverty. This poverty is so abysmal that many outsiders can grow rich on it.

Out in the jungles, the forest people cultivate maize. They burn-beat the land, and the harvest supplies only enough food to last four months of the year. This means that for most of the year, they must make a living off side-line occupations. Bad years see the feeble among them, the children and the old, starve to death.

So they cut bamboo for the paper industry. They weave baskets and make handicraft products. They collect herbs, leaves and resin for the market. The state forestry officials make a good profit off them. By twisting the laws and using corrupt methods, they squeeze goods, services and money from the poor of the forests. Merchants buy handicraft and forestry products at a low price, but in return charge shamelessly exorbitant prices for goods sold to the natives. They loan money at usurious rates of interest. Workers in construction and road building projects are recruited from the forests at a bargain price.

It is this unbearable oppression and abysmal poverty that make the armed squads the appropriate form of political organization.

"What happened ten years ago when we began our struggle against the contractors for better working conditions? The police showed up. They raped the women, they looted the houses, they arrested people. They beat people, and ripped out their fingernails. Burnt them with hot irons. The armed squads are necessary to defend the people and keep the organizations alive.

"We do not carry arms for the purpose of attacking our enemies or killing them. In April, 1979, Subbanna's squad happened upon plain-clothes policemen from the police bivouac at Regalla in Moddulagudem village. Sub-Inspector Babu Rao fell on his knees and begged for mercy. He thought we were going to shoot him. We explained our political line. We do not kill anyone unnecessarily. We do not wish to kill. We told the sub-inspector that he wronged the people. We explained to him why the people had to struggle for a better life and why solidarity was necessary in that struggle. We asked him to consider carefully where his interests really lay, and whom he should be serving. Everyone in Moddulagudem had assembled around us. Afterwards, we shook hands with Sub-Inspector Babu Rao, and he was allowed to go."

The job of the armed squads is to popularize the revolutionary line and to take up the people's problems. Each squad is made up of a squad leader and four squad members. They live in the forests outside the villages. Each squad is responsible for fifteen villages, on whom they are totally dependent. The squad gets food from the villages and, in the dry season, water. In each village, a few boys maintain contact with the armed squads.

Initially, revolutionary students went out into the forests. Once there, they were forced to arm themselves. They first had only clubs, but were later able to get firearms. Now 90 percent of the squad members are natives of the forest villages. They constitute a local defense against the authorities.

A village committee is formed in every village. It is based on the *ryotu-kuli-sangham*. These organizations are legal. Each member pays twenty-five paise per year. Between 50 percent and 60 percent of the villagers are paying members. But almost all of them support the struggle, and this is why it is possible to move with such safety despite the police troops.

The armed squads are the Party's defense organization. In the past, the Party (which is never referred to as anything besides "Party") consisted mainly of city people. The policy in the past resulted in the recruitment of a very few poor villagers into the Party. Only one out of a hundred was admitted. But that policy has been changed. What is important is not one's ability to read, but one's class consciousness, loyalty, political awareness and serve-the-people spirit. There are now four or five members in every village. An important discussion is now in progress about how best to organize sympathizers.

"The mass organizations are being expanded in the villages. That comprises our legal activity. At the same time, our capacity for armed resistance to police attack is being strengthened. The state-employed forestry officials have not dared show their faces here for the last seven or eight years. They have now been granted permission to perform the useful part of their work. Those who oppressed the people are gone. Instead, there are now many sympathizers among the officials working here. They perform good forestry work which serves the people.

"The armed squads teach new, improved farming methods. They help people carry out irrigation projects. Just in this area alone, we have seen to it that thirty irrigation reservoirs have been built. This improves conditions for the people. Of course, the authorities try to hinder these initiatives.

"Cultural work is an important part of our work. Within the squads and Party we hold regular sessions of instruction. Everyone learns to read and write. Naturally, we also have political education. All the meetings we hold in the villages have cultural programs. We popularize the new poems and songs. After the meetings we dance. As you have seen, we have many agitation-dances. We work with the vernacular and popular melodies. Since there are few who can read, we have also set up about fifty evening schools in the villages. But when Indira Gandhi cracked down with the Emergency in 1975, large forces of police troops were sent to crush these schools. The police were rough with anyone who knew how to read. They considered the ability to read a sign that the person in question had been poisoned with communism. The teachers were brutally tortured. We still haven't been able to reopen the schools. But we intend to do it as soon as the number of squads increases and we can protect them more effectively.

"We think it important not to confine ourselves to local issues. We have arranged meetings and demonstrations to protest the plunder of India by social imperialism, and Moscow's invasion of Afghanistan. We have also held solidarity meetings for Kampuchea. Kampuchea's struggle is of deep concern to us. There are so many similarities in our situations."

The Indian peasant movement is very large. The agrarian revolution is on the rise. These armed squads are only a small part of this growing movement. One may wonder about their future. Will they be destroyed by bigger, more powerful forces? To date, the armed squads of Andhra Pradesh have not had to face either napalm or helicopters. This is not to say that the police have been content with combing the forests and torturing captured squad members for information. They have also poisoned the waterholes and wells in the forests during the dry season. They have already tried to divide the people up in the mountains into strategic hamlets, and if the squads begin to develop into a larger guerrilla force, the police troops will certainly use everything they have got against them. Knowing this, is it at all possible to build a movement out in the forest strong enough to consolidate a base area?

"Our road is not that followed by Che Guevara. Ours is the road of the mass line. It is our political work among the masses that is decisive. The weapons are only a necessity. But a necessity which is slowly growing into a guerilla army."

In the woods outside the village of Madagudem in Narsampet taluk, Warangal district, squad leader Madhu talks of a struggle which has been going on in these forests for ten years already. He is a native of Nalagonda district. He grew up hearing stories about the Telengana struggle.

"The peasants and landless farm laborers fought for land and freedom. But the leadership of the Communist Party and the leading cadres betrayed the struggle and began to compromise."

In secondary school he began to read political literature. He graduated from school in 1967 and became a student organizer. He was responsible for work with the student movement in the city of Khammam. In May 1969, he left for the forest. In August of the same year, he was arrested while on a courier mission in Khammam. He remained in prison until December 1972. In April, 1973, he returned to the squad and since then has worked in the forest. He is now squad leader. The police want him, dead or alive. When he speaks of the armed squads and the growing guerrilla struggle, it is not without experience.

"In the spring of 1969, when we first went out into the forest, we were only thirteen in Khammam district. Since then, seventy-five of us have been shot and more than 2,000 arrested. Today, we stand stronger than ever. Thanks to the mass line!"

On our way down from the camp in the Eastern Ghats, a middle-aged man approaches us as we are taking a break by the Godavari River. He is a bamboo-cutter of the Koya tribe and almost entirely naked. He wears only a goji, a scant loin-cloth. He laughs and opens wide his arms. He is wiry and strong.

"Lal salam!" he says. "Revolutionary greetings! The world is ours!"

And After Six More Years?

What about the bamboo-cutters? Was that just a phrase? "The future belongs to the common man." A literary ending of a book; a couple of words that looked good and closed the volume. Or does also in reality the future of India belong to people such as this?

Six years have passed and I reread what I then wrote. There is a pattern but no predestination. Many futures are possible. Scenarios they are called when intelligence officers and generals play. But I don't share their bias. I see the world differently and I don't use their words. I am still convinced that the only future in India fit for human beings is that future that belongs to the bamboo-cutter by the Godavari River and to all his hundreds of millions of class brothers.

As I write this I am listening to the radio. There are communal riots in Gujarat. Poor Hindus and poor Muslims kill each other. For the love of God and morality.

"I have seen the future. It is one of Race and Religion," said Richard Wright thirty years ago.

But the killings and the violence in Ahmedabad is nothing strange. There in the Muslim districts was a center for the textile industry that was built up during the British period and continued to expand well into the nineteen-sixties. During that time the industry needed more workers and Hindu families were moving in. Now there is crisis in the industry and unemployment among the workers. But as long as the poor Hindus and poor Muslims kill each other the textile barons will be safe. Race and religion serve as pillars in a crumbling state. Now as in the years of Independence.

Until. . . until religion and/or race themselves become the slogans of social upheaval. Because even if there is no conscious political movement expressing social conflict, the conflict is there; religion can serve as the ideology of revolt, as in Germany during the Sixteenth century and in present day Iran. Thomas Münzer interpreted the word of God as revolution, but he was not using religion for other aims; he was a truly God-fearing and believing man, as are the Islamic fundamentalists of today who interpret the word of God in a similar way. But to me—standing outside the religions even though I have respect both for the Münzers and the fundamentalists—the underlying order remains. The pattern is clearly visible. And I see no reason to change my mind and view the world slanted like a general at play. Whatever the ideological expressions and their own beliefs, the people remain the driving force in history.

In 1958 I started work on this book. Six years ago I wrote it. If I had begun the writing today I would have written it much the same. I would have used the same—or closely similar—arguments and examples. On the other hand, a second book about India will be different. Whenever you come to the river for the first time, it is there for you to see it; but you can not step into the same stream twice. You can never write the same book a second time.

I hope to write that second book on India. I would then take up another side of the discussion about India I have been involved in since Kali talked to me nearly forty years ago; since I first came to India almost thirty years ago.

To be sure, I would also write about southern Indian temple architecture and on the theories of caste/class, language/nationality and religion/politics. The book, however, would mainly deal with *urban India*: the huge cities; India's large-scale industry and its working class; the emerging high-technology-India and its managerial elite, an elite both dependent and in conflict with the imperialist and social-imperialist forces struggling for influence and profit in India; and the growing slumbelts surrounding the cities, inhabited by constantly increasing superfluous millions of pauperized peasants and other useless, broken human refuse, a slum continuously seeking to eat its way in towards the central districts, while the authorities of the elite try to fend it off. Urban India, where high technology and science go hand in hand with general impoverishment, where the relation of city and country has become the same as in classical antiquity, when the cities were tax collection centers. Urban India, a place where the rural hungry are drawn, since it is only in the cities they may find food.

There, in the slum, the bamboo-cutter's brother looks for a job. After having been taken by the trafficker in girls and sold to a brothel on GT Road, his sister has ended up there a cheap prostitute. She has grown frail and sickly. And it is there, in those slums—and not at the university or government offices—that the forces capable of liberating India and transforming it into a rich land for its people is growing. This, however, is not the entire truth; it is but one possible truth. This reservation is important.

For there is also a second possibility in the slum's prospects. That of race and religion; communalism organized into pogroms serving the established order. On October 31, 1984, Indira Gandhi was shot by members of her own bodyguard. Following that, pogroms which served the interests of the government broke out against the Sikhs. Once again Delhi reeked of the burnt flesh of human beings. The pogroms were organized by leaders of the Congress Party (I).* And it was the oppressed, the poor and untouchables of the slum who were used to do the killing. The ruling class needs the slum at times like this. The slum can overthrow its rulers, however, if its inhabitants are awakened from their degradation through struggle for their real interests.

That Indira Gandhi was shot at that place and time may be considered an accidental occurrence of history, but that she was almost certain to be assassinated was obvious to anyone who had observed her policies of the year before. In the press sycophants spoke of her talent. But she wasn't talented, she was shrewd and domineering. Her shrewdness was to be her downfall, and in dying she dragged thousands of victims with her.

During the 1960s and 1970s Indira Gandhi had followed a populistic course. She was in power to serve the poor.

She was her father's daughter, defender of the poor and India's Indira. Her son and designated successor, Sanjay, organized around himself elements of the lumpen proletariat and lumpen bourgeoisie in a manner reminiscent of 1850 France. He was to be the fourth of the great Nehru Dynasty and, what is more, like his mother, to have a fine-sounding name: Gandhi. Even if his name had nothing whatever to do with the great Gandhi, he would be known as Father of his Country. As for Indira, she cynically made use of temple and religion to drape herself in holiness in the people's eyes, just as for Europeans she played up her family's European upbringing and tradition. With the proclamation of the state of emergency, she created what many among traditionally conservative Europeans, the new left and those close to Moscow called a strong government. Those opposed to her were jailed for being anti-

* See the banned booklet published by the People's Union for Democratic Rights and the People's Union for Civil Rights, "Who are the guilty? Report of a Joint Inquiry into the Causes and Impact of the Riots in Delhi from 31 October to 10 November."

national, and in all the government-controlled media Indira had herself proclaimed beloved by the people.

In time she came to believe in her own popularity and decided to hold general elections. She lost. When her opponents came to power, however, they proved to be just as corrupt as her own party members—and disunited to boot. She was returned to power in 1980, as it was said, to give India a government that worked.

But now things were different. Sanjay died—of foolhardiness. One might say from incipient delusions of grandeur. It proved impossible to make the crisis disappear through magic. The general economic situation kept growing worse, social inequality ever more glaring. The green revolution resulted in fewer farmers dividing among them larger harvests, while increasing numbers were thrown into deepening poverty. In Afghanistan, Moscow had got rid of the 'friendly' Daud and even replaced the more or less independent comprador-communist leaders with Karmal, who was flown in after Soviet troops had finished off the former head of state and had begun to occupy the country. In a number of Indian provinces a greater degree of regional autonomy was being demanded. It was time to dump economic populism. In its place Indira attempted to rule with a militant, chauvinistic nationalism aimed against Pakistan, and by beginning to come out as a Hindu and play directly on the issue of religion. The more Indira Gandhi used chauvinism and religion, however, the more divided India became.

The Punjab was the Sikhs' stronghold. It is a fertile agricultural region, and below the ideological struggle for Sikh rights lies a real struggle over river water. The Akali government had been Sikh, but after Indira won there in 1980, it fell from power. In order to regain the lucrative government offices, the Akali politicians, now in opposition, raised the issue of river water that they had neglected while in office.

To sabotage the Akali Party's efforts, Indira Gandhi had given support to the most extreme of all Sikh leaders, Sant Bhindrawale. He advocated the use of terror in the cause of religion. The question of water now became a religious issue. Indira Gandhi herself supported the Hindu religious reactionaries. She played one extreme off against the other; they were to keep each other in check. She had reckoned shrewdly that this would make her own position more secure and that she would in this way be able to strengthen the state. The riots soon grew into a war of religion with many wounded and dead. The police shot Sikhs in the Punjab, and Sikhs the world over began to support the demand for an independent Sikh state, Khalistan. Now the Soviet Union was supporting Indira Gandhi in return for her military and political pressure on Pakistan, thereby destabilizing a base area for many of the Afghani patriots fighting the Soviet occupation forces. In response, the United States, Canada and Great Britain gave some support to those demanding an independent Khalistan.

It soon became clear that Indira Gandhi's shrewd attempt to divide-and-rule had unleashed forces she could not control. The terrorism and murder increased; poor Hindus and poor Sikhs killed each other. Sant Bhindrawale, who had long since ceased to do Indira's bidding and who had begun a holy war, entrenched himself in the Golden Temple. When Indira Gandhi insisted on being shrewd instead of politically wise, when she sent the Indian Army on "Operation Bluestar" to storm and occupy the Sikhs' most holy temple (neither Mussolini nor Hitler ever stormed the Vatican), anyone with even a little knowledge of current Indian politics knew that she had signed her own death warrant. It was just a question of where and when it would be carried out. In the meantime she continued her centralizing policies by striking against the Muslims and deposing Farooq Abdullah's government in Jammu and Kashmir. Claiming it was for the good of the nation, she then tried to eliminate N.T. Rama Rao in Andhra Pradesh. But as the weeks passed, her policies met with setback after setback. Following the storming of the Golden Temple, opposition grew even among the masses who had previously supported her. She lost in Andhra Pradesh. The Hindu-Muslim conflict began to assume a class character. It looked as if Indira Gandhi was headed for the political defeat of her career in October 1984.

With her death, however, the scene changed. By letting herself be killed, she could also serve as a martyr. Across the entire Hindu belt of northern India and for the majority of Hindus, her image was suddenly transformed. The emotions could be utilized. Now she could be mourned to the advantage of the state. It was to safeguard the regime that the lumpen apparatus Sanjay organized within Congress (I) swung into action.

This was the classic pogrom, the kind the Black Hundreds used to organize—a politically motivated orgy of violence to preserve the established power.

First there were the carefully prepared rumors: Sikhs had danced in the streets when Indira Gandhi was murdered. Sikhs had congratulated each other. Sikhs had passed out sweets to celebrate the assassination. Sikhs were now busy poisoning wells. They had come in trains from the Punjab to Old Delhi Station. They stood silent and motionless on the platforms. When workers at the station wondered why no one left the train and looked, they saw that all the railroad cars were full of dead Hindus. To assure wide diffusion of these rumors the government apparatus was also used. In some places police cars drove around with loudspeakers blaring, urging people not to drink the poisoned water; they screamed out the news of the dead people in the trains.

Yet, one needs more than just organizers and victims for a pogrom. There must also be the masses who can be led into the orgies of bloodshed. In Delhi, as in Old Russia, it was the down-and-out, the poor, the oppressed themselves who could be used. They had been driven from their land and from their original slum quarters. They were now housed in controlled slum districts.

From areas such as these, tightly controlled by the party apparatus, the assailants were transported into the city by car. Out in the suburbs attacks started against Sikhs in one neighborhood after the other. Then it began: "Blood for blood!" For a week it was open season on Sikhs. Party officials indicated which shops were Sikh-owned and where they lived. Downtrodden street-sweepers, peasants chased from their land, the browbeaten and persecuted, were sent against the Sikhs. Shops and dwellings were burnt down. Girls and women were raped, men beaten to death. They were drenched in gasoline and set on fire. Now there was murder on the trains from the Punjab. But it was Sikhs who were dragged out of the cars and beaten to death when the trains made stops.

Everything that happened is carefully recorded; the names and addresses of the involved party officials and politicians are documented.

The pogroms that took place in northern India during the first week of November 1984 were in the interest of the state. They were brilliant (not just shrewd) steps in a successful attempt at stabilizing and centralizing the regime. Indira Gandhi's son, Rajiv, was known to be an honest technician, to have clean hands. He was installed as his mother's successor on October 31. The dynasty was now a reality. He was not just prime minister, he was also minister of defense. Naturally, he condemned the killings. It is said that he forbade them. But the army made no genuine, organized effort to restore law and order. The government's moralizing repudiation of the violence, coupled with an inability to act in the face of what in some quarters is portrayed as "the people's spontaneous outburst of rage and sorrow," are standard ingredients in program tactics.

The time was at hand for new elections: emotions were at a boil, the opposition seemingly paralyzed. The opposition had concentrated on the individual Indira Gandhi, and now she had become a martyr and a saint, beyond attack. Rajiv Gandhi naturally won a landslide victory.

His image is that of a selfless technocrat, advised by a youthful, computerized elite. India is about to experience a technical-scientific revolution. Indira's populism, as well as Sanjay's lumpen-bourgeois apparatus, has been put back in the wings. Now is the time for reason and elitism.

It is undoubtedly the millions of downtrodden, poor, superfluous peasants who comprise the main force which *can* create a future for India. Notice, I didn't write *will*, but *can*. For religion, caste, language can all be utilized by the ruling class to make the oppressed and exploited quite harmless. In the slums and dung-heap villages, they can be egged on to tear each other apart like starving wild animals in their cages. It is a classic method used frequently in the history of southern Asia. Now, however, as this century draws to an end, technical and scientific advances have cleared a path leading to a new, brave world of another sort, a world where mass misery has been done away with by helping the unfortunate out of their earthly wretchedness, a world where they have been annihilated. This is possible because, for the first time, the masses are becoming unnecessary for the existence of the elite.

There are four hundred million of these increasingly superfluous people in India. I do not doubt the ruling elite's cold-blooded determination to abolish underdevelopment and poverty in this way, physically eliminating the impoverished majority that day it becomes politically possible for them to do so. Nor do I doubt that their determination will be rationalized with ideology and cloaked in ideals.

Thus, a number of evil paths also stand open.

Still, one need not be a romantic to maintain that the masses are the motive force in history. The ruling classes are parasitic, even when they hold the power over knowledge and technology in their grip. For the ruling class *always* holds sway (among other things) by virtue of its control over the technology, knowledge, religion and beliefs of their particular society. They determine not just the laws but, as Strindberg pointed out, the laws of thought—in Sweden, as in India. It is by virtue of this power that they, in their class interest, can unleash the most down-trodden street-sweepers of the Bhangi caste or the dispossessed peasants in pogroms and wars of religion. Each time the people through struggle realize this, lift their gaze and look around, each time they consciously use their power in their own interest, established society is over-thrown and the course of world history altered.

Now for the first time, however, the masses in the Third World (and later in our own societies) are faced with the ultimate decision. They may choose to remain unaware, which not only keeps them exploited, but also leads to their annihilation; and they may choose conscious action, for the liberation of not just one class but of all mankind.

Any political or aesthetic ideology that in this situation disregards the vast majority and declares it to be backward or at present negligible, during the current technical-scientific leap, any ideology that replaces the many with the few, objectively serves the class interest of the elites and contributes to the development of the conceptual models that can serve to legitimize this mass murder. These ideologies might come labelled communist or socialist, liberal, radical or humanitarian; it might be developed at Marxist seminars on some imperialist university campus, in the think tanks of the military-industrial complex or by party congresses in the countries pulling the strings of the new ruling class.

There are a number of political movements in India which view the peasant masses as the main force in a protracted, revolutionary struggle for power. I have been criticized in India for not coming out clearly in support of one or another of these movements—or, rather, for not coming out against all except one. But I am a Swedish, not an Indian writer, and even if I were, in the present situation I would probably work within the united revolutionary writers' association, supporting the Naxalbari way and the people's culture. I would participate in the on-going efforts to build up an all-India revolutionary culture front serving the people, regardless of caste, religion or language, but still without coming out in direct support of any one particular organization. For the fact is that after the tremendous losses in terms of dead and jailed since 1967, after the splits and confusion caused among other things by developments in China, those accused of being Naxalites are now implementing Mao Zedong's analysis of the Indian people's potential, an analysis condemned in Beijing, as in New Delhi, Moscow and Washington. Haltingly they advance. They are still divided.

But around India, in Assam, Tripura, West Bengal, Uttar Pradesh, Andhra Pradesh, Madhya Pradesh, Maharashtra, Bihar and other provinces, tremendous class struggles are now taking place; these are seldom reflected in the official media. The struggle for a minimum wage has mobilized millions of day-laborers. The poor peasants are taking back large tracts of land—by force. Loggers, plantation hands and mining workers have gone out. They have taken up the struggle for more than the basic material demands; they have fought for their rights and their *izzat*, their honor. And this can be decisive. The scorned and degraded masses demand their land and human dignity back. They are rising up even in the sense that they are no longer willing to bow their heads and step aside when the mighty come along. The struggle for dignity and self-respect is revolutionary.

These class struggles have taken place almost everywhere with the help of weapons, with popular violence against that of the rulers. Hundreds of usurers, landowners, corrupt policemen and bureaucrats have been arrested and brought before the people gathered in judgement.

In several areas there exist various organized armed groups to protect the people from the mighty and their state. Notorious exploiters have been publically humiliated. They have been stripped, forced to walk through the rural communities dressed only in their underwear, and in this way put to shame. The smallest child could see that the mighty are naked.

New, broad-based democratic organizations have been built up outside the control of, and directed against, those in power. The revolutionary cultural movement faces a growing task. Poetry and music are as vital to the people's liberation struggle as weapons. Without songs the weapons would remain untouched! It is not without reason that the authorities come down so hard on the poets. Civil rights organizations based in the cities document the torture and excesses, and occasionally force the authorities to respect the law. Other times, as in the case of the thorough investigation of the pogroms in Delhi between October 31 and November 10, the authorities intervene by confiscating the report and banning its publication. The names of the guilty appear in the report. The women's struggle against rape has grown into a mass movement. Long before the Bhopal catastrophe the revolutionary environmental movement in India showed how Union Carbide and other multinational companies were poisoning the people for profit.

Local, provincial and more or less nationwide organizations and parties grow. They work in a variety of ways. Some work both inside and outside established political institutions, others only outside; some claim that the general armed struggle has already begun and organized their own armed forces, others argue that the time has not yet come; some defend the execution of individual class enemies—notorious usurers, landowners and policemen—arguing that these executions are necessary and serve, others condemn such executions as individual terrorism. This debate is rooted in the reality of rural hunger and has been going on for a long time in India. The local disparities are great and the organizations numerous, although only a few are more or less nationwide. They are a reflection of the real struggle now taking place in the Indian countryside, and these organizations are beginning to lead that struggle. What these organizations have in common is not just that they have taken the Naxalbari path in theory, but that in their practice they are also beginning to deal seriously with the issues of local power, the question of how the large cities can be surrounded in a protracted struggle from the countryside. Unity, however, is still just a possibility. In this situation I, as a writer, inevitably take a stand in my work. I am not unaware of this, thereby serving the ruling classes; I am no aesthete on some cloud high above the social order. A neutral observer I am not.

It was leading Communists, even those who went to pains to call themselves revolutionary Marxists, who utilized the government apparatus of West Bengal to kill rebellious peasants in Naxalbari. They were trying to suppress the peasant movement and to represent their victims to the world as provocateurs, madmen and agents, in order to continue administering the state in the interest of the ruling class. You might say that their analysis was wrong; they weren't able to view the situation as Marx had viewed the Paris Commune. In other words, an error of theory. But that is not the case. Their attitude was characteristic and fateful. It revealed the actual class character of the organization. Parties that call themselves communist (like those that call themselves socialist, democratic, leftist, republican or revolutionary) can serve the interests of the ruling class. And now, when the question is actually posed whether the small elites are to establish for themselves a brave new world by eliminating the majority of the population, the dark, starving peasant masses, I am not a curious, neutral observer from a distance.

Nevertheless, it is not my business to intervene from on high, to say which of the struggling organizations in the Indian countryside is right and which is wrong. This the Indian people will do through their actions. We are not talking about small sects here, but of great mass organizations that mobilize millions of people in political and social struggle. When they prove that their line is correct, it won't be millions but hundreds of millions they mobilize in organized movements.

In this book I have mentioned two of the best known leaders of this revolutionary movement: Satyanaraian Singh and Chandrapulla Reddy. Each led one large group. I knew them both. Chandrapulla Reddy was wanted by the police, a price on his head, when one long night in spring 1980 we sat drinking tea in a safe-house in Bombay. He himself spoke of this constant disunity:

"You could say that when the communist movement in India split, first between Dange's people and the rest of us, and then between those who really sought the path of revolution in India and those who actually stood against the people, when objectively it became necessary to build a new party, there were none among us who somehow found ourselves at the head of the revolutionary splinter groups. There were none of us, although we were old communists, with more than local, or at best state-level, experience. No one, not even Charu Mazumdar, a charismatic leader for his followers, had national standing. One cannot ignore the personal characteristics of these party leaders, and our lack of broad perspective contributed to our allowing the different conditions in various parts of India to grow into real, often antagonistic contradictions within the movement. One cannot deny my own responsibility or that of the leaders of the other organizations. Perhaps in time we shall overcome this."

Later he and Satyanaraian got together and their organizations joined forces. Following this there arose new differences over policy and these led to new factionalism. But in October 1984 Satyanaraian Singh, who had just split the organization he headed, died of a heart attack. In November 1984, Chandrapulla Reddy also died of a heart attack, just as he was once again contributing to breaking up his party, this time due to differences with the majority in Andhra.

I respected them both as individuals and grieve their passing. But with them, a generation of traditional leadership is gone, a generation of leaders unable to rise above their constant factionalism. Thus their passing also represents a milestone. They prepared the way. With their deaths, the new road became more accessible.

They, however, are not the only ones mentioned in this book who have died these past five years. I wrote about the poet Cherabandu Raju. He died poor and persecuted.

Once dead, the ruling class tried to buy the repute of the corpse by presenting the dead man with an award, a prize from Andhra Pradesh Academy. But his widow refused the money. She was poor, but she didn't sell Cherabandu Raju's honor. She was as proud as he.

> My reply to you is a resolute NO! As Cherabandu Raju's life-companion for two decades, I can confidently say that I know his every thought and emotion. His adherence to our great cause, the people's armed revolution, was total and unreserved. His words served this cause even prior to 1970. He was not merely an adversary of this or that regime, he opposed today's exploitative system itself, that system to which the Academy and other similar institutions belong.... To accept an award from the Academy is to disavow and dishonor his person as well as the popular masses for whom he wrote and sang, those who stood by him through good times and bad.
>
> B. Syamala
> Hyderabad, A.P.

Literature and art are not ornamentation, not mere decoration of reality. The revolutionary struggle depicted in Cherabandu Raju's poetry was of fundamental importance. The struggle for a People's Culture is also the struggle for the insight that makes it possible for the poor and exploited to stand up in human dignity.

Singing the Poetry of the People

In the heat of the afternoon of June 15, 1983, one of the world's great poets suffered a heart attack and died. He was 73. In the Swedish press, however, there was not even a short notice to be read. Perhaps there was some short not tucked away in the French or British papers; if there was, I didn't see it.

The silence in Europe is not surprising, seeing as the poet died in Madras and was Asian, an Indian. What is more, he was a Communist—not some Goulash Communist, Eurocommunist or communist of some other variety of radish politics, however. He was a real communist, red straight through. He died in Madras. His language was Telugu, a major, beautifully poetic language with a rich literature. But it is an Asian language, and its great and long cultural tradition is not French, British or American. Cultured Europe, which gets itself into a tizzy over the opinion of this or that/Parisian cafe scribbler on the structure of poetry, doesn't even know the name of the language 40,000,000 southern Indians use to give expression to their experiences, knowledge and emotion.

The obituarist D. Anjaneyulu writing in *Indian Express*, June 16, 1983, concluded with the words: "He was for Andhra Pradesh what Nazrul Islam was for Bangladesh, Pablo Neruda for Latin America and Mayakovsky for Soviet Russia. He remains poet of the revolution, the ever ephemeral herald of the future."

Goethe, of course, was right when speaking with Eckermann on Wednesday January 27, 1827, he stated that one had to look out over the world so as not to fall into the delusion that what one wrote was the only poetry and was of particular value. But unfortunately he was mistaken when he claimed that the epoch of world literature was at hand. One hundred and fifty years after that discussion, the epoch of world literature is still so far off that one can safely assume that Europeans who work with literature do not even recognize the name of that great poet who died in Madras in the summer of 1983.

His people knew and loved him by the name Sri Sri. Because of his language he was also reluctantly loved by his class enemies. They considered him a renegade, a flouter of religion and a caste-breaker. His full name was Srirangam Srinivasa Rao, and he was born into an orthodox middle class family in Visakhapatnam on January 2, 1910. It was there he attended school. Later he studied at Madras Christian College and received a degree in Zoology in 1930. By then he already had a reputation as a poet, a promising—if romantic and slightly reactionary—youth. In 1928, at the age of 28, he had made his debut with *Prabhava*, a thin, little volume of confidently constructed, romantically religious poetry in traditional style.

This was a great period for Andhra's literature. In later Indian literature history the two decades 1915-1935 in Andhra are compared with the age of Pericles in Athens or the Elizabethan period in England. The poets of the Andhra Renaissance, people such as Veerasalingam Panthulu, had shattered the ossified written language and recaptured the spoken tongue for literature. A constellation of great poets, unknown in Europe, created an extensive body of literature: lyric and epic poetry, religious hymns and topical poems. This was also a time for novels and dramatic works in Telugu.

Sri Sri's break through came in 1933 with *Suptaasthikalu*. His rejection of orthodoxy and reaction signalled an attachment to romantic modernism, and, at the same time, a return toward the popular, religious, Shivaitic poetry.

Now he became a bard of the new technology and industrialism, vitalist and machine-worshipper, socialist and revolutionary. It was labor that created the world and all its wealth. It was the working people who would make themselves free and build the world of tomorrow. In forceful language, with total formal control of both the popular tongue and Sanskritized Telugu, and with a sovereign ability to use speech sound and meter, he gave youth of the thirties the message to *crush the old state and rip apart its web of lies.*

At the same time he turned his attention to foreign poetry; he was as free in his outward reflection as he was deeply-rooted in his people and their language. He was influenced by poets such as Nazrul Islam and Harin Chatto, but also by Shelley and Swinburne, Rupert Brooke and

Siegfried Sassoon, Baudelaire, Pasternak and Mayakovsky.

He earned a living at a variety of jobs, seldom remaining long. He drank heavily and lived hard. He worked as a journalist at *Andhra Praba* in Madras and *Meezaan* in Hyderabad. He freelanced for the press and radio, did a stint as a civilian employee in the Air force, and then in the forties began working as a librettist and a dialogue writer for the southern Indian film industry in Madras.

During the thirties his political awareness grew. The mounting threat of world fascism, the first socialist state—the Soviet Union of the five-year plans, the Spanish Civil War, Japan's war on the Chinese people transformed him. Romantic revolutionism evolved into the need for the dictatorship of the proletariat. The poetic world-perspective became proletarian internationalism, uniting the southern Indian agricultural laborer with the Czech miner, the Irish sailor and the cotton-harvesting plantation black in the American south.

Now it was Aragon who influenced his style and determined his direction. From modernism and surrealistic experimentation, Sri Sri consciously turned to the masses to learn of his true roots in the people's language and culture. Thus Sri Sri learned from Andhra's despised peasants and outcastes, from their rich culture and highly-evolved folk songs: The bardic Burrakatha lyrics (where the story teller, the singer, performs with the jester as well as the commentator, who both accompany themselves on burra instruments) and the Madiga Songs. The lyrics of the outcastes also liberated his poetry. His sureness of style grew, while his poetry spoke ever more clearly of subjects held to be base and unpoetic by the artistic poets: kerosene lamps, soap fragments and small, small puppies.

In the democratic writers' association, The Progressive Writers' Movement, formed by the Communist Party during the Second World War, Sri Sri became one of the leaders in Andhra. When he opened the third annual meeting of progressive Andhra writers in Rajhamundry in December 1945, eighty Telugu writers took part in the three days of deliberations and appearances. They represented nine hundred writers organized in sixteen sections across all Andhra (as well as the Nizams of Hyderabad).

Sri Sri was not merely an intellectual; he also took part in practical political actions, participated in the Party's election campaigns and was elected to the legislative assembly. He was active in the world peace movement and visited Helsinki, Paris and Moscow.

As the most prominent of the revolutionary poets in Andhra, he naturally also incurred the most ferocious attacks. During the 1955 election campaign in Andhra, he was assailed with such vehemence in the press and at meetings by the remorselessly implaccable supporters of the Congress for Cultural Freedom that he suffered a nervous breakdown. But these champions of individual freedom were not to be rid of him; Sri Sri recovered from his illness and continued to write. He grew increasingly disappointed with the official Indian Communist movement, which was adapting itself to parliamentarism and middle class existence, while forgetting the poor.

Then came the Naxalbari revolt in 1967. Spring thunder rumbled across the plain and lightning struck. Now, this wasn't parliamentary or middle class, it wasn't a matter of sitting at international meetings or drinking vodka with Russians, it was the poor peasants of India in revolt. It was communists who broke with the corrupt party, turning to the masses, taking the Indian people's road, the road to revolution, from the Coal Revolt and Wahhabi Rebellion, from Santhal and 1857, from Moplah and Telengana, men and women who, if necessary, were willing to die for the cause of the people. There followed Srikakulam here in Andhra and peasant revolt smoldered across the land. If one seeks heroes, look no further—heroes such as Charu Mazumdar, weaver of the revolution's red scarf, and Vempatapu Satyanarayana and Adibhatla Kailasam, brilliant jewels of Andhra, and all the other thousands of immortal martyrs of whom the poor now sing.

When Sri Sri turned 60 and it was time for the grand, official homage, students came and publically posed their question to the assembled poets:

"Which side are you on, you poets? On the side of the struggling poor masses or that of the cruel government?"

In Germany, the young radical students had lived to see their beloved Goethe become the poet of indifferentism. Sri Sri was great, a Goethe of his time and one with his people. He did not become indifferent. 1970 was the jubilee year, the year of homage. From the Chief Minister of Andhra Pradesh, the poor national poet was to receive a great prize, a large amount of money and the acclamation of the powerful. But Sri Sri spurned the honor and the money, choosing instead to participate in the founding of Viplava Rachayitya Sangham, the Revolutionary Writers' Association, which openly advocated the Naxalbari way.

In the years that followed he took part in the efforts of the Revolutionary Writers' Association and worked toward the establishment of the All-India Revolutionary Writers' Association. He defied the authorities. They were even obliged to imprison him a short time, this national poet they had once tried to coopt. And all the while he wrote.

For the poetry movement in Andhra, for thousands of poets and millions of listeners and readers, Sri Sri's work from the years after 1970, collected in *Maro Prasthanam*, is a fantastically young, creative continuation of one of Indian literature's great and liberating lifeworks.

Now he is dead. Even European workers and students who have never heard of him are the poorer for it. But the revolutionary poetry movement for the liberation of India's people, which he served and inspired, goes on stronger than ever.

INDEX

GLOSSARY

ahisma	non-violence
atavika	forest people
babu	clerk or official
Bhil-woman	woman from Bhil tribe
chapatie	flat, circular, fried bread
chamar	untouchable who works with leather
charpoy	bedspread, bamboo mat
chowkidar	watchman
Congress (I)	created by split in Congress Party engineered by Mrs. Gandhi
CPI	Communist Party of India
CPI(M)	Communist Party of India (Marxist)
CPI(ML)	Communist Party of India (Marxist-Leninist)
dacoit	bandit
dora	king, lord; boss
ghee	clarified butter
goonda	retainers of landlord used to terrorize poor
guru	spiritual teacher
harijans	'children of god,' Gandhi's new word for the untouchables
howdah	elephant saddle

jagir	land given by government
jagirdar	landowner holding a jagir
kisan sabha	"peasant association"; a peasant movement during freedom struggle
lathi	three or four foot long club carried by police
maidan	open space near village, used for meetings
mamul	bribery
MISA	Maintenance of Internal Security Act, passed by Indira Gandhi
mofussil	rural areas
Naxalites	revolutionaries inspired by the Naxalbari peasant revolt; participants in movement organized by the CPI (ML)
panchayat	village council
peepul	sacred fig tree
pucca	permanent, well-made; esp. of house made of stone or brick
Raj	rule, kingdom. Used of the British Raj.
RAW	Research and Analysis Wing, secret police organization set up by Indira Gandhi
RSS	Rashtriya Swayamsevak Sangh; a Hindu nationalist organization
ryotu-kuli-sangham	peasant-worker association
sahib	colonialist term of respect, used by Indians of Europeans
sati	suicide of widow on funeral pyre of husband
Shaivite	follower of Shiva
shamiana	canopy, tent room
shoe	to beat with shoes, especially humiliating form of physical abuse
SIDA	Swedish International Development Agency
stupa	a Buddhist monument
swadeshi	movement to boycott foreign goods (lit., 'own-country things')
swaraj	independence
toddy	sap of palm tree, used to make intoxicating liquor
twice-born	reincarnated
vellama	a land-owning caste
zamindar	landowner

Jan Myrdal, one of the leading figures in contemporary Swedish culture, has written more than thirty books, including fiction, plays and books on literature, art and politics. He has also made a number of feature films and TV documentaries. His books include *Report from a Chinese Village*, *The Silk Road* and *Confessions of a Disloyal European*. He writes regularly for all of Stockholm's newspapers and lectures on international affairs at the Royal Defence Academy.

Gun Kessle, a painter, photographer and graphic artist, studied at the Royal Academy of Fine Art in Sweden. She has exhibited at Stockholm's Museum of Modern Art, National Museum and Museum of Far Eastern Antiquities. She has published a number of books in Sweden, has been a member of the board of the Swedish Union of Artists, and is editor of the Swedish arts magazine *Past and Present*.